Dedicated to Gabriela and Teresa

The Presidency and the Constitution: Cases and Controversies

Michael A. Genovese
Loyola Chair of Leadership, Loyola Marymount University

and

Robert J. Spitzer
Distinguished Service Professor of Political Science, SUNY Cortland

palgrave
macmillan

THE PRESIDENCY AND THE CONSTITUTION
© Michael A. Genovese, 2005.

First published in 2005 by
PALGRAVE MACMILLAN™
175 Fifth Avenue, New York, N.Y. 10010 and
Houndmills, Basingstoke, Hampshire, England RG21 6XS
Companies and representatives throughout the world.

PALGRAVE MACMILLAN is the global academic imprint of the Palgrave Macmillan division of St. Martin's Press, LLC and of Palgrave Macmillan Ltd. Macmillan® is a registered trademark in the United States, United Kingdom and other countries. Palgrave is a registered trademark in the European Union and other countries.

ISBN 1–4039–6673–7 hardback
ISBN 1–4039–6674–5 paperback

Library of Congress Cataloging-in-Publication Data

Genovese, Michael A.
    The presidency and the Constitution : cases and controversies / Michael A. Genovese, Robert J. Spitzer.
        p. cm.
    Includes bibliographical references and index.
    ISBN 1–4039–6673–7—ISBN 1–4039–6674–5 (pbk.)
        1. Executive power—United States—Cases. 2. Constitutional law—United States—Cases. I. Spitzer, Robert J., 1953– II. Title.

KF5050.A7G46 2005
342′.73062—dc22   2004065497

A catalogue record for this book is available from the British Library.

Design by Newgen Imaging Systems (P) Ltd., Chennai, India.

First edition: August 2005

10 9 8 7 6 5 4 3 2 1

Printed in the United States of America.

Contents

Preface

The first and most important purpose of this book is to do something that, with one exception,[1] has not been done before: to bring together under one cover the important court cases that address the constitutional powers and limits of the American presidency. We do this mindful of two important qualifiers: that court cases alone do not define presidential power and authority, and that all three branches of government participate in the process of constitutional interpretation; that is to say, the courts do not possess a monopoly over the interpretation of constitutional meaning, despite popular impressions to the contrary.[2]

Without question, a fulsome treatment of presidential powers arising from law would include not only court cases, but also statutory law enacted by the Congress, as well as executive orders and other issuances emanating from the executive branch. We deliberated, even agonized over whether to include such legal issuances, but ultimately decided against doing so, for both principled and pragmatic reasons.

The principled reason informs us that, despite the shared nature of constitutional interpretation just referenced, the courts in the United States are nevertheless recognized as serving the pivotal interpretive and adjudicative role with regard to constitutional and legal authority. In recent decades, the rise of judicial activism of both the left and the right, and the country's increasing disposition to bring all manner of disputes to the courts for resolution, has resulted in a proliferation of important court rulings affecting the presidency. The unprecedented final resolution of the hotly disputed presidential election of 2000 in the case of *Bush v. Gore* and the three cases from 2004 regarding the legal status and rights of detainees held in connection with the ongoing war on terrorism exemplify the judiciary's singular role. In short, a case-law examination of the presidency is not only a useful but a necessary contribution to a fuller understanding of the presidency in the American separation-of-powers system.

The pragmatic reason for our editorial decision was our desire to produce a book that was comprehensive yet limited in length and therefore accessible to many readers. Moreover, we wanted to do more than reprint edited cases. Thus, this book begins with two chapters that lay out the broad political and developmental context of presidential power and court interaction. The subsequent nine case chapters each have an introduction that offers main themes, and each case also has an introduction—all of which, we hope, will make this book more user friendly, especially for those who have little experience with the often cumbersome text of court cases. Obviously, any meaningful inclusion of statutes, executive orders, and the like would have vastly expanded the size of this volume and inhibited our ability to offer pedagogical commentary. As it is, we have tightly edited these cases, focusing on that text that bears most directly on how the courts have viewed presidential power. Of the nearly fifty cases presented here, most are from the Supreme Court, but a few are lower federal court rulings whose decisions have been upheld on appeal and that have meaningfully addressed broader questions of presidential power. In addition, we warn the reader that matters of form and style in the writing of court cases have changed over 200 years, so the reader will observe some stylistic differences in the cases.

We wish to express our gratitude to those who have played a role in advancing this project. David Pervin has been an engaging, thoughtful, and committed editor for us at Palgrave Macmillan, and we extend to him our warmest and most sincere gratitude, as well as to Palgrave's Theresa Lee and Donna Cherry. Michael Genovese wishes to thank his research assistants, Melissa Branda, Theresa Tran, and Chris Zepeda, for their important contributions. Robert Spitzer similarly thanks Julío Fernandez, Deb Dintino, and Jerry O'Callaghan for their important contributions, and also expresses special felicitations to Mellissa Mitchell, Shannon Long, and Skye Wilson. And we both reserve our most heartfelt admiration, gratitude, and love to our respective wives, Gabriela and Teresa, to whom this book is dedicated. We are just smart enough to realize how fortunate we are to have married these wonderful women.

About the Authors

Michael A. Genovese (Ph.D. University of Southern California, 1979) holds the Loyola Chair of Leadership, is Professor of Political Science, and Director of the Institute for Leadership Studies at Loyola Marymount University. He has written sixteen books, including *The Paradoxes of the American Presidency*, Oxford University Press (2nd edition 2004, with Thomas E. Cronin); The *Presidency and Domestic Policy*, CQ Press (2000, with William W. Lammers), *The Power of the American Presidency, 1789–2000*, Oxford University Press (2001); *The Presidential Dilemma*, Longman (2nd ed. 2003), and *The Encyclopedia of the American Presidency*, Facts-on-File (2005). Professor Genovese has won over a dozen university and national teaching awards, and frequently appears as a political commentator on television and radio. He is also Associate Editor of the journal, *White House Studies*, has lectured for the United States Embassy abroad, and is editor of Palgrave Macmillan Publishing's, "The Evolving American Presidency" book series. In 2004–05, he served as the President of Presidency Research Group of the American Political Science Association.

Robert J. Spitzer (Ph.D. Cornell University, 1980) is Distinguished Service Professor of Political Science at the State University of New York, College at Cortland. His books include *The Presidency and Public Policy* (1983), *The Right to Life Movement and Third Party Politics* (1987), *The Presidential Veto* (1988), *President and Congress* (1993), *Media and Public Policy* (1993), *The Politics of Gun Control* (1995; 2nd ed. 1998; 3rd ed. 2004), *Politics and Constitutionalism* (2000), *The Right to Bear Arms* (2001), and *Essentials of American Politics* (co-authored, 2002; 2nd ed. 2005). He is also Series Editor for the book series "American Constitutionalism" for SUNY Press. In 2003 he received the State University of New York's Chancellor's Award for Excellence in Scholarship. Spitzer is the author of over 200 articles and papers appearing in many publications on a variety of American politics subjects, and is former President of the Presidency Research Group of the American Political Science Association. He also served as a member of the New York State Commission on the Bicentennial of the U.S. Constitution, and has testified before Congress on several occasions.

CHAPTER **1** | # Introduction

Episode 1

With the Chief Justice presiding over a packed Senate Chamber and a worldwide television audience viewing with nervous anticipation, the clerk began to call the roll:

Senator Abraham . . .
      "guilty"
Senator Akaka . . .
      "not guilty"
Senator Allard . . .
      "guilty"
Senator Ashcroft . . .
      "guilty"
Senator Baucus . . .
      "not guilty"
Senator Bayh . . .
      "not guilty"

As the yeas and nays echoed throughout the chamber, it became clear that although President Clinton was impeached by the Republican-controlled House of Representatives (only the second president in history, but the first elected president to be impeached), the Republican-controlled Senate could not muster the two-thirds vote needed to convict. In the end, the Republicans could not even get a majority to vote in favor of any of the articles of impeachment.

Clinton escaped. Again.

Thus ended one of the most dramatic, contentious, and sleazy episodes in American political history—with a whimper, not a bang.

It was a tale of sex, lies, but unlike Richard Nixon, no tapes.

President Clinton lied to the American public, lied under oath, covered up, embarrassed himself, and demeaned the office of the presidency. But did these transgressions rise to the level of impeachable offenses? Apparently. Did they justify removal from office? Apparently not.

Episode 2

In the aftermath of the September 11, 2001, terrorist attack against the United States, President George W. Bush, through his attorney general, John Ashcroft, ordered the detention of U.S. citizens without charging them with any crime, and even denied them access to an attorney.

The president claimed that such steps were (a) necessary given the risks of terrorism and (b) perfectly legal given the president's implied and expressed constitutional authority as commander in chief.

Critics charged the president with abuse of power and violation of the constitutional rights of the U.S.

citizen, and questioned the source of such claims of power, arguing that the Constitution was the supreme law of the land and the president could not subvert or negate guaranteed constitutional rights and liberties merely on his own whim.

These two cases illustrate the intersection between *law* and *politics*.

They also serve as an example of how ours is a system of three branches—not one. In a separation-of-powers system, all three branches play—or should play—a role.

Ours is a *system*, Madisonian in design, that separates and shares power. No one branch holds all the cards. Although the president may be politically well positioned to exercise *leadership* (the ability to mobilize support and influence events and opinions), the Congress is given a stronger *power* hand. The Constitution grants most of the substantive *powers* to the Congress: to pass legislation, raise armies, tax, regulate commerce, declare war, and so on. The president plays a role in making policy: formally, through the constitutional duties to report from time to time on the state of the union and through the use and threat of the *veto*; informally, through the exercise of rhetoric, political bargaining, party leadership, and coalition building.

The courts also play a significant, but different, political role. Shrouded in mystery, adamant in insisting they only follow "the law," the courts are nonetheless often called on to settle political and policy disputes in the American system.

In chapter 6 of his *Democracy in America*, Alexis de Tocqueville, an insightful nineteenth-century French observer of American government and culture, noted that

the judicial organization of the United States is the institution which a stranger has the greatest difficulty in understanding. He hears the authority of a judge invoked in the political occurrences of every day, and he naturally concludes that, in the United States, the judges are important political functionaries: nevertheless, when he examines the nature of the tribunals, they offer at the first glance nothing which is contrary to the usual habits and privileges of those bodies; and the magistrates seem

to him to interfere in public affairs only by chance, but by a chance which recurs every day.[1]

If anyone doubts the role politics plays in the judicial process, she need only look to the Supreme Court's role in the 2000 presidential election. Contradicting its own oft-stated preference for states' rights, a Republican majority gave the presidency to Republican George W. Bush in a decision that astounded court watchers and stretched the bounds of credulity to the near-breaking point.

Yes, the courts are political. One becomes a judge through political appointment, judges do take politics into account (even though they usually deny it), and judicial rulings often have profound political and policy consequences. If politics played little or no role in court decisions, presidents and governors would not be as concerned with getting ideological soul mates onto the courts.

This book examines presidential power as defined, and redefined, by the Supreme Court. The presidency was designed over two hundred years ago as an office of limited power, based on the rule of law within a constitutional framework. In the last two centuries, many questions dealing with the scope and limitations of presidential power have come before the courts for resolution, and in recent decades, most important political controversies have made their way to the courts. From interbranch struggles for power to presidential selection, to campaign financing, to executive privilege, to war powers, hardly an issue arises for the modern presidency that does not eventually find itself framed as a legal problem to be addressed by the courts.

This book offers to you, the reader, a "case-law" examination of the presidency. We recognize at the outset, however, that this approach does not provide a complete or definitive examination of the American presidency, as much of what composes presidential power extends well beyond that which is dealt with by the courts. Yet much of what comprises the modern strong presidency arises from, or is legitimized by, favorable court rulings. Further, because both institutional legitimacy and politics arise from the law, this case-law look at the presidency provides an *institutional* view of the office and its powers that we consider the gateway to understanding the modern American chief executive.

Beyond the mere presentation of cases, however, we argue that, with the exception of a few court cases from the nineteenth century, the institution of the presidency almost always prevails in court challenges. This is an argument of no little consequence, for in a nation of laws, the law itself is arguably the greatest power of all, especially when it is bestowed by America's "law-keepers," the courts. In turn, this presidency bias poses an important and underappreciated explanation for the ever-spiraling power of the executive branch, the future consequences of which will be explored in the final chapter of this book.

How, then, is presidential power defined by the Supreme Court?

In order to understand the role of the presidency and presidential power within a constitutional framework as interpreted by the Court, we first need to examine the invention of the presidency, the president's constitutional place, and the development of presidential power over time.

From Divine Right of Kings to Servant of the People

The Europe from which the framers of the U.S. Constitution and their ancestors fled was a world of kings and hereditary monarchies. In England, a nascent Parliament was in the process of a long, slow, and at times violent march designed to wrestle power away from the king and give it first to representatives of the landed barons and later to representatives of the people.

When the Americas were first colonized, the Age of the Divine Right of Kings was giving way to more limited and representative forms of power. During the Age of Divine Right of Kings, monarchs could *rule* or *command*. After all, they claimed an authority based on the will of God. To challenge the monarch was to challenge God. This was very firm ground on which monarchs stood.

But as the church and the barons challenged monarchical power, a long, slow transformation took place. The Age of the Divine Right of Kings derived from God, was slowly replaced by the Age of the Divine Right of the People (expressed as democracy) through their chosen representatives.[2]

In this new configuration, authority and legitimacy that once came from God now came from something called "the People." This new secular base of authority made it more difficult for leaders to gain compliance. Consent replaced command; leadership replaced rule; influence and persuasion replaced orders. Government officials had to *lead*, not merely command. Eventually rule of the people through elected representatives made the government the servant of the people; all were servants of the Constitution as supreme law of the land. "In America," the revolutionary author Tom Paine pointed out, "the law is king."

The American Revolution took place in the middle of this transformation. At the time of the colonists' break with Great Britain, antimonarchical sentiment was strong. Thomas Jefferson's Declaration of Independence was, in addition to being an eloquent expression of democratic and revolutionary faith, a laundry list of charges leveled against a tyrannical king. And propagandist supreme Tom Paine stigmatized England's King George III as "the Royal Brute of Britain."

Antiexecutive feelings were so strong that when the postrevolutionary leadership assembled to form a government, their Articles of Confederation contained *no executive*! So weak and ineffective were the articles that Noah Webster author of the first American dictionary said they were "but a name, and our confederation a cobweb." Over time however, the absence of an executive proved unworkable, and leaders slowly yielded to grudging acceptance of the inevitability of an executive officer.

But this new executive would be no strong, independent, monarchical executive. The new nation was willing, if reluctant, to accept the necessity of an executive, but the fear of tyranny continued to lead in the direction of a very limited and constrained office.

Several European political theorists opened the framers' imaginations to new possibilities for governing. John Locke's *Second Treatise on Government*

(1690) and Montesquieu's *The Spirit of the Laws* (1748) were especially influential.

From their understanding of history, the framers drew several lessons. In studying the collapse of ancient Greek (Athenian) democracy, the founders deepened their already profound suspicions of democracy. Thus, they were determined to prevent what some framers referred to as mobocracy. A tyranny of the people was just as frightening as a tyranny of the monarchy. From their examination of the Roman republic and its collapse from the weight of empire, the founders understood how delicate was the balance between the Senate and the will of the emperor. An emperor armed as tribune of the people, bent on imperial pursuits, led to a tyranny just as dangerous as monarchy and mobocracy.

Although less understood, the lessons the framers drew from the Native Americans clearly had an impact on the writing of the Constitution. The framers looked across the Atlantic and saw hereditary monarchies; they looked down the road and saw a sophisticated, democratic, egalitarian government in action: the Iroquois Confederation. This union of six tribes/nations, organized along lines similar to a separation-of-powers system, was the model for Ben Franklin's 1754 Albany Plan of Union and was studied by several of the framers.

The experience with colonial governors further added to the framers' storehouse of knowledge. Those states with weak executives, states dominated by the legislature with a defanged governor, seemed less well run than New York, for example, which had a fairly strong, independent governor. Such examples softened the founders' fears of executive tyranny. Thus, antiexecutive sentiments slowly began to subside, and there developed a growing recognition that although executive tyranny was still to be feared, an enfeebled executive was also a danger to good government.

Under the Articles, the national government was weak and ineffective. In each state, minor revolts of debtors threatened property and order. The most famous of these was Shays' Rebellion (1787). The minirevolutions put a fear into the propertied classes. Some longed for the imposed order of a monarchy. "Shall we have a king?" John Jay asked of George Washington during the rebellion.

This was not the first time Washington had been approached with such a suggestion. A few years earlier, in 1782, army units stationed in Newburgh, New York, threatened to meet and make Washington monarch. But Washington found out about the Newburgh Conspiracy and quickly put an end to it. The impact of these pushes toward monarchy further persuaded the framers of a need for an executive in America.

As the framers met in Philadelphia, most of those present recognized (some quite reluctantly) the need for an independent executive with *some* power. But how much? No useful model existed anywhere in the known world. They would have to invent one.

Inventing the Presidency

The American Revolution against Great Britain was in large part a revolution against authority. Historian Bernard Bailyn said the rebellion against Britain made resistance to authority "a doctrine according to godliness."[3] The colonists were for the most part defiant, independent, egalitarian, and individualistic. The symbols and rallying cries were anti-authority in nature. Once it became necessary to establish a new government, reestablishing the respect for authority so necessary for an effective government was difficult.

Reconstructing authority, especially executive authority, was a slow, painful process. By 1787, when the framers met in Philadelphia "for the sole and express purpose of revising the Articles of Confederation . . .[in order to] render the federal constitution adequate to the exigencies of government and the preservation of the Union," there was general agreement that a limited executive was necessary to promote good government. But what kind of executive? One person or several? How should he be selected? What powers should he have?[4]

No decision at the constitutional convention was more difficult to reach than the scope and nature of the executive. The framers went through proposals, counterproposals, decisions, reconsiderations, postponements, reversals—until finally a presidency was invented.[5]

The confusion reflected what political scientist Harvey C. Mansfield Jr. referred to as the framers' "ambivalence of executive power."[6] There were widespread and divergent views on the creation of an executive office. Initially, most delegates were considered "congressionalists," hoping to create a government with a strong Congress and a plural executive with very limited power. Delegate George Mason proposed a three-person executive, one chosen from each region of the nation. Delegate Roger Sherman described this plural executive as "no more than an institution for carrying the will of the legislature into effect" (James Madison's Notes of the Convention).

But there were also advocates for a strong, unitary executive. Alexander Hamilton initially wanted to institute a version of the British system of government on American soil, along with a monarch. However, there was little support for such a proposal, and Hamilton quickly backed away.

James Madison, often referred to as the father of the U.S. Constitution, had surprisingly little impact on the invention of the presidency, even going so far as to write in a letter to George Washington shortly before the convention: "I have scarcely ventured as yet to form my own opinion either of the manner in which [the executive] ought to be constituted or of the authorities with which it ought to be clothed."

Probably the most influential framer on the invention of the presidency was James Wilson of Pennsylvania. At first, Wilson sought the direct popular election of the president, but eventually he lost that battle and instead helped develop what became the Electoral College. He also greatly influenced the choice of a single over a plural executive.

In the end, the framers wanted to strike a balance in executive power. Making the presidency too strong would jeopardize liberty; making the office too weak would jeopardize good government. But just how to achieve balance remained a thorny issue.

Unlike the Congress and the judiciary, for which there was ample precedent to guide the framers, the presidency was truly new, invented in Philadelphia, different from any executive office that preceded it.

The president would not be a king or sovereign. Instead, he would swear to protect and defend a higher authority: the Constitution.

The framers faced several key questions. First, how many? Should it be a single (unitary) or plural executive? Initial sympathy for a plural executive eventually gave way to a single executive, primarily because that was the best way to assign responsibility (and blame) for the execution of policy. The second question was how to choose the executive. Some proposed popular election, which was rejected because the framers feared the president might become tribune of the people. Others promoted selection by the Congress, but this was rejected on grounds that it might make the president the servant of the Congress, and it would undermine the separation of powers. Finally, the framers invented an Electoral College as the best of several unappealing alternatives.

Next, how long a term of office? Should the president serve for life? A fixed term? Two years, four years, six years? If for a fixed term, should he be eligible for reelection? After much hemming and hawing, the framers decided on a four-year term with reeligibility as an option. But the president could be removed—impeached—for certain not very clearly delineated offenses.

The toughest question related to how much power the president should be given. In a way, the framers deftly avoided this issue. Because they could not reach a clear consensus on the president's power, they decided to create a bare skeleton of authority. They left many areas vague and ambiguous; they left gaping silences throughout Article II, the article dealing with the presidency. How could the framers—so afraid of the mob and the monarchy—leave so important an issue so poorly answered? The answer is George Washington.

Any examination of the invention of the presidency that does not take George Washington into account is remiss. Each day, as debate after debate took place, the men of Philadelphia could look at the man presiding over the convention, secure in the knowledge that whatever else became of the presidency, George Washington would be its first officeholder. So confident were the framers (and the public as well) of Washington's skills, integrity, and republican sentiments, they felt comfortable leaving the presidency unfinished and incomplete.

They would leave it to Washington to fill in the gaps and set the proper precedents.

After the convention, delegate Pierce Butler acknowledged Washington's influence in this excerpt from a letter to Weedon Butler:

I am free to acknowledge that his powers [the President's] are full great, and greater than I was disposed to make them. Nor, entre nous, do I believe they would have been so great had not many of the members cast their eyes towards George Washington as President; and shaped their ideas of the powers to be given to a President by their opinions of his virtue.

Of course, Washington would not always be the president. Thus, although the framers trusted Washington, could they trust all of his successors? Leaving the presidency unfinished opened the door for future problems in the executive branch. Ben Franklin pointed to this when he noted, "The first man, put at the helm, will be a good one. Nobody knows what sort may come afterwards."

Washington, then, is the chief reason why the presidency is so elastic. The office was left half finished with the expectation that Washington would fill in the gaps. In many ways he did. But openings were left that future presidents were able to exploit on the road to an expanding conception of executive power.

The presidency that emerged from the Philadelphia convention was an office with "very little plainly given, very little clearly withheld . . . the Convention . . . did not define: it deferred."[7] This meant that the presidency would be shaped, defined, and created by those people who occupied the office and the times and demands of different eras. The framers thus invented a very "personal presidency," and much of the history of presidential power stems from the way presidents have understood and attempted to use the office to attain their goals. As political commentator Alan Wolfe has written: "The American presidency has been a product of practice, not theory. Concrete struggles between economic and political forces have been responsible for shaping it, not maxims

from Montesquieu."[8] The unsettled nature of the presidency was a marked characteristic of this peculiar office and, to some, of the genius of the framers. The Constitution that emerged from the Philadelphia convention was less an act of clear design and intent and more a "mosaic of everyone's second choices."[9] The presidency, left unfinished and only partially formed, had yet to be truly invented.

The President of the Constitution

The framers invented a presidency of some strength, but little independent power. They put the president in a position to lead (influence, persuade), but not command (order).

What exactly did the framers create? What structure or skeleton of power and government did the founders of the U.S. system design? The Constitution does not clearly spell out the powers the president possessed. The framers did not leave us clueless, but they did not give us a clear road map either. Justice Robert Jackson, in his *Youngstown Sheet & Tube Co. v. Sawyer* (1952) concurrence, wrote:

A judge, like an executive adviser, may be surprised at the poverty of really useful and unambiguous authority applicable to concrete problems of executive power as they actually present themselves. Just what our forefathers did envision, or would have envisioned had they foreseen modern conditions, must be divined from materials almost as enigmatic as the dreams Joseph was called upon to interpret for Pharaoh. A century and a half of partisan debate and scholarly speculation yields no net result but only supplies more or less apt quotations from respected sources on each side of any question. They largely cancel each other. And court decisions are indecisive because of the judicial practice of dealing with the largest questions in the most narrow way.

The chief mechanisms the framers established in the constitutional framework to control as well as to empower the executive are: (1) *limited government*, a reaction against the arbitrary, expansive powers of the king or state, and a protection of personal liberty; (2) *rule of law*, so that only on the basis of legal or constitutional grounds could the government act; (3) *separation of powers*, so that the three branches of government each would have a defined sphere of power; and (4) *checks and balances*, so that each branch could limit or control the powers of the other branches of government.

In this structure, what *powers* and *resources* has the president? Limited powers. Constitutionally, the United States faces a paradox: The Constitution both *empowers* and *restrains* government. In fact, the Constitution does not clearly spell out the power of the presidency. Article I is devoted to the Congress, the first and constitutionally the most powerful branch of government. Article II, the executive article, deals with the presidency. The president's constitutional power cupboard is—compared to that of the Congress—nearly bare. Section 1 gives the "executive power" to the president but does not reveal whether this is a grant of tangible power or merely a title. Section 2 makes the president commander in chief of the armed forces, but this is a power that can be used only when the military is "called into the actual Service of the United States," a power that also belongs to the Congress. Further, in Article I the Constitution also reserves for the Congress the power to *declare* war. Section 2 of Article II gives the president absolute power to grant reprieves and pardons; the power to make treaties (with the advice and consent of the Senate); and the power to nominate ambassadors, judges, and other public ministers (with the advice and consent of the Senate). Section 3 calls for the president to inform the Congress on the state of the union and to recommend measures to the Congress, grants the president the power to receive ambassadors, and imposes on the president the duty to see that the laws are faithfully executed. And the president is granted to power to veto legislation in Article I (although Congress may override the veto by two-thirds vote of both houses).[10] These powers are significant, but in and of themselves they do not suggest a very strong or independent institution, and certainly not a national leadership position.

The rule of law was, in many ways, a revolutionary concept. The only way the government could legitimately act was on the basis of law. But was this possible? Several questions can be raised about a constitutional system restrained by the rule of law: Could "the government" be bound by the rule of law? Could a "president" be bound by the rule of law? James Madison wrote that "the natural province of the executive magistrate is to execute the laws, as that of the legislature is to make laws. All his acts, therefore, properly executive, must presuppose the existence of the laws to be executed."[11] And today, can a president who leads the world's only superpower be bound by the rule of law? In modern terms, the question is: Can a 21st century superpower be bound by an 18th century Constitution?

The Constitution was written in and for a quieter time, when wars were limited, transportation and communication were slow, the United States was a new and, by world standards, insignificant nation. Today we are the world's only superpower. Can a Constitution written for a small, minor nation guide a hyperpower in a globalized world?

Presidential Power and the Constitution

Presidential power, when viewed from a constitutional perspective, is both specific and obscure: specific in that some elements of presidential power are clearly spelled out (e.g., the veto power, a pardon power); obscure in that the limits and boundaries of presidential power are either ill-defined or open to vast differences in interpretation (e.g., the president's power in foreign affairs and his power over the military). In an effort to understand presidential power, the Constitution is a starting point, but it provides few definitive answers. The Constitution, as it relates to the power of the president, raises more questions than it answers.

The skeletal provisions of Article II have left the words open to definition and redefinition by courts and presidents. This skeletal wording leaves it up to an aggressive chief executive and a willing Supreme Court to shape the actual parameters of such powers. The loose construction of the words of the Constitution, such as "the executive power shall be vested in a president . . . take care that the laws be faithfully executed . . .," has been used to view the powers of the president in expansive or elastic terms.

In effect, history has rewritten the Constitution. For two centuries, we have been debating just what the words of the Constitution mean, and this debate is by no means over. The words are "flexible" enough to mean different things in different situations. Thus, one can see the elasticity of options open for both the Supreme Court and the president. On the whole, though, a more "expansive" view of presidential power has taken precedence over a more "restrictive" view. The history of the meaning of presidential power through the Constitution has been one of the expansion of power and the enlargement of the meaning of the words of the Constitution.

The Constitution gives us an outline of the powers of the president, but not a picture. The president is much more than the Constitution leads us to believe. As political scientists David E. Haight and Larry D. Johnston write: "the Presidency is above all an integrated institution, all of whose parts interlock with one another. Any description that discusses these parts individually cannot help being partially misleading."[12] Thus, one cannot simply look at the Constitution and define and describe "presidential power." The presidency is more than the sum of its constitutional parts.

Presidential power exists in two forms: *formal* and *informal*. To understand presidential power, one must understand how both the formal and informal powers work and interact and how the combination of the two can lead to dominance by a president who, given the proper conditions and abilities, is able to exploit his power source.

Formal Powers

The formal powers of the president are derived essentially from the Constitution. Those powers extend, however, beyond the strictly legalistic or specifically granted powers that find their source in the literal reading of the words of the Constitution. Additionally, presidents may have:

Enumerated powers: Those that the Constitution expressly grants;

Implied powers: Those that may be inferred from power expressly granted;

Resulting powers: Those that result when several enumerated powers are added together;

Inherent powers: Those powers in the field of external affairs that the Supreme Court has declared do not depend on constitutional grants but grow out of the existence of the national government.

Informal Powers

The informal powers of the president find their source in the "political" as opposed to the "constitutional." They are the powers that are not spelled out in the Constitution, are acquired through politics, or are "missing" from the Constitution. Presidential scholar Richard Neustadt, in his classic work *Presidential Power*, discusses the informal power of the president to "persuade." Neustadt and others feel that the power to persuade is the most important of all the presidential powers.

These informal powers of the president rely on his ability to engage in the personal part of politics. All presidents have and can use their formal powers, but the informal powers require skill at persuasion, personal manipulation, and mobilization. Although these skills may be difficult to cultivate, in the long run, changing the minds of people may be more powerful than ordering someone into compliance. Some historians can see, in the informal powers of the president, the dividing line between those characterized as "great" or aggressive and those who rate less well. The great presidents have been able and willing to exploit the informal powers at their disposal.

Thus, the president has two types of power: formal, the ability to command, and informal, the ability to persuade. The president's formal powers are limited and (often) shared. The president's informal powers are a function of skill, situation, and the political times. Although the formal power of the president remains fairly constant over time, the informal powers are quite variable, dependent on the skill of each individual president. This is not to suggest that the president's formal powers are static—over time, presidential power has increased significantly—but the pace of change has been such that it was well over a hundred years before the presidency assumed primacy in the U.S. political system.

Ratification: Is the President a King?

The invention of the presidency in Philadelphia was the first step in the creation process. The system of government still had to be ratified by the states. And one of the chief bones of contention was the presidency: Could the president become a king?

Two opposing camps formed: the federalists, who supported the ratification, and the antifederalists, most of whom sought a more democratic and decentralized government and who were most suspicious of presidential power. Hamilton, Madison, and John Jay began writing broadsides in support of the new Constitution (*The Federalist Papers*), noting the limits on presidential power. The antifederalists raised concerns about the presidency evolving into a monarchy. Edmund Randolph of Virginia said the presidency could be "the foetus of monarchy"; George Mason of Virginia saw the presidency as an "elective monarchy"; and Patrick Henry of Virginia thought the new presidency "squints toward monarchy."

Thomas Jefferson, American minister in Paris, was uneasy about some aspects of the new Constitution. "Reason and experience," he wrote to John Adams in November 1787,

> prove to us that a chief magistrate, so continuable, is an officer for life. When one or two generations shall have proved that this is an office for life, it becomes on every succession worthy of intrigue,

of bribery, of force, and even of foreign interference. It will be of great consequence to France and England to have America governed by a Galloman or Angloman. Once in office, and possessing the military force of the union, without either the aid or the check of a council, he would not easily be dethroned, even if the people could be induced to withdraw their votes from him. I wish that at the end of the 4 years they had made him for ever ineligible a second time.

Alexander Hamilton, chief advocate of energy in the executive, countered the antifederalist view, arguing that "a feeble execution is but another phrase for a bad execution; and a government ill executed, whatever it may be in theory, must be, in practice, a bad government." (*The Federalist*, No. 69). And "energy" was both a crucial "character in the definition of good government" and the defining attribute of the executive itself.

Hamilton's direct challenge to the antifederalist charges, a comparison between the newly created president and the king of England, that appeared in *The Federalist*, No. 69, suggests that:

> The president of the United States would be an officer elected by the people for *four* years; the King of Great Britain is a perpetual and *hereditary* prince. The one would be amenable to personal punishment and disgrace [through impeachment]; the person of the other is . . . inviolable. The one would have a *qualified* negative upon the acts of the legislative body; the other as an *absolute* negative. The one would have a right to command the military and naval forces of the nation; the other, in addition to this right, possessed that of *declaring* war [a right reserved to congress in the Constitution], and of *raising* and *regulating* fleets and armies [likewise, a responsibility of Congress] by his own authority. The one would have a concurrent power [with the Senate] in the formation of treaties; the other is the *sole possessor* of the power of making treaties. The one would have a like concurrent authority in appointing to office; the other is the sole author of all appointments. The one can confer no privileges whatsoever; the

other can make denizens of aliens, noblemen of commoners; can erect corporations with all the rights incident to corporate bodies. The one can prescribe no rules concerning the commerce of currency of the nation; the other is in several respects the arbiter of commerce. . . . The one has not particle of spiritual jurisdiction; the other is supreme head and governor of the national church! What answer shall we give to those who would persuade us that things so unlike resemble each other? The same that ought to be given to those who tell us that a government, the sole power of which would be in the hands of the elective and periodical servants of the people, is an aristocracy, a monarchy, and a despotism.

In the end, the federalist arguments won out, and the Constitution was ratified. But the suspicions raised by the antifederalists did not disappear. They would help shape the debate on presidential power for decades to come. And who is to say when a president exceeds constitutional limits? The Congress? The president himself as judge in his own case? Or the Court?

The Courts Judge

Ever since *Marbury v. Madison* (1803), the Supreme Court has claimed (it is nowhere expressly granted in the Constitution) the right to review and overturn acts of the Congress and the president. Although several presidents have questioned the Court's power in this area, few have had the nerve to defy the Court. Is the Supreme Court, then, the final arbiter of the Constitution? Not really. There is a continuous struggle for power, and often presidents find ways to get around the Court. The Congress, too, legislates to give meaning to the Constitution as it sees fit.[13]

The presidency is a complex, multidimensional, contradictory, paradoxical *office*. It is embedded in a *system*—the separation of powers—that limits and frustrates the use of power. The office has been occupied by *individuals* from a wide range of backgrounds, possessing varied skills, motives, and ambitions. They served under drastically different conditions and *circumstances*. It should not then surprise us that the history of the presidency reflects the ebb and flow of power.

Strong, determined presidents like Clinton and George W. Bush often clash with the Congress and to a lesser extent, with the courts in an effort to exert their will on the political system.[14] Andrew Jackson and Woodrow Wilson clashed with the Congress; Thomas Jefferson and Franklin Roosevelt enjoyed congressional support but were nevertheless rebuffed by the Court; and Harry Truman and Richard Nixon invoked broad claims of power that were rejected by the Court. Beyond the familiar executive appetite for power, the cause for conflicts between the president and the Courts is, in part, also attributable to the fact that ours is a system of separated but shared, autonomous but overlapping, power. There is no central repository of constitutional authority, no single organ of political power. The elaborate enumeration-of-power scheme is not a self-executing machine, and its implementation occurs within a political environment in which individuals and institutions vie and compete for power:[15] Competition may produce cooperation, but it has been known, particularly in recent years, to yield gridlock and deadlock; on occasion, it results in unregenerate conflict and open warfare. Resolution of these conflicts, which have produced constitutional crises and landmark cases, frequently has fallen to the Supreme Court. In this context the Court has faced important questions about the nature and scope of presidential authority, some of which are unanswered by resort to the constitutional text alone and require resort to the legislative history of the Constitutional Convention: Is the Vesting Clause, which vests executive power in the presidency, a conferral of substantive authority? Or is it a reference to the title of the chief executive and the enumerated powers and duties of the office? Does the commander-in-chief clause authorize the president to initiate military hostilities? Should it be read in conjunction with the War Clause? Other constitutional questions about presidential powers arise as a result of silences in the Constitution: Can the president terminate treaties? Can the president lay claim to what is variously known as inherent or emergency power prerogative?

The President and the Court: Conflict and Cooperation

A variety of activities are consumed under the rubric of relations between the Supreme Court and the president; among these are conflict and cooperation. In an effort to highlight the patterns of interaction between the two branches, it is useful to look at this interinstitutional link as a series of relationships that are more or less likely to produce conflict or cooperation. By separating Supreme Court–president relations into four key relationships, one can begin to see when courts and presidents are likely to work together, or at cross purposes.

Traditionally, court activity is looked at on a case-by-case method, or as it relates to one specific policy area (race, criminal rights, etc.). This book attempts to take a broader, more theoretical perspective of relations between the judiciary and the president. We organize Court–president relations in such a way as to allow us to make generalized statements about conflict and cooperation. It should be noted that this model involves cases at both the Supreme Court and lower federal court levels, and many of the cases referred to in the book did not reach the Supreme Court.

Four key relationships shape the Court–president connection. One dimension is the split between *domestic and foreign policy*. The second consists of *normal versus emergency conditions*. The third dimension includes court composition, with a split between *majoritarian and antimajoritarian* courts. The fourth, one that does not apply to every case, but is a potent predictor when present, is the *intent of Congress*. These four relationships comprise the major points of conflict and interaction, and through these relationships and conditions, we can see when and why the courts are both willing and unwilling to "take on" the president. The model represents an attempt to discern the relative

potencies of four sets of interrelated variables and seeks to be predictive in that, through its application, one can see under which conditions the court and president are likely to engage in public conflict and cooperation.

Domestic versus Foreign Policy Decisions

The first relationship, the domestic versus foreign policy dyad, is adapted from a fairly common distinction in political science. It is based on the "two presidencies" theory of presidential power.[16] This theory, described by political scientist Aaron Wildavsky, contends: "the United States has one President, but it has two presidencies; one presidency is for domestic affairs, the other is concerned with defense and foreign policy. Since World War II, Presidents have had much greater success in controlling the nation's defense and foreign policies than in dominating its domestic policies."[17]

Although some social scientists have disputed the tenability of this argument, most would agree that presidents maintain greater influence and success in foreign than in domestic policy.[18]

By approaching the two presidencies' problem from a president–Congress perspective, Wildavsky taps an important part of the relationship he seeks to analyze. But an additional way to look at the relative potencies of domestic versus foreign policy variables of presidential power is to do so from a Supreme Court–president perspective. If Wildavsky is correct, and if his thesis stands the test of Supreme Court analysis, the Court will allow the president more leeway in foreign policy and defense (war) matters than it will in domestic politics.[19] Although not all matters can be categorized neatly into the domestic or foreign policy realms, the distinction will prove to be both useful and instructive for our analysis.[20]

The Supreme Court itself has recognized the difference between domestic and foreign affairs when in *United States v. Curtiss-Wright Export Corporation* (299 U.S. 304 1938) it said: "we first consider the difference between the powers of the Federal government in respect of foreign or external affairs and those in respect of domestic or internal affairs. That there are differences between them and that these differences are fundamental, may not be doubted."

Normal versus Emergency Conditions

The second relationship, normal conditions versus emergency conditions, suggests that the Court is more likely to engage in conflict with a president under normal conditions than under emergency conditions.

Supreme Court decisions are not made in a vacuum. Justices read the newspapers, talk with friends, and are susceptible to many of the same influences everyone else must face. They know when a president has public support; they know when he does not. They know when the nation is facing an emergency. In short, they know when to "back off" and let the president exercise "prerogative" (at least they usually do).

Justices also know what conditions face a president. Thankfully, most of the time we do not face national emergencies. But there have been times when the nation has faced grave national crises. Foreign wars, a Civil War, economic crises, and terrorism have all plagued our nation. The Court has not been immune from the everyday pressures associated with being part of a government in crisis. In short, the "nature of the times" seem to affect justices' voting decisions.

The logic behind the normal versus emergency condition dyad rests on the belief that in times of crisis or emergency, the other actors in the political system will recognize the need for strong executive action (Locke's "prerogative") and usually will support the president in his actions. During crisis situations, the power of the president "should" be greater than it is in normal times.[21]

Majoritarian versus Antimajoritarian Courts

The next distinction, the majoritarian versus antimajoritarian dyad, deals with the partisan makeup of the Supreme Court. A majoritarian court is one whose members were appointed by the same political party as the president; an antimajoritarian court is one in which the party in opposition to the president controls a majority of the seats on the Court. The distinction contends that the partisan makeup of the Court is important in explaining conflict and cooperation between the Court and the president. An "antimajoritarian" Court is more likely to conflict with a president than is a majoritarian Court. A majoritarian Court is one that has a majority of its members appointed by the party of the incumbent president. The members need not be appointed by the incumbent himself, only by a president of the same party as the incumbent. An antimajoritarian Court is one which has a majority of its members appointed by the out party, that is, by the party other than the incumbent president's party.

The importance of the majoritarian versus antimajoritarian dyad becomes apparent when we approach the Court from a political perspective—that is, when we look at the Court as a "political institution." If politics plays a part in the outcome of judicial decision making, as we here suggest (and how could one look on *Bush v. Gore*, for example, and *not* see the politics of the case?), then the partisan makeup of the Court will influence the behavior of justices and will thus help determine when a Court is likely to conflict with a president and when it is unlikely to do so. Courts of the same partisan makeup as the president are less likely to conflict with him than will Courts whose majority is made up of a hostile or opposing party.

The Intent of Congress

When the Congress speaks, it weighs heavily on Court decisions. A president is at his strongest when he speaks *with* the Congress. He is at his most vulnerable when he defies the will of the Congress. The logic of this was best expressed by Justice Jackson, in his concurring opinion in *Youngstown Sheet & Tube Co. v. Sawyer* (343 U.S. 579 1952): "When the President acts pursuant to an express or implied authorization of Congress, his authority is at its maximum, for it includes all that he possesses in his own right plus all that Congress can delegate." Jackson later writes that "[w]hen the President acts in absence of either a congressional grant or denial of authority, he can only rely upon his own independent powers, but there is a zone of twilight in which he and Congress may have concurrent authority, or in which its distribution is uncertain." Finally, Jackson sees the president's power at its lowest ebb "[w]hen the President takes measures incompatible with the expressed or implied will of Congress."

One would thus expect that the Court will be most likely to conflict with a president when the following factors come into play: on domestic policy under normal conditions, when there is an antimajoritarian Court, and when the Congress has opposed the president's position. The Court will be least likely to conflict with a president when faced with: foreign policy under emergency conditions, when there is a majoritarian court, and when the Congress supports the president's position.

The Inevitability of Conflict

Conflict and interaction are built into our political system. Power is designed to counteract power. Thus, presidents and the Supreme Court will both complement and conflict with one another. But history has painted a picture of the president, more often than not, dominating the Court, emerging victorious from conflicts. In the conflicts between presidents and Courts, one can see more than fights over institutional supremacy; one can see battles over ideas of progress and legitimacy, law and politics, power and authority.

The history of the republic consists of far more than simply a history of Court–president conflicts and interaction, yet our history has been spotted with a number of dramatic judicial–executive confrontations. As constitutional scholar Edward S. Corwin has said, the Constitution is "an invitation to struggle," and struggle it has produced. Presidents and the Courts have met in political and legal battle over a variety of topics.

The President and the Court in Perspective

Throughout history, but especially in times of crisis or economic and political dislocation and change, the branches of government clash. When strong presidents confront a determined Congress or Supreme Court, a constitutional crisis can ensue. Thomas Jefferson clashed with the holdover Federalists on the Supreme Court; Andrew Jackson clashed with the Congress over the issue of a national bank and other matters; Lincoln was rebuffed by the Supreme Court regarding some of his decisions arising from the Civil War; FDR faced a series of Court setbacks; Richard Nixon was corraled by the Court over Watergate; and Bill Clinton lost a number of battles with the Court, as has George W. Bush.

More often than not, however, Supreme Courts have bowed to claims of presidential power. The history of Supreme Court–president relations is, we argue here, primarily one of the nation's highest court aiding and abetting an expansive view of presidential power. Although the Supreme Court has occasionally halted presidential action or declared a presidential act unconstitutional, it has more frequently labored to approve or legitimize the growth of presidential power. And even when particular sitting presidents have been rebuked by the Court, the institution of the presidency most often gains power.

The framers of the Constitution intended the Supreme Court to serve, along with the presidency, as a major check on the anticipated excesses of the national legislature. The Court, they hoped, would comprise wise, virtuous, and well-educated statesmen who would interpret and preserve the Constitution, especially from legislative encroachment. Yet two centuries later, the Court–president axis has, we argue, elevated the power of both, leaving the Congress weaker, relatively speaking, as compared with the other two branches. In the next chapter, we present instructive cases of three key presidents who clashed with the Supreme Court at pivotal moments in the country's history.

Court–President Clashes: The Cases of Abraham Lincoln, Franklin Roosevelt, and Bill Clinton*

CHAPTER **2**

Over the course of U.S. history, there have been a number of significant clashes between presidents and Courts. Three of the most important were the challenges posed by the presidencies of Abraham Lincoln, Franklin Delano Roosevelt, and William Jefferson Clinton. Although each poses a different set of circumstances and issues, each is an exemplar of how interactions between the president and the judiciary have shaped these presidencies. Most of the cases mentioned in this chapter are reprinted in the chapters to come. We offer these three accounts to provide an instructive narrative underscoring the interplay of law, politics, and interbranch jockeying.

President Lincoln and the Court

Lincoln did not believe in a dominant role for the American presidency, at least not in normal times. As a Whig Party member in earlier years, he believed the Congress should take the lead, and he believed in a strong cabinet. He also thought presidents should rarely use the veto power.

Lincoln, however, came to office in extraordinary times. In one sense, he owed his election in 1860 to Chief Justice Roger B. Taney, for the Taney Court's controversial 1857 *Dred Scott* decision split the Democratic Party into northern and southern wings over the issue of slavery. Lincoln rose to prominence because he opposed the Taney Court decision, and he won election because of the Democratic schism.

Lincoln's expansion of presidential powers came because of the wartime emergencies he faced soon after he took office. He would defer to the Congress and his cabinet on domestic matters but would use his powers as commander in chief to the fullest. Indeed, he would push them beyond the boundaries the country had hitherto known.

Fellow members of Lincoln's Republican Party were determined to reform the Supreme Court as Lincoln came to the office. Some wanted to call a national convention to modify the power of the Court through a constitutional amendment. Others pushed a "court-packing" scheme that would have enlarged the Court to thirteen members. Still others proposed even more radical remedies.

Lincoln chose a more elusive and generally a politically successful approach. He would do what he deemed necessary to fight and win the Civil War and would, whenever possible, try to prevent the court's interference by denying it an opportunity to become involved in controversial cases. Lincoln exercised broad constitutional power, and in nearly every instance he sought congressional approval only after he acted unilaterally, primarily because circumstances forced him to act. With the Congress and public opinion on his side, the Court usually did not challenge Lincoln.

Yet Lincoln clashed with the Court on some occasions, and the federal judiciary ruled against him in several cases (although many of these came after his assassination). His wartime leadership expanded the scope of executive power and tested the Court's ability to restrain a president in times of war or crisis.

Faced with the secession crisis in 1861, Lincoln, with the Congress out of session, proclaimed a blockade of southern ports and ordered the navy to enforce it. The blockade-running shipowners whose ships were seized went to court and challenged the legality of Lincoln's orders. The owners claimed that under international law, a blockade was legal only in a declared state of war. Yet no such declaration existed. Hence, they claimed, Lincoln's blockade was illegal and unconstitutional until July 1861, when the Congress sanctioned the conflict, and Lincoln's actions.

Crucial constitutional questions were raised as this case came before the Court. Was the blockade valid without a congressional declaration of war? Can a president commit the nation to military action without congressional approval? Are undeclared wars sanctioned by the U.S. Constitution?

The Court ruled (5 to 4) that a state of war had existed at the time of the blockade, thus justifying a resort to these means of subduing a "hostile force." Lincoln "won," yet only by a narrow margin. Still, the case established significant constitutional precedent. In effect, a president may determine the existence of an emergency and can take whatever measures are necessary to meet it. A president cannot declare war, yet as commander in chief he may

commit the nation to military action, especially in an ongoing domestic crisis. The president, at least in certain cases, can wage a "defensive war."

Had this case been brought up soon after the event itself, Lincoln might not have won. The Supreme Court delayed hearing the blockade cases for a year. By the time of the decision Lincoln had made three appointments to the Court; they constituted three of the five pro-Lincoln, or pro-presidential power, votes. Chief Justice Taney voted against Lincoln's position. Lincoln's initial war-making acts were thus held valid, the blockade was legitimated, the condemnation of the seized ships was sustained, and a convenient dual theory of the Civil War was outlined: It was both an insurrection, hostility within a nation, yet it had the status of a state of hostilities between independent nations.

During this time Lincoln created a national army out of state militias, calling up 75,000 volunteers for three months of military service, which the law authorized him to do. But he went beyond the law a short time later when he called up 42,000 volunteers to serve for three years in the army, thereby doubling the army's size and necessitating major spending for unauthorized projects. The Congress later gave him retroactive approval, yet he was exercising his powers to their fullest. He also suspended the right of habeas corpus (a court order stipulated in the Constitution directing an official having a person in custody to produce the person in court and explain to the judge why he or she is being held).

The central issue in another clash that Lincoln had with Chief Justice Taney rested on whether the Constitution expanded in wartime to provide enlarged presidential discretion and authority. Lincoln insisted necessity forced him to take whatever measures were needed to subdue the enemy. On this and similar occasions, Lincoln believed measures otherwise unconstitutional might become lawful by being indispensable for the preservation of the Constitution through the preservation of the nation. Usually, however, Lincoln insisted that the Constitution did provide the necessary authority for him to act as he had acted.

The Constitution, Lincoln believed, was nothing without the nation. National survival was his prime duty. Preserving all the rights and liberties provided for in the Constitution was a secondary duty, at least for the time being.

Chief Justice Roger B. Taney disagreed. He wrote the president saying he had no constitutional power to suspend the writ of habeas corpus. A president certainly "does not faithfully execute the laws if he takes upon himself legislative power, by suspending the writ of habeas corpus, and the judicial power also by arresting and imprisoning a person (John Merryman) without due process of law."[1] Taney lectured Lincoln that Merryman should be set free and that the President should reconsider his misuse of powers belonging to Congress.

Lincoln ignored Taney's judgment, although later in a special message to the Congress he asked: "Are all the laws but one to go unexecuted and the government itself go to pieces lest that one be violated?" which is a classic validation of executive power beyond the law for the alleged needs of national security. Taney's verdict was not a Supreme Court decision, as it came in a directive from Taney acting as a circuit court judge and thus had less binding force than had it come as a Court decision. More important, in this case Lincoln enjoyed pubic opinion support and popular acquiescence for his extension of executive power. Even Taney conceded he could not match the president's power.

Lincoln, through his secretary of state, instituted censorship and military arrest and trials, and continued to ignore or even suspend habeas corpus requirements in cases of persons accused of aiding the Confederacy. Throughout this period Lincoln resisted the federal courts, and Taney in particular, on the ground that a president's duty to obey judicial rulings may be suspended, in special circumstances, by the higher responsibility to "preserve, protect, and defend the Constitution." One part of the Constitution may be disregarded temporarily, he implied, in order to save the government as a whole.

What lesson can be drawn from this clash between Taney and Lincoln? At first glance it was simply a question of Taney as Supreme Court Justice striving to preserve respect for the law. Lincoln as president was determined to preserve the Union. Constitutional historians draw additional verdicts.

Clinton Rossiter comes close to saying that if a president has pubic support, he can virtually disregard both the Constitution and federal courts: "The one great precedent [here] is what Lincoln did, not what Taney said. Future Presidents will know where to look for historical support. So long as public opinion sustains the President, as a sufficient amount of it sustained Lincoln in his shadowy tilt with Taney and throughout the rest of the war, he has nothing to fear from displeasure of the courts. . . ."[2]

Others concluded that Lincoln's sweeping assertions of authority revealed an inability of the Congress and the Court to curb a dynamic president determined to act decisively in times of emergency. His leadership stunned even some of those who sympathized with the northern cause. Thus, the abolitionist Wendell Phillips called Lincoln an "unlimited despot." Lincoln may have lacked mass backing for certain of his war policies and civil liberties violations, yet he counted on the popular acquiescence that proved to sustain his leadership.

Taney died in October 1864, just before Lincoln won reelection to the White House. Two years later Taney, who while in office could never curb Lincoln's sweeping definition of emergency powers, won at least a symbolic victory in the Supreme Court in the case of *Ex parte Milligan* (1866), which vindicated the Taney judgment in *Ex parte Merryman* (1861). The Court, with Lincoln dead and at least a couple of Lincoln appointees now voting with the majority, ruled that the president's use of military courts outside the war zone was unconstitutional.

As long as civil courts are open and operating, the Court said, an accused is entitled to a civil trial by jury. The Congress had not clearly authorized the imposition of martial law. Thus, Lincoln and the executive branch had acted unconstitutionally.

Note, however, that this after-the-fact slap-on-the-wrist decision came a full year or so after the Civil War was over. It had not restrained or affected Lincoln or his presidential performance. Many analysts point to this decision as typical of the timidity of the Court or of its inability to act as a reliable check on a president during wartime. If the Court was unable or unwilling to restrain a prudent leader like Lincoln, would it be able to restrain a deter-mined, guileful, and ambitious future president? Will future presidents learn from the Lincoln lesson that emergency actions in the gray area of the Constitution are unlikely to be met with Court resistance, at least not during the emergency or during their lifetime?

Lincoln scholar Richard N. Current disputes the suggestion that Lincoln was a despot or an American Cromwell. Lincoln, he writes, continued to be sensitive to the constitutional limits on executive action. Not only did he retain his Whiggish habits of deferring rather than dictating to Congress, he almost never used the veto and he continued to consult widely. Lincoln would sometimes even acknowledge that he had little legal basis for what he had done, and he would ask Congress for appro-priate authority:

> Never did Lincoln show any hankering for the perquisite or trappings of exalted power. If absolute power corrupts absolutely, he was absolutely safe from corruption. As a young man, he warned against future politicians of a dictatorial bent. . . .
>
> Such, in actual life, were the concerns of the Lincoln whose image, more or less distorted, later presidents were to exploit. When, regardless of their party, they represented themselves as true followers, they were indeed doing as he had done, for he had said again and again that he was the true follower of the honored dead of both parties of the past. But when his successors asserted the broadest presidential power and took him as their prototype, they were making a very dubious use of history and biography. . . . Neither by word nor by deed did he give any real justification for the idea of "executive privilege" or of an "imper-ial president."[3]

Franklin D. Roosevelt and the Court

Like most strong presidents, Franklin D. Roosevelt had a series of clashes with the Court. Like Lincoln, FDR came to office during an emergency, and the

times demanded extraordinary leadership. Roosevelt was more than happy to provide it. The Supreme Court, however, would not always approve his interpretation of what needed to be done.

Roosevelt's New Deal emergency relief and recovery programs had their presumed constitutional basis in emergency executive powers or in the power of the Congress to provide for the general welfare and to regulate interstate commerce. The combined efforts of FDR and a generally cooperative Congress became the most far-reaching assertion to date of national emergency leadership.

The Supreme Court of the early Roosevelt years was hardly a body receptive to FDR's spacious uses of executive and federal power. Most of its mem-bers were appointees from the Republican Harding, Coolidge, and Hoover years.

Roosevelt's first two years passed without notable clashes with the Court. This changed in 1935. Between early 1935 and mid-1936, the Court ruled against the New Deal in several decisions. Among other actions, it held unconstitutional important parts of the National Industrial Recovery Act, the Railroad Retirement Act, a Federal Farm Mortgage Relief Act, the Agricultural Adjustment Act, and the Bituminous Coal Conservation Act. The Court also told Roosevelt he was without inherent power, which FDR had claimed, to remove a federal trade commissioner.

The Supreme Court was not the only part of the federal judiciary hostile to Roosevelt. Federal district judges granted hundreds of injunctions restraining officers of the federal government from carrying out various congressional acts.

To Roosevelt and his advisers, the Court's actions amounted to a reckless, partisan, and irresponsible claim of judicial supremacy. The Court had virtually nullified vital, core chunks of the New Deal recov-ery effort. Robert H. Jackson, a top FDR Justice Department official who would later become a Supreme Court member, describes the Court's attack on the New Deal: "In striking at New Deal laws the Court allowed its language to run riot. It attempted to engraft its own nineteenth cen-tury laissez faire philosophy upon a Constitution intended by its founders to endure for ages. . . . The

Court not merely challenged the policies of the New Deal but erected judicial barriers to the reasonable exercise of legislative powers, both state and national, to meet he urgent needs of a twentieth-century community."[4]

Then came 1936. Roosevelt won reelection by a landslide. It was a defeat for the Court almost as much as it was a Roosevelt victory. Tensions were high. Senator Burton K. Wheeler (D. Montana) proposed a constitutional amendment that would allow the Congress to override a Supreme Court decision merely by reenacting it by a two-thirds vote in both houses. Neither FDR nor his advisers wanted to go that far, yet they warned that some means had to be found to adapt the legal system and judicial interpretation to contemporary national needs.

On February 5, 1937, a frustrated Roosevelt, emboldened no doubt by his impressive reelection victory, introduced his famous reorganization, or "court-packing," plan to the Congress. Thomas Jefferson, Andrew Jackson, and Theodore Roosevelt all had altered or threatened to alter the size of the Court; thus Roosevelt's actions were not unprecedented. Yet the scope of his proposal, which would have had the effect of expanding the size of the Court from nine to fifteen, was an almost revolutionary effort.

FDR's plan recommended that if a federal judge (Supreme Court or lower courts) who had served at least ten years waited more than six months after his seventieth birthday to resign or retire, a president could add a new judge to the bench. If implemented, this plan would have allowed the president to appoint as many as six new justices to the Supreme Court and 44 judges to the lower courts.

Roosevelt's objective was obvious. Although claiming he sought efficiency and elimination of crowded backlogs facing the courts, everyone realized he was seeking to gain quick control of the Supreme Court. He told friends that what the Court needed was some Roosevelt appointments: "Then we might get some good decisions out of them." He had had no opportunity to appoint a justice in his first term, and he believed he had no choice but to act now, and to act boldly.

The plan stirred angry protests. Even Roosevelt Democrats worried it might destroy the independence of the judiciary. Several Roosevelt confidants, such as James Farley, Harry Hopkins, and Rexford Tugwell, disagreed with FDR's strategy. The less than candid reasons he gave for the plan damaged his credibility. Chief Justice Charles Evans Hughes blasted the Roosevelt scheme, saying that adding members to the Court would hinder rather than promote efficiency in Supreme Court operations. Most of the members of the then sitting Court resented FDR's attempt to make the Court more submissive to his political will. Justice Louis Brandeis, the Court's eldest member, was irked by the arbitrary and indiscriminate attack on age. Still, the plan was given reasonably serious consideration in the Congress—a Congress controlled by Democrats—until the Senate Judiciary Committee wrote a scathing report on the measure, which helped defeat it.[5]

Other reasons for the plan's defeat came as a result of post 1936 election changes by and on the Court itself. The Court began upholding as constitutional key New Deal measures that came before it. Two of the justices (Hughes and Roberts) shifted sides. Then in May 1937 one of the conservatives announced his retirement. These developments gave FDR pretty much what he wanted, a likely 6 to 3 working majority. Other developments in the Congress also were at work, but the end result was a defeat for FDR's devious plan.

Scholars often say Roosevelt lost the battle yet won the war. Plainly his 1936 election victory combined with his subsequent campaign to alter the Court's size had an impact on the Court. "A switch in time," it was said, "saved nine." The presidential power of appointment combined with congressional authority to determine the Court's size proved to be useful guns behind the door. Still, this episode was acutely embarrassing for the Roosevelt presidency as historian William E. Leuchtenburg wrote:

Nevertheless, in the end, FDR got what he wanted and won significant changes: Roosevelt, denied the opportunity to make any appointments to the Supreme Court in his first term, was able before he was through to name eight justices and elevate Harlan Fiske Stone to the chief justiceship. The new Court, the Roosevelt Court as it was called, took so broad a view of the commerce and taxing powers that scholars speak of the Constitutional Revolution of 1937, for since that time the Court has not struck down a single significant piece of social legislation. Of all the many consequences of FDR's Court-packing endeavor, by far the most significant was the legitimization of the twentieth-century state.[6]

As with Lincoln, Franklin Roosevelt's most important ally in his conflicts with the Court was public opinion. Ultimately, the Court came to legitimize Roosevelt's more sweeping use of national power because he enjoyed the support of the public. Whether public opinion should sway the judgments of the judiciary is of course another matter, and one of the most profoundly debated aspects of the role of the Court and constitutional review in our democratic republic.

Roosevelt enjoyed even stronger public support for the foreign policy and wartime measures he initiated. Conservative Republican George Sutherland, a Harding appointee to the court, shared Roosevelt's view of a strong president for foreign policy. Justice Sutherland said in the *U.S. v. Curtiss-Wright Export Corporation* case in 1936 that in foreign policy, "with its important, complicated, delicate and manifold problems, the president alone has the power to speak or listen as a representative of the nation." The Congress had delegated broad powers in foreign affairs to the president and even extended the normal pattern. Sutherland called the president the "sole organ" of the nation and came close to calling him "the sovereign." It appeared from this decision that virtually any delegation of foreign policy power to a president would be upheld.

Political scientist David Gray Adler summarizes the decision's impact: "There can be little doubt that the opinion in *United States v. Curtiss-Wright Export Corp.* in 1936 has been the Court's principal contribution to the growth of executive power over foreign affairs. Its declaration that the president is the "sole organ of foreign affairs" is a powerful, albeit unfortunate, legacy of the case. Even when

the sole-organ doctrine has not been invoked by name, its spirit, indeed its talismanic aura, has provided a common thread in a pattern of cases that has exalted presidential power above constitutional norms."[7]

Once again in 1942, in *Ex parte Quirin*, the Supreme Court expanded presidential power in a period of wartime. The case involved the manner in which eight German saboteurs who had landed on American shores with explosives should be tried. Franklin Roosevelt ordered a secret military trial and closed the civil courts to saboteurs. Judicial scholar David J. Danelski explains this complex, fascinating, and tortured case well, but his conclusion is of primary concern here: "For the executive branch, the Saboteurs' Case was a constitutional and propaganda victory; it expanded Executive power, and it allayed pubic fears of subversion. For the Supreme Court, it was an institutional defeat. If there is any lesson to be learned from the case, it is that the Court should be wary of departing from its established rules and practices, even in times of national crisis, for at such times the Court is especially susceptible to co-optation by the executive."[8]

In 1944, another significant delegation of power was added to the list of precedents for presidential emergency leadership. The Court, in the *Korematsu v. U.S.* case (in which the Court approved the actions of the executive branch when in the early 1940s it forced West Coast Japanese Americans to relocate to the Rocky Mountain region) gave the president foreign policy or national security powers even when these powers extended into the domestic arena.[9] A president's war powers were found to take precedence even over the constitutional rights of U.S. citizens on American soil. As it did in the *Curtiss-Wright* decision, the Court based much of its decision on the reality of congressional approval of the president's action. Also, Roosevelt still had public opinion on his side. When a president has both the Congress and the public supporting an initiative or a policy, the Court is very likely to legitimize it as constitutional.

Two later presidents, Harry Truman and Richard Nixon, sometimes found themselves in the situation where neither the Congress nor the public stood by them. The Court is more tempted to strike down presidential actions when a president stands alone. Such was Truman's fate in the 1952 *Youngstown Sheet & Tube Co. v. Sawyer* case. Nixon suffered a series of defeats before the Court, including his impoundment policy, wiretapping, and the famous tapes case, *U.S. v. Nixon* (1974).

On balance, it is clear the Court will limit presidents only when they ignore congressional mandates, attempt to alter the structure of government, or seriously tread on individual liberties. (Even then the Court may find rationales for supporting an extension of presidential power.) The Court becomes more bold than it otherwise might be when presidents lose the backing of the American pubic. Still, the judicial history of noninterference with the growth of presidential power contains just enough exceptions to make it unpredictable.

Bill Clinton and the Courts

During the Clinton presidency, a number of constitutional confrontations, if not crises, took place that ultimately affected the political strength and independence of the presidency. Although Clinton emerged from these confrontations damaged but still in office, the institution of the presidency was, to some degree, battered. The degree to which the presidency may or may not have been damaged cannot be adequately judged this close to the events. But some argued that the presidency emerged from these confrontations wounded and limping.

As political scientist Richard M. Pious notes, "Clinton fared poorly in the courts, losing almost all the cases. . . . Yet winning or losing in the courts was not really what Clinton's political strategy depended upon."[10] Clinton was fighting a battle for public opinion. In this, Clinton defeated independent counsel Ken Starr and his Republican attackers in a landslide. He saved his presidency but left behind a damaged institution.

In a case of sex, lies, and videotaped depositions, the Republican-controlled Congress, hell-bent on destroying the president, became hyperpartisan,

hypercritical, and excessive in its attacks against Clinton. When it was revealed that many of the president's critics in the Congress were guilty of transgressions similar to those of the president, their case, their integrity, and their credibility crumbled. They tried too hard, cut too many corners, and were too intent on getting Clinton. In the end, their extremism and poor judgment showed.

The Court too can be faulted for some questionable decisions, most notably its failure to postpone the Paula Jones civil lawsuit until after President Clinton left office.

The high drama of the impeachment and Senate trial of William Jefferson Clinton, while attracting the most attention, was but one of a number of examples of how the intersection of law and politics forced all three branches of government to confront issues, answer questions, and resolve disputes usually dealt with more informally.

Sometimes President Clinton, sometimes the Congress, and on occasion the Court pressed claims and privilege to such an extent and without the benefit of the normal bargaining regime that the Court was asked to render a final judgment. Normally, when faced with interbranch disputes, a president and the Congress would publicly lambaste their adversaries, face a stalemate, but eventually reach an accommodation, incorporating a bargain of some kind to resolve the dispute. Such a political resolution would leave unsettled the ultimate claims of power and reinforce the give-and-take regime of bargaining and compromising characteristic of a well-functioning separation-of-powers system.

But during the Clinton years, each side became so entrenched in its positions, so hyperpartisan, and so unwilling to bargain or compromise that many issues were pressed to the end of the legal system, to be "decided" once and perhaps for all. That President Clinton lost most of these battles means that the presidency lost some of its flexibility, some of its bargaining position, and some of its independence.

Law, politics, public opinion, institutional positioning, and personal posturing all contributed to each of the three branches becoming involved in disputes over presidential power and independence. Here the president, the Congress, and the Courts all came together to decide the fate of a president, the presidency, and the system of separation of powers.[11] What distinguishes the Clinton case from the previous two is the greater inclination of political adversaries to use the Courts as a venue to resolve political disputes and the greater willingness of the Courts to accept such appeals.

In the next nine chapters, readers can judge for themselves how, and in what ways, the courts' responses to challenges arising from presidential use of power have evolved.

Separation of Powers

Although nowhere is it mentioned in the Constitution itself, the separation of powers is the principle hinge on which the American system rests. Power is separated—that is, no one branch controls or dominates; each shares power.

The presidency is part of a system. This system consists of a constellation of political participants: the Congress, courts, public, media, interest groups, and bureaucrats, all of whom share a claim to power. The president is a part of this system, often a vital part, yet a president is not in control of the system.

Ours is a constitutional system of shared, separated, overlapping, dispersed, and fragmented powers. No one influential figure controls the levers of power; they are spread out across the system. This lessens the likelihood of tyranny. But it also makes achieving necessary change difficult. The system is slow and cumbersome, designed to make leadership deliberate and usually difficult as well.

Essentially, the framers wanted to counteract two fears: the fear of the *mob* (democracy or mobocracy) and the fear of the *monarchy* (centralized, tyrannical, executive power). In fact, the menacing image of England's King George III—against whom the colonists rebelled and whom Tom Paine called "the Royal Brute of Britain"—served the framers as a powerful reminder of the dangers of a strong executive. Thus, to contain power, they set up an executive office that was constitutionally rather *weak* (the Congress had, on paper at least, most of the power), dependent on the *rule of law*, with a *separation of powers* in order to ensure a system of *checks and balances*.

For James Madison, the chief architect of the Constitution, a government with too much power was a dangerous government. Seeing himself as a keen student of history, he believed that human nature drove men—at this time, only men were allowed to enter the public arena—to pursue self-interest, and, therefore, a system of government designed to have "ambition checked by ambition" set within rather strict limits was the only hope to establish a stable government that did not endanger liberty. Realizing that "enlightened statesmen" would not always guide the nation, Madison embraced a checks-and-balance system of separate but overlapping and shared powers. His concern to have a government with controlled and limited powers is seen throughout his writings, but nowhere is it more vivid than when he wrote in *The Federalist*, No. 51, "You must first enable the government to control the governed; and in the next place, oblige it to control itself."

Yes, government had to have enough power to govern, but no, it could not have enough power to overwhelm liberty. If one branch could check another, tyranny might be thwarted.

In the early days of the fledgling republic, each branch struggled to establish itself and its power and independence within this new government. Marbury v. Madison *marked one of the essential steps in the*

Supreme Court's efforts to establish itself as a viable coequal branch to the Congress and the executive.

The case arose as a function of the first transfer of political power from one party, the Federalists, to another, the Jeffersonian Republicans. Federalist president John Adams made a series of eleventh-hour judicial appointments in an effort to stack the courts with Federalist judges. The appointment of William Marbury was signed by the president, but not delivered to the nominee. Marbury sued Secretary of State James Madison, seeking his commission.

John Marshall, the new Chief Justice of the Supreme Court and a Federalist, recognized both the precarious position in which the Court was put and the rare opportunity to establish judicial power. If the Court ordered Madison to deliver Marbury's commission, President Thomas Jefferson would surely have ignored the order, thereby diminishing—perhaps forever—the power, respect, and independence of the judiciary.

In the end, Marshall and the Court decided against Marbury on a technicality, but in doing so—and by giving Jefferson no option to respond—Marshall established the authority of the Court to declare acts of the Congress and the president unconstitutional. This authority, judicial review, made the Court the arbiter of the Constitution. And while the Court would not declare an act of the Congress unconstitutional for another fifty years, it was the assumption of this power in Marbury v. Madison *that gave Court decisions legitimacy for the next two centuries. For this reason,* Marbury v. Madison *stands out as one of the most important Supreme Court cases in history.*

Marbury v. Madison
5 U.S. 137 (1803)

Mr. Chief Justice Marshall delivered the opinion of the court.

At the last term, on the affidavits then read and filed with the clerk, a rule was granted in this case, requiring the secretary of state to show cause why a mandamus should not issue, directing him to deliver to William Marbury his commission as a justice of the peace for the county of Washington, in the district of Columbia.

No cause has been shown, and the present motion is for a mandamus . . .

1. Has the applicant a right to the commission he demands? . . .

His right originates in an act of congress passed in February 1801, concerning the district of Columbia.

After dividing the district into two counties, the eleventh section of this law enacts, "that there shall be appointed in and for each of the said counties, such number of discreet persons to be justices of the peace as the president of the United States shall, from time to time, think expedient, to continue in office for five years."

It appears from the affidavits, that in compliance with this law, a commission for William Marbury as a justice of peace for the county of Washington was signed by John Adams, then president of the United States; after which the seal of the United States was affixed to it; but the commission has never reached the person for whom it was made out. In order to determine whether he is entitled to this commission, it becomes necessary to inquire whether he has been appointed to the office. For if he has been appointed, the law continues him in office for five years, and he is entitled to the possession of those evidences of office, which, being completed, became his property . . .

The commission being signed, the subsequent duty of the secretary of state is prescribed by law, and not to be guided by the will of the president. He is to affix the seal of the United States to the commission, and is to record it.

This is not a proceeding which may be varied, if the judgment of the executive shall suggest one more eligible, but is a precise course accurately marked out by law, and is to be strictly pursued. It is the duty of the secretary of state to conform to the law, and in this he is an officer of the United States, bound to obey the laws. He acts, in this respect, as has been very properly stated at the bar, under the authority of law, and not by the instructions of the president. It is a ministerial act which the law enjoins on a particular officer for a particular purpose . . .

It is therefore decidedly the opinion of the court, that when a commission has been signed by the president, the appointment is made; and that the commission is complete when the seal of the United States has been affixed to it by the secretary of state.

Where an officer is removable at the will of the executive, the circumstance which completes his appointment is of no concern; because the act is at any time revocable; and the commission may be arrested, if still in the office. But when the officer is not removable at the will of the executive, the appointment is not revocable and cannot be annulled. It has conferred legal rights which cannot be resumed.

The discretion of the executive is to be exercised until the appointment has been made. But having once made the appointment, his power over the office is terminated in all cases, where by law the officer is not removable by him. The right to the office is then in the person appointed, and he has the absolute, unconditional power of accepting or rejecting it.

Mr. Marbury, then, since his commission was signed by the president and sealed by the secretary of state, was appointed; and as the law creating the office gave the officer a right to hold for five years independent of the executive, the appointment was not revocable; but vested in the officer legal rights which are protected by the laws of his country.

To withhold the commission, therefore, is an act deemed by the court not warranted by law, but violative of a vested legal right.

This brings us to the second inquiry; which is,

2. If he has a right, and that right has been violated, do the laws of his country afford him a remedy?

The very essence of civil liberty certainly consists in the right of every individual to claim the protection of the laws, whenever he receives an injury. One of the first duties of government is to afford that protection. In Great Britain the king himself is sued in the respectful form of a petition, and he never fails to comply with the judgment of his court . . .

The government of the United States has been emphatically termed a government of laws, and not of men. It will certainly cease to deserve this high appellation, if the laws furnish no remedy for the violation of a vested legal right.

If this obloquy is to be cast on the jurisprudence of our country, it must arise from the peculiar character of the case.

It behooves us then to inquire whether there be in its composition any ingredient which shall exempt from legal investigation, or exclude the injured party from legal redress . . .

Is it in the nature of the transaction? Is the act of delivering or withholding a commission to be considered as a mere political act belonging to the executive department alone, for the performance of which entire confidence is placed by our constitution in the supreme executive; and for any misconduct respecting which, the injured individual has no remedy.

That there may be such cases is not to be questioned; but that every act of duty to be performed in any of the great departments of government constitutes such a case, is not to be admitted . . .

It follows then that the question, whether the legality of an act of the head of a department be examinable in a court of justice or not, must always depend on the nature of that act.

If some acts be examinable, and others not, there must be some rule of law to guide the court in the exercise of its jurisdiction.

In some instances there may be difficulty in applying the rule to particular cases; but there cannot, it is believed, be much difficulty in laying down the rule.

By the constitution of the United States, the president is invested with certain important political powers, in the exercise of which he is to use his own discretion, and is accountable only to his country in his political character, and to his own conscience. To aid him in the performance of these duties, he is authorized to appoint certain officers, who act by his authority and in conformity with his orders.

In such cases, their acts are his acts; and whatever opinion may be entertained of the manner in which executive discretion may be used, still there exists, and can exist, no power to control that discretion. The subjects are political. They respect the nation, not individual rights, and being entrusted to the executive, the decision of the executive is conclusive. The application of this remark will be perceived by adverting to the act of congress for establishing the department of foreign affairs. This officer, as his duties were prescribed by that act, is to conform precisely to the will of the president. He is the mere organ by whom that will is communicated. The acts of such an officer, as an officer, can never be examinable by the courts.

But when the legislature proceeds to impose on that officer other duties; when he is directed peremptorily to perform certain acts; when the rights of individuals are dependent on the performance of those acts; he is so far the officer of the law; is amenable to the laws for his conduct; and cannot at his discretion sport away the vested rights of others . . .

If this be the rule, let us inquire how it applies to the case under the consideration of the court.

The power of nominating to the senate, and the power of appointing the person nominated, are political powers, to be exercised by the president according to his own discretion. When he has made an appointment, he has exercised his whole power, and his discretion has been completely applied to the case . . .

The question whether a right has vested or not, is, in its nature, judicial, and must be tried by the judicial authority, If, for example, Mr. Marbury had taken the oaths of a magistrate, and proceeded to act as one; in consequence of which a suit had been instituted against him, in which his defence had depended on his being a magistrate; the validity of his appointment must have been determined by judicial authority.

So, if he conceives that by virtue of his appointment he has a legal right either to the commission which has been made out for him or to a copy of that commission, it is equally a question examinable in a court, and the decision of the court upon it must depend on the opinion entertained of his appointment . . .

It is then the opinion of the court . . .

2. That, having this legal title to the office, he has a consequent right to the commission; a refusal to deliver which is a plain violation of that right, for which the laws of his country afford him a remedy. . . .

Still, to render the mandamus a proper remedy, the officer to whom it is to be directed, must be one to whom, on legal principles, such writ may be directed; and the person applying for it must be without any other specific and legal remedy.

. . . The intimate political relation, subsisting between the president of the United States and the heads of departments, necessarily renders any legal investigation of the acts of one of those high officers peculiarly irksome, as well as delicate; and excites some hesitation with respect to the propriety of entering into such investigation.

. . . The province of the court is, solely, to decide on the rights of individuals, not to inquire how the executive, or executive officers, perform duties in which they have discretion. Questions, in their nature political, or which are, by the constitution and laws, submitted to the executive, can never be made in this court.

But, if this be not such a question; if so far from being an intrusion into the secrets of the cabinet, it respects a paper, which, according to law, is upon record, and to a copy of which the law gives a right, on the payment of ten cents; if it be no intermeddling with a subject, over which the executive can be considered as having exercised any control; what is there in the exalted station of the officer, which shall bar a citizen from asserting, in a court of justice, his legal rights, or shall forbid a court to listen to the claim; or to issue a mandamus, directing the performance of a duty, not depending on executive discretion, but on particular acts of congress and the general principles of law?

. . . It is not by the office of the person to whom the writ is directed, but the nature of the thing to be done, that the propriety or impropriety of issuing a mandamus is to be determined . . .

This, then, is a plain case of a mandamus, either to deliver the commission, or a copy of it from the record; and it only remains to be inquired, whether it can issue from this court.

During the Korean War, President Truman, facing a labor dispute that shut down the steel industry, issued Executive Order 10340, seizing the mills and keeping them open. Truman claimed that the mills were a vital element in the war effort and that as commander in chief he had the authority (inherent power) to seize the mills and maintain steel production. After issuing the executive order, Truman delivered a message to the Congress informing them of his action, but the Congress took no action.

The steel companies immediately brought suit to restrain the government from seizing their mills, on the grounds that the president did not have the proper authority to seize private property and that he exceeded his constitutional authority.

Youngstown Sheet & Tube Co. v. Sawyer
343 U.S. 579 (1952)

. . . Mr. Justice Black delivered the opinion of the Court.

We are asked to decide whether the President was acting within his constitutional power when he issued an order directing the Secretary of Commerce to take possession of and operate most of the Nation's steel mills. The mill owners argue that the President's order amounts to lawmaking, a legislative function which the Constitution has expressly confided to the Congress and not to the President. The Government's position is that the order was made on findings of the President that his action was necessary to avert a national catastrophe which would inevitably result from a stoppage of steel production, and that in meeting this grave emergency the President was acting within the aggregate of his constitutional powers as the Nation's Chief Executive and the Commander in Chief of the Armed Forces of the United States. The issue emerges here from the following series of events . . .

The President's power, if any, to issue the order must stem either from an act of Congress or from the Constitution itself. There is no statute that expressly authorizes the President to take possession of property as he did here. Nor is there any act of Congress to which our attention has been directed from which such a power can fairly be implied. Indeed, we do not understand the Government to rely on statutory authorization for this seizure. There are two statutes which do authorize the President to take both personal and real property under certain conditions. However, the Government admits that these conditions were not met and that the President's order was not rooted in either of the statutes. The Government refers to the seizure provisions of one of these statutes (201 (b) of the Defense Production Act) as "much too cumbersome, involved, and time-consuming for the crisis which was at hand."

Moreover, the use of the seizure technique to solve labor disputes in order to prevent work stoppages was not only unauthorized by any congressional enactment; prior to this controversy, Congress had refused to adopt that method of settling labor disputes. When the Taft-Hartley Act was under consideration in 1947, Congress rejected an amendment which would have authorized such governmental seizures in cases of emergency. Apparently it was thought that the technique of seizure, like that of compulsory arbitration, would interfere with the process of collective bargaining. Consequently, the plan Congress adopted in that Act did not provide for seizure under any circumstances. Instead, the plan sought to bring about settlements by use of the customary devices of mediation, conciliation, investigation by boards of inquiry, and public reports. In some instances temporary injunctions were authorized to provide cooling-off periods. All this failing, unions were left free to strike after a secret vote by employees as to whether they wished to accept their employers' final settlement offer.

It is clear that if the President had authority to issue the order he did, it must be found in some provision of the Constitution. And it is not claimed that express constitutional language grants this power to the President. The contention is that presidential power should be implied from the aggregate of his powers under the Constitution. Particular reliance is placed on provisions in Article II which say that "The executive Power shall be vested in a President . . ."; that "he shall take Care that the Laws be faithfully executed"; and that he "shall be Commander in Chief of the Army and Navy of the United States."

The order cannot properly be sustained as an exercise of the President's military power as Commander in Chief of the Armed Forces. The Government attempts to do so by citing a number of cases upholding broad powers in military commanders engaged in day-to-day fighting in a theater of war. Such cases need not concern us here. Even though "theater of war" be an expanding concept, we cannot with faithfulness to our constitutional system hold that the Commander in Chief of the Armed Forces has the ultimate power as such to take possession of private property in order to keep labor disputes from stopping production. This is a job for the Nation's lawmakers, not for its military authorities.

Nor can the seizure order be sustained because of the several constitutional provisions that grant executive power to the President. In the framework of our Constitution, the President's power to see that the laws are faithfully executed refutes the idea that he is to be a lawmaker. The Constitution limits his functions in the lawmaking process to the recommending of laws he thinks wise and the vetoing of laws he thinks bad. And the Constitution is neither silent nor equivocal about who shall make laws which the President is to execute. The first section of the first article says that "All legislative Powers herein granted shall be vested in a Congress of the United States . . . ." After granting many powers to the Congress, Article I goes on to provide that Congress may "make all Laws which shall be necessary and proper for carrying into Execution the foregoing Powers, and all other Powers vested by this Constitution in the Government of the United States, or in any Department or Officer thereof."

The President's order does not direct that a congressional policy be executed in a manner prescribed by Congress—it directs that a presidential policy be executed in a manner prescribed by the President. The preamble of the order itself, like that of many statutes, sets out reasons why the President believes certain policies should be adopted, proclaims these policies as rules of conduct to be followed, and again, like a statute, authorizes a government official to promulgate additional rules and regulations consistent with the policy proclaimed and needed to carry that policy into execution. The power of Congress to adopt such public policies as those proclaimed by the order is beyond question. It can authorize the taking of private property for public use. It can make laws regulating the relationships between employers and employees, prescribing rules designed to settle labor disputes, and fixing wages and working conditions in certain fields of our economy. The Constitution does not subject this lawmaking power of Congress to presidential or military supervision or control.

It is said that other Presidents without congressional authority have taken possession of private business enterprises in order to settle labor disputes. But even if this be true, Congress has not thereby lost its exclusive constitutional authority to make laws necessary and proper to carry out the powers vested by the

Constitution "in the Government of the United States, or any Department or Officer thereof."

The Founders of this Nation entrusted the lawmaking power to the Congress alone in both good and bad times. It would do no good to recall the historical events, the fears of power and the hopes for freedom that lay behind their choice. Such a review would but confirm our holding that this seizure order cannot stand.

The judgment of the District Court is Affirmed.

Mr. Justice Frankfurter, concurring . . .

Congress in 1947 was again called upon to consider whether governmental seizure should be used to avoid serious industrial shutdowns. Congress decided against conferring such power generally and in advance, without special Congressional enactment to meet each particular need. Under the urgency of telephone and coal strikes in the winter of 1946, Congress addressed itself to the problems raised by "national emergency" strikes and lockouts. The termination of wartime seizure powers on December 31, 1946, brought these matters to the attention of Congress with vivid impact. A proposal that the President be given powers to seize plants to avert a shutdown where the "health or safety" of the Nation was endangered, was thoroughly canvassed by Congress and rejected. No room for doubt remains that the proponents as well as the opponents of the bill which became the Labor Management Relations Act of 1947 clearly understood that as a result of that legislation the only recourse for preventing a shutdown in any basic industry, after failure of mediation, was Congress. Authorization for seizure as an available remedy for potential dangers was unequivocally put aside. The Senate Labor Committee, through its Chairman, explicitly reported to the Senate that a general grant of seizure powers had been considered and rejected in favor of reliance on ad hoc legislation, as a particular emergency might call for it. An amendment presented in the House providing that, where necessary "to preserve and protect the public health and security," the President might seize

any industry in which there is an impending curtailment of production, was voted down after debate, by a vote of more than three to one . . .

. . . On a balance of considerations, Congress chose not to lodge this power in the President. It chose not to make available in advance a remedy to which both industry and labor were fiercely hostile . . .

In any event, nothing can be plainer than that Congress made a conscious choice of policy in a field full of perplexity and peculiarly within legislative responsibility for choice. In formulating legislation for dealing with industrial conflicts, Congress could not more clearly and emphatically have withheld authority than it did in 1947 . . . Instead of giving him even limited powers, Congress in 1947 deemed it wise to require the President, upon failure of attempts to reach a voluntary settlement, to report to Congress if he deemed the power of seizure a needed shot for his locker. The President could not ignore the specific limitations of prior seizure statutes. No more could he act in disregard of the limitation put upon seizure by the 1947 Act . . .

. . . But it is now claimed that the President has seizure power by virtue of the Defense Production Act of 1950 and its Amendments. And the claim is based on the occurrence of new events—Korea and the need for stabilization, etc.—although it was well known that seizure power was withheld by the Act of 1947, and although the President, whose specific requests for other authority were in the main granted by Congress, never suggested that in view of the new events he needed the power of seizure which Congress in its judgment had decided to withhold from him. The utmost that the Korean conflict may imply is that it may have been desirable to have given the President further authority, a freer hand in these matters. Absence of authority in the President to deal with a crisis does not imply want of power in the Government. Conversely the fact that power exists in the Government does not vest it in the President . . .

No authority that has since been given to the President can by any fair process of statutory construction be deemed to withdraw the restriction or change the will of Congress as expressed by a body of enactments, culminating in the Labor Management Relations Act of 1947 . . .

Apart from his vast share of responsibility for the conduct of our foreign relations, the embracing function of the President is that "he shall take Care that the Laws be faithfully executed. . . ." Art. II, 3. The nature of that authority has for me been comprehensively indicated by Mr. Justice Holmes. "The duty of the President to see that the laws be executed is a duty that does not go beyond the laws or require him to achieve more than Congress sees fit to leave within his power." *Myers v. United States, 272 U.S. 52, 177* . . .

To be sure, the content of the three authorities of government is not to be derived from an abstract analysis. The areas are partly interacting, not wholly disjointed. The Constitution is a framework for government. Therefore the way the framework has consistently operated fairly establishes that it has operated according to its true nature. Deeply embedded traditional ways of conducting government cannot supplant the Constitution or legislation, but they give meaning to the words of a text or supply them. It is an inadmissibly narrow conception of American constitutional law to confine it to the words of the Constitution and to disregard the gloss which life has written upon them. In short, a systematic, unbroken, executive practice, long pursued to the knowledge of the Congress and never before questioned, engaged in by Presidents who have also sworn to uphold the Constitution, making as it were such exercise of power part of the structure of our government, may be treated as a gloss on "executive Power" vested in the President by 1 of Art. II . . .

Down to the World War II period, then, the record is barren of instances comparable to the one before us. Of twelve seizures by President Roosevelt prior to the enactment of the War Labor Disputes Act in June, 1943, three were sanctioned by existing law, and six others were effected after Congress, on December 8, 1941, had declared the existence of a state of war. In this case, reliance on the powers that

flow from declared war has been commendably disclaimed by the Solicitor General. Thus the list of executive assertions of the power of seizure in circumstances comparable to the present reduces to three in the six-month period from June to December of 1941. We need not split hairs in comparing those actions to the one before us, though much might be said by way of differentiation. Without passing on their validity, as we are not called upon to do, it suffices to say that these three isolated instances do not add up, either in number, scope, duration or contemporaneous legal justification, to the kind of executive construction of the Constitution revealed in the Midwest Oil case. Nor do they come to us sanctioned by long-continued acquiescence of Congress giving decisive weight to a construction by the Executive of its powers . . .

Mr. Justice Jackson, concurring in the judgment and opinion of the Court . . .

The actual art of governing under our Constitution does not and cannot conform to judicial definitions of the power of any of its branches based on isolated clauses or even single Articles torn from context. While the Constitution diffuses power the better to secure liberty, it also contemplates that practice will integrate the dispersed powers into a workable government. It enjoins upon its branches separateness but interdependence, autonomy but reciprocity. Presidential powers are not fixed but fluctuate, depending upon their disjunction or conjunction with those of Congress. We may well begin by a somewhat over-simplified grouping of practical situations in which a President may doubt, or others may challenge, his powers, and by distinguishing roughly the legal consequences of this factor of relativity.

1. When the President acts pursuant to an express or implied authorization of Congress, his authority is at its maximum, for it includes all that he possesses in his own right plus all that Congress can delegate. In these circumstances, and in these only, may he be said (for what it may be worth) to personify the federal sovereignty. If his act is held unconstitutional under these circumstances, it

usually means that the Federal Government as an undivided whole lacks power. A seizure executed by the President pursuant to an Act of Congress would be supported by the strongest of presumptions and the widest latitude of judicial interpretation, and the burden of persuasion would rest heavily upon any who might attack it.

2. When the President acts in absence of either a congressional grant or denial of authority, he can only rely upon his own independent powers, but there is a zone of twilight in which he and Congress may have concurrent authority, or in which its distribution is uncertain. Therefore, congressional inertia, indifference or quiescence may sometimes, at least as a practical matter, enable, if not invite, measures on independent presidential responsibility. In this area, any actual test of power is likely to depend on the imperatives of events and contemporary imponderables rather than on abstract theories of law.

3. When the President takes measures incompatible with the expressed or implied will of Congress, his power is at its lowest ebb, for then he can rely only upon his own constitutional powers minus any constitutional powers of Congress over the matter. Courts can sustain exclusive presidential control in such a case only by disabling the Congress from acting upon the subject. Presidential claim to a power at once so conclusive and preclusive must be scrutinized with caution, for what is at stake is the equilibrium established by our constitutional system.

Into which of these classifications does this executive seizure of the steel industry fit? It is eliminated from the first by admission, for it is conceded that no congressional authorization exists for this seizure. That takes away also the support of the many precedents and declarations which were made in relation, and must be confined, to this category.

Can it then be defended under flexible tests available to the second category? It seems clearly eliminated from that class because Congress has not left seizure of private property an open field but has covered it by three statutory policies inconsistent with this seizure. In cases where the purpose is to supply needs of the Government itself, two courses are provided: one, seizure of a plant which fails to comply with obligatory orders placed by the Government; another, condemnation of facilities, including temporary use under the power of eminent domain. The third is applicable where it is the general economy of the country that is to be protected rather than exclusive governmental interests. None of these were invoked. In choosing a different and inconsistent way of his own, the President cannot claim that it is necessitated or invited by failure of Congress to legislate upon the occasions, grounds and methods for seizure of industrial properties.

This leaves the current seizure to be justified only by the severe tests under the third grouping, where it can be supported only by any remainder of executive power after subtraction of such powers as Congress may have over the subject. In short, we can sustain the President only by holding that seizure of such strike-bound industries is within his domain and beyond control by Congress. Thus, this Court's first review of such seizures occurs under circumstances which leave presidential power most vulnerable to attack and in the least favorable of possible constitutional postures . . .

The Solicitor General seeks the power of seizure in three clauses of the Executive Article, the first reading, "The executive Power shall be vested in a President of the United States of America." Lest I be thought to exaggerate, I quote the interpretation which his brief puts upon it: "In our view, this clause constitutes a grant of all the executive powers of which the Government is capable." If that be true, it is difficult to see why the forefathers bothered to add several specific items, including some trifling ones.

The example of such unlimited executive power that must have most impressed the forefathers was the prerogative exercised by George III, and the description of its evils in the Declaration of Independence leads me to doubt that they were creating their new

Executive in his image. Continental European examples were no more appealing. And if we seek instruction from our own times, we can match it only from the executive powers in those governments we disparagingly describe as totalitarian. I cannot accept the view that this clause is a grant in bulk of all conceivable executive power but regard it as an allocation to the presidential office of the generic powers thereafter stated.

The clause on which the Government next relies is that "The President shall be Commander in Chief of the Army and Navy of the United States . . . ." These cryptic words have given rise to some of the most persistent controversies in our constitutional history. Of course, they imply something more than an empty title. But just what authority goes with the name has plagued presidential advisers who would not waive or narrow it by nonassertion yet cannot say where it begins or ends. It undoubtedly puts the Nation's armed forces under presidential command. Hence, this loose appellation is sometimes advanced as support for any presidential action, internal or external, involving use of force, the idea being that it vests power to do anything, anywhere, that can be done with an army or navy.

That seems to be the logic of an argument tendered at our bar—that the President having, on his own responsibility, sent American troops abroad derives from that act "affirmative power" to seize the means of producing a supply of steel for them. To quote, "Perhaps the most forceful illustration of the scope of Presidential power in this connection is the fact that American troops in Korea, whose safety and effectiveness are so directly involved here, were sent to the field by an exercise of the President's constitutional powers." Thus, it is said, he has invested himself with "war powers."

I cannot foresee all that it might entail if the Court should indorse this argument. Nothing in our Constitution is plainer than that declaration of a war is entrusted only to Congress. Of course, a state of war may in fact exist without a formal declaration. But no doctrine that the Court could promulgate would seem to me more sinister and alarming

than that a President whose conduct of foreign affairs is so largely uncontrolled, and often even is unknown, can vastly enlarge his mastery over the internal affairs of the country by his own commitment of the Nation's armed forces to some foreign venture. I do not, however, find it necessary or appropriate to consider the legal status of the Korean enterprise to discountenance argument based on it.

Assuming that we are in a war *de facto*, whether it is or is not a war de jure, does that empower the Commander in Chief to seize industries he thinks necessary to supply our army? The Constitution expressly places in Congress power "to raise and support Armies" and "to provide and maintain a Navy." This certainly lays upon Congress primary responsibility for supplying the armed forces. Congress alone controls the raising of revenues and their appropriation and may determine in what manner and by what means they shall be spent for military and naval procurement. I suppose no one would doubt that Congress can take over war supply as a Government enterprise. On the other hand, if Congress sees fit to rely on free private enterprise collectively bargaining with free labor for support and maintenance of our armed forces, can the Executive, because of lawful disagreements incidental to that process, seize the facility for operation upon Government-imposed terms?

There are indications that the Constitution did not contemplate that the title Commander in Chief of the Army and Navy will constitute him also Commander in Chief of the country, its industries and its inhabitants. He has no monopoly of "war powers," whatever they are . . .

We should not use this occasion to circumscribe, much less to contract, the lawful role of the President as Commander in Chief. I should indulge the widest latitude of interpretation to sustain his exclusive function to command the instruments of national force, at least when turned against the outside world for the security of our society. But, when it is turned inward, not because of rebellion but because of a lawful economic struggle between industry and labor, it should have no such indulgence. His command power is not such an absolute as might be implied from that office in a militaristic system but is subject to limitations consistent with a constitutional Republic whose law and policy-making branch is a representative Congress. The purpose of lodging dual titles in one man was to insure that the civilian would control the military, not to enable the military to subordinate the presidential office . . .

The third clause in which the Solicitor General finds seizure powers is that "he shall take Care that the Laws be faithfully executed . . . ." That authority must be matched against words of the Fifth Amendment that "No person shall be . . . deprived of life, liberty or property, without due process of law. . . ." One gives a governmental authority that reaches so far as there is law, the other gives a private right that authority shall go no farther. These signify about all there is of the principle that ours is a government of laws, not of men, and that we submit ourselves to rulers only if under rules.

The Solicitor General lastly grounds support of the seizure upon nebulous, inherent powers never expressly granted but said to have accrued to the office from the customs and claims of preceding administrations. The plea is for a resulting power to deal with a crisis or an emergency according to the necessities of the case, the unarticulated assumption being that necessity knows no law.

Loose and irresponsible use of adjectives colors all nonlegal and much legal discussion of presidential powers. "Inherent" powers, "implied" powers, "incidental" powers, "plenary" powers, "war" powers and "emergency" powers are used, often interchangeably and without fixed or ascertainable meanings.

The vagueness and generality of the clauses that set forth presidential powers afford a plausible basis for pressures within and without an administration for presidential action beyond that supported by those whose responsibility it is to defend his actions in court. The claim of inherent and unrestricted presidential powers has long been a persuasive dialectical weapon in political controversy. While it is not surprising that counsel should grasp support from such unadjudicated claims of power, a judge cannot accept self-serving press statements of the attorney for one of the interested parties as authority in answering a constitutional question, even if the advocate was himself. But prudence has counseled that actual reliance on such nebulous claims stop short of provoking a judicial test . . .

The appeal, however, that we declare the existence of inherent powers ex necessitate to meet an emergency asks us to do what many think would be wise, although it is something the forefathers omitted. They knew what emergencies were, knew the pressures they engender for authoritative action, knew, too, how they afford a ready pretext for usurpation. We may also suspect that they suspected that emergency powers would tend to kindle emergencies. Aside from suspension of the privilege of the writ of habeas corpus in time of rebellion or invasion, when the public safety may require it, they made no express provision for exercise of extraordinary authority because of a crisis. I do not think we rightfully may so amend their work, and, if we could, I am not convinced it would be wise to do so, although many modern nations have forthrightly recognized that war and economic crises may upset the normal balance between liberty and authority. Their experience with emergency powers may not be irrelevant to the argument here that we should say that the Executive, of his own volition, can invest himself with undefined emergency powers . . .

Great Britain also has fought both World Wars under a sort of temporary dictatorship created by legislation. As Parliament is not bound by written constitutional limitations, it established a crisis government simply by delegation to its Ministers of a larger measure than usual of its own unlimited power, which is exercised under its supervision by Ministers whom it may dismiss. This has been called the "high-water mark in the voluntary surrender of liberty," but, as Churchill put it, "Parliament stands custodian of these surrendered liberties, and its most sacred duty will be to restore them in their fullness when victory has crowned our exertions and our perseverance." Thus, parliamentary control made emergency powers compatible with freedom.

This contemporary foreign experience may be inconclusive as to the wisdom of lodging emergency powers somewhere in a modern government. But it suggests that emergency powers are consistent with free government only when their control is lodged elsewhere than in the Executive who exercises them. That is the safeguard that would be nullified by our adoption of the "inherent powers" formula. Nothing in my experience convinces me that such risks are warranted by any real necessity, although such powers would, of course, be an executive convenience.

In the practical working of our Government we already have evolved a technique within the framework of the Constitution by which normal executive powers may be considerably expanded to meet an emergency. Congress may and has granted extraordinary authorities which lie dormant in normal times but may be called into play by the Executive in war or upon proclamation of a national emergency. In 1939, upon congressional request, the Attorney General listed ninety-nine such separate statutory grants by Congress of emergency or wartime executive powers. They were invoked from time to time as need appeared. Under this procedure we retain Government by law—special, temporary law, perhaps, but law nonetheless. The public may know the extent and limitations of the powers than can be asserted, and persons affected may be informed from the statute of their rights and duties.

In view of the ease, expedition and safety with which Congress can grant and has granted large emergency powers, certainly ample to embrace this crisis, I am quite unimpressed with the argument that we should affirm possession of them without statute. Such power either has no beginning or it has no end. If it exists, it need submit to no legal restraint. I am not alarmed that it would plunge us straightaway into dictatorship, but it is at least a step in that wrong direction.

As to whether there is imperative necessity for such powers, it is relevant to note the gap that exists between the President's paper powers and his real powers. The Constitution does not disclose the measure of the actual controls wielded by the modern presidential office. That instrument must be understood as an Eighteenth-Century sketch of a government hoped for, not as a blueprint of the Government that is. Vast accretions of federal power, eroded from that reserved by the States, have magnified the scope of presidential activity. Subtle shifts take place in the centers of real power that do not show on the face of the Constitution.

Executive power has the advantage of concentration in a single head in whose choice the whole Nation has a part, making him the focus of public hopes and expectations. In drama, magnitude and finality his decisions so far overshadow any others that almost alone he fills the public eye and ear. No other personality in public life can begin to compete with him in access to the public mind through modern methods of communications. By his prestige as head of state and his influence upon public opinion he exerts a leverage upon those who are supposed to check and balance his power which often cancels their effectiveness.

Moreover, rise of the party system has made a significant extra constitutional supplement to real executive power. No appraisal of his necessities is realistic which overlooks that he heads a political system as well as a legal system. Party loyalties and interests, sometimes more binding than law, extend his effective control into branches of government other than his own and he often may win, as a political leader, what he cannot command under the Constitution. Indeed, Woodrow Wilson, commenting on the President as leader both of his party and of the Nation, observed, "If he rightly interpret the national thought and boldly insist upon it, he is irresistible . . . . His office is anything he has the sagacity and force to make it." I cannot be brought to believe that this country will suffer if the Court refuses further to aggrandize the presidential office, already so potent and so relatively immune from judicial review, at the expense of Congress.

But I have no illusion that any decision by this Court can keep power in the hands of Congress if it is not wise and timely in meeting its problems. A crisis that challenges the President equally, or perhaps primarily, challenges Congress. If not good law, there was worldly wisdom in the maxim attributed to Napoleon that "The tools belong to the man who can use them." We may say that power to legislate for emergencies belongs in the hands of Congress, but only Congress itself can prevent power from slipping through its fingers.

. . . With all its defects, delays and inconveniences, men have discovered no technique for long preserving free government except that the Executive be under the law, and that the law be made by parliamentary deliberations . . .

MR. CHIEF JUSTICE VINSON, with whom MR. JUSTICE REED and MR. JUSTICE MINTON join, dissenting . . .

In passing upon the question of Presidential powers in this case, we must first consider the context in which those powers were exercised.

Those who suggest that this is a case involving extraordinary powers should be mindful that these are extraordinary times. A world not yet recovered from the devastation of World War II has been forced to face the threat of another and more terrifying global conflict.

. . . In 1950, when the United Nations called upon member nations "to render every assistance" to repel aggression in Korea, the United States furnished its vigorous support. For almost two full years, our armed forces have been fighting in Korea, suffering casualties of over 108,000 men. Hostilities have not abated . . . Congressional support of the action in Korea has been manifested by provisions for increased military manpower and equipment and for economic stabilization, as hereinafter described . . .

Congress also directed the President to build up our own defenses. Congress, recognizing the "grim fact . . . that the United States is now engaged in a struggle for survival" and that "it is imperative that we now take those necessary steps to make our strength equal to the peril of the hour," granted authority to draft men into the armed forces. As a result, we now have over 3,500,000 men in our armed forces.

Appropriations for the Department of Defense, which had averaged less than $13 billion per year for the three years before attack in Korea, were increased by Congress to $48 billion for fiscal year 1951 and to $60 billion for fiscal year 1952 . . . The bulk of the increase is for military equipment and supplies—guns, tanks, ships, planes, and ammunition—all of which require steel . . .

Congress recognized the impact of these defense programs upon the economy. Following the attack in Korea, the President asked for authority to requisition property and to allocate and fix priorities for scarce goods. In the Defense Production Act of 1950, Congress granted the powers requested and, in addition, granted power to stabilize prices and wages and to provide for settlement of labor disputes arising in the defense program . . .

The President has the duty to execute the foregoing legislative programs. Their successful execution depends upon continued production of steel and stabilized prices for steel. Accordingly, when the collective bargaining agreements between the Nation's steel producers and their employees, represented by the United Steel Workers, were due to expire on December 31, 1951, and a strike shutting down the entire basic steel industry was threatened, the President acted to avert a complete shutdown of steel production . . .

. . . April 9, 1952, the President addressed the following Message to Congress:

"To the Congress of the United States:

"The Congress is undoubtedly aware of the recent events which have taken place in connection with the management-labor dispute in the steel industry. These events culminated in the action which was taken last night to provide for temporary operation of the steel mills by the Government.

"I took this action with the utmost reluctance. The idea of Government operation of the steel mills is thoroughly distasteful to me and I want to see it ended as soon as possible. However, in the situation which confronted me yesterday, I felt that I could make no other choice. The other alternatives appeared to be even worse—so much worse that I could not accept them.

"One alternative would have been to permit a shutdown in the steel industry. The effects of such a shut-down would have been so immediate and damaging with respect to our efforts to support our Armed Forces and to protect our national security that it made this alternative unthinkable.

"The only way that I know of, other than Government operation, by which a steel shut-down could have been avoided was to grant the demands of the steel industry for a large price increase. I believed and the officials in charge of our stabilization agencies believed that this would have wrecked our stabilization program. I was unwilling to accept the incalculable damage which might be done to our country by following such a course.

"Accordingly, it was my judgment that Government operation of the steel mills for a temporary period was the least undesirable of the courses of action which lay open. In the circumstances, I believed it to be, and now believe it to be, my duty and within my powers as President to follow that course of action.

"It may be that the Congress will deem some other course to be wiser . . ."

Twelve days passed without action by Congress. On April 21, 1952, the President sent a letter to the President of the Senate in which he again described the purpose and need for his action and again stated his position that "The Congress can, if it wishes, reject the course of action I have followed in this matter." Congress has not so acted to this date.

Meanwhile, plaintiffs instituted this action in the District Court to compel defendant to return possession of the steel mills seized under Executive Order 10340 . . . We also assume without deciding that the courts may go behind a President's finding of fact that an emergency exists. But there is not the slightest basis for suggesting that the President's finding in this case can be undermined. Plaintiffs moved for a preliminary injunction before answer or hearing. Defendant opposed the motion, filing uncontroverted affidavits of Government officials describing the facts underlying the President's order . . .

Accordingly, if the President has any power under the Constitution to meet a critical situation in the absence of express statutory authorization, there is no basis whatever for criticizing the exercise of such power in this case . . .

In passing upon the grave constitutional question presented in this case, we must never forget, as Chief Justice Marshall admonished, that the Constitution is "intended to endure for ages to come, and, consequently, to be adapted to the various crises of human affairs," and that "[i]ts means are adequate to its ends." Cases do arise presenting questions which could not have been foreseen by the Framers. In such cases, the Constitution has been treated as a living document adaptable to new situations. But we are not called upon today to expand the Constitution to meet a new situation. For, in this case, we need only look to history and time-honored principles of constitutional law—principles that have been applied consistently by all branches of the Government throughout our history. It is those who assert the invalidity of the Executive Order who seek to amend the Constitution in this case.

A review of executive action demonstrates that our Presidents have on many occasions exhibited the leadership contemplated by the Framers when they made the President Commander in Chief, and imposed upon him the trust to "take Care that the Laws be faithfully executed." With or without explicit statutory authorization, Presidents have at such times dealt with national emergencies by acting promptly and resolutely to enforce legislative programs, at least to save those programs until Congress could act. Congress and the courts have responded to such executive initiative with consistent approval . . .

Focusing now on the situation confronting the President on the night of April 8, 1952, we cannot but conclude that the President was performing his duty under the Constitution to "take Care that the Laws be faithfully executed"—a duty described by President Benjamin Harrison as "the central idea of the office."

The President reported to Congress the morning after the seizure that he acted because a work stoppage in steel production would immediately imperil the safety of the Nation by preventing execution of the legislative programs for procurement of military equipment. And, while a shutdown could be averted by granting the price concessions requested by plaintiffs, granting such concessions would disrupt the price stabilization program also enacted by Congress. Rather than fail to execute either legislative program, the President acted to execute both.

Much of the argument in this case has been directed at straw men. We do not now have before us the case of a President acting solely on the basis of his own notions of the public welfare. Nor is there any question of unlimited executive power in this case. The President himself closed the door to any such claim when he sent his Message to Congress stating his purpose to abide by any action of Congress, whether approving or disapproving his seizure action. Here, the President immediately made sure that Congress was fully informed of the temporary action he had taken only to preserve the legislative programs from destruction until Congress could act.

The absence of a specific statute authorizing seizure of the steel mills as a mode of executing the laws—both the military procurement program and the anti-inflation program—has not until today been thought to prevent the President from executing the laws. Unlike an administrative commission confined to the enforcement of the statute under which it was created, or the head of a department when administering a particular statute, the President is a constitutional officer charged with taking care that a "mass of legislation" be executed. Flexibility as to mode of execution to meet critical situations is a matter of practical necessity. This practical construction of the "Take Care" clause, advocated by John Marshall, was adopted by this Court in In re Neagle, In re Debs and other cases cited *supra*.

There is no statute prohibiting seizure as a method of enforcing legislative programs. Congress has in no wise indicated that its legislation is not to be executed by the taking of private property (subject of course to the payment of just compensation) if its legislation cannot otherwise be executed. Indeed, the Universal Military Training and Service Act authorizes the seizure of any plant that fails to fill a Government contract or the properties of any steel producer that fails to allocate steel as directed for defense production. And the Defense Production Act authorizes the President to requisition equipment and condemn real property needed without delay in the defense effort. Where Congress authorizes seizure in instances not necessarily crucial to the defense program, it can hardly be said to have disclosed an intention to prohibit seizures where essential to the execution of that legislative program.

. . . The President's action served the same purposes as a judicial stay entered to maintain the status quo in order to preserve the jurisdiction of a court . . .

In United States v. Midwest Oil Co., *supra*, this Court approved executive action where, as here, the President acted to preserve an important matter until Congress could act—even though his action in that case was contrary to an express statute. In this case, there is no statute prohibiting the action taken by the President in a matter not merely important but threatening the very safety of the Nation. Executive inaction in such a situation, courting national disaster, is foreign to the concept of energy and initiative in the Executive as created by the Founding Fathers. The Constitution was itself "adopted in a period of grave emergency. . . . While emergency does not create power, emergency may furnish the occasion for the exercise of power." The Framers knew, as we should know in these times of peril, that there is real danger in

Executive weakness. There is no cause to fear Executive tyranny so long as the laws of Congress are being faithfully executed. Certainly there is no basis for fear of dictatorship when the Executive acts, as he did in this case, only to save the situation until Congress could act.

Plaintiffs place their primary emphasis on the Labor Management Relations Act of 1947, hereinafter referred to as the Taft-Hartley Act, but do not contend that that Act contains any provision prohibiting seizure . . .

Plaintiffs admit that the emergency procedures of Taft-Hartley are not mandatory. Nevertheless, plaintiffs apparently argue that, since Congress did provide the 80-day injunction method for dealing with emergency strikes, the President cannot claim that an emergency exists until the procedures of Taft-Hartley have been exhausted. This argument was not the basis of the District Court's opinion and, whatever merit the argument might have had following the enactment of Taft-Hartley, it loses all force when viewed in light of the statutory pattern confronting the President in this case.

In Title V of the Defense Production Act of 1950 . . .

Title V authorized the President to initiate labor-management conferences and to take action appropriate to carrying out the recommendations of such conferences and the provisions of Title V. (502.) Due regard is to be given to collective bargaining practice and stabilization policies and no action taken is to be inconsistent with Taft-Hartley and other laws. (503.) . . .

The President authorized the Wage Stabilization Board (WSB), which administers the wage stabilization functions of Title IV of the Defense Production Act, also to deal with labor disputes affecting the defense program. When extension of the Defense Production Act was before Congress in 1951, the Chairman of the Wage Stabilization Board described in detail the relationship between the Taft-Hartley procedures applicable to labor disputes imperiling the national health and safety and the new WSB disputes procedures especially devised for settlement of labor disputes growing out of the needs of the defense program. Aware that a technique separate from Taft-Hartley had been devised, members of Congress attempted to divest the WSB of its disputes power. These attempts were defeated in the House, were not brought to a vote in the Senate, and the Defense Production Act was extended through June 30, 1952, without change in the disputes powers of the WSB. Certainly this legislative creation of a new procedure for dealing with defense disputes negatives any notion that Congress intended the earlier and discretionary Taft-Hartley procedure to be an exclusive procedure.

Accordingly, as of December 22, 1951, the President had a choice between alternate procedures for settling the threatened strike in the steel mills: one route created to deal with peacetime disputes; the other route specially created to deal with disputes growing out of the defense and stabilization program. There is no question of bypassing a statutory procedure because both of the routes available to the President in December were based upon statutory authorization. Both routes were available in the steel dispute . . .

When the President acted on April 8, he had exhausted the procedures for settlement available to him. Taft-Hartley was a route parallel to, not connected with, the WSB procedure. The strike had been delayed 99 days as contrasted with the maximum delay of 80 days under Taft-Hartley. There had been a hearing on the issues in dispute and bargaining which promised settlement up to the very hour before seizure had broken down. Faced with immediate national peril through stoppage in steel production on the one hand and faced with destruction of the wage and price legislative programs on the other, the President took temporary possession of the steel mills as the only course open to him consistent with his duty to take care that the laws be faithfully executed.

Plaintiffs' property was taken and placed in the possession of the Secretary of Commerce to prevent any interruption in steel production. It made no difference whether the stoppage was caused by a union-management dispute over terms and conditions of employment, a union-Government dispute over wage stabilization or a management-Government dispute over price stabilization. The President's action has thus far been effective, not in settling the dispute, but in saving the various legislative programs at stake from destruction until Congress could act in the matter . . .

Amid inflationary pressures, President Jimmy Carter signed Executive Order 12092 on November 1, 1978. This order directed the Council on Wage and Price Stability to develop noninflationary, voluntary wage and price standards for the U.S. economy. The chairman of the council was charged with monitoring compliance.

In March 1979, the AFL-CIO challenged the order, arguing that it interfered with the right to collective bargaining and that, in issuing the order, the president had exceeded his authority. The government claimed that the president was acting on statutory authority delegated to him by the Congress. This ruling of the District of Columbia Circuit was appealed to the Supreme Court, but it refused to hear the appeal.

AFL-CIO v. Kahn
618 F.2d 784 (D.C. Cir. 1979)

. . . Wright, Chief Judge: This case presents the question whether Congress has authorized the President to deny Government contracts above $5 million to companies that fail or refuse to comply with the voluntary wage and price standards. We answer that question in the affirmative . . .

We note at the outset our disagreement with the contention that this case presents the same issue decided by the Supreme Court in Youngstown Sheet & Tube Co. v. Sawyer. In Youngstown President Truman argued that he could constitutionally seize and operate the steel mills, which had been closed by a labor dispute, under his "inherent

powers" to deal with national emergencies and wartime situations. In arguing for the validity of Executive Order 12092, however, the Government relies entirely upon authority said to be delegated by statute, and makes no appeal to constitutional powers of the Executive that have not been confirmed by legislation. Thus, although both cases involve challenges to Executive actions, they raise sharply different legal questions. Although the separation of powers between Congress and the President was the dominant issue in Youngstown, here we primarily face a difficult problem of statutory interpretation. Appellees' challenge to the Executive Order is directed at the procurement aspect of the Order, not at the Council's authority under COWPSA [Council on Wage and Price Stability Act] to promulgate voluntary standards. Thus the central issue in this case is whether the FPASA [Federal Property and Administrative Services Act of 1949] indeed grants to the President the powers he has asserted . . .

The most important provision of the Act for this case, Section 205, provides that the President "may prescribe such policies and directives, not inconsistent with the provisions of this Act, as he shall deem necessary to effectuate the provisions of said Act." Because this language is open-ended, it is important to examine its genesis. The initial Hoover Commission study of procurement recommended that a General Services Agency oversee Government acquisitions, and that the Agency be placed within the Executive Office of the President to bolster its authority and to ensure central direction of the bureaucracy. Congress, however, was reluctant to saddle the relatively small Executive Office with such a vast administrative burden, so it set up the General Services Administration as an independent agency. But in response to the Hoover Commission's concern that the strength of the presidency support the new agency, Congress added Section 205 to guarantee that "Presidential policies and directives shall govern—not merely guide—" the agencies under the FPASA. We believe that by emphasizing the leadership role of the President in setting Government-wide procurement policy on matters common to all agencies, Congress intended that the President play a direct and active part in supervising the Government's management functions . . .

To define the President's powers under Section 205(a), some content must be injected into the general phrases "not inconsistent with" the FPASA and "to effectuate the provisions" of the Act. The congressional declaration of policy for the FPASA sets forth the goal of an "economical and efficient system for procurement and supply." Section 201 directs that the Administrator of General Services chart policy and procure supplies in a manner "advantageous to the Government in terms of economy, efficiency, or service, and with due regard to the program activities of the agencies concerned." This language recognizes that the Government generally must have some flexibility to seek the greatest advantage in various situations. "Economy" and "efficiency" are not narrow terms; they encompass those factors like price, quality, suitability, and availability of goods or services that are involved in all acquisition decisions. Similar concerns can be seen in the specific direction to contracting officers in Section 303(b) that contracts should be awarded to bidders whose terms "will be most advantageous to the Government, price and other factors considered" . . .

In light of the imprecise definition of presidential authority under the FPASA, it is useful to consider how the procurement power has been exercised under the Act. As the Commission on Government Procurement pointed out in its 1972 report, Congress itself has frequently imposed on the procurement process social and economic programs somewhat removed from a strict view of efficiency and economy. More significant for this case, however, several Executive actions taken explicitly or implicitly under Section 205 of the FPASA have also imposed additional considerations on the procurement process. Of course, the President's view of his own authority under a statute is not controlling, but when that view has been acted upon over a substantial period of time without eliciting congressional reversal, it is "entitled to great respect."

As the Supreme Court observed this Term, the "construction of a statute by those charged with its execution should be followed unless there are compelling indications that it is wrong" . . .

In February 1964, President Johnson directed by Executive Order that federal contractors not "discriminate against persons because of their age except upon the basis of a bona fide occupational qualification, retirement plan, or statutory requirement" . . .

Executive Order 11141 . . . Although the Order can now be justified under the Age Discrimination in Employment Act of 1967, 29 U.S.C. §§ 621–634 (1976), and the Age Discrimination Act of 1975, 42 U.S.C. §§ 6101–6107 (1976), for the first three years of its operation this Order was apparently based on only the FPASA. The Executive Order itself simply cites "the authority vested in [the President] by the Constitution and statutes of the United States". . .

Since 1941, though, the most prominent use of the President's authority under the FPASA has been a series of anti-discrimination requirements for Government contractors. The early anti-discrimination orders were issued under the President's war powers and special wartime legislation, but for the period from 1953 to 1964 only the FPASA could have provided statutory support for the Executive action . . .

The anti-discrimination orders were not tested in the courts until 1964, when the Third Circuit held that they did not grant a private right of action to an employee alleging racial discrimination in work assignment. The court concluded that those orders were a proper exercise of presidential authority under Section 205 of the FPASA and the "declaration of policy" in the Defense Production Act of 1950. In a 1967 ruling on the private cause of action question, the Fifth Circuit observed that the FPASA supported President Kennedy's 1961 Order directing affirmative action by contractors to hire minority workers . . .

[T]he District Court misapprehended the President's statutory powers in this case. Any order based on Section 205(a) must accord with the values of "economy" and "efficiency." Because there is a sufficiently close nexus between those criteria and the procurement compliance program established by Executive Order 12092, we find that program to be authorized by the FPASA.

The District Court was alarmed by the prospect of Government contracts being diverted from low bidders who are not in compliance with the wage and price standards to higher bidders. The result, it might seem, could be an unwarranted drain on the public fisc. Yet it is important to consider the procurement compliance program in its real-world setting. Much Government procurement takes place through the processes of negotiation rather than formal advertisement and competitive bidding. Military procurement, which is the largest single component of Government purchasing, is conducted almost exclusively through negotiated arrangements. In the context of a negotiated contract, the procurement program announced by Executive Order 12092 will likely have the direct and immediate effect of holding down the Government's procurement costs . . .

Firms that meet the President's price and pay standards will be reducing their overall rate of increase in costs and prices. By directing procurement toward such firms an incentive will be provided to large numbers of Government suppliers to meet the standards. To the extent that this occurs, the inflationary element in overall Government procurement costs will be lessened, and the cost of procurement reduced . . .

We do not deny that under Executive Order 12092 there may be occasional instances where a low bidder will not be awarded a contract. Nevertheless, we find no basis for rejecting the President's conclusion that any higher costs incurred in those transactions will be more than off-set by the advantages gained in negotiated contracts and in those cases where the lowest bidder is in compliance with the voluntary standards and his bid is lower than it would have been in the absence of standards. Consequently, we conclude that Executive Order 12092 is in accord

with the "economy and efficiency" touchstone of the FPASA. By acting to restrain procurement costs across the entire Government, the President was within his Section 205(a) powers . . .

We wish to emphasize the importance to our ruling today of the nexus between the wage and price standards and likely savings to the Government. As is clear from the terms and history of the statute and from experience with its implementation, our decision today does not write a blank check for the President to fill in at his will. The procurement power must be exercised consistently with the structure and purposes of the statute that delegates that power . . .

The question presented by this case, however, is not whether in some abstract sense President Carter's program is mandatory or voluntary, but whether it is barred by Section 3(b) of COWPSA. In our view, that provision refers to the sort of mandatory economic controls imposed during World War II, the Korean War, and the early 1970s. The statute covers "prices, rents, wages, salaries, [and] corporate dividends," a likely reference to a similar list in Section 203(a) of the Economic Stabilization Act Amendments of 1971 which established legally enforceable wage and price controls. Because COWPSA was enacted just a few months after the Economic Stabilization Act expired, it is reasonable to conclude that the language of Section 3(b) looks back to the provisions of the earlier Act. In addition, the standards in Executive Order 12092, which cover only wages and prices, are not as extensive as the list in Section 3(b). Consequently, we do not think the procurement compliance program falls within the coverage of Section 3(b), but rather is a halfway measure outside the contemplation of Congress in that enactment. This interpretation is reinforced by the fact that Executive Order 12092, unlike the earlier wage and price programs, makes no provision for civil or criminal penalties or injunctions . . .

Perhaps more important, Section 3(b) is irrelevant to the President's procurement compliance program. The statutory provision states that "[nothing] in this

Act authorizes mandatory economic controls." Executive Order 12092 relies on COWPSA for the Council's power to establish the voluntary wage and price standards, but the Order rests on the FPASA for implementation of the procurement compliance program. Since we think the procurement feature of the President's Order is supported by FPASA, it is of no concern that Section 3(b) may not also grant him that authority . . .

Finally, it is important to point out that just two months ago the Congress approved a one-year extension of COWPSA, a tripling of its budget, and a sixfold increase in its staff. The legislative history of this 1979 extension of COWPSA, which was approved while this suit was pending in the District Court, contains several assertions that Congress did not intend to make any statement on the issues raised in this case. Yet it strains credulity to maintain that COWPSA bars the procurement compliance program when Congress has just extended that statute knowing that the Council it established is charged with implementing the wage and price guidelines on which the procurement program is based. Congress can reverse incorrect Executive interpretations of its statutes and has used that power in the past. Congress, fully aware of the procurement program, renewed COWPSA without significant modification. In this context, a court could only in the most extreme case find that the Executive has violated the statute . . .

Consequently, the order of the District Court is reversed and its injunction is vacated.

We note our disagreement with the view taken by Judge MacKinnon in his lengthy dissent as to the role of Congress with respect to this case. We do not think it without any significance at all that the FPASA has not been revised in reaction to Executive Orders by Presidents Eisenhower, Kennedy, Johnson, and Nixon that explicitly or implicitly relied on the statute, and which deployed the procurement power in pursuit of ends that might not strictly be defined as economy or efficiency . . .

DISSENT: MacKINNON . . . I can find no license in the President's important but modest powers under the 1949 Act to support his imposition of wage and price controls on federal government contractors. Moreover, I believe that were the majority's construction of section 205(a) correct, then the 1949 Act would amount to an unconstitutional delegation of legislative authority to the executive branch. Accordingly, I dissent . . .

As government has grown larger and more complex, the Congress has attempted to give wide discretion to the executive branch in implementing policy while attempting to maintain some control of executive branch activities. One way the Congress has sought to maintain its authority is by granting the executive flexibility while reserving the right to overturn or stop presidential acts through what has been called the "legislative veto." The legislative veto is a provision attached to enabling legislation that permits Congress to overturn, or veto, an executive branch regulation or action.

In 1974, Jagdish Rai Chadha, a student from Kenya who had overstayed his visa, received permission from the Immigration and Naturalization Service (INS) to extend his stay in the United States. The Congress overturned this decision using a legislative veto. Chadha sued, arguing that the legislative veto was unconstitutional.

INS v. Chadha
462 U.S. 919 (1983)

. . . Chief Justice Burger delivered the opinion of the Court.

. . . [This case] presents a challenge to the constitutionality of the provision in 244(c)(2) of the Immigration and Nationality Act, 66 Stat. 216, as amended, 8 U.S.C. 1254(c)(2), authorizing one House of Congress, by resolution, to invalidate the decision of the Executive Branch, pursuant to authority delegated by Congress to the Attorney General of the United States, to allow a particular deportable alien to remain in the United States . . .

B

Severability

Congress . . . contends that the provision for the one-House veto in 244(c)(2) cannot be severed from 244. Congress argues that if the provision for the one-House veto is held unconstitutional, all of 244 must fall. If 244 in its entirety is violative of the Constitution, it follows that the Attorney General has no authority to suspend Chadha's deportation under 244(a)(1) and Chadha would be deported. From this, Congress argues that Chadha lacks standing to challenge the constitutionality of the one-House veto provision because he could receive no relief even if his constitutional challenge proves successful.

Only recently this Court reaffirmed that the invalid portions of a statute are to be severed " '[u]nless it is evident that the Legislature would not have enacted those provisions which are within its power, independently of that which is not.' " *Buckley v. Valeo, 424 U.S. 1, 108* (1976), quoting *Champlin Refining Co. v. Corporation Comm'n of Oklahoma, 286 U.S. 210, 234* (1932). Here, however, we need not embark on that elusive inquiry since Congress itself has provided the answer to the question of severability in 406 of the Immigration and Nationality Act, note following 8 U.S.C. 1101, which provides:

"If any particular provision of this Act, or the application thereof to any person or circumstance, is held invalid, *the remainder of the Act and the application of such provision to other persons or circumstances shall not be affected thereby.*"

This language is unambiguous and gives rise to a presumption that Congress did not intend the validity of the Act as a whole, or of any part of the Act, to depend upon whether the veto clause of 244(c)(2) was invalid. The one-House veto provision in 244(c)(2) is clearly a "particular provision" of the Act as that language is used in the severability clause. Congress clearly intended "the remainder of the Act" to stand if "any particular provision"

were held invalid. Congress could not have more plainly authorized the presumption that the provision for a one-House veto in 244(c)(2) is severable from the remainder of 244 and the Act of which it is a part . . .

The presumption as to the severability of the one-House veto provision in 244(c)(2) is supported by the legislative history of 244. That section and its precursors supplanted the long-established pattern of dealing with deportations like Chadha's on a case-by-case basis through private bills . . .

The proposal to permit one House of Congress to veto the Attorney General's suspension of an alien's deportation was incorporated in the Immigration and Nationality Act of 1952, Pub. L. 414, 244(a), 66 Stat. 214. Plainly, Congress' desire to retain a veto in this area cannot be considered in isolation but must be viewed in the context of Congress' irritation with the burden of private immigration bills. This legislative history is not sufficient to rebut the presumption of severability raised by 406 because there is insufficient evidence that Congress would have continued to subject itself to the onerous burdens of private bills had it known that 244(c)(2) would be held unconstitutional.

A provision is further presumed severable if what remains after severance "is fully operative as a law." *Champlin Refining Co. v. Corporation Comm'n, supra, at 234.* There can be no doubt that 244 is "fully operative" and workable administrative machinery without the veto provision in 244(c)(2). Entirely independent of the one-House veto, the administrative process enacted by Congress authorizes the Attorney General to suspend an alien's deportation under 244(a). Congress' oversight of the exercise of this delegated authority is preserved since all such suspensions will continue to be reported to it under 244(c)(1). Absent the passage of a bill to the contrary, deportation proceedings will be canceled when the period specified in 244(c)(2) has expired. Clearly, 244 survives as a workable administrative mechanism without the one-House veto . . .

III

A

We turn now to the question whether action of one House of Congress under 244(c)(2) violates strictures of the Constitution. We begin, of course, with the presumption that the challenged statute is valid. Its wisdom is not the concern of the courts; if a challenged action does not violate the Constitution, it must be sustained . . .

By the same token, the fact that a given law or procedure is efficient, convenient, and useful in facilitating functions of government, standing alone, will not save it if it is contrary to the Constitution. Convenience and efficiency are not the primary objectives—or the hallmarks—of democratic government and our inquiry is sharpened rather than blunted by the fact that congressional veto provisions are appearing with increasing frequency in statutes which delegate authority to executive and independent agencies . . .

Justice White undertakes to make a case for the proposition that the one-House veto is a useful "political invention," post, at 972, and we need not challenge that assertion. We can even concede this utilitarian argument although the long range political wisdom of this "invention" is arguable. It has been vigorously debated, and it is instructive to compare the views of the protagonists . . . But policy arguments supporting even useful "political inventions" are subject to the demands of the Constitution which defines powers and, with respect to this subject, sets out just how those powers are to be exercised.

Explicit and unambiguous provisions of the Constitution prescribe and define the respective functions of the Congress and of the Executive in the legislative process. Since the precise terms of those familiar provisions are critical to the resolution of these cases, we set them out verbatim. Article I provides:

"All legislative Powers herein granted shall be vested in a Congress of the United States, which shall consist of a Senate and House of Representatives." Art. I, 1.

"Every Bill which shall have passed the House of Representatives and the Senate, shall, before it becomes a law, be presented to the President of the United States . . ." Art. I, 7, cl. 2.

"Every Order, Resolution, or Vote to which the Concurrence of the Senate and House of Representatives may be necessary (except on a question of Adjournment) shall be presented to the President of the United States; and before the Same shall take Effect, shall be approved by him, or being disapproved by him, shall be repassed by two thirds of the Senate and House of Representatives, according to the Rules and Limitations prescribed in the Case of a Bill." Art. I, 7, cl. 3.

These provisions of Art. I are integral parts of the constitutional design for the separation of powers . . . We see that the purposes underlying the Presentment Clauses, Art. I, 7, cls. 2, 3, and the bicameral requirement of Art. I, 1, and 7, cl. 2, guide our resolution of the important question presented in these cases. The very structure of the Articles delegating and separating powers under Arts. I, II, and III exemplifies the concept of separation of powers, and we now turn to Art. I.

B

The Presentment Clauses

The records of the Constitutional Convention reveal that the requirement that all legislation be presented to the President before becoming law was uniformly accepted by the Framers. Presentment to the President and the Presidential veto were considered so imperative that the draftsmen took special pains to assure that these requirements could not be circumvented. During the final debate on Art. I, 7, cl. 2, James Madison expressed concern that it might easily be evaded by the simple expedient of calling a proposed law a "resolution" or "vote" rather than a "bill." 2 Farrand . . . Art. I, 7, cl. 3 . . . was added.

The decision to provide the President with a limited and qualified power to nullify proposed legislation by veto was based on the profound conviction of the Framers that the powers conferred on Congress were the powers to be most carefully circumscribed. It is beyond doubt that lawmaking was a power to be shared by both Houses and the President. In The Federalist No. 73 . . . , Hamilton focused on the President's role in making laws:

"If even no propensity had ever discovered itself in the legislative body to invade the rights of the Executive, the rules of just reasoning and theoretic propriety would of themselves teach us that the one ought not to be left to the mercy of the other, but ought to possess a constitutional and effectual power of self-defence" . . .

The President's role in the lawmaking process also reflects the Framers' careful efforts to check whatever propensity a particular Congress might have to enact oppressive, improvident, or ill-considered measures. The President's veto role in the legislative process was described later during public debate on ratification:

"It establishes a salutary check upon the legislative body, calculated to guard the community against the effects of faction, precipitancy, or of any impulse unfriendly to the public good, which may happen to influence a majority of that body.
". . . The primary inducement to conferring the power in question upon the Executive is, to enable him to defend himself; the secondary one is to increase the chances in favor of the community against the passing of bad laws, through haste, inadvertence, or design." The Federalist No. 73, *supra*, at 458 (A. Hamilton).

. . . The Court also has observed that the Presentment Clauses serve the important purpose of assuring that a "national" perspective is grafted on the legislative process:

"The President is a representative of the people just as the members of the Senate and of the House are, and it may be, at some times, on some subjects, that the President elected by all the people is rather more representative of them all than are the members of either body of the Legislature whose constituencies are local and not countrywide. . . ." *Myers v. United States, supra,* at 123.

C

Bicameralism

The bicameral requirement of Art. I, 1, 7, was of scarcely less concern to the Framers than was the Presidential veto and indeed the two concepts are interdependent. By providing that no law could take effect without the concurrence of the prescribed majority of the Members of both Houses, the Framers reemphasized their belief, already remarked upon in connection with the Presentment Clauses, that legislation should not be enacted unless it has been carefully and fully considered by the Nation's elected officials . . .

These observations are consistent with what many of the Framers expressed, none more cogently than Madison in pointing up the need to divide and disperse power in order to protect liberty:

"In republican government, the legislative authority necessarily predominates. The remedy for this inconveniency is to divide the legislature into different branches; and to render them, by different modes of election and different principles of action, as little connected with each other as the nature of their common functions and their common dependence on the society will admit." The Federalist No. 51 . . .

We see therefore that the Framers were acutely conscious that the bicameral requirement and the Presentment Clauses would serve essential constitutional functions. The President's participation in the legislative process was to protect the Executive Branch from Congress and to protect the whole people from improvident laws. The division of the Congress into two distinctive bodies assures that the legislative power would be exercised only after opportunity for full study and debate in separate settings. The President's unilateral veto power, in turn, was limited by the power of two-thirds of both Houses of Congress to overrule a veto thereby precluding final arbitrary action of one person. See *id.*, at 99–104. It emerges clearly that the prescription for legislative action in Art. I, 1, 7, represents the Framers' decision that the legislative power of the Federal Government be exercised in accord with a single, finely wrought and exhaustively considered, procedure.

IV

The Constitution sought to divide the delegated powers of the new Federal Government into three defined categories, Legislative, Executive, and Judicial, to assure, as nearly as possible, that each branch of government would confine itself to its assigned responsibility. The hydraulic pressure inherent within each of the separate Branches to exceed the outer limits of its power, even to accomplish desirable objectives, must be resisted.

Although not "hermetically" sealed from one another . . . the powers delegated to the three Branches are functionally identifiable. When any Branch acts, it is presumptively exercising the power the Constitution has delegated to it . . . When the Executive acts, he presumptively acts in an executive or administrative capacity as defined in Art. II. And when, as here one House of Congress purports to act, it is presumptively acting within its assigned sphere.

Beginning with this presumption, we must nevertheless establish that the challenged action under 244(c)(2) is of the kind to which the procedural requirements of Art. I, 7, apply. Not every action taken by either House is subject to the bicameralism and presentment requirements of Art. I . . . Whether actions taken by either House are, in law and fact, an exercise of legislative power depends not on their form but upon "whether they contain matter which is properly to be regarded as legislative in its

character and effect." S. Rep. No. 1335, 54th Cong., 2d Sess., 8 (1897).

Examination of the action taken here by one House pursuant to 244(c)(2) reveals that it was essentially legislative in purpose and effect. In purporting to exercise power defined in Art. I, 8, cl. 4, to "establish an uniform Rule of Naturalization," the House took action that had the purpose and effect of altering the legal rights, duties, and relations of persons, including the Attorney General, Executive Branch officials and Chadha, all outside the Legislative Branch. Section 244(c)(2) purports to authorize one House of Congress to require the Attorney General to deport an individual alien whose deportation otherwise would be canceled under 244. The one-House veto operated in these cases to overrule the Attorney General and mandate Chadha's deportation; absent the House action, Chadha would remain in the United States. Congress has acted and its action has altered Chadha's status.

The legislative character of the one-House veto in these cases is confirmed by the character of the congressional action it supplants. Neither the House of Representatives nor the Senate contends that, absent the veto provision in 244(c)(2), either of them, or both of them acting together, could effectively require the Attorney General to deport an alien once the Attorney General, in the exercise of legislatively delegated authority, had determined the alien should remain in the United States. Without the challenged provision in 244(c)(2), this could have been achieved, if at all, only by legislation requiring deportation. Similarly, a veto by one House of Congress under 244(c)(2) cannot be justified as an attempt at amending the standards set out in 244(a)(1), or as a repeal of 244 as applied to Chadha. Amendment and repeal of statutes, no less than enactment, must conform with Art. I.

The nature of the decision implemented by the one-House veto in these cases further manifests its legislative character. After long experience with the clumsy, time-consuming private bill procedure, Congress made a deliberate choice to delegate to the Executive Branch, and specifically to the

Attorney General, the authority to allow deportable aliens to remain in this country in certain specified circumstances. It is not disputed that this choice to delegate authority is precisely the kind of decision that can be implemented only in accordance with the procedures set out in Art. I. Disagreement with the Attorney General's decision on Chadha's deportation—that is, Congress' decision to deport Chadha—no less than Congress' original choice to delegate to the Attorney General the authority to make that decision, involves determinations of policy that Congress can implement in only one way; bicameral passage followed by presentment to the President. Congress must abide by its delegation of authority until that delegation is legislatively altered or revoked.

Finally, we see that when the Framers intended to authorize either House of Congress to act alone and outside of its prescribed bicameral legislative role, they narrowly and precisely defined the procedure for such action. There are four provisions in the Constitution, explicit and unambiguous, by which one House may act alone with the unreviewable force of law, not subject to the President's veto:

(a) The House of Representatives alone was given the power to initiate impeachments. Art. I, 2, cl. 5;

(b) The Senate alone was given the power to conduct trials following impeachment on charges initiated by the House and to convict following trial. Art. I, 3, cl. 6;

(c) The Senate alone was given final unreviewable power to approve or to disapprove Presidential appointments. Art. II, 2, cl. 2;

(d) The Senate alone was given unreviewable power to ratify treaties negotiated by the President. Art. II, 2, cl. 2.

Clearly, when the Draftsmen sought to confer special powers on one House, independent of the other House, or of the President, they did so in explicit, unambiguous terms. These carefully defined exceptions from presentment and bicameralism underscore the difference between the legislative functions of Congress and other unilateral but important and binding one-House acts provided for in the Constitution. These exceptions are narrow, explicit, and separately justified; none of them authorize the action challenged here. On the contrary, they provide further support for the conclusion that congressional authority is not to be implied and for the conclusion that the veto provided for in 244(c)(2) is not authorized by the constitutional design of the powers of the Legislative Branch.

Since it is clear that the action by the House under 244(c)(2) was not within any of the express constitutional exceptions authorizing one House to act alone, and equally clear that it was an exercise of legislative power, that action was subject to the standards prescribed in Art. I . . .

V

We hold that the congressional veto provision in 244(c)(2) is severable from the Act and that it is unconstitutional. Accordingly, the judgment of the Court of Appeals is

Affirmed . . .

Justice Powell, concurring in the judgment.

The Court's decision, based on the Presentment Clauses, Art. I, 7, cls. 2 and 3, apparently will invalidate every use of the legislative veto. The breadth of this holding gives one pause. Congress has included the veto in literally hundreds of statutes, dating back to the 1930s. Congress clearly views this procedure as essential to controlling the delegation of power to administrative agencies. One reasonably may disagree with Congress' assessment of the veto's utility, but the respect due its judgment as a coordinate branch of Government cautions that our holding should be no more extensive than necessary to decide these cases. In my view, the cases may be decided on a narrower ground. When Congress finds that a particular person does not satisfy the statutory criteria for permanent residence in this country it has assumed a judicial function in violation of the principle of separation of powers. Accordingly, I concur only in the judgment.

I

A

The Framers perceived that "[t]he accumulation of all powers legislative, executive and judiciary in the same hands, whether of one, a few or many, and whether hereditary, self appointed, or elective, may justly be pronounced the very definition of tyranny." The Federalist No. 47 . . . (J. Madison). Theirs was not a baseless fear. Under British rule, the Colonies suffered the abuses of unchecked executive power that were attributed, at least popularly, to a hereditary monarchy . . . During the Confederation, the States reacted by removing power from the executive and placing it in the hands of elected legislators. But many legislators proved to be little better than the Crown. "The supremacy of legislatures came to be recognized as the supremacy of faction and the tyranny of shifting majorities. The legislatures confiscated property, erected paper money schemes, [and] suspended the ordinary means of collecting debts." Levi . . . at 374–375.

One abuse that was prevalent during the Confederation was the exercise of judicial power by the state legislatures. The Framers were well acquainted with the danger of subjecting the determination of the rights of one person to the "tyranny of shifting majorities" . . .

It was to prevent the recurrence of such abuses that the Framers vested the executive, legislative, and judicial powers in separate branches. Their concern that a legislature should not be able unilaterally to impose a substantial deprivation on one person was expressed not only in this general allocation of power, but also in more specific provisions, such as the Bill of Attainder Clause, Art. I, 9, cl. 3. As the Court recognized in *United States v. Brown, 381 U.S. 437, 442* (1965), "the Bill of Attainder Clause was intended not as a narrow, technical . . . prohibition, but rather as an implementation of the

separation of powers, a general safeguard against legislative exercise of the judicial function, or more simply—trial by legislature." This Clause, and the separation-of-powers doctrine generally, reflect the Framers' concern that trial by a legislature lacks the safeguards necessary to prevent the abuse of power.

B

The Constitution does not establish three branches with precisely defined boundaries . . . But where one branch has impaired or sought to assume a power central to another branch, the Court has not hesitated to enforce the doctrine. See Buckley v. Valeo, *supra*, at 123.

Functionally, the doctrine may be violated in two ways. One branch may interfere impermissibly with the other's performance of its constitutionally assigned function. See *Nixon v. Administrator of General Services, 433 U.S. 425, 433* (1977); *United States v. Nixon, 418 U.S. 683* (1974). Alternatively, the doctrine may be violated when one branch assumes a function that more properly is entrusted to another. See Youngstown Sheet & Tube Co. v. Sawyer, *supra*, at 587 . . . These cases present the latter situation.

II

. . . On its face, the House's action appears clearly adjudicatory. The House did not enact a general rule; rather it made its own determination that six specific persons did not comply with certain statutory criteria. It thus undertook the type of decision that traditionally has been left to other branches. Even if the House did not make a de novo determination, but simply reviewed the Immigration and Naturalization Service's findings, it still assumed a function ordinarily entrusted to the federal courts. See 5 U.S.C. 704 (providing generally for judicial review of final agency action); cf. Foti v. INS, 375 U.S. 21 (1963) (holding that courts of appeals have jurisdiction to review INS decisions denying suspension of deportation) . . .

Loan Receipt
Liverpool John Moores University
Library Services

of this
action
;ht to
decid-
orted,
raints
of the
iciary
ound
ect to
coun-
, that
icates
at on
most
es of
s of
"the

uliar
ules
1 of
1 to

6 Cranch 87, 136 (1810). In my view, when
Congress undertook to apply its rules to Chadha, it
exceeded the scope of its constitutionally prescribed
authority. I would not reach the broader question
whether legislative vetoes are invalid under the
Presentment Clauses . . .

JUSTICE WHITE, dissenting.

Today the Court not only invalidates 244(c)(2) of
the Immigration and Nationality Act, but also sounds
the death knell for nearly 200 other statutory provisions in which Congress has reserved a "legislative
veto." For this reason, the Court's decision is of
surpassing importance. And it is for this reason that
the Court would have been well advised to decide
the cases, if possible, on the narrower grounds of
separation of powers, leaving for full consideration
the constitutionality of other congressional review
statutes operating on such varied matters as war
powers and agency rulemaking, some of which
concern the independent regulatory agencies . . .

The history of the legislative veto also makes clear
that it has not been a sword with which Congress
has struck out to aggrandize itself at the expense of
the other branches—the concerns of Madison and
Hamilton. Rather, the veto has been a means of
defense, a reservation of ultimate authority necessary if Congress is to fulfill its designated role under
Art. I as the Nation's lawmaker. While the President
has often objected to particular legislative vetoes,
generally those left in the hands of congressional
Committees, the Executive has more often agreed
to legislative review as the price for a broad
delegation of authority. To be sure, the President
may have preferred unrestricted power, but that
could be precisely why Congress thought it
essential to retain a check on the exercise of
delegated authority.

For all these reasons, the apparent sweep of the
Court's decision today is regrettable. The Court's
Art. I analysis appears to invalidate all legislative
vetoes irrespective of form or subject. Because the
legislative veto is commonly found as a check upon
rulemaking by administrative agencies and upon
broad-based policy decisions of the Executive
Branch, it is particularly unfortunate that the Court
reaches its decision in cases involving the exercise of
a veto over deportation decisions regarding particular individuals. Courts should always be wary of
striking statutes as unconstitutional; to strike an
entire class of statutes based on consideration of a
somewhat atypical and more readily indictable
exemplar of the class is irresponsible . . .

III

. . . I agree with the Court that the President's qualified veto power is a critical element in the distribution of powers under the Constitution, widely
endorsed among the Framers, and intended to serve
the President as a defense against legislative
encroachment and to check the "passing of bad
laws, through haste, inadvertence, or design." The
Federalist No. 73 . . . (A. Hamilton) . . . I also
agree that the bicameral approval required by Art. I,
1, 7, "was of scarcely less concern to the Framers

than was the Presidential veto," . . . and that the need to divide and disperse legislative power figures significantly in our scheme of Government. All of this, Part III of the Court's opinion, is entirely unexceptionable.

It does not, however, answer the constitutional question before us. The power to exercise a legislative veto is not the power to write new law without bicameral approval or Presidential consideration. The veto must be authorized by statute and may only negative what an Executive department or independent agency has proposed. On its face, the legislative veto no more allows one House of Congress to make law than does the Presidential veto confer such power upon the President . . .

A

The terms of the Presentment Clauses suggest only that bills and their equivalent are subject to the requirements of bicameral passage and presentment to the President . . .

Although the Clause does not specify the actions for which the concurrence of both Houses is "necessary," the proceedings at the Philadelphia Convention suggest its purpose was to prevent Congress from circumventing the presentation requirement in the making of new legislation . . . The chosen language, Madison's comment, and the brevity of the Convention's consideration, all suggest a modest role was intended for the Clause and no broad restraint on congressional authority was contemplated. See Stewart . . . This reading is consistent with the historical background of the Presentment Clause itself which reveals only that the Framers were concerned with limiting the methods for enacting new legislation . . . There is no record that the Convention contemplated, let alone intended, that these Art. I requirements would someday be invoked to restrain the scope of congressional authority pursuant to duly enacted law . . .

When the Convention did turn its attention to the scope of Congress' lawmaking power, the Framers were expansive. The Necessary and Proper Clause, Art. I, 8, cl. 18, vests Congress with the power "[t]o make all Laws which shall be necessary and proper for carrying into Execution the foregoing Powers [the enumerated powers of 8] and all other Powers vested by this Constitution in the Government of the United States, or in any Department or Officer thereof." It is long settled that Congress may "exercise its best judgment in the selection of measures, to carry into execution the constitutional powers of the government," and "avail itself of experience, to exercise its reason, and to accommodate its legislation to circumstances." McCulloch v. Maryland, 4 Wheat. 316, 415–416, 420 (1819).

B

The Court heeded this counsel in approving the modern administrative state. The Court's holding today that all legislative-type action must be enacted through the lawmaking process ignores that legislative authority is routinely delegated to the Executive Branch, to the independent regulatory agencies, and to private individuals and groups . . .

This Court's decisions sanctioning such delegations make clear that Art. I does not require all action with the effect of legislation to be passed as a law . . .

. . . These cases establish that by virtue of congressional delegation, legislative power can be exercised by independent agencies and Executive departments without the passage of new legislation. For some time, the sheer amount of law—the substantive rules that regulate private conduct and direct the operation of government—made by the agencies has far outnumbered the lawmaking engaged in by Congress through the traditional process. There is no question but that agency rulemaking is lawmaking in any functional or realistic sense of the term. The Administrative Procedure Act, 5 U.S.C. 551(4), provides that a "rule" is an agency statement "designed to implement, interpret, or prescribe law or policy." When agencies are authorized to prescribe law through substantive rulemaking, the administrator's regulation is not only due deference, but is accorded "legislative effect." . . . These regulations bind courts and officers of the Federal Government, may pre-empt state law . . . and grant rights to and impose obligations on the public. In sum, they have the force of law.

If Congress may delegate lawmaking power to independent and Executive agencies, it is most difficult to understand Art. I as prohibiting Congress from also reserving a check on legislative power for itself. Absent the veto, the agencies receiving delegations of legislative or quasi-legislative power may issue regulations having the force of law without bicameral approval and without the President's signature. It is thus not apparent why the reservation of a veto over the exercise of that legislative power must be subject to a more exacting test. In both cases, it is enough that the initial statutory authorizations comply with the Art. I requirements.

Nor are there strict limits on the agents that may receive such delegations of legislative authority so that it might be said that the Legislature can delegate authority to others but not to itself. While most authority to issue rules and regulations is given to the Executive Branch and the independent regulatory agencies, statutory delegations to private persons have also passed this Court's scrutiny . . . Assuming Currin and Rock Royal Co-operative remain sound law, the Court's decision today suggests that Congress may place a "veto" power over suspensions of deportation in private hands or in the hands of an independent agency, but is forbidden to reserve such authority for itself. Perhaps this odd result could be justified on other constitutional grounds, such as the separation of powers, but certainly it cannot be defended as consistent with the Court's view of the Art. I presentment and bicameralism commands . . .

The Court also takes no account of perhaps the most relevant consideration: However resolutions of disapproval under 244(c)(2) are formally characterized, in reality, a departure from the status quo occurs only upon the concurrence of opinion among the House, Senate, and President. Reservations of legislative authority to be exercised by Congress should be upheld if the exercise of such reserved authority is consistent with the distribution of and limits upon legislative power that Art. I provides . . .

The central concern of the presentment and bicameralism requirements of Art. I is that when a departure from the legal status quo is undertaken, it is done with the approval of the President and both Houses of Congress—or, in the event of a Presidential veto, a two-thirds majority in both Houses. This interest is fully satisfied by the operation of 244(c)(2). The President's approval is found in the Attorney General's action in recommending to Congress that the deportation order for a given alien be suspended. The House and the Senate indicate their approval of the Executive's action by not passing a resolution of disapproval within the statutory period. Thus, a change in the legal status quo—the deportability of the alien—is consummated only with the approval of each of the three relevant actors. The disagreement of any one of the three maintains the alien's pre-existing status: the Executive may choose not to recommend suspension; the House and Senate may each veto the recommendation. The effect on the rights and obligations of the affected individuals and upon the legislative system is precisely the same as if a private bill were introduced but failed to receive the necessary approval . . .

Thus understood, 244(c)(2) fully effectuates the purposes of the bicameralism and presentment requirements. I now briefly consider possible objections to the analysis.

First, it may be asserted that Chadha's status before legislative disapproval is one of nondeportation and that the exercise of the veto, unlike the failure of a private bill, works a change in the status quo. This position plainly ignores the statutory language. At no place in 244 has Congress delegated to the Attorney General any final power to determine which aliens shall be allowed to remain in the United States. Congress has retained the ultimate power to pass on such changes in deportable status . . .

Second, it may be said that this approach leads to the incongruity that the two-House veto is more suspect than its one-House brother. Although the idea may be initially counterintuitive, on close analysis, it is not at all unusual that the one-House veto is of more certain constitutionality than the two-House version. If the Attorney General's action is a proposal for legislation, then the disapproval of but a single House is all that is required to prevent its passage. Because approval is indicated by the failure to veto, the one-House veto satisfies the requirement of bicameral approval. The two-House version may present a different question . . .

Third, it may be objected that Congress cannot indicate its approval of legislative change by inaction. In the Court of Appeals' view, inaction by Congress "could equally imply endorsement, acquiescence, passivity, indecision, or indifference," . . . and the Court appears to echo this concern . . . This objection appears more properly directed at the wisdom of the legislative veto than its constitutionality. The Constitution does not and cannot guarantee that legislators will carefully scrutinize legislation and deliberate before acting. In a democracy it is the electorate that holds the legislators accountable for the wisdom of their choices. It is hard to maintain that a private bill receives any greater individualized scrutiny than a resolution of disapproval under 244(c)(2). Certainly the legislative veto is no more susceptible to this attack than the Court's increasingly common practice of according weight to the failure of Congress to disturb an Executive or independent agency's action . . .

. . . The legislative veto provision does not "preven[t] the Executive Branch from accomplishing its constitutionally assigned functions." First, it is clear that the Executive Branch has no "constitutionally assigned" function of suspending the deportation of aliens . . . Nor can it be said that the inherent function of the Executive Branch in executing the law is involved. The Steel Seizure Case resolved that the Art. II mandate for the President to execute the law is a directive to enforce the law which Congress has written . . . "The duty of the President to see that the laws be executed is a [462 U.S. 919, 1001] duty that does not go beyond the laws or require him to achieve more than

Congress sees fit to leave within his power." *Myers v. United States . . . 272 U.S., at 177* (Holmes, J., dissenting) . . . Here, 244 grants the Executive only a qualified suspension authority, and it is only that authority which the President is constitutionally authorized to execute.

. . . In comparison to private bills, which must be initiated in the Congress and which allow a Presidential veto to be overridden by a two-thirds majority in both Houses of Congress, 244 augments rather than reduces the Executive Branch's authority . . .

Nor does 244 infringe on the judicial power, as JUSTICE POWELL would hold. Section 244 makes clear that Congress has reserved its own judgment as part of the statutory process. Congressional action does not substitute for judicial review of the Attorney General's decisions. The Act provides for judicial review of the refusal of the Attorney General to suspend a deportation and to transmit a recommendation to Congress. *INS v. Jong Ha Wang, 450 U.S. 139* (1981) (per curiam). But the courts have not been given the authority to review whether an alien should be given permanent status; review is limited to whether the Attorney General has properly applied the statutory standards for essentially denying the alien a recommendation that his deportable status be changed by the Congress. Moreover, there is no constitutional obligation to provide any judicial review whatever for a failure to suspend deportation . . .

I do not suggest that all legislative vetoes are necessarily consistent with separation-of-powers principles. A legislative check on an inherently executive function, for example, that of initiating prosecutions, poses an entirely different question. But the legislative veto device here—and in many other settings—is far from an instance of legislative tyranny over the Executive. It is a necessary check on the unavoidably expanding power of the agencies, both Executive and independent, as they engage in exercising authority delegated by Congress . . .

JUSTICE REHNQUIST, with whom JUSTICE WHITE joins, dissenting. . . .

In 1996, the Congress enacted the Line Item Veto Act, a bill that, for the first time in history, gave the president a limited ability to block the enactment of certain spending provisions within legislation. Under the law, the president could "cancel" limited spending provisions of a bill up to five days after signing it into law. The canceled provisions would remain canceled unless the Congress voted to resurrect them, by simple majority vote. If it did so, the provisions would be sent to the president for signature or veto; if vetoed, the Congress could then override the veto(es) by a two-thirds vote. This awkward procedure was constructed to counter criticism that the presidential veto could be altered only by constitutional amendment. President Bill Clinton used the power in 1997, prompting a court challenge. In its decision, the Court majority rejected the power as a violation of the Constitution's Presentment Clause, as the power allowed the president to, in effect, rewrite legislation presented to him by the Congress, even though the bills in question technically became law with presidential signature before the president then excised selected spending items.

Clinton v. City of New York
524 U.S. 417 (1998)

Justice Stevens delivered the opinion of the Court. . . .

The Line Item Veto Act gives the President the power to "cancel in whole" three types of provisions that have been signed into law: "(1) any dollar amount of discretionary budget authority; (2) any item of new direct spending; or (3) any limited tax benefit." 2 U.S.C. § 691(a) (1994 ed., Supp. II). . . .

The Act requires the President to adhere to precise procedures whenever he exercises his cancellation authority. In identifying items for cancellation he must . . . transmit a special message to Congress notifying it of each cancellation within five calendar days (excluding Sundays) after the enactment of the canceled provision. See §691(a)(B). It is undisputed that the President meticulously followed these procedures in these cases.

A cancellation takes effect upon receipt by Congress of the special message from the President. See §691b(a). If, however, a "disapproval bill" pertaining to a special message is enacted into law, the cancellations set forth in that message become "null and void." *Ibid.* The Act sets forth a detailed expedited procedure for the consideration of a "disapproval bill," see §691d, but no such bill was passed for either of the cancellations involved in these cases. A majority vote of both Houses is sufficient to enact a disapproval bill. The Act does not grant the President the authority to cancel a disapproval bill, see §691(c), but he does, of course, retain his constitutional authority to veto such a bill. . . .

In both legal and practical effect, the President has amended two Acts of Congress by repealing a portion of each. "[R]epeal of statutes, no less than enactment, must conform with Art. I." *INS v. Chadha, 462 U.S. 919, 954* (1983). There is no provision in the Constitution that authorizes the President to enact, to amend, or to repeal statutes. Both Article I and Article II assign responsibilities to the President that directly relate to the lawmaking process, but neither addresses the issue presented by these cases. The President "shall from time to time give to the Congress Information on the State of the Union, and recommend to their Consideration such Measures as he shall judge necessary and expedient. . . ." Art. II, §3. Thus, he may initiate and influence legislative proposals. Moreover, after a bill has passed both Houses of Congress, but "before it become[s] a Law," it must be presented to the President. If he approves it, "he shall sign it, but if not he shall return it, with his Objections to that House in which it shall have originated, who shall enter the Objections at large on their Journal, and proceed to reconsider it." Art. I, §7, cl. 2. His "return" of a bill, which is usually described as a "veto," is subject to being overridden by a two-thirds vote in each House.

There are important differences between the President's "return" of a bill pursuant to Article I, §7, and the exercise of the President's cancellation authority pursuant to the Line Item Veto Act. The constitutional return takes place before the bill becomes law; the statutory cancellation occurs after the bill becomes law. The constitutional return is of the entire bill; the statutory cancellation is of only a part. Although the Constitution expressly authorizes the President to play a role in the process of enacting statutes, it is silent on the subject of unilateral Presidential action that either repeals or amends parts of duly enacted statutes.

There are powerful reasons for construing constitutional silence on this profoundly important issue as equivalent to an express prohibition. The procedures governing the enactment of statutes set forth in the text of Article I were the product of the great debates and compromises that produced the Constitution itself. Familiar historical materials provide abundant support for the conclusion that the power to enact statutes may only "be exercised in accord with a single, finely wrought and exhaustively considered, procedure." Chadha, *462 U.S., at 951.* Our first President understood the text of the Presentment Clause as requiring that he either "approve all the parts of a Bill, or reject it in toto." What has emerged in these cases from the President's exercise of his statutory cancellation powers, however, are truncated versions of two bills that passed both Houses of Congress. They are not the product of the "finely wrought" procedure that the Framers designed. . . .

The Government advances two related arguments to support its position that despite the unambiguous provisions of the Act, cancellations do not amend or repeal properly enacted statutes in violation of the Presentment Clause. First, relying primarily on *Field v. Clark, 143 U.S. 649* (1892), the Government contends that the cancellations were merely exercises of discretionary authority granted to the President by the Balanced Budget Act and the Taxpayer Relief Act read in light of the previously enacted Line Item Veto Act. Second, the Government submits that the substance of the authority to cancel tax and spending items "is, in practical effect, no more and no less than the power to "decline to spend" specified sums of money, or to "decline to implement" specified tax measures." Brief for Appellants 40. Neither argument is persuasive.

In Field v. Clark, the Court upheld the constitutionality of the Tariff Act of 1890. Act of Oct. 1, 1890, 26 Stat. 567. That statute contained a "free list" of almost 300 specific articles that were exempted from import duties "unless otherwise specially provided for in this act." 26 Stat. 602. Section 3 was a special provision that directed the President to suspend that exemption for sugar, molasses, coffee, tea, and hides "whenever, and so often" as he should be satisfied that any country producing and exporting those products imposed duties on the agricultural products of the United States that he deemed to be "reciprocally unequal and unreasonable. . . ." 26 Stat. 612, quoted in Field , *143 U.S., at 680.* The section then specified the duties to be imposed on those products during any such suspension. . . .

This passage identifies three critical differences between the power to suspend the exemption from import duties and the power to cancel portions of a duly enacted statute. First, the exercise of the suspension power was contingent upon a condition that did not exist when the Tariff Act was passed: the imposition of "reciprocally unequal and unreasonable" import duties by other countries. In contrast, the exercise of the cancellation power within five days after the enactment of the Balanced Budget and Tax Reform Acts necessarily was based on the same conditions that Congress evaluated when it passed those statutes. Second, under the Tariff Act, when the President determined that the contingency had arisen, he had a duty to suspend; in contrast, while it is true that the President was required by the Act to make three determinations before he canceled a provision, see 2 U.S.C. § 691(a)(A) (1994 ed., Supp. II), those determinations did not qualify his discretion to cancel or not to cancel. Finally, whenever the President suspended an exemption under the Tariff Act, he was executing the policy that Congress had embodied in the statute. In contrast, whenever the President cancels an item of new direct spending or a limited tax benefit he is rejecting the policy judgment made by Congress and relying on his own policy judgment. Thus, the conclusion in Field v. Clark that the suspensions mandated by the Tariff Act were not exercises of legislative power does not undermine our opinion that cancellations pursuant to the Line Item Veto Act are the functional equivalent of partial repeals of Acts of Congress that fail to satisfy Article I, §7. . . .

The Line Item Veto Act authorizes the President himself to effect the repeal of laws, for his own policy reasons, without observing the procedures set out in Article I, §7. The fact that Congress intended such a result is of no moment. Although Congress presumably anticipated that the President might cancel some of the items in the Balanced Budget Act and in the Taxpayer Relief Act, Congress cannot alter the procedures set out in Article I, §7, without amending the Constitution.

Neither are we persuaded by the Government's contention that the President's authority to cancel new direct spending and tax benefit items is no greater than his traditional authority to decline to spend appropriated funds. The Government has reviewed in some detail the series of statutes in which Congress has given the Executive broad discretion over the expenditure of appropriated funds. For example, the First Congress appropriated "sum[s] not exceeding" specified amounts to be spent on various Government operations. See, e.g., Act of Sept. 29, 1789, ch. 23, §1, 1 Stat. 95; Act of Mar. 26, 1790, ch. 4, §1, 1 Stat. 104; Act of Feb. 11, 1791, ch. 6, 1 Stat. 190. In those statutes, as in later years, the President was given wide discretion with respect to both the amounts to be spent and how the money would be allocated among different functions. It is argued that the Line Item Veto Act merely confers comparable discretionary authority over the expenditure of appropriated funds. The critical difference between this statute and all of its predecessors, however, is that unlike any of them, this Act gives the President the unilateral power to change the text of duly enacted statutes. None of the Act's predecessors could even arguably have been construed to authorize such a change.

Although they are implicit in what we have already written, the profound importance of these cases makes it appropriate to emphasize three points.

First, we express no opinion about the wisdom of the procedures authorized by the Line Item Veto Act. Many members of both major political parties who have served in the Legislative and the Executive Branches have long advocated the enactment of such procedures for the purpose of "ensur[ing] greater fiscal accountability in Washington." H. R. Conf. Rep. 104–491, p. 15 (1996). The text of the Act was itself the product of much debate and deliberation in both Houses of Congress and that precise text was signed into law by the President. We do not lightly conclude that their action was unauthorized by the Constitution. We have, however, twice had full argument and briefing on the question and have concluded that our duty is clear.

Second, although appellees challenge the validity of the Act on alternative grounds, the only issue we address concerns the "finely wrought" procedure commanded by the Constitution. *Chadha, 462 U.S., at 951.* We have been favored with extensive debate about the scope of Congress' power to delegate law-making authority, or its functional equivalent, to the President. The excellent briefs filed by the parties and their amici curiae have provided us with valuable historical information that illuminates the delegation issue but does not really bear on the narrow issue that is dispositive of these cases. Thus, because we conclude that the Act's cancellation provisions violate Article I, §7, of the Constitution, we find it unnecessary to consider the District Court's alternative holding that the Act "impermissibly disrupts the balance of powers among the three branches of government." 985 F. Supp., at 179. 43

Third, our decision rests on the narrow ground that the procedures authorized by the Line Item Veto Act are not authorized by the Constitution. The Balanced Budget Act of 1997 is a 500-page document that became "Public Law 105–33" after three procedural steps were taken: (1) a bill containing its exact text was approved by a majority of the Members of the House of Representatives; (2) the Senate approved precisely the same text; and (3) that text was signed into law by the President. The

Constitution explicitly requires that each of those three steps be taken before a bill may "become a law." Art. I, §7. If one paragraph of that text had been omitted at any one of those three stages, Public Law 105–33 would not have been validly enacted. If the Line Item Veto Act were valid, it would authorize the President to create a different law-one whose text was not voted on by either House of Congress or presented to the President for signature. Something that might be known as "Public Law 105–33 as modified by the President" may or may not be desirable, but it is surely not a document that may "become a law" pursuant to the procedures designed by the Framers of Article I, §7, of the Constitution.

If there is to be a new procedure in which the President will play a different role in determining the final text of what may "become a law," such change must come not by legislation but through the amendment procedures set forth in Article V of the Constitution.

The judgment of the District Court is affirmed.

It is so ordered. . . .

JUSTICE SCALIA, with whom JUSTICE O'CONNOR joins, and with whom JUSTICE BREYER joins as to Part III, concurring in part and dissenting in part. . . .

I agree with the Court that the New York appellees have standing to challenge the President's cancellation of §4722(c) of the Balanced Budget Act of 1997 as an "item of new direct spending." . . . Unlike the Court, however, I do not believe that Executive cancellation of this item of direct spending violates the Presentment Clause.

The Presentment Clause requires, in relevant part, that "[e]very Bill which shall have passed the House of Representatives and the Senate, shall, before it becomes a Law, be presented to the President of the United States; If he approve he shall sign it, but if not he shall return it," U.S. Const., Art. I, §7, cl. 2. There is no question that enactment of the Balanced Budget Act complied with these requirements: the

House and Senate passed the bill, and the President signed it into law. It was only after the requirements of the Presentment Clause had been satisfied that the President exercised his authority under the Line Item Veto Act to cancel the spending item. Thus, the Court's problem with the Act is not that it authorizes the President to veto parts of a bill and sign others into law, but rather that it authorizes him to "cancel"—prevent from "having legal force or effect"—certain parts of duly enacted statutes. . . .

I turn, then, to the crux of the matter: whether Congress's authorizing the President to cancel an item of spending gives him a power that our history and traditions show must reside exclusively in the Legislative Branch. I may note, to begin with, that the Line Item Veto Act is not the first statute to authorize the President to "cancel" spending items. In *Bowsher v. Synar, 478 U.S. 714 (1986),* we addressed the constitutionality of the Balanced Budget and Emergency Deficit Control Act of 1985, 2 U.S.C. §901 et seq. (1982 ed., Supp. III), which required the President, if the federal budget deficit exceeded a certain amount, to issue a "sequestration" order mandating spending reductions specified by the Comptroller General. §902. The effect of sequestration was that "amounts sequestered . . . shall be permanently cancelled," §902(a)(4) (ed). We held that the Act was unconstitutional, not because it impermissibly gave the Executive legislative power, but because it gave the Comptroller General, an officer of the Legislative Branch over whom Congress retained removal power, "the ultimate authority to determine the budget cuts to be made," *478 U.S., at 733,* "functions . . . plainly entailing execution of the law in constitutional terms." *Id.,* at 732–733. The President's discretion under the Line Item Veto Act is certainly broader than the Comptroller General's discretion was under the 1985 Act, but it is no broader than the discretion traditionally granted the President in his execution of spending laws.

Insofar as the degree of political, "law-making" power conferred upon the Executive is concerned, there is not a dime's worth of difference between Congress's authorizing the President to cancel a spending item, and Congress's authorizing money to be spent on a particular item at the President's discretion. And the latter has been done since the Founding of the Nation. . . .

The short of the matter is this: Had the Line Item Veto Act authorized the President to "decline to spend" any item of spending contained in the Balanced Budget Act of 1997, there is not the slightest doubt that authorization would have been constitutional. What the Line Item Veto Act does instead-authorizing the President to "cancel" an item of spending-is technically different. But the technical difference does not relate to the technicalities of the Presentment Clause, which have been fully complied with; and the doctrine of unconstitutional delegation, which is at issue here, is preeminently not a doctrine of technicalities. The title of the Line Item Veto Act, which was perhaps designed to simplify for public comprehension, or perhaps merely to comply with the terms of a campaign pledge, has succeeded in faking out the Supreme Court. The President's action it authorizes in fact is not a line item veto and thus does not offend Art. I, §7; and insofar as the substance of that action is concerned, it is no different from what Congress has permitted the President to do since the formation of the Union.

I would hold that the President's cancellation of §4722(c) of the Balanced Budget Act as an item of direct spending does not violate the Constitution. Because I find no party before us who has standing to challenge the President's cancellation of §968 of the Taxpayer Relief Act, I do not reach the question whether that violates the Constitution.

For the foregoing reasons, I respectfully dissent.

Selection/Election

The 2000 presidential election in the United States was a cynic's paradise and a democrat's nightmare. With a plot seemingly taken from a baroque Graham Greene novel of colonial corruption and imperial arrogance, Election 2000 challenged many of the sacred assumptions Americans once held about the integrity of the electoral process and the legitimacy of their governmental system. Called into question were the core democratic values Americans long took for granted.

Election 2000 was anything but ordinary. Indeed, it was an international embarrassment for the United States. After decades of monitoring elections in other countries to ensure democratic standards, the United States found itself trying to explain to others why the leader of the free world could not even get a vote count right!

Arguably the closest, certainly the longest, demonstrably the costliest presidential campaign in history, this contest will be remembered for the strange thirty-six-day election aftermath, in which five Supreme Court justices finally selected the candidate, from their own party, who lost the popular vote and actually may have lost the Electoral College vote. It was not supposed to be this way—not in America.

How is one to understand and put into proper perspective the peculiarities of Election 2000? The postelection swirl of events perplexed rather than enlightened. So many ups and downs, so many possible outcomes hanging on a single judge's decision or the interpretation of what to do about dangling, dimpled, or pregnant chads.

As political scientists James Ceaser and Andrew Busch note, "There were two major questions at that moment that no one could answer: who would win, and who would decide who would win."[1] We now know that George W. Bush won; we also know that it was the U.S. Supreme Court that ultimately handed him the presidency. In the end, Bush became president in one of the closest elections in presidential history.

How did it come to pass that the United States Supreme Court selected the president of the United States? What rules and laws apply to the selection/election of presidents? How much guidance does the Constitution give? Few public issues in the United States escape judicial scrutiny. If the integrity of our democracy is to be maintained, the "process" must be above politics. But can it ever be truly above or apart from politics?

Politics has always had its slimy side, and often money has played a key role in questions of political corruption. Over time, Congress has attempted to control the flow of money into the political process, but with little success.

One such effort, the Federal Election Campaign Act of 1971, with its 1974 amendments, sought to limit political contributions and to limit expenditures, and called for timely reporting of contributions. The act was challenged on a variety of grounds, but the "free speech" question quickly came to center stage in this per curiam opinion.

Buckley v. Valeo
424 U.S. 1 (1976)

. . . B. The Merits

Appellants urge that since Congress has given the Commission wide-ranging rulemaking and enforcement powers with respect to the substantive provisions of the Act, Congress is precluded under the principle of separation of powers from vesting in itself the authority to appoint those who will exercise such authority. Their argument is based on the language of Art. II, 2, cl. 2, of the Constitution . . .

Appellants' argument is that this provision is the exclusive method by which those charged with executing the laws of the United States may be chosen . . .

Appellee Commission and amici in support of the Commission urge that the Framers of the Constitution, while mindful of the need for checks and balances among the three branches of the National Government, had no intention of denying to the Legislative Branch authority to appoint its own officers. Congress, either under the Appointments Clause or under its grants of substantive legislative authority and the Necessary and Proper Clause in Art. I, is in their view empowered to provide for the appointment to the Commission in the manner which it did because the Commission is performing "appropriate legislative functions." . . .

1. Separation of Powers

. . . Our inquiry of necessity touches upon the fundamental principles of the Government established by the Framers of the Constitution, and all litigants and all of the courts which have addressed themselves to the matter start on common ground in the recognition of the intent of the Framers that the powers of the three great branches of the National Government be largely separate from one another.

James Madison, writing in the Federalist No. 47, defended the work of the Framers against the charge that these three governmental powers were not entirely separate from one another in the proposed Constitution. He asserted that while there was some admixture, the Constitution was nonetheless true to Montesquieu's well-known maxim that the legislative, executive, and judicial departments ought to be separate and distinct:

"The reasons on which Montesquieu grounds his maxim are a further demonstration of his meaning. 'When the legislative and executive powers are united in the same person or body,' says he, 'there can be no liberty, because apprehensions may arise lest the same monarch or senate should enact tyrannical laws to execute them in a tyrannical manner.' Again: 'Were the power of judging joined with the legislative, the life and liberty of the subject would be exposed to arbitrary control, for the judge would then be the legislator. Were it joined to the executive power, the judge might behave with all the violence of an oppressor.' . . ."

Yet it is also clear from the provisions of the Constitution itself, and from the Federalist Papers, that the Constitution by no means contemplates total separation of each of these three essential branches of Government. The President is a participant in the lawmaking process by virtue of his authority to veto bills enacted by Congress. The Senate is a participant in the appointive process by virtue of its authority to refuse to confirm persons nominated to office by the President. The men who met in Philadelphia in the summer of 1787 were practical statesmen, experienced in politics, who viewed the principle of separation of powers as a vital check against tyranny. But they likewise saw that a hermetic sealing off of the three branches of Government from one another would preclude the establishment of a Nation capable of governing itself effectively . . . The Framers regarded the checks and balances that they had built into the tripartite Federal Government as a self-executing safeguard against the encroachment or aggrandizement of one branch at the expense of the other . . .

More closely in point to the facts of the present case is this Court's decision in *Springer v. Philippine Islands, 277 U.S. 189* (1928), where the Court held that the legislature of the Philippine Islands could not provide for legislative appointment to executive agencies.

2. The Appointments Clause

The principle of separation of powers was not simply an abstract generalization in the minds of the Framers: it was woven into the document that they drafted in Philadelphia in the summer of 1787. Article I, 1, declares: "All legislative Powers herein granted shall be vested in a Congress of the United States." Article II, 1, vests the executive power "in a President of the United States of America," and Art. III, 1, declares that "The judicial Power of the United States, shall be vested in one supreme Court, and in such inferior Courts as the Congress may from time to time ordain and establish." The further concern of the Framers of the Constitution with maintenance of the separation of powers is found in the so-called "Ineligibility" and "Incompatibility" Clauses contained in Art. I, 6 . . .

It is in the context of these cognate provisions of the document that we must examine the language of Art. II. 2, cl. 2, which appellants contend provides the only authorization for appointment of those to whom substantial executive or administrative authority is given by statute . . .

The Appointments Clause could, of course, be read as merely dealing with etiquette or protocol in describing "Officers of the United States," but the drafters had a less frivolous purpose in mind. This conclusion is supported by language from *United States v. Germaine, 99 U.S. 508, 509–510 (1879)*:

"The Constitution for purposes of appointment very clearly divides all its officers into two classes. The primary class requires a nomination by the President and confirmation by the Senate. But foreseeing that when offices became numerous, and sudden removals necessary, this mode might be inconvenient, it was provided that, in regard to officers inferior to those specially mentioned, Congress might by law vest their appointment in the President alone, in the courts of law, or in the heads of departments. That all persons who can be said to hold an office under the government about to be established under the Constitution were intended to be included within one or the other of these modes of appointment there can be but little doubt."

We think that the term "Officers of the United States" as used in Art. II, defined to include "all persons who can be said to hold an office under the government" in United States v. Germaine, *supra*, is a term intended to have substantive meaning. We think its fair import is that any appointee exercising significant authority pursuant to the laws of the United States is an "Officer of the United States," and must, therefore, be appointed in the manner prescribed by 2, cl. 2, of that Article . . .

Although two members of the Commission are initially selected by the President, his nominations are subject to confirmation not merely by the Senate, but by the House of Representatives as well. The remaining four voting members of the Commission are appointed by the President pro tempore of the Senate and by the Speaker of the House. While the second part of the Clause authorizes Congress to vest the appointment of the officers described in that part in "the Courts of Law, or in the Heads of Departments," neither the Speaker of the House nor the President pro tempore of the Senate comes within this language.

The phrase "Heads of Departments," used as it is in conjunction with the phrase "Courts of Law," suggests that the Departments referred to are themselves in the Executive Branch or at least have some connection with that branch. While the Clause expressly authorizes Congress to vest the appointment of certain officers in the "Courts of Law," the absence of similar language to include Congress must mean that neither Congress nor its officers were included within the language "Heads of Departments" in this part of cl. 2.

Thus with respect to four of the six voting members of the Commission, neither the President, the head of any department, nor the Judiciary has any voice in their selection.

The Appointments Clause specifies the method of appointment only for "Officers of the United States" whose appointment is not "otherwise provided for" in the Constitution. But there is no provision of the Constitution remotely providing any alternative means for the selection of the members of the Commission or for anybody like them. Appellee Commission has argued . . . that the Appointments Clause of Art. II should not be read to exclude the "inherent power of Congress" to appoint its own officers to perform functions necessary to that body as an institution. But there is no need to read the Appointments Clause contrary to its plain language in order to reach the result . . . Ranking nonmembers, such as the Clerk of the House of Representatives, are elected under the internal rules of each House and are designated by statute as "officers of the Congress." . . . Nothing in our holding with respect to Art. II, 2, cl. 2, will deny to Congress "all power to appoint its own inferior officers to carry out appropriate legislative functions."

Appellee Commission and amici contend somewhat obliquely that because the Framers had no intention of relegating Congress to a position below that of the co-equal Judicial and Executive Branches of the National Government, the Appointments Clause must somehow be read to include Congress or its officers as among those in whom the appointment power may be vested. But the debates of the Constitutional Convention, and the Federalist Papers, are replete with expressions of fear that the Legislative Branch of the National Government will aggrandize itself at the expense of the other two branches. The debates during the Convention, and the evolution of the draft version of the Constitution, seem to us to lend considerable support to our reading of the language of the Appointments Clause itself.

An interim version of the draft Constitution had vested in the Senate the authority to appoint Ambassadors, public Ministers, and Judges of the Supreme Court, and the language of Art. II as finally adopted is a distinct change in this regard. We believe that it was a deliberate change made by the Framers with the intent to deny Congress any authority itself to appoint those who were "Officers of the United States." . . .

Appellee Commission and amici urge that because of what they conceive to be the extraordinary authority reposed in Congress to regulate elections, this case stands on a different footing than if Congress had exercised its legislative authority in another field. There is, of course, no doubt that Congress has express authority to regulate congressional elections, by virtue of the power conferred in Art. I, 4. This Court has also held that it has very broad authority to prevent corruption in national Presidential elections. *Burroughs v. United States*, *290 U.S. 534* (1934). But Congress has plenary authority in all areas in which it has substantive legislative jurisdiction, *McCulloch v. Maryland*, *4 Wheat. 316* (1819), so long as the exercise of that authority does not offend some other constitutional restriction. We see no reason to believe that the authority of Congress over federal election practices is of such a wholly different nature from the other grants of authority to Congress that it may be employed in such a manner as to offend well-established constitutional restrictions stemming from the separation of powers.

The position that because Congress has been given explicit and plenary authority to regulate a field of activity, it must therefore have the power to appoint those who are to administer the regulatory statute is both novel and contrary to the language of the Appointments Clause. Unless their selection is elsewhere provided for, all officers of the United States are to be appointed in accordance with the Clause. Principal officers are selected by the President with the advice and consent of the Senate. Inferior officers Congress may allow to be appointed by the President alone, by the heads of departments, or by the Judiciary. No class or type of officer is excluded because of its special functions. The President appoints judicial as well as executive officers.

Neither has it been disputed—and apparently it is not now disputed—that the Clause controls the appointment of the members of a typical administrative agency even though its functions, as this Court recognized in *Humphrey's Executor v. United States, 295 U.S. 602, 624* (1935), may be "predominantly quasi-judicial and quasi-legislative" rather than executive. The Court in that case carefully emphasized that although the members of such agencies were to be independent of the Executive in their day-to-day operations, the Executive was not excluded from selecting them . . .

We are also told by appellees and amici that Congress had good reason for not vesting in a Commission composed wholly of Presidential appointees the authority to administer the Act, since the administration of the Act would undoubtedly have a bearing on any incumbent President's campaign for re-election. While one cannot dispute the basis for this sentiment as a practical matter, it would seem that those who sought to challenge incumbent Congressmen might have equally good reason to fear a Commission which was unduly responsive to members of Congress whom they were seeking to unseat. But such fears, however rational, do not by themselves warrant a distortion of the Framers' work.

Appellee Commission and amici finally contend . . . that whatever shortcomings the provisions for the appointment of members of the Commission might have under Art. II, Congress had ample authority under the Necessary and Proper Clause of Art. I to effectuate this result. We do not agree. The proper inquiry when considering the Necessary and Proper Clause is not the authority of Congress to create an office or a commission, which is broad indeed, but rather its authority to provide that its own officers may make appointments to such office or commission . . .

. . . Congress could not, merely because it concluded that such a measure was "necessary and proper" to the discharge of its substantive legislative authority, pass a bill of attainder or ex post facto law contrary to the prohibitions contained in 9 of Art. I.

No more may it vest in itself, or in its officers, the authority to appoint officers of the United States when the Appointments Clause by clear implication prohibits it from doing so.

The trilogy of cases from this Court dealing with the constitutional authority of Congress to circumscribe the President's power to remove officers of the United States is entirely consistent with this conclusion. In *Myers v. United States, 272 U.S. 52* (1926), the Court held that Congress could not by statute divest the President of the power to remove an officer in the Executive Branch whom he was initially authorized to appoint . . .

In the later case of Humphrey's Executor, where it was held that Congress could circumscribe the President's power to remove members of independent regulatory agencies, the Court was careful to note that it was dealing with an agency intended to be independent of executive authority "except in its selection." *295 U.S. at 625* (emphasis in original). *Wiener v. United States, 357 U.S. 349* (1958), which applied the holding in Humphrey's Executor to a member of the War Claims Commission, did not question in any respect that members of independent agencies are not independent of the Executive with respect to their appointments . . .

3. The Commission's Powers

Thus, on the assumption that all of the powers granted in the statute may be exercised by an agency whose members have been appointed in accordance with the Appointments Clause, the ultimate question is which, if any, of those powers may be exercised by the present voting Commissioners, none of whom was appointed as provided by that Clause. Our previous description of the statutory provisions, see *supra,* at 109–113, disclosed that the Commission's powers fall generally into three categories: functions relating to the flow of necessary information—receipt, dissemination, and investigation; functions with respect to the Commission's task of fleshing out the statute—rulemaking and advisory opinions; and functions necessary to ensure compliance with the statute and rules—informal procedures, administrative determinations and hearings, and civil suits.

Insofar as the powers confided in the Commission are essentially of an investigative and informative nature, falling in the same general category as those powers which Congress might delegate to one of its own committees, there can be no question that the Commission as presently constituted may exercise them . . .

But when we go beyond this type of authority to the more substantial powers exercised by the Commission, we reach a different result. The Commission's enforcement power, exemplified by its discretionary power to seek judicial relief, is authority that cannot possibly be regarded as merely in aid of the legislative function of Congress. A lawsuit is the ultimate remedy for a breach of the law, and it is to the President, and not to the Congress, that the Constitution entrusts the responsibility to "take Care that the Laws be faithfully executed." Art. II, 3 . . .

We hold that these provisions of the Act, vesting in the Commission primary responsibility for conducting civil litigation in the courts of the United States for vindicating public rights, violate Art. II, 2, cl. 2, of the Constitution. Such functions may be discharged only by persons who are "Officers of the United States" within the language of that section.

All aspects of the Act are brought within the Commission's broad administrative powers: rule-making, advisory opinions, and determinations of eligibility for funds and even for federal elective office itself. These functions, exercised free from day-to-day supervision of either Congress or the Executive Branch, are more legislative and judicial in nature than are the Commission's enforcement powers, and are of kinds usually performed by independent regulatory agencies or by some department in the Executive Branch under the direction of an Act of Congress. Congress viewed these broad powers as essential to effective and impartial administration of the entire substantive framework of the Act. Yet each of these functions also represents the performance of a significant governmental duty exercised pursuant to a public law. While the

President may not insist that such functions be delegated to an appointee of his removable at will, Humphrey's Executor v. United States . . . none of them operates merely in aid of congressional authority to legislate or is sufficiently removed from the administration and enforcement of public law to allow it to be performed by the present Commission. These administrative functions may therefore be exercised only by persons who are "Officers of the United States." . . .

Americans are accustomed to waking up on the day after a presidential election and knowing who will be at the helm of government. On November 8, 2000, the campaign had officially ended, but a new contest was just beginning, and it would not be resolved for five weeks.

At issue were the vote totals in the state of Florida. That race was too close to call, and Vice President Al Gore, behind by a few hundred votes, asked for a recount. The strategy of the Bush team was to delay and thus make inevitable the selection of Bush as president.

As events in Florida unfolded at a bewildering pace, as each day seemed to bring a decision that favored one candidate, only to be reversed the next, as the outcome seemed as uncertain as the process seemed to be confusing, both camps began to believe that the outcome ultimately would be decided in the courts: either Florida's or the U.S. Supreme Court.

A political time bomb was ticking, but no one knew for sure who would ignite the final flame. As the days passed, time, or the shortness of time, would dictate events. The Supreme Court felt it had to cast the final deciding vote in the 2000 election; and although politically, no one should have been surprised that this Republican court sided with Bush, constitutional scholars had reason to feel surprise at the ground on which this Court decided.

Bush v. Gore
531 U.S. 98 (2000)

Per Curiam . . .

This case has shown that punch card balloting machines can produce an unfortunate number of ballots which are not punched in a clean, complete way by the voter. After the current counting, it is likely legislative bodies nationwide will examine ways to improve the mechanisms and machinery for voting.

The individual citizen has no federal constitutional right to vote for electors for the President of the United States unless and until the state legislature chooses a statewide election as the means to implement its power to appoint members of the Electoral College. U.S. Const., Art. II, §1. This is the source for the statement in *McPherson v. Blacker, 146 U.S. 1, 35* (1892), that the State legislature's power to select the manner for appointing electors is plenary; it may, if it so chooses, select the electors itself, which indeed was the manner used by State legislatures in several States for many years after the Framing of our Constitution . . . History has now favored the voter, and in each of the several States the citizens themselves vote for Presidential electors. When the state legislature vests the right to vote for President in its people, the right to vote as the legislature has prescribed is fundamental; and one source of its fundamental nature lies in the equal weight accorded to each vote and the equal dignity owed to each voter. The State, of course, after granting the franchise in the special context of Article II, can take back the power to appoint electors . . .

The right to vote is protected in more than the initial allocation of the franchise. Equal protection applies as well to the manner of its exercise. Having once granted the right to vote on equal terms, the State may not, by later arbitrary and disparate treatment, value one person's vote over that of another . . .

There is no difference between the two sides of the present controversy on these basic propositions. Respondents say that the very purpose of vindicating the right to vote justifies the recount procedures now at issue. The question before us, however, is whether the recount procedures the Florida Supreme Court has adopted are consistent with its obligation to avoid arbitrary and disparate

treatment of the members of its electorate. Much of the controversy seems to revolve around ballot cards designed to be perforated by a stylus but which, either through error or deliberate omission, have not been perforated with sufficient precision for a machine to count them. In some cases a piece of the card—a chad—is hanging, say by two corners. In other cases there is no separation at all, just an indentation.

The Florida Supreme Court has ordered that the intent of the voter be discerned from such ballots . . . The recount mechanisms implemented in response to the decisions of the Florida Supreme Court do not satisfy the minimum requirement for non-arbitrary treatment of voters necessary to secure the fundamental right. Florida's basic command for the count of legally cast votes is to consider the "intent of the voter." *Gore v. Harris*, ___ So. 2d, at ___ (slip op., at 39). This is unobjectionable as an abstract proposition and a starting principle. The problem inheres in the absence of specific standards to ensure its equal application. The formulation of uniform rules to determine intent based on these recurring circumstances is practicable and, we conclude, necessary.

. . . The search for intent can be confined by specific rules designed to ensure uniform treatment . . .

The want of those rules here has led to unequal evaluation of ballots in various respects . . . As seems to have been acknowledged at oral argument, the standards for accepting or rejecting contested ballots might vary not only from county to county but indeed within a single county from one recount team to another . . .

The State Supreme Court ratified this uneven treatment. It mandated that the recount totals from two counties, Miami-Dade and Palm Beach, be included in the certified total. The court also appeared to hold *sub silentio* that the recount totals from Broward County, which were not completed until after the original November 14 certification by the Secretary of State, were to be considered part of the new certified vote totals even though the county certification was not contested by

Vice President Gore. Yet each of the counties used varying standards to determine what was a legal vote. Broward County used a more forgiving standard than Palm Beach County, and uncovered almost three times as many new votes, a result markedly disproportionate to the difference in population between the counties.

In addition, the recounts in these three counties were not limited to so-called undervotes but extended to all of the ballots. The distinction has real consequences. A manual recount of all ballots identifies not only those ballots which show no vote but also those which contain more than one, the so-called overvotes. Neither category will be counted by the machine. This is not a trivial concern. At oral argument, respondents estimated there are as many as 110,000 overvotes statewide. As a result, the citizen whose ballot was not read by a machine because he failed to vote for a candidate in a way readable by a machine may still have his vote counted in a manual recount; on the other hand, the citizen who marks two candidates in a way discernable by the machine will not have the same opportunity to have his vote count, even if a manual examination of the ballot would reveal the requisite indicia of intent. Furthermore, the citizen who marks two candidates, only one of which is discernable by the machine, will have his vote counted even though it should have been read as an invalid ballot. The State Supreme Court's inclusion of vote counts based on these variant standards exemplifies concerns with the remedial processes that were under way.

That brings the analysis to yet a further equal protection problem. The votes certified by the court included a partial total from one county, Miami-Dade. The Florida Supreme Court's decision thus gives no assurance that the recounts included in a final certification must be complete. Indeed, it is respondent's submission that it would be consistent with the rules of the recount procedures to include whatever partial counts are done by the time of final certification, and we interpret the Florida Supreme Court's decision to permit this . . . This accommodation no doubt results

from the truncated contest period established by the Florida Supreme Court in *Bush I*, at respondents' own urging. The press of time does not diminish the constitutional concern. A desire for speed is not a general excuse for ignoring equal protection guarantees.

In addition to these difficulties the actual process by which the votes were to be counted under the Florida Supreme Court's decision raises further concerns. That order did not specify who would recount the ballots . . .

The recount process, in its features here described, is inconsistent with the minimum procedures necessary to protect the fundamental right of each voter in the special instance of a statewide recount under the authority of a single state judicial officer. Our consideration is limited to the present circumstances, for the problem of equal protection in election processes generally presents many complexities.

The question before the Court is not whether local entities, in the exercise of their expertise, may develop different systems for implementing elections. Instead, we are presented with a situation where a state court with the power to assure uniformity has ordered a statewide recount with minimal procedural safeguards. When a court orders a statewide remedy, there must be at least some assurance that the rudimentary requirements of equal treatment and fundamental fairness are satisfied.

Given the Court's assessment that the recount process underway was probably being conducted in an unconstitutional manner, the Court stayed the order directing the recount so it could hear this case and render an expedited decision. The contest provision, as it was mandated by the State Supreme Court, is not well calculated to sustain the confidence that all citizens must have in the outcome of elections. The State has not shown that its procedures include the necessary safeguards . . .

Upon due consideration of the difficulties identified to this point, it is obvious that the recount cannot be conducted in compliance with the requirements of equal protection and due process without substantial additional work. . . .

The Supreme Court of Florida has said that the legislature intended the State's electors to "participat[e] fully in the federal electoral process," as provided in 3 U.S.C. §5. ___ So. 2d. That statute, in turn, requires that any controversy or contest that is designed to lead to a conclusive selection of electors be completed by December 12. That date is upon us, and there is no recount procedure in place under the State Supreme Court's order that comports with minimal constitutional standards. Because it is evident that any recount seeking to meet the December 12 date will be unconstitutional for the reasons we have discussed, we reverse the judgment of the Supreme Court of Florida ordering a recount to proceed . . .

Seven Justices of the Court agree that there are constitutional problems with the recount ordered by the Florida Supreme Court that demand a remedy . . .

None are more conscious of the vital limits on judicial authority than are the members of this Court, and none stand more in admiration of the Constitution's design to leave the selection of the President to the people, through their legislatures, and to the political sphere. When contending parties invoke the process of the courts, however, it becomes our unsought responsibility to resolve the federal and constitutional issues the judicial system has been forced to confront.

The judgment of the Supreme Court of Florida is reversed, and the case is remanded for further proceedings not inconsistent with this opinion . . .

It is so ordered.

Chief Justice Rehnquist, with whom *Justice Scalia* and *Justice Thomas* join, concurring. We join the *per curiam* opinion. We write separately because we believe there are additional grounds that require us to reverse the Florida Supreme Court's decision . . .

In most cases, comity and respect for federalism compel us to defer to the decisions of state courts on issues of state law. That practice reflects our understanding that the decisions of state courts are definitive pronouncements of the will of the States as sovereigns . . .

In Florida, the legislature has chosen to hold statewide elections to appoint the State's 25 electors. Importantly, the legislature has delegated the authority to run the elections and to oversee election disputes to the Secretary of State (Secretary), Fla. Stat. §97.012(1) (2000), and to state circuit courts, §§102.168(1), 102.168(8). Isolated sections of the code may well admit of more than one interpretation, but the general coherence of the legislative scheme may not be altered by judicial interpretation so as to wholly change the statutorily provided apportionment of responsibility among these various bodies. In any election but a Presidential election, the Florida Supreme Court can give as little or as much deference to Florida's executives as it chooses, so far as Article II is concerned, and this Court will have no cause to question the court's actions. But, with respect to a Presidential election, the court must be both mindful of the legislature's role under Article II in choosing the manner of appointing electors and deferential to those bodies expressly empowered by the legislature to carry out its constitutional mandate.

In order to determine whether a state court has infringed upon the legislature's authority, we necessarily must examine the law of the State as it existed prior to the action of the court. Though we generally defer to state courts on the interpretation of state law—see, *e.g., Mullaney v. Wilbur, 421 U.S. 684* (1975)—there are of course areas in which the Constitution requires this Court to undertake an independent, if still deferential, analysis of state law . . .

The scope and nature of the remedy ordered by the Florida Supreme Court jeopardizes the "legislative wish" to take advantage of the safe harbor provided by 3 U.S.C. §5. *Bush v. Palm Beach County Canvassing Bd., ante,* at 6. December 12, 2000, is the last date for a final determination of the Florida electors that will satisfy §5. Yet in the late afternoon of December 8th—four days before this deadline—the Supreme Court of Florida ordered recounts of tens of thousands of so-called "under-votes" spread through 64 of the State's 67 counties. This was done in a search for elusive—perhaps delusive—certainty as to the exact count of 6 million votes. But no one claims that these ballots have not previously been tabulated; they were initially read by voting machines at the time of the election, and thereafter reread by virtue of Florida's automatic recount provision. No one claims there was any fraud in the election. The Supreme Court of Florida ordered this additional recount under the provision of the election code giving the circuit judge the authority to provide relief that is "appropriate under such circumstances." Fla. Stat. §102.168(8) (2000).

Surely when the Florida Legislature empowered the courts of the State to grant "appropriate" relief, it must have meant relief that would have become final by the cut-off date of 3 U.S.C. §5. In light of the inevitable legal challenges and ensuing appeals to the Supreme Court of Florida and petitions for certiorari to this Court, the entire recounting process could not possibly be completed by that date . . .

Justice Stevens, with whom *Justice Ginsburg and Justice Breyer* join, dissenting.

The Constitution assigns to the States the primary responsibility for determining the manner of select-ing the Presidential electors. See Art. II, §1, cl. 2. When questions arise about the meaning of state laws, including election laws, it is our settled prac-tice to accept the opinions of the highest courts of the States as providing the final answers. On rare occasions, however, either federal statutes or the Federal Constitution may require federal judicial intervention in state elections. This is not such an occasion.

The federal questions that ultimately emerged in this case are not substantial. Article II provides that "[e]ach *State* shall appoint, in such Manner as the Legislature *thereof* may direct, a Number of Electors." *Ibid.* (emphasis added). It does not create state legislatures out of whole cloth, but rather takes

them as they come—as creatures born of, and constrained by, their state constitutions.

Lest there be any doubt, we stated over 100 years ago in *McPherson v. Blacker, 146 U.S. 1, 25* (1892), that "[w]hat is forbidden or required to be done by a State" in the Article II context "is forbid-den or required of the legislative power under state constitutions as they exist." In the same vein, we also observed that "[t]he [State's] legislative power is the supreme authority except as limited by the constitution of the State." *Ibid.*; cf. *Smiley v. Holm, 285 U.S. 355, 367* (1932) . . .

It hardly needs stating that Congress, pursuant to 3 U.S.C. §5, did not impose any affirmative duties upon the States that their governmental branches could "violate." Rather, §5 provides a safe harbor for States to select electors in contested elections "by judicial or other methods" established by laws prior to the election day. Section 5, like Article II, assumes the involvement of the state judiciary in interpreting state election laws and resolving elec-tion disputes under those laws. Neither §5 nor Article II grants federal judges any special authority to substitute their views for those of the state judi-ciary on matters of state law . . .

Admittedly, the use of differing substandards for determining voter intent in different counties employing similar voting systems may raise serious concerns. Those concerns are alleviated—if not eliminated—by the fact that a single impartial magistrate will ultimately adjudicate all objections arising from the recount process. Of course, as a general matter, "[t]he interpretation of constitu-tional principles must not be too literal. We must remember that the machinery of government would not work if it were not allowed a little play in its joints." *Bain Peanut Co. of Tex. v. Pinson, 282 U.S. 499, 501* (1931) . . .

Even assuming that aspects of the remedial scheme might ultimately be found to violate the Equal Protection Clause, I could not subscribe to the majority's disposition of the case. As the majority explicitly holds, once a state legislature determines to select electors through a popular vote, the right to have one's vote counted is of constitutional stature. As the majority further acknowledges, Florida law holds that all ballots that reveal the intent of the voter constitute valid votes. Recognizing these principles, the majority nonetheless orders the termination of the contest proceeding before all such votes have been tabulated. Under their own reasoning, the appropriate course of action would be to remand to allow more specific procedures for implementing the legislature's uniform general standard to be established.

In the interest of finality, however, the majority effectively orders the disenfranchisement of an unknown number of voters whose ballots reveal their intent—and are therefore legal votes under state law—but were for some reason rejected by ballot-counting machines. It does so on the basis of the deadlines set forth in Title 3 of the United States Code. *Ante*, at 11. But, as I have already noted, those provisions merely provide rules of decision for Congress to follow when selecting among conflicting slates of electors. *Supra*, at 2. They do not prohibit a State from counting what the majority concedes to be legal votes until a bona fide winner is determined . . . Thus, nothing prevents the majority, even if it properly found an equal protection violation, from ordering relief appropriate to remedy that violation without depriving Florida voters of their right to have their votes counted. As the majority notes, "[a] desire for speed is not a general excuse for ignoring equal protection guarantees." . . .

Finally, neither in this case, nor in its earlier opinion in *Palm Beach County Canvassing Bd. v. Harris, 2000 WL 1725434* (Fla., Nov. 21, 2000), did the Florida Supreme Court make any substantive change in Florida electoral law . . .

What must underlie petitioners' entire federal assault on the Florida election procedures is an unstated lack of confidence in the impartiality and capacity of the state judges who would make the critical decisions if the vote count were to proceed. Otherwise, their position is wholly without merit. The endorsement of that position by the majority of this Court can only lend credence to the most cynical appraisal of the work of judges throughout the land. It is confidence in the men and women who administer the judicial system that is the true backbone of the rule of law. Time will one day heal the wound to that confidence that will be inflicted by today's decision. One thing, however, is certain. Although we may never know with complete certainty the identity of the winner of this year's Presidential election, the identity of the loser is perfectly clear. It is the Nation's confidence in the judge as an impartial guardian of the rule of law.

I respectfully dissent . . .

Administrative Powers

Article II, Section I, of the Constitution opens with these words: "The executive power shall be vested in a President of the United States of America." Does this merely assign a title to this office, vest the office with a responsibility, or grant the office real and tangible power? Elsewhere in the Constitution (Article II, Section 3), the language reads, "he shall take care that the laws be faithfully executed."

Together these two constitutional provisions, along with the appointment (Section 2) and other powers, make the president the chief executive officer of the government. And the chief executive is more than a mere title; it implies real and substantive powers. But what was the scope of this authority? What were its limitations? As these powers were not clearly spelled out in the Constitution, political and legal battles, primarily between the president and the Congress, have occurred over the course of the nation's history over the administrative powers of the presidency.

Was the president to be sole master of his own house, or did the Congress have a role? Many offices within the executive branch are appointed by the president with the "advice and consent of the Senate." Must the Senate also consent when one of these offices is removed? How much independent power does a president wield in "faithfully executing the law"? The separation of powers calls for the sharing of powers as well as the separation; how involved should the Congress or courts be in what presidents consider to be managerial and executive matters and thus under presidential control?

The tug-of-war between presidents and the Congress is especially visible in the administrative power arena. Some of these battles have taken place largely for political reasons (e.g., the post–Civil War passage of the Tenure in Office Act as a prelude to the impeachment of Andrew Johnson); others were struggles over significant policy or procedural matters (e.g., must a president show "cause" in removing an executive branch officer?). In the area of administrative power, one can see where both the separation and the sharing of power can lead to political as well as institutional conflict.

As the chief executive officer, the president is required to make a series of personnel decisions on hiring and firing. Is the president's removal power restricted to showing cause? Must a president demonstrate malfeasance in order to remove an official from office? In this case, the president removed a general appraiser of merchandise without citing any cause, as the enabling stature seemed to call for.

The Court sided with the president, arguing that terms of office are not fixed for life and that, with the exception of constitutionally created offices that indeed are appointed for life (e.g., judges), the president should be granted some flexibility in removing officers.

Shurtleff v. United States
189 U.S. 311 (1903)

. . . Mr. Justice Peckham . . . delivered the opinion of the court: . . .

The office of general appraiser of merchandise was created by the 12th section of the act of Congress. . . . The material portion of that section reads as follows:

> 'Sec. 12. That there shall be appointed by the President, by and with the advice and consent of the Senate, nine general appraisers of merchandise, each of whom shall receive a salary of seven thousand dollars a year. Not more than five of such general appraisers shall be appointed from the same political party. They shall not be engaged in any other business, avocation, or employment, and may be removed from office at any time by the President for inefficiency, neglect of duty, or malfeasance in office. . . .'

There is, of course, no doubt of the power of Congress to create such an office . . .

It must be presumed that the President did not make the removal for any cause assigned in the statute, because there was given to the officer no notice or opportunity to defend. The question then arises, Can the President exercise the power of removal for any other causes than those mentioned in the statute? In other words, Is he restricted to a removal for those causes alone, or can he exercise his general power of removal without such restriction?

. . . We assume, for the purposes of this case only, that Congress could attach such conditions to the removal of an officer appointed under this statute as to it might seem proper; and, therefore, that it could provide that the officer should only be removed for the causes stated, and for no other, and after notice and an opportunity for a hearing. Has Congress, by the 12th section of the above act, so provided?

It cannot now be doubted that, in the absence of constitutional or statutory provision, the President can, by virtue of his general power of appointment, remove an officer, even though appointed by and with the advice and consent of the Senate . . . To take away this power of removal in relation to an inferior office created by statute, although that statute provided for an appointment thereto by the President and confirmation by the Senate, would require very clear and explicit language. It should not be held to be taken away by mere inference or implication. Congress has regarded the office as of sufficient importance to make it proper to fill it by an appointment to be made by the President and confirmed by the Senate. It has thereby classed it as appropriately coming under the direct supervision of the President, and to be administered by officers appointed by him (and confirmed by the Senate) with reference to his constitutional responsibility to see that the laws are faithfully executed . . .

The appellant contends that, because the statute specified certain causes for which the officer might be removed, it thereby impliedly excluded and denied the right to remove for any other cause, and that the President was therefore by the statute prohibited from any removal excepting for the causes, or some of them, therein defined . . . We are of opinion that, as thus used, the maxim does not justify the contention of the appellant. We regard it as inapplicable to the facts herein. The right of removal would exist if the statute had not contained a word upon the subject. It does not exist by virtue of the grant, but it inheres in the right to appoint, unless limited by constitution or statute. It requires plain language to take it away . . .

In making removals from office it must be assumed that the President acts with reference to his constitutional duty to take care that the laws are faithfully executed, and we think it would be a mistaken view to hold that the mere specification in the statute of some causes for removal thereby excluded the right of the President to remove for any other reason which he, acting with a due sense of his official responsibility, should think sufficient.

By the 4th section of article 2 of the Constitution it is provided that all civil officers shall be removed from office on impeachment for, and conviction of, treason, bribery, or other high crimes and misde- meanors. No one has ever supposed that the effect of this section was to prevent their removal for other causes deemed sufficient by the President. No such inference could be reasonably drawn from such language.

We are not unmindful of the force of the con- tention that, if the power of removal is not limited to the causes specified in the statute, that then those words providing for a removal for inefficiency, neglect of duty, or malfeasance in office fulfill no function, because without them the President has unlimited power of removal, and with them he still has the same power.

It may be said, however, that there is some use for the provision for removal for the causes named in the statute. A removal for any of those causes can only be made after notice and an opportunity to defend; and therefore, if a removal is made without such notice, there is a conclusive presumption that the officer was not removed for any of those causes, and his removal cannot be regarded as the least imputation on his character for integrity or capacity . . . It is true that, under this construction, it is possible that officers may be removed for causes unconnected with the proper administration of the office. That is the case with most of the other offi- cers in the government. The only restraint in cases such as this must consist in the responsibility of the President, under his oath of office, to so act as shall be for the general benefit and welfare . . .

The right of removal . . . would exist as inherent in the power of appointment unless taken away in plain and unambiguous language. This has not been done, and although language has been used from which we might speculate or guess that possi- bly Congress did intend the meaning contended for by appellant, yet it has not in fact expressed that meaning in words plain enough to call upon the courts to determine that such intention existed.

Does the president have the exclusive authority to remove executive officers of the United States when they are appointed with the advice and consent of the Senate?

Louis Myers was appointed by the president as a postmaster. This appointment was approved by the Senate. Three years later, his resignation was demanded. He refused, and was soon removed from office by the Postmaster General, acting as directed by the president.

Myers brought suit. The law said that "Postmasters . . . shall be appointed and may be removed by the President by and with the advice and consent of the Senate, and shall hold their offices for four years unless sooner removed or suspended accord- ing to law." As the Senate did not consent of Myers's removal, the appellant seemed to have a strong case. The government asserted that the removal require- ment was not valid and that the president was free to remove officers without the consent of the Senate.

Myers v. United States 272 U.S. 52 (1926)

. . . Mr. Chief Justice TAFT delivered the opinion of the Court.

This case presents the question whether under the Constitution the President has the exclusive power of removing executive officers of the United States whom he has appointed by and with the advice and consent of the Senate . . .

The question where the power of removal of executive officers . . . was vested, was presented early in the first session of the First Congress. There is no express provision respecting removals in the Constitution, except as section 4 of article 2 . . . provides for removal from office by impeachment. The subject was not discussed in the Constitutional Convention . . .

In the House of Representatives of the First Congress, on Tuesday, May 18, 1789, Mr. Madison moved in the committee of the whole that there should be established three executive departments, one of Foreign Affairs, another of the Treasury, and a third of War, at the head of each of which there should be a Secretary, to be appointed by the President by and with the advice and consent of the Senate, and to be removable by the President. The committee agreed to the establishment of a

Department of Foreign Affairs, but a discussion ensued as to making the Secretary removable by the President . . . 'The question was now taken and carried, by a considerable majority, in favor of declaring the power of removal to be in the President.' 1 Annals of Congress, 383.

On June 16, 1789, the House resolved itself into a committee of the whole on a bill proposed by Mr. Madison for establishing an executive department to be denominated the Department of Foreign Affairs . . . "to be removable from office by the President of the United States." . . . After a very full discussion the question was put; Shall the words "to be removable by the President" be struck out? It was determined in the negative—yeas 20, nays 34 . . .

On June 22, in the renewal of the discussion:

> 'Mr. Benson moved to amend the bill, by altering the second clause, so as to imply the power of removal to be in the President alone . . .

'Mr. Benson stated that his objection to the clause 'to be removable by the President' arose from an idea that the power of removal by the President hereafter might appear to be exercised by virtue of a legislative grant only, and consequently be subjected to legislative instability, when he was well satisfied in his own mind that it was fixed by a fair legislative construction of the Constitution'. . .

Mr. Madison admitted the objection . . . He said:

> 'They certainly may be construed to imply a legislative grant of the power. He wished everything like ambiguity expunged . . . and therefore seconded the motion. Gentlemen have all along proceeded on the idea that the Constitution vests the power in the President . . .

Mr. Benson's first amendment to alter the second clause by the insertion of the italicized words, made that clause read as follows:

> 'That there shall be in the State Department an inferior officer to be . . . called the chief clerk

in . . . and *who, whenever the principal officers shall be removed from office by the President of the United States*, or in any other case of vacancy, shall, during such vacancy, have charge and custody of all records, books and papers appertaining to said department.'

The first amendment was then approved by a vote of 30 to 18. . . . Mr. Benson then moved to strike out in the first clause the words "to be removable by the President," in pursuance of the purpose he had already declared, and this second motion of his was carried by a vote of 31 to 19 . . .

The bill as amended . . . was then passed by a vote of 29 to 22 . . .

. . . After the bill as amended had passed the House, it was sent to the Senate, where it was discussed in secret session, without report. The critical vote there was upon the striking out of the clause recognizing and affirming the unrestricted power of the President to remove. The Senate divided by 10 to 10, requiring the deciding vote of the Vice President, John Adams, who voted against striking out, and in favor of the passage of the bill as it had left the House. Ten of the Senators had been in the Constitutional Convention, and of them 6 voted that the power of removal was in the President alone. The bill, having passed as it came from the House, was signed by President Washington and became a law. Act July 27, 1789 . . .

. . . Mr. Madison insisted that article 2 by vesting the executive power in the President was intended to grant to him the power of appointment and removal of executive officers except as thereafter expressly provided in that article . . . He said:

> . . . 'If there is any point in which the separation of the legislative and executive powers ought to be maintained with great caution, it is that which relates to officers and offices.' Annals of Congress, 581 . . .

. . . The reasonable construction of the Constitution must be that the branches should be kept separate in all cases in which they were not expressly blended, and the Constitution should be expounded to blend them no more than it affirmatively requires . . .

The vesting of the executive power in the President was essentially a grant of the power to execute the laws. But the President alone and unaided could not execute the laws. He must execute them by the assistance of subordinates . . . As he is charged specifically to take care that they be faithfully executed, the reasonable implication, even in the absence of express words, was that as part of his executive power he should select those who were to act for him under his direction in the execution of the laws. The further implication must be, in the absence of any express limitation respecting removals, that as his selection of administrative officers is essential to the execution of the laws by him, so must be his power of removing those for whom he cannot continue to be responsible . . . It was urged that the natural meaning of the term "executive power" granted the President included the appointment and removal of executive subordinates. If such appointments and removals were not an exercise of the executive power, what were they? They certainly were not the exercise of legislative or judicial power in government as usually understood . . .

The requirement of the second section of article 2 that the Senate should advise and consent to the presidential appointments, was to be strictly construed . . . The executive power was given in general terms strengthened by specific terms where emphasis was regarded as appropriate, and was limited by direct expressions where limitation was needed, and the fact that no express limit was placed on the power of removal by the executive was convincing indication that none was intended. This is the same construction of article 2 as that of Alexander Hamilton . . .

The history of the clause by which the Senate was given a check upon the President's power of appointment makes it clear that it was not prompted by any desire to limit removals . . . The important purpose of those who brought about the restriction was to lodge in the Senate, where the small states had equal representation with the larger states, power to prevent the President from making too many appointments from the larger states . . . The formidable opposition to the Senate's veto on the President's power of appointment indicated that in construing its effect, it should not be extended beyond its express application to the matter of appointments . . .

It was pointed out in this great debate that the power of removal, though equally essential to the executive power is different in its nature from that of appointment . . . A veto by the Senate—a part of the legislative branch of the government—upon removals is a much greater limitation upon the executive branch, and a much more serious blending of the legislative with the executive, than a rejection of a proposed appointment. It is not to be implied. The rejection of a nominee of the President for a particular office does not greatly embarrass him in the conscientious discharge of his high duties . . . because the President usually has an ample field from which to select for office, according to his preference, competent and capable men. The Senate has full power to reject newly proposed appointees whenever the President shall remove the incumbents. Such a check enables the Senate to prevent the filling of offices with bad or incompetent men, or with those against whom there is tenable objection.

The power to prevent the removal of an officer who has served under the President is different from the authority to consent to or reject his appointment. When a nomination is made, it may be presumed that the Senate is, or may become, as well advised as to the fitness of the nominee as the President, but in the nature of things the defects in ability or intelligence or loyalty in the administration of the laws of one who has served as an officer under the President are facts as to which the President, or his trusted subordinates, must be better informed than the Senate, and the power to remove him may therefor be regarded as confined for very sound and practical reasons, to the governmental authority which has administrative control.

... Another argument urged against the constitutional power of the President alone to remove executive officers is that, in the absence of an express power of removal granted to the President, power to make provision for removal of all such officers is vested in the Congress by section 8 of article 1.

Mr. Madison, mistakenly thinking that an argument like this was advanced by Roger Sherman, took it up and answered it as follows:

> 'He seems to think (if I understand him rightly) that the power of displacing from office is subject to legislative discretion, because, it having a right to create, it may limit or modify as it thinks proper. I shall not say but at first view this doctrine may seem to have some plausibility. But when I consider that the Constitution clearly intended to maintain a marked distinction between the legislative, executive and judicial powers of government, and when I consider that, if the Legislature has a power such as is contended for, they may subject and transfer at discretion powers from one department of our government to another, they may, on that principle, exclude the President altogether from exercising any authority in the removal of officers, they may give to the Senate alone, or the President and Senate combined, they may vest it in the whole Congress, or they may reserve it to be exercised by this house. When I consider the consequences of this doctrine, and compare them with the true principles of the Constitution, I own that I cannot subscribe to it. . . .' Annals of Congress . . .

The constitutional construction that excludes Congress from legislative power to provide for the removal of superior officers finds support in the second section of article 2 . . . This is 'but the Congress may by law vest the appointment of such inferior officers, as they think proper, in the President alone, in the Courts of Law, or in the Heads of Departments.' These words, it has been held by this court, give to Congress the power to limit and regulate removal of such inferior officers by heads of departments when it exercises its constitutional power to lodge the power of appointment with

them . . . By the plainest implication it excludes congressional dealing with appointments or removals of executive officers not falling within the exception and leaves unaffected the executive power of the President to appoint and remove them . . .

... It could never have been intended to leave to Congress unlimited discretion to vary fundamentally the operation of the great independent executive branch of government and thus most seriously to weaken it. It would be a delegation by the convention to Congress of the function of defining the primary boundaries of another of the three great divisions of government . . .

It is reasonable to suppose also that had it been intended to give to Congress power to regulate or control removals in the manner suggested, it would have been . . . specifically enumerated . . . The difference between the grant of legislative power under article 1 to Congress which is limited to powers therein enumerated, and the more general grant of the executive power to the President under article 2 is significant. The fact that the executive power is given in general terms strengthened by specific terms where emphasis is appropriate, and limited by direct expressions where limitation is needed, and that no express limit is placed on the power of removal by the executive is a convincing indication that none was intended.

It is argued that the denial of the legislative power to regulate removals in some way involves the denial of power to prescribe qualifications for office, or reasonable classification for promotion, and yet that has been often exercised. We see no conflict between the latter power and that of appointment and removal, provided of course that the qualifications do not so limit selection and so trench upon executive choice as to be in effect legislative designation. As Mr. Madison said in the First Congress:

> 'The powers relative to offices are partly legislative and partly executive. The Legislature creates the office, defines the powers, limits its duration, and annexes a compensation. This done, the legislative power ceases. They ought to have nothing

to do with designating the man to fill the office. That I conceive to be of an executive nature'. . .

. . . Mr. Madison and his associates pointed out with great force the unreasonable character of the view that the convention intended, without express provision, to give to Congress or the Senate, in case of political or other differences, the means of thwarting the executive in the exercise of his great powers and in the bearing of his great responsibility by fastening upon him, as subordinate executive officers, men who by their inefficient service under him, by their lack of loyalty to the service, or by their different views of policy might make his taking care that the laws be faithfully executed most difficult or impossible.

As Mr. Madison said in the debate in the First Congress:

> 'Vest this power in the Senate jointly with the President, and you abolish at once that great principle of unity and responsibility in the executive department, which was intended for the security of liberty and the public good. If the President should possess alone the power of removal from office, those who are employed in the execution of the law will be in their proper situation, and the chain of dependence be preserved; the lowest officers, the middle grade, and the highest will depend, as they ought, on the President, and the President on the community.' 1 Annals of Congress, 499 . . .

Made responsible under the Constitution for the effective enforcement of the law, the President needs as an indispensable aid to meet it the disciplinary influence upon those who act under him of a reserve power of removal. But it is contended that executive officers appointed by the President with the consent of the Senate are bound by the statutory law, and are not his servants to do his will, and that his obligation to care for the faithful execution of the laws does not authorize him to treat them as such. The degree of guidance in the discharge of their duties that the President may exercise over

executive officers varies with the character of their service as prescribed in the law under which they act. The highest and most important duties which his subordinates perform are those in which they act for him. In such cases they are exercising not their own but his discretion. This field is a very large one. It is sometimes described as political. Kendall v. United States, 12 . . . Each head of a department is and must be the President's alter ego in the matters of that department where the President is required by law to exercise authority . . .

. . . But this is not to say that there are not strong reasons why the President should have a like power to remove his appointees charged with other duties than those above described. The ordinary duties of officers prescribed by statute come under the general administrative control of the President by virtue of the general grant to him of the executive power, and he may properly supervise and guide their construction of the statutes under which they act in order to secure that unitary and uniform execution of the laws which article 2 of the Constitution evidently contemplated in vesting general executive power in the President alone. Laws are often passed with specific provision for adoption of regulations by a department or bureau head to make the law workable and effective. The ability and judgment manifested by the official thus empowered, as well as his energy and stimulation of his subordinates, are subjects which the President must consider and supervise in his administrative control. Finding such officers to be negligent and inefficient, the President should have the power to remove them. Of course there may be duties so peculiarly and specifically committed to the discretion of a particular officer as to raise a question whether the President may overrule or revise the officer's interpretation of his statutory duty in a particular instance. Then there may be duties of a quasi judicial character imposed on executive officers and members of executive tribunals whose decisions after hearing affect interests of individuals, the discharge of which the President cannot in a particular case properly influence or control. But even in such a case he may consider the decision after its rendition as a reason for removing the officer, on the ground that the discretion regularly entrusted to that officer by statute has not been on the whole intelligently or wisely exercised. Otherwise he does not discharge his own constitutional duty of seeing that the laws be faithfully executed . . .

For the reasons given, we must therefore hold that the provision of the law of 1876 by which the unrestricted power of removal of first-class postmasters is denied to the President is in violation of the Constitution and invalid. This leads to an affirmance of the judgment of the Court of Claims . . .

The separate opinion of Mr. Justice McReynolds . . .

Nothing short of language clear beyond serious disputation should be held to clothe the President with authority wholly beyond congressional control arbitrarily to dismiss every officer whom he appoints except a few judges. There are no such words in the Constitution, and the asserted inference conflicts with the heretofore accepted theory that this government is one of carefully enumerated powers under an intelligible charter . . .

If the phrase 'executive power' infolds the one now claimed, many others heretofore totally unsuspected may lie there awaiting future supposed necessity, and no human intelligence can define the field of the President's permissible activities. 'A masked battery of constructive powers would complete the destruction of liberty.'. . .

The Legislature may create post offices and prescribe qualifications, duties, compensation, and term. And it may protect the incumbent in the enjoyment of his term unless in some way restrained therefrom. The real question, therefore, comes to this: Does any constitutional provision definitely limit the otherwise plenary power of Congress over postmasters, when they are appointed by the President with the consent of the Senate? . . .

. . . Congress, in the exercise of its unquestioned power, may deprive the President of the right either to appoint or to remove any inferior officer, by vesting the authority to appoint in another . . . He must utilize the force which Congress gives. He cannot, without permission, appoint the humblest clerk or expend a dollar of the public funds.

It is well to emphasize that our present concern is with the removal of an 'inferior officer,' within article 2, 2, of the Constitution, which the statute positively prohibits without consent of the Senate . . . We are not dealing with an ambassador, public minister, consul, judge, or 'superior officer.'. . . From its first session down to the last one Congress has consistently asserted its power to prescribe conditions concerning the removal of inferior officers. The executive has habitually observed them, and this court has affirmed the power of Congress therein . . .

. . . Congress may vest the power to appoint and remove all of them in the head of a department and thus exclude them from presidential authority. From 1789 to 1836 the Postmaster General exercised these powers, as to all postmasters . . . For 40 years the President functioned and met his duty to 'take care that the laws be faithfully executed' without the semblance of power to remove any postmaster. So I think the supposed necessity and theory of government are only vapors . . .

. . . The Constitution empowers the President to appoint ambassadors, other public ministers, consuls, judges of the Supreme Court and superior officers, and no statute can interfere therein. But Congress may authorize both appointment and removal of all inferior officers without regard to the President's wishes—even in direct opposition to them . . .

. . . If it were possible to spell out of the debate and action of the first Congress on the bill to establish the Department of Foreign Affairs some support for the present claim of the United States, this would be of little real consequence, for the same Congress on at least two occasions took the opposite position, and time and time again subsequent Congresses have done the same thing. It would be amazing for this court to base the interpretation of a constitutional provision upon a single doubtful congressional interpretation, when there have been dozens of them extending through 135 years, which are directly to the contrary effect . . .

Congress has long and vigorously asserted its right to restrict removals and there has been no common executive practice based upon a contrary view. The President has often removed, and it is admitted that he may remove, with either the express or implied assent of Congress; but the present theory is that he may override the declared will of that body. This goes far beyond any practice heretofore approved or followed; it conflicts with the history of the Constitution, with the ordinary rules of interpretation, and with the construction approved by Congress since the beginning and emphatically sanctioned by this court. To adopt it would be revolutionary . . .

It is beyond the ordinary imagination to picture 40 or 50 capable men, presided over by George Washington, vainly discussing, in the heat of a Philadelphia summer, whether express authority to require opinions in writing should be delegated to a President in whom they had already vested the illimitable executive power here claimed . . .

The claim advanced for the United States is supported by no opinion of this court, and conflicts with Marbury v. Madison (1803), *supra*, concurred in by all, including Mr. Justice Paterson . . .

. . . The court must have appreciated that, unless it found Marbury had the legal right to occupy the office irrespective of the President's will, there would be no necessity for passing upon the much-controverted and farreaching power of the judiciary to declare an act of Congress without effect . . .

If the framers of the Constitution had intended 'the executive power,' in article 2, 1, to include all power of an executive nature, they would not have added the carefully defined grants of section 2 . . . That the general words of a grant are limited, when followed by those of special import, is an established canon; and an accurate writer would hardly think of emphasizing a general grant by adding special and narrower ones without explanation. . . .

. . . Those who maintain that article 2, 1, was intended as a grant of every power of executive nature not specifically qualified or denied, must show that the term 'executive power' had some definite and commonly accepted meaning in 1787. This court has declared that it did not include all powers exercised by the King of England; and, considering the history of the period, none can say that it had then (or afterwards) any commonly accepted and practical definition. If any one of the descriptions of 'executive power' known in 1787 had been substituted for it, the whole plan would have failed. Such obscurity would have been intolerable to thinking men of that time . . .

Mr. Justice BRANDEIS, dissenting . . .

The separation of the powers of government did not make each branch completely autonomous. It left each in some measure, dependent upon the others, as it left to each power to exercise, in some respects, functions in their nature executive, legislative and judicial. Obviously the President cannot secure full execution of the laws, if Congress denies to him adequate means of doing so. Full execution may be defeated because Congress declines to create offices indispensable for that purpose; or because Congress, having created the office, declines to make the indispensable appropriation; or because Congress, having both created the office and made the appropriation, prevents, by restrictions which it imposes, the appointment of officials who in quality and character are indispensable to the efficient execution of the law . . .

Checks and balances were established in order that this should be 'a government of laws and not of men.' As White said in the House in 1789, an uncontrollable power of removal in the Chief Executive 'is a doctrine not to be learned in American governments.' Such power had been denied in colonial charters, and even under proprietary grants and royal commissions. It had been denied in the thirteen states before the framing of the federal Constitution. The doctrine of the separation of powers was adopted by the convention of 1787 not to promote efficiency but to preclude the exercise of arbitrary power. The purpose was not to avoid friction, but, by means of the inevitable friction incident to the distribution of the governmental powers among three departments, to save the people from autocracy. In order to prevent arbitrary executive action, the Constitution provided in terms that presidential appointments be made with the consent of the Senate, unless Congress should otherwise provide; and this clause was construed by Alexander Hamilton in The Federalist, No. 77, as requiring like consent to removals . . .

Mr. Justice HOLMES, dissenting . . .

We have to deal with an office that owes its existence to Congress and that Congress may abolish to-morrow. Its duration and the pay attached to it while it lasts depend on Congress alone. Congress alone confers on the President the power to appoint to it and at any time may transfer the power to other hands. With such power over its own creation, I have no more trouble in believing that Congress has power to prescribe a term of life for it free from any interference than I have in accepting the undoubted power of Congress to decree its end. I have equally little trouble in accepting its power to prolong the tenure of an incumbent until Congress or the Senate shall have assented to his removal. The duty of the President to see that the laws be executed is a duty that does not go beyond the laws or require him to achieve more than Congress sees fit to leave within his power . . .

This case helped establish limits on the president's removal power. In 1925, President Calvin Coolidge appointed William E. Humphrey to the Federal Trade Commission (FTC). The conservative Humphrey clashed with the liberal Franklin D. Roosevelt, who tried to oust Humphrey from the FTC.

After failed efforts to coax Humphrey to leave his post, FDR wrote to Humphrey asking him to step down. Humphrey refused. FDR removed him and appointed a replacement. Humphrey sued. But Humphrey died in 1934, and his executor, Samuel Rathban, continued with the suit.

Two questions were before the Court: (1) Was the president's power to remove officials restricted to malfeasance in office; and (2) if so, was such a limitation on the president constitutional? This case was a follow-up to Myers v. United States *wherein the president was granted fairly wide latitude in removal. The Supreme Court in* Humphrey *ruled unanimously against the president, arguing that he had exceeded his authority in discharging Humphrey. This case established limits on the president's removal power.*

Humphrey's Executor v. United States
295 U.S. 602 (1935)

. . . Justice SUTHERLAND delivered the opinion of the Court. . . .

If the commission finds the method of competition is one prohibited by the act, it is directed to make a report in writing stating its findings as to the facts, and to issue and cause to be served a cease and desist order. If the order is disobeyed, the commission may apply to the appropriate Circuit Court of Appeals for its enforcement. The party subject to the order may seek and obtain a review in the Circuit Court of Appeals in a manner provided by the act.

. . . The question . . . by the provisions of section 1 of the Federal Trade Commission Act . . . already quoted, the President's power is limited to removal for the specific causes enumerated therein. The negative contention of the government is based principally upon the decision of this court in *Shurtleff v. United States, 189 U.S. 311.* That case involved the power of the President to remove a general appraiser of merchandise appointed under the Act . . . 'may be removed from office at any time by the President for inefficiency, neglect of duty, or malfeasance in office.' The President removed Shurtleff without assigning any cause therefor. The Court . . . would give the appraiser the right to hold office during his life or until found guilty of some act specified in the statute . . .

The commission is to be nonpartisan; and it must, from the very nature of its duties, act with entire impartiality. It is charged with the enforcement of no policy except the policy of the law. Its duties are neither political nor executive, but predominantly quasi judicial and quasi legislative. Like the Interstate Commerce Commission, its members are called upon to exercise the trained judgment of a body of experts "appointed by law and informed by experience." . . .

Thus, the language of the act, the legislative reports, and the general purposes of the legislation as reflected by the debates, all combine to demonstrate the congressional intent to create a body of experts who shall gain experience by length of service; a body which shall be independent of executive authority, except in its selection, and free to exercise its judgment without the leave or hindrance of any other official or any department of the government. To the accomplishment of these purposes, it is clear that Congress was of opinion that length and certainty of tenure would vitally contribute. And to hold that, nevertheless, the members of the commission continue in office at the mere will of the President, might be to thwart, in large measure, the very ends which Congress sought to realize by definitely fixing the term of office.

We conclude that the intent of the act is to limit the executive power of removal to the causes enumerated, the existence of none of which is claimed here; and we pass to the second question.

Second. To support its contention that the removal provision of section 1, as we have just construed it, is an unconstitutional interference with the executive power of the President, the government's chief reliance is Myers v. United States . . . Nevertheless, the narrow point actually decided was only that the President had power to remove a postmaster of the first class, without the advice and consent of the Senate as required by act of Congress. In the course of the opinion of the court, expressions occur which tend to sustain the government's contention, but these are beyond the point involved and, therefore, do not come within the rule of stare

decisis. In so far as they are out of harmony with the views here set forth, these expressions are disapproved . . . The office of a postmaster is so essentially unlike the office now involved that the decision in the Myers Case cannot be accepted as controlling our decision here. A postmaster is an executive officer restricted to the performance of executive functions. He is charged with no duty at all related to either the legislative or judicial power. The actual decision in the Myers Case finds support in the theory that such an officer is merely one of the units in the executive department and, hence, inherently subject to the exclusive and illimitable power of removal by the Chief Executive, whose subordinate and aid he is. Putting aside dicta . . . the necessary reach of the decision goes far enough to include all purely executive officers. It goes no farther; much less does it include an officer who occupies no place in the executive department and who exercises no part of the executive power vested by the Constitution in the President.

The Federal Trade Commission is an administrative body created by Congress to carry into effect legislative policies embodied in the statute in accordance with the legislative standard therein prescribed, and to perform other specified duties as a legislative or as a judicial aid. Such a body cannot in any proper sense be characterized as an arm or an eye of the executive. Its duties are performed without executive leave and, in the contemplation of the statute, must be free from executive control. In administering the provisions of the statute in respect of "unfair methods of competition," that is to say, in filling in and administering the details embodied by that general standard, the commission acts in part quasi legislatively and in part quasi judicially. In making investigations and reports thereon for the information of Congress under section 6, in aid of the legislative power, it acts as a legislative agency. Under section 7, which authorizes the commission to act as a master in chancery under rules prescribed by the court, it acts as an agency of the judiciary. To the extent that it exercises any executive function, as distinguished from executive power in the constitutional sense, it does so in the discharge and effectuation of its quasi legislative or quasi judicial powers, or as an agency of the legislative or judicial departments of the government. If Congress is without authority to prescribe causes for removal of members of the trade commission and limit executive power of removal accordingly, that power at once becomes practically all-inclusive in respect of civil officers with the exception of the judiciary provided for by the Constitution. The Solicitor General, at the bar, apparently recognizing this to be true, with commendable candor, agreed that his view in respect of the removability of members of the Federal Trade Commission necessitated a like view in respect of the Interstate Commerce Commission and the Court of Claims. We are thus confronted with the serious question whether not only the members of these quasi legislative and quasi judicial bodies, but the judges of the legislative Court of Claims, exercising judicial power . . . continue in office only at the pleasure of the President.

We think it plain under the Constitution that illimitable power of removal is not possessed by the President in respect of officers of the character of those just named. The authority of Congress, in creating quasi legislative or quasi judicial agencies, to require them to act in discharge of their duties independently of executive control cannot well be doubted; and that authority includes, as an appropriate incident, power to fix the period during which they shall continue, and to forbid their removal except for cause in the meantime. For it is quite evident that one who holds his office only during the pleasure of another cannot be depended upon to maintain an attitude of independence against the latter's will.

The fundamental necessity of maintaining each of the three general departments of government entirely free from the control or coercive influence, direct or indirect, of either of the others, has often been stressed and is hardly open to serious question. So much is implied in the very fact of the separation of the powers of these departments by the Constitution; and in the rule which recognizes their essential coequality. The sound application of a principle that makes one master in his own house precludes him from imposing his control in the house of another who is master there . . .

The power of removal here claimed for the President falls within this principle, since its coercive influence threatens the independence of a commission, which is not only wholly disconnected from the executive department, but which, as already fully appears, was created by Congress as a means of carrying into operation legislative and judicial powers, and as an agency of the legislative and judicial departments.

In the light of the question now under consideration, we have re-examined the precedents referred to in the Myers Case, and find nothing in them to justify a conclusion contrary to that which we have reached . . . not only purely executive, but the officer one who was responsible to the President, and to him alone, in a very definite sense. A reading of the debates shows that the President's illimitable power of removal was not considered in respect of other than executive officers. And it is pertinent to observe that when, at a later time, the tenure of office for the Comptroller of the Treasury was under consideration, Mr. Madison quite evidently thought that, since the duties of that office were not purely of an executive nature but partook of the judiciary quality as well, a different rule in respect of executive removal might well apply . . . .

In Marbury v. Madison, *supra*, 1 Cranch, 137, at pages 162, 165–166, it is made clear that Chief Justice Marshall was of opinion that a justice of the peace for the District of Columbia was not removable at the will of the President; and that there was a distinction between such an officer and officers appointed to aid the President in the performance of his constitutional duties. In the latter case, the distinction he saw was that 'their acts are his acts' and his will, therefore, controls; and, by way of illustration, he adverted to the act establishing the Department of Foreign Affairs, which was the subject of the 'decision of 1789.'

The result of what we now have said is this: Whether the power of the President to remove an officer shall prevail over the authority of Congress to condition the power by fixing a definite term and precluding a removal except for cause will depend upon the character of the office; the Myers decision, affirming the power of the President alone to make the removal, is confined to purely executive officers; and as to officers of the kind here under consideration, we hold that no removal can be made during the prescribed term for which the officer is appointed, except for one or more of the causes named in the applicable statute.

To the extent that, between the decision in the Myers Case . . . there shall remain a field of doubt, we leave such cases as may fall within it for future consideration and determination as they may arise.

In accordance with the foregoing, the questions submitted are answered . . .

Is a president liable for damages when acting in his capacity as president? In Nixon v. Fitzgerald, *the Court was confronted with this question as it related to considerations of presidential immunity in a claim of civil damages. Ernest Fitzgerald sued President Richard M. Nixon, claiming that the president removed him from his civilian job in the Air Force because Fitzgerald was a "whistle blower," who was exposing cost overruns in testimony to Congress.*

The Court, siding with the president, argued that the president had absolute immunity from damages for acts committed in his official capacity as president. Two later cases, Harlow v. Fitzgerald *(1982) and* Clinton v. Jones *(1997), shed further light upon this question.*

Nixon v. Fitzgerald
457 U.S. 731 (1982)

Justice Powell delivered the opinion of the Court.

The plaintiff in this lawsuit seeks relief in civil damages from a former President of the United States. The claim rests on actions allegedly taken in the former President's official capacity during his tenure in office. The issue before us is the scope of the immunity possessed by the President of the United States . . .

This Court consistently has recognized that government officials are entitled to some form of immunity from suits for civil damages. In *Spalding v. Vilas, 161 U.S. 483* (1896), the Court considered the immunity available to the Postmaster General in a suit for damages based upon his official acts. Drawing upon principles of immunity developed in English cases at common law, the Court concluded that "[t]he interests of the people" required a grant of absolute immunity to public officers. *Id.,* at 498. In the absence of immunity, the Court reasoned, executive officials would hesitate to exercise their discretion in a way "injuriously affect[ing] the claims of particular individuals,". . . even when the public interest required bold and unhesitating action. Considerations of "public policy and convenience" therefore compelled a judicial recognition of immunity from suits arising from official acts . . .

Our decisions concerning the immunity of government officials from civil damages liability have been guided by the Constitution, federal statutes, and history. Additionally, at least in the absence of explicit constitutional or congressional guidance, our immunity decisions have been informed by the common law . . . This Court necessarily also has weighed concerns of public policy, especially as illuminated by our history and the structure of our government . . .

. . . Because the Presidency did not exist through most of the development of common law, any historical analysis must draw its evidence primarily from our constitutional heritage and structure. Historical inquiry thus merges almost at its inception with the kind of "public policy" analysis appropriately undertaken by a federal court. This inquiry involves policies and principles that may be considered implicit in the nature of the President's office in a system structured to achieve effective government under a constitutionally mandated separation of powers.

Here a former President asserts his immunity from civil damages claims of two kinds. He stands named as a defendant in a direct action under the Constitution and in two statutory actions under federal laws of general applicability. In neither case has Congress taken express legislative action to subject the President to civil liability for his official acts.

Applying the principles of our cases to claims of this kind, we hold that petitioner, as a former President of the United States, is entitled to absolute immunity from damages liability predicated on his official acts. We consider this immunity a functionally mandated incident of the President's unique office, rooted in the constitutional tradition of the separation of powers and supported by our history. Justice Story's analysis remains persuasive:

> "There are . . . incidental powers, belonging to the executive department, which are necessarily implied from the nature of the functions, which are confided to it. Among these, must necessarily be included the power to perform them. . . . The president cannot, therefore, be liable to arrest, imprisonment, or detention, while he is in the discharge of the duties of his office; and for this purpose his person must be deemed, in civil cases at least, to possess an official inviolability."
> 3 J. Story, Commentaries on the Constitution of the United States.

The President occupies a unique position in the constitutional scheme. Article II, 1, of the Constitution provides that "[t]he executive Power shall be vested in a President of the United States. . . ." This grant of authority establishes the President as the chief constitutional officer of the Executive Branch, entrusted with supervisory and policy responsibilities of utmost discretion and sensitivity. These include the enforcement of federal law—it is the President who is charged constitutionally to "take Care that the Laws be faithfully executed"; the conduct of foreign affairs—a realm in which the Court has recognized that "[i]t would be intolerable that courts, without the relevant

information, should review and perhaps nullify actions of the Executive taken on information properly held secret"; and management of the Executive Branch—a task for which "imperative reasons requir[e] an unrestricted power [in the President] to remove the most important of his subordinates in their most important duties."

In arguing that the President is entitled only to qualified immunity, the respondent relies on cases in which we have recognized immunity of this scope for governors and cabinet officers . . . We find these cases to be inapposite. The President's unique status under the Constitution distinguishes him from other executive officials.

Because of the singular importance of the President's duties, diversion of his energies by concern with private lawsuits would raise unique risks to the effective functioning of government. As is the case with prosecutors and judges—for whom absolute immunity now is established—a President must concern himself with matters likely to "arouse the most intense feelings.". . . Yet, as our decisions have recognized, it is in precisely such cases that there exists the greatest public interest in providing an official "the maximum ability to deal fearlessly and impartially with" the duties of his office. *Ferri v. Ackerman* . . . This concern is compelling where the officeholder must make the most sensitive and far-reaching decisions entrusted to any official under our constitutional system. Nor can the sheer prominence of the President's office be ignored. In view of the visibility of his office and the effect of his actions on countless people, the President would be an easily identifiable target for suits for civil damages. Cognizance of this personal vulnerability frequently could distract a President from his public duties, to the detriment of not only the President and his office but also the Nation that the Presidency was designed to serve . . .

Courts traditionally have recognized the President's constitutional responsibilities and status as factors counseling judicial deference and restraint. For example, while courts generally have looked to the common law to determine the scope of an official's evidentiary privilege, we have recognized that the Presidential privilege is "rooted in the separation of powers under the Constitution.". . . It is settled law that the separation-of-powers doctrine does not bar every exercise of jurisdiction over the President of the United States . . . But our cases also have established that a court, before exercising jurisdiction, must balance the constitutional weight of the interest to be served against the dangers of intrusion on the authority and functions of the Executive Branch . . . When judicial action is needed to serve broad public interests—as when the Court acts, not in derogation of the separation of powers, but to maintain their proper balance, cf. *Youngstown Sheet & Tube Co. v. Sawyer* . . . or to vindicate the public interest in an ongoing criminal prosecution, see *United States v. Nixon* . . . —the exercise of jurisdiction has been held warranted. In the case of this merely private suit for damages based on a President's official acts, we hold it is not.

In defining the scope of an official's absolute privilege, this Court has recognized that the sphere of protected action must be related closely to the immunity's justifying purposes. Frequently our decisions have held that an official's absolute immunity should extend only to acts in performance of particular functions of his office . . . But the Court also has refused to draw functional lines finer than history and reason would support . . . In view of the special nature of the President's constitutional office and functions, we think it appropriate to recognize absolute Presidential immunity from damages liability for acts within the "outer perimeter" of his official responsibility.

Under the Constitution and laws of the United States the President has discretionary responsibilities in a broad variety of areas, many of them highly sensitive. In many cases it would be difficult to determine which of the President's innumerable "functions" encompassed a particular action. In this case, for example, respondent argues that he was dismissed in retaliation for his testimony to Congress— a violation of 5 U.S.C. 7211 (1976 . . .) and 18 U.S.C. 1505. The Air Force, however, has claimed that the underlying reorganization was

undertaken to promote efficiency. Assuming that petitioner Nixon ordered the reorganization in which respondent lost his job, an inquiry into the President's motives could not be avoided under the kind of "functional" theory asserted both by respondent and the dissent. Inquiries of this kind could be highly intrusive. Here respondent argues that petitioner Nixon would have acted outside the outer perimeter of his duties by ordering the discharge of an employee who was lawfully entitled to retain his job in the absence of " 'such cause as will promote the efficiency of the service.' ". . . no federal official could, within the outer perimeter of his duties of office, cause Fitzgerald to be dismissed without satisfying this standard in prescribed statutory proceedings.

This construction would subject the President to trial on virtually every allegation that an action was unlawful, or was taken for a forbidden purpose. Adoption of this construction thus would deprive absolute immunity of its intended effect. It clearly is within the President's constitutional and statutory authority to prescribe the manner in which the Secretary will conduct the business of the Air Force . . . See 10 U.S.C. 8012(b). Because this mandate of office must include the authority to prescribe reorganizations and reductions in force, we conclude that petitioner's alleged wrongful acts lay well within the outer perimeter of his authority.

A rule of absolute immunity for the President will not leave the Nation without sufficient protection against misconduct on the part of the Chief Executive. There remains the constitutional remedy of impeachment. In addition, there are formal and informal checks on Presidential action that do not apply with equal force to other executive officials. The President is subjected to constant scrutiny by the press. Vigilant oversight by Congress also may serve to deter Presidential abuses of office, as well as to make credible the threat of impeachment. Other incentives to avoid misconduct may include a desire to earn reelection, the need to maintain prestige as an element of Presidential influence, and a President's traditional concern for his historical stature.

The existence of alternative remedies and deterrents establishes that absolute immunity will not place the President "above the law." For the President, as for judges and prosecutors, absolute immunity merely precludes a particular private remedy for alleged misconduct in order to advance compelling public ends . . .

Chief Justice Burger, concurring.

I join the Court's opinion, but I write separately to underscore that the President immunity derives from and is mandated by the constitutional doctrine of separation of powers. Indeed, it has been taken for granted for nearly two centuries. In reaching this conclusion we do well to bear in mind that the focus must not be simply on the matter of judging individual conduct in a fact-bound setting; rather, in those familiar terms of John Marshall, it is a Constitution we are expounding. Constitutional adjudication often bears unpalatable fruit. But the needs of a system of government sometimes must outweigh the right of individuals to collect damages. . . .

The immunity of a President from civil suits is not simply a doctrine derived from this Court's interpretation of common law or public policy. Absolute immunity for a President for acts within the official duties of the Chief Executive is either to be found in the constitutional separation of powers or it does not exist. The Court today holds that the Constitution mandates such immunity and I agree. . . .

JUSTICE WHITE, with whom JUSTICE BRENNAN, JUSTICE MARSHALL, and JUSTICE BLACKMUN join, dissenting . . .

The Court now applies the dissenting view in Butz to the Office of the President: A President, acting within the outer boundaries of what Presidents normally do, may, without liability, deliberately cause serious injury to any number of citizens even though he knows his conduct violates a statute or tramples on the constitutional rights of those who are injured. Even if the President in this case ordered Fitzgerald fired by means of a trumped-up

reduction in force, knowing that such a discharge was contrary to the civil service laws, he would be absolutely immune from suit . . . He would be immune regardless of the damage he inflicts, regardless of how violative of the statute and of the Constitution he knew his conduct to be, and regardless of his purpose . . .

We have not taken such a scatter-gun approach in other cases. Butz held that absolute immunity did not attach to the office held by a member of the President's Cabinet but only to those specific functions performed by that officer for which absolute immunity is clearly essential. Members of Congress are absolutely immune under the Speech or Debate Clause of the Constitution, but the immunity extends only to their legislative acts . . . Members of Congress, for example, repeatedly importune the executive branch and administrative agencies outside hearing rooms and legislative halls, but they are not immune if in connection with such activity they deliberately violate the law . . . Judges are absolutely immune from liability for damages, but only when performing a judicial function, and even then they are subject to criminal liability . . . The absolute immunity of prosecutors is likewise limited to the prosecutorial function. A prosecutor who directs that an investigation be carried out in a way that is patently illegal is not immune . . .

. . . The decision thus has all the earmarks of a constitutional pronouncement—absolute immunity for the President's office is mandated by the Constitution. Although the Court appears to disclaim this, *ante*, at 748–749, n. 27, it is difficult to read the opinion coherently as standing for any narrower proposition: Attempts to subject the President to liability either by Congress through a statutory action or by the courts through a Bivens . . . proceeding would violate the separation of powers. Such a generalized absolute immunity cannot be sustained when examined in the traditional manner and in light of the traditional judicial sources . . .

[A]ll that can be concluded is that absolute immunity from civil liability for the President finds no support in constitutional text or history, or in the explanations of the earliest commentators. This is too weak a ground to support a declaration by this Court that the President is absolutely immune from civil liability, regardless of the source of liability or the injury for which redress is sought. This much the majority implicitly concedes since history and text, traditional sources of judicial argument, merit only a footnote in the Court's opinion . . .

No bright line can be drawn between arguments for absolute immunity based on the constitutional principle of separation of powers and arguments based on what the Court refers to as "public policy." This necessarily follows from the Court's functional interpretation of the separation-of-powers doctrine . . .

. . . Petitioner argues that public policy favors absolute immunity because absent such immunity the President's ability to execute his constitutionally mandated obligations will be impaired. The convergence of these two lines of argument is superficially apparent from the very fact that in both instances the approach of the Court has been characterized as a "functional" analysis.

The difference is only one of degree. While absolute immunity might maximize executive efficiency and therefore be a worthwhile policy, lack of such immunity may not so disrupt the functioning of the Presidency as to violate the separation-of-powers doctrine. Insofar as liability in this case is of congressional origin, petitioner must demonstrate that subjecting the President to a private damages action will prevent him from "accomplishing [his] constitutionally assigned functions." Insofar as liability is based on a Bivens action, perhaps a lower standard of functional disruption is appropriate. Petitioner has surely not met the former burden; I do not believe that he has met the latter standard either . . .

. . . The President has been held to be subject to judicial process at least since 1807. *United States v. Burr* . . .

. . . If there is a separation-of-powers problem here, it must be found in the nature of the remedy and not in the process involved. . . .

The possibility of liability may, in some circumstances, distract officials from the performance of their duties and influence the performance of those duties in ways adverse to the public interest. But when this "public policy" argument in favor of absolute immunity is cast in these broad terms, it applies to all officers, both state and federal: All officers should perform their responsibilities without regard to those personal interests threatened by the possibility of a lawsuit . . . Inevitably, this reduces the public policy argument to nothing more than an expression of judicial inclination as to which officers should be encouraged to perform their functions with "vigor," although with less care . . .

The functional approach to the separation-of-powers doctrine and the Court's more recent immunity decisions converge on the following principle: The scope of immunity is determined by function, not office. The wholesale claim that the President is entitled to absolute immunity in all of his actions stands on no firmer ground than did the claim that all Presidential communications are entitled to an absolute privilege, which was rejected in favor of a functional analysis, by a unanimous Court in *United States v. Nixon* . . . Therefore, whatever may be true of the necessity of such a broad immunity in certain areas of executive responsibility, the only question that must be answered here is whether the dismissal of employees falls within a constitutionally assigned executive function, the performance of which would be substantially impaired by the possibility of a private action for damages. I believe it does not. . . .

Absolute immunity is appropriate when the threat of liability may bias the decisionmaker in ways that are adverse to the public interest. But as the various regulations and statutes protecting civil servants from arbitrary executive action illustrate, this is an area in which the public interest is demonstrably on the side of encouraging less "vigor" and more "caution" on the part of decisionmakers . . . Absolute immunity would be nothing more than a judicial declaration of policy that directly contradicts the policy of protecting civil servants reflected in the statutes and regulations . . .

The majority fails to recognize the force of what the Court has already done in this area. Under the above principles, the President could not claim that there are no circumstances under which he would be subject to a Bivens-type action for violating respondent's constitutional rights. Rather, he must assert that the absence of absolute immunity will substantially impair his ability to carry out particular functions that are his constitutional responsibility. For the reasons I have presented above, I do not believe that this argument can be successfully made under the circumstances of this case . . .

JUSTICE BLACKMUN, with whom JUSTICE BRENNAN and JUSTICE MARSHALL join, dissenting . . .

I join JUSTICE WHITE's dissent. For me, the Court leaves unanswered his unanswerable argument that no man, not even the President of the United States, is absolutely and fully above the law . . .

Nor can I understand the Court's holding that the absolute immunity of the President is compelled by separation-of-powers concerns, when the Court at the same time expressly leaves open the possibility that the President nevertheless may be fully subject to congressionally created forms of liability. These two concepts, it seems to me, cannot coexist . . .

In an offshoot of Nixon v. Fitzgerald, *two of President Nixon's subordinates, Bryce Harlow and Alexander Butterfield, were alleged to be a part of a conspiracy to violate the rights of A. Ernest Fitzgerald, an Air Force employee who had "blown the whistle" on cost overruns and was subsequently dismissed from employment, allegedly as a punishment for whistle-blowing. The defendant's claim to have acted in good faith failed.*

Harlow & Butterfield v. Fitzgerald 457 U.S. 800 (1982)

. . . Justice Powell delivered the opinion of the Court.

The issue in this case is the scope of the immunity available to the senior aides and advisers of the President of the United States in a suit for damages based upon their official acts . . .

For executive officials in general, however, our cases make plain that qualified immunity represents the norm. In *Scheuer v. Rhodes* . . . we acknowledged that high officials require greater protection than those with less complex discretionary responsibilities. Nonetheless, we held that a governor and his aides could receive the requisite protection from qualified or good-faith immunity . . . In *Butz v. Economou, supra*, we extended the approach of Scheuer to high federal officials of the Executive Branch . . . Discussing in detail the considerations that also had underlain our decision in *Scheuer*, we explained that the recognition of a qualified immunity defense for high executives reflected an attempt to balance competing values: not only the importance of a damages remedy to protect the rights of citizens, but also "the need to protect officials who are required to exercise their discretion and the related public interest in encouraging the vigorous exercise of official authority.". . . Without discounting the adverse consequences of denying high officials an absolute immunity from private lawsuits alleging constitutional violations—consequences found sufficient in *Spalding v. Vilas* . . . to warrant extension to such officials of absolute immunity from suits at common law—we emphasized our expectation that insubstantial suits need not proceed to trial . . .

Petitioners argue that they are entitled to a blanket protection of absolute immunity as an incident of their offices as Presidential aides. In deciding this claim we do not write on an empty page. In *Butz v. Economou, supra*, the Secretary of Agriculture—a Cabinet official directly accountable to the President—asserted a defense of absolute official immunity from suit for civil damages. We rejected his claim. In so doing we did not question the power or the importance of the Secretary's office. Nor did we doubt the importance to the President of loyal and efficient subordinates in executing his duties of office. Yet we found these factors, alone, to be insufficient to justify absolute immunity. "[T]he greater power of [high] officials," we reasoned, "affords a greater potential for a regime of lawless conduct." . . .

Having decided in *Butz* that Members of the Cabinet ordinarily enjoy only qualified immunity from suit, we conclude today that it would be equally untenable to hold absolute immunity an incident of the office of every Presidential subordinate based in the White House. Members of the Cabinet are direct subordinates of the President, frequently with greater responsibilities, both to the President and to the Nation, than White House staff. The considerations that supported our decision in *Butz* apply with equal force to this case . . .

In disputing the controlling authority of *Butz*, petitioners rely on the principles developed in *Gravel v. United States, 408 U.S. 606* . . . In Gravel we endorsed the view that "it is literally impossible . . . for Members of Congress to perform their legislative tasks without the help of aides and assistants" and that "the day-to-day work of such aides is so critical to the Members' performance that they must be treated as the latter's alter egos . . . ." . . . Having done so, we held the Speech and Debate Clause derivatively applicable to the "legislative acts" of a Senator's aide that would have been privileged if performed by the Senator himself . . .

Petitioners contend that the rationale of Gravel mandates a similar "derivative" immunity for the chief aides of the President of the United States. Emphasizing that the President must delegate a large measure of authority to execute the duties of his office, they argue that recognition of derivative absolute immunity is made essential by all the considerations that support absolute immunity for the President himself.

Petitioners' argument is not without force. Ultimately, however, it sweeps too far. If the President's aides are derivatively immune because they are essential to the functioning of the Presidency, so should the Members of the Cabinet—Presidential subordinates some of whose essential roles are acknowledged by the Constitution itself—be absolutely immune. Yet we implicitly rejected such derivative immunity in *Butz*. Moreover, in general our cases have followed a "functional" approach to immunity law. We have recognized that the judicial, prosecutorial, and legislative functions require absolute immunity. But this protection has extended no further than its justification would warrant. In Gravel, for example, we emphasized that Senators and their aides were absolutely immune only when performing "acts legislative in nature," and not when taking other acts even "in their official capacity." . . .

Petitioners also assert an entitlement to immunity based on the "special functions" of White House aides. This form of argument accords with the analytical approach of our cases. For aides entrusted with discretionary authority in such sensitive areas as national security or foreign policy, absolute immunity might well be justified to protect the unhesitating performance of functions vital to the national interest. But a "special functions" rationale does not warrant a blanket recognition of absolute immunity for all Presidential aides in the performance of all their duties. This conclusion too follows from our decision in *Butz*, which establishes that an executive official's claim to absolute immunity must be justified by reference to the public interest in the special functions of his office, not the mere fact of high station.

Butz also identifies the location of the burden of proof. The burden of justifying absolute immunity rests on the official asserting the claim. We have not of course had occasion to identify how a Presidential aide might carry this burden. But the general requisites are familiar in our cases. In order to establish entitlement to absolute immunity a Presidential aide first must show that the responsibilities of his office embraced a function so sensitive as to require a total shield from liability. He then must demonstrate that he was discharging the protected function when performing the act for which liability is asserted.

Applying these standards to the claims advanced by petitioners Harlow and Butterfield, we cannot conclude on the record before us that either has shown that "public policy requires [for any of the functions of his office] an exemption of [absolute] scope." Nor, assuming that petitioners did have functions for which absolute immunity would be warranted, could we now conclude that the acts charged in this lawsuit—if taken at all—would lie within the protected area . . .

Even if they cannot establish that their official functions require absolute immunity, petitioners assert that public policy at least mandates an application of the qualified immunity standard that would permit the defeat of insubstantial claims without resort to trial. We agree . . .

Qualified or "good faith" immunity is an affirmative defense that must be pleaded by a defendant official. *Gomez v. Toledo, 446 U.S. 635* (1980). Decisions of this Court have established that the "good faith" defense has both an "objective" and a "subjective" aspect. The objective element involves a presumptive knowledge of and respect for "basic, unquestioned constitutional rights." *Wood v. Strickland, 420 U.S. 308, 322* (1975). The subjective component refers to "permissible intentions." Characteristically the Court has defined these elements by identifying the circumstances in which qualified immunity would not be available. Referring both to the objective and subjective elements, we have held that qualified immunity would be defeated if an official "knew or reasonably should have known that the action he took within his sphere of official responsibility would violate the constitutional rights of the [plaintiff], or if he took the action with the malicious intention to cause a deprivation of constitutional rights or other injury . . ."

The subjective element of the good-faith defense frequently has proved incompatible with our admonition in *Butz* that insubstantial claims should not proceed to trial. Rule 56 of the Federal Rules of Civil Procedure provides that disputed questions of fact ordinarily may not be decided on motions for summary judgment. And an official's subjective good faith has been considered to be a question of fact that some courts have regarded as inherently requiring resolution by a jury.

In the context of *Butz'* attempted balancing of competing values, it now is clear that substantial costs attend the litigation of the subjective good faith of government officials. Not only are there the general costs of subjecting officials to the risks of trial—distraction of officials from their governmental duties, inhibition of discretionary action, and deterrence of able people from public service. There are special costs to "subjective" inquiries of this kind. Immunity generally is available only to officials performing discretionary functions. In contrast with the thought processes accompanying "ministerial" tasks, the judgments surrounding discretionary action almost inevitably are influenced by the decisionmaker's experiences, values, and emotions. These variables explain in part why questions of subjective intent so rarely can be decided by summary judgment. Yet they also frame a background in which there often is no clear end to the relevant evidence. Judicial inquiry into subjective motivation therefore may entail broad-ranging discovery and the deposing of numerous persons, including an official's professional colleagues. Inquiries of this kind can be peculiarly disruptive of effective government.

Consistently with the balance at which we aimed in *Butz*, we conclude today that bare allegations of malice should not suffice to subject government officials either to the costs of trial or to the burdens of broad-reaching discovery. We therefore hold that government officials performing discretionary functions, generally are shielded from liability for civil damages insofar as their conduct does not violate clearly established statutory or constitutional rights of which a reasonable person would have known. See *Procunier v. Navarette, 434 U.S. 555, 565* (1978); *Wood v. Strickland, 420 U.S., at 322* . . .

CHIEF JUSTICE BURGER, dissenting . . .

In this case the Court decides that senior aides of the President do not have derivative immunity from the President. I am at a loss, however, to reconcile this conclusion with our holding in *Gravel v. United States* . . .

We very properly recognized in *Gravel* that the central purpose of a Member's absolute immunity would be "diminished and frustrated" if the legislative aides were not also protected by the same broad immunity . . .

. . . Without absolute immunity for these "elbow aides," who are indeed "alter egos," a Member could not effectively discharge all of the assigned constitutional functions of a modern legislator.

The Court has made this reality a matter of our constitutional jurisprudence. How can we conceivably hold that a President of the United States, who represents a vastly larger constituency than does any Member of Congress, should not have "alter egos" with comparable immunity? To perform the constitutional duties assigned to the Executive would be "literally impossible, in view of the complexities of the modern [Executive] process . . . without the help of aides and assistants." . . . These words reflect the precise analysis of *Gravel*, and this analysis applies with at least as much force to a President. The primary layer of senior aides of a President— like a Senator's "alter egos"—are literally at a President's elbow, with offices a few feet or at most a few hundred feet from his own desk. The President, like a Member of Congress, may see those personal aides many times in one day. They are indeed the President's "arms" and "fingers" to aid in performing his constitutional duty to see "that the laws [are] faithfully executed." Like a Member of Congress, but on a vastly greater scale, the President cannot personally implement a fraction of his own policies and day-to-day decisions . . .

Precisely the same public policy considerations on which the Court now relies in *Nixon v. Fitzgerald*, and that we relied on only recently in *Gravel*, are fully applicable to senior Presidential aides . . . In addition, exposure to civil liability for official acts will result in constant judicial questioning, through judicial proceedings and pretrial discovery, into the inner workings of the Presidential Office beyond

that necessary to maintain the traditional checks and balances of our constitutional structure . . .

. . . The *Gravel* Court took note of the burdens on congressional aides: the stress of long hours, heavy responsibilities, constant exposure to harassment of the political arena. Is the Court suggesting the stresses are less for Presidential aides? By construing the Constitution to give only qualified immunity to senior Presidential aides we give those key "alter egos" only lawsuits, winnable lawsuits perhaps, but lawsuits nonetheless, with stress and effort that will disperse and drain their energies and their purses . . .

Butz v. Economou . . . does not dictate that senior Presidential aides be given only qualified immunity. Butz held only that a Cabinet officer exercising discretion was not entitled to absolute immunity; we need not abandon that holding. A senior Presidential aide works more intimately with the President on a daily basis than does a Cabinet officer, directly implementing Presidential decisions literally from hour to hour . . .

The Court's analysis in *Gravel* demonstrates that the question of derivative immunity does not and should not depend on a person's rank or position in the hierarchy, but on the function performed by the person and the relationship of that person to the superior . . . The function of senior Presidential aides, as the "alter egos" of the President, is an integral, inseparable part of the function of the President . . .

In 1970, the Federal Bureau of Investigation received information indicating that a radical organization known as the East Coast Conspiracy to Save Lives (ECCSL) might be planning to blow up a tunnel in Washington, D.C., along with other activities. Acting on this information, Attorney General John Mitchell ordered a warrantless wiretap on the telephone of one of the organization's members.

Claiming that the wiretaps were authorized "in the exercise of [the President's] authority relating to national security" alone, the government asserted a bold defense of presidential power to engage in domestic surveillance. The defendant, Keith Forsyth, claimed that his Fourth Amendment rights had been violated.

Does the president possess these expansive powers, and is the attorney general liable for damages if the president, through his agent, violated the rights of a U.S. citizen?

Mitchell v. Forsyth
472 U.S. 511 (1985)

. . . Justice White delivered the opinion of the Court.

This is a suit for damages stemming from a warrantless wiretap authorized by petitioner, a former Attorney General of the United States. The case presents . . . whether the Attorney General is absolutely immune from suit for actions undertaken in the interest of national security . . .

. . . The Government response was accompanied by an affidavit, sworn to by then Attorney General Richard Kleindienst, averring that the surveillance to which Forsyth had been subjected was authorized "in the exercise of [the President's] authority relating to the national security . . ."

Shortly thereafter, this Court ruled that the Fourth Amendment does not permit the use of warrantless wiretaps in cases involving domestic threats to the national security. *United States v. United States District Court, 407 U.S. 297* . . . (Keith). In the wake of the Keith decision, Forsyth filed this lawsuit against John Mitchell . . . Forsyth alleged that the surveillance to which he had been subjected violated both the Fourth Amendment and Title III of the Omnibus Crime Control and Safe Streets Act of 1968, 18 U.S.C. 2510–2520, which sets forth comprehensive standards governing the use of wiretaps and electronic surveillance by both governmental and private agents. He asserted that both the constitutional and statutory provisions provided him with a private right of action; he sought compensatory, statutory, and punitive damages . . .

. . . The District Court rejected Mitchell's argument that under this standard he should be held immune from suit for warrantless national security wiretaps authorized before this Court's decision in Keith: that decision was merely a logical extension of general Fourth Amendment principles and in particular of the ruling in *Katz v. United States, 389 U.S. 347* (1967), in which the Court held for the first time that electronic surveillance unaccompanied by physical trespass constituted a search subject to the Fourth Amendment's warrant requirement. Mitchell and the Justice Department, the court suggested, had chosen to "gamble" on the possibility that this Court would create an exception to the warrant requirement if presented with a case involving national security. Having lost the gamble, Mitchell was not entitled to complain of the consequences. The court therefore denied Mitchell's motion for summary judgment, granted Forsyth's motion for summary judgment on the issue of liability, and scheduled further proceedings on the issue of damages . . .

We first address Mitchell's claim that the Attorney General's actions in furtherance of the national security should be shielded from scrutiny in civil damages actions by an absolute immunity similar to that afforded the President, judges, prosecutors, witnesses, and officials performing "quasi-judicial" functions . . . We conclude that the Attorney General is not absolutely immune from suit for damages arising out of his allegedly unconstitutional conduct in performing his national security functions.

As the Nation's chief law enforcement officer, the Attorney General provides vital assistance to the President in the performance of the latter's constitutional duty to "preserve, protect, and defend the Constitution of the United States." U.S. Const., Art. II, 1, cl. 8. Mitchell's argument, in essence, is that the national security functions of the Attorney General are so sensitive, so vital to the protection of our Nation's well-being, that we cannot tolerate any risk that in performing those functions he will be chilled by the possibility of personal liability for acts that may be found to impinge on the constitutional rights of citizens . . .

Our decisions in this area leave no doubt that the Attorney General's status as a Cabinet officer is not in itself sufficient to invest him with absolute immunity: the considerations of separation of powers that call for absolute immunity for state and federal legislators and for the President of the United States do not demand a similar immunity for Cabinet officers or other high executive officials. See *Harlow v. Fitzgerald, 457 U.S. 800* (1982); *Butz v. Economou, supra*. Mitchell's claim, then, must rest not on the Attorney General's position within the Executive Branch, but on the nature of the functions he was performing in this case. See *Harlow v. Fitzgerald, supra*, at 810–811. Because Mitchell was not acting in a prosecutorial capacity in this case, the situations in which we have applied a functional approach to absolute immunity questions provide scant support for blanket immunization of his performance of the "national security function."

First, in deciding whether officials performing a particular function are entitled to absolute immunity, we have generally looked for a historical or common-law basis for the immunity in question . . . Mitchell points to no analogous historical or common-law basis for an absolute immunity for officers carrying out tasks essential to national security.

Second, the performance of national security functions does not subject an official to the same obvious risks of entanglement in vexatious litigation as does the carrying out of the judicial or "quasi-judicial" tasks that have been the primary wellsprings of absolute immunities. The judicial process is an arena of open conflict, and in virtually every case there is, if not always a winner, at least one loser. It is inevitable that many of those who lose will pin the blame on judges, prosecutors, or witnesses and will bring suit against them in an effort to relitigate the underlying conflict. See *Bradley v. Fisher, 13 Wall. 335, 348* . . . National security tasks, by contrast, are carried out in secret; open conflict and overt winners and losers are rare. Under such circumstances, it is far more likely that actual abuses will go uncovered than that fancied abuses will give rise to unfounded and burdensome

litigation. Whereas the mere threat of litigation may significantly affect the fearless and independent performance of duty by actors in the judicial process, it is unlikely to have a similar effect on the Attorney General's performance of his national security tasks.

Third, most of the officials who are entitled to absolute immunity from liability for damages are subject to other checks that help to prevent abuses of authority from going unredressed. Legislators are accountable to their constituents . . . and the judicial process is largely self-correcting: procedural rules, appeals, and the possibility of collateral challenges obviate the need for damages actions to prevent unjust results. Similar built-in restraints on the Attorney General's activities in the name of national security, however, do not exist. And despite our recognition of the importance of those activities to the safety of our Nation and its democratic system of government, we cannot accept the notion that restraints are completely unnecessary . . .

We emphasize that the denial of absolute immunity will not leave the Attorney General at the mercy of litigants with frivolous and vexatious complaints. Under the standard of qualified immunity articulated in *Harlow v. Fitzgerald*, the Attorney General will be entitled to immunity so long as his actions do not violate "clearly established statutory or constitutional rights of which a reasonable person would have known." . . . We do not believe that the security of the Republic will be threatened if its Attorney General is given incentives to abide by clearly established law . . .

Accordingly, we hold that a district court's denial of a claim of qualified immunity, to the extent that it turns on an issue of law, is an appealable "final decision" within the meaning of 28 U.S.C. 1291 notwithstanding the absence of a final judgment . . .

Under *Harlow v. Fitzgerald*, Mitchell is immune unless his actions violated clearly established law . . . Forsyth complains that in November 1970, Mitchell authorized a warrantless wiretap aimed at gathering intelligence regarding a domestic threat to national security—the kind of wiretap that the Court subsequently declared to be illegal. *Keith, 407 U.S. 297* (1972). The question of Mitchell's immunity turns on whether it was clearly established in November 1970, well over a year before *Keith* was decided, that such wiretaps were unconstitutional. We conclude that it was not . . .

. . . The District Court's conclusion that Mitchell is not immune because he gambled and lost on the resolution of this open question departs from the principles of Harlow. Such hindsight-based reasoning on immunity issues is precisely what Harlow rejected. The decisive fact is not that Mitchell's position turned out to be incorrect, but that the question was open at the time he acted. Hence, in the absence of contrary directions from Congress, Mitchell is immune from suit for his authorization of the Davidon wiretap notwithstanding that his actions violated the Fourth Amendment . . .

Justice Stevens, concurring in the judgment . . .

In my opinion, when Congress has legislated in a disputed area, that legislation is just as relevant to any assertion of official immunity as to the analysis of the question whether an implied cause of action should be recognized.

In Title III of the Omnibus Crime Control and Safe Streets Act of 1968, Congress enacted comprehensive legislation regulating the electronic interception of wire and oral communications. See 18 U.S.C. 2510–2520. One section of that Act, 2511(3) . . . (1976 ed.), specifically exempted "any wire or oral communication intercepted by authority of the President" for national security purposes. In *United States v. United States District Court, 407 U.S. 297* (1972) . . . the Court held that certain wiretaps authorized by the Attorney General were covered by the proviso in 2511(3) and therefore exempt from the prohibitions in Title III . . . .

The Court's determination in this case and in Keith that Attorney General Mitchell was exercising the discretionary "power of the President" in the area of national security when he authorized these episodes of surveillance inescapably leads to the conclusion that absolute immunity attached to the special function then being performed by Mitchell. In *Harlow v. Fitzgerald* . . . the Court explicitly noted that absolute immunity may be justified for Presidential "aides entrusted with discretionary authority in such sensitive areas as national security or foreign policy . . . to protect the unhesitating performance of functions vital to the national interest." . . . In "such 'central' Presidential domains as foreign policy and national security" the President cannot "discharge his singularly vital mandate without delegating functions nearly as sensitive as his own." . . .

Here, the President expressly had delegated the responsibility to approve national security wiretaps to the Attorney General. The Attorney General determined that the wiretap in this case was essential to gather information about a conspiracy that might be plotting to kidnap a Presidential adviser and sabotage essential facilities in Government buildings. That the Attorney General was too vigorous in guaranteeing the personal security of a Presidential aide and the physical integrity of important Government facilities does not justify holding him personally accountable for damages in a civil action that has not been authorized by Congress.

When the Attorney General, the Secretary of State, and the Secretary of Defense make erroneous decisions on matters of national security and foreign policy, the primary liabilities are political. Intense scrutiny, by the people, by the press, and by Congress, has been the traditional method for deterring violations of the Constitution by these high officers of the Executive Branch. Unless Congress authorizes other remedies, it presumably intends the retributions for any violations to be undertaken by political action. Congress is in the best position to decide whether the incremental deterrence added by a civil damages remedy outweighs the adverse effect that the exposure to personal liability may have on governmental decisionmaking . . .

. . . The availability of qualified immunity is hardly comforting when it took 13 years for the federal courts to determine that the plaintiff's claim in this case was without merit . . .

If the Attorney General had violated the provisions of Title III . . . he would have no immunity. Congress, however, had expressly refused to enact a civil remedy against Cabinet officials exercising the President's powers described in 2511(3). In that circumstance, I believe the Cabinet official is entitled to the same absolute immunity as the President of the United States. Indeed, it is highly doubtful whether the rationale of *Bivens v. Six Unknown Federal Narcotics Agents, 403 U.S. 388* (1971), even supports an implied cause of action for damages after Congress has enacted legislation comprehensively regulating the field of electronic surveillance but has specifically declined to impose a remedy for the national security wiretaps described in 2511(3) . . .

In 1994, Paula Corbin Jones filed suit against President Clinton in the U.S. District Court for the Eastern District of Arkansas, alleging that in May 1991, as governor of Arkansas, Clinton made unwanted sexual advances toward her while she was an employee of the state of Arkansas. The suit claimed sexual harassment, denial of equal protection, infliction of emotional distress, and character defamation. Ms. Jones claimed that Clinton had an Arkansas State trooper bring her to a hotel room during a conference, where he made sexual advances toward her, which she rejected. She further alleged that as a result of this rejection, her superiors punished her by treating her in a "hostile and rude manner." Clinton's lawyers filed a motion to dismiss, arguing that a sitting president cannot be sued, even for actions that occurred prior to office. The president sought temporary immunity from the suit while he was in office, a position that would have allowed Jones to resume her suit after his term. The case traveled up from the district court to the Eighth Circuit Court of Appeals and finally to the Supreme Court. The Supreme Court's decision that the president enjoys no immunity, even temporary,

from civil suit for unofficial acts was a factor that led to the impeachment proceedings against Clinton.

Although Paula Corbin Jones was supported by a variety of right-wing organizations, the case nonetheless raised serious legal as well as political questions. Could a sitting president be compelled to face a civil suit while in office? Could a claim against a sitting president be temporarily postponed until he left office? And if a president is compelled to face all civil charges, what impact might that have on the operation of the presidency?

The Supreme Court finally decided these questions. Justice John Paul Stevens wrote for a unanimous Court and determined that the claim that "the Constitution affords the president temporary immunity from civil damages litigation arising out of events that occurred before he took office—cannot be sustained on the basis of precedent." While admitting that a sitting president's time and attention might be compromised in addressing civil charges at trial, the Justices nonetheless dismissed the concern that such incidents would unduly interfere with a president in the performance of his official duties. The Supreme Court remanded the case to the district court, and it was dismissed on April 1, 1998. The judge determined that Ms. Jones had failed to establish her claims of sexual harassment. Jones appealed to the Eighth Circuit and on November 13, 1998, Clinton agreed to settle the case out of court for $850,000.

Clinton v. Jones
520 U.S. 681 (1997)

Justice Stevens delivered the opinion of the Court.

This case raises a constitutional and a prudential question concerning the Office of the President of the United States. Respondent, a private citizen, seeks to recover damages from the current occupant of that office based on actions allegedly taken before his term began. The President submits that in all but the most exceptional cases the Constitution requires federal courts to defer such litigation until his term ends and that, in any event, respect for the office warrants such a stay. Despite the force of the arguments supporting the

President's submissions, we conclude that they must be rejected . . .

While our decision to grant the petition expressed no judgment concerning the merits of the case, it does reflect our appraisal of its importance. The representations made on behalf of the Executive Branch as to the potential impact of the precedent established by the Court of Appeals merit our respectful and deliberate consideration . . .

The principal rationale for affording certain public servants immunity from suits for money damages arising out of their official acts is inapplicable to unofficial conduct. In cases involving prosecutors, legislators, and judges we have repeatedly explained that the immunity serves the public interest in enabling such officials to perform their designated functions effectively without fear that a particular decision may give rise to personal liability . . .

That rationale provided the principal basis for our holding that a former President of the United States was "entitled to absolute immunity from damages liability predicated on his official acts," *Fitzgerald, 457 U.S., at 749.* Our central concern was to avoid rendering the President "unduly cautious in the discharge of his official duties." *457 U.S., at 752* . . .

This reasoning provides no support for an immunity for unofficial conduct. As we explained in *Fitzgerald,* "the sphere of protected action must be related closely to the immunity's justifying purposes." *Id.,* at 755. Because of the President's broad responsibilities, we recognized in that case an immunity from damages claims arising out of official acts extending to the "outer perimeter of his authority." *Id.,* at 757. But we have never suggested that the President, or any other official, has an immunity that extends beyond the scope of any action taken in an official capacity . . .

Moreover, when defining the scope of an immunity for acts clearly taken within an official capacity, we have applied a functional approach. "Frequently our decisions have held that an official's absolute immunity should extend only to acts in performance of particular functions of his office." *Id.,* at 755. Hence, for example, a judge's absolute immunity does not extend to actions performed in a purely administrative capacity. See *Forrester v. White, 484 U.S. 219, 229–230* (1988). As our opinions have made clear, immunities are grounded in "the nature of the function performed, not the identity of the actor who performed it." *Id.,* at 229.

Petitioner's effort to construct an immunity from suit for unofficial acts grounded purely in the identity of his office is unsupported by precedent . . .

Petitioner's strongest argument supporting his immunity claim is based on the text and structure of the Constitution. He does not contend that the occupant of the Office of the President is "above the law," in the sense that his conduct is entirely immune from judicial scrutiny. The President argues merely for a postponement of the judicial proceedings that will determine whether he violated any law. His argument is grounded in the character of the office that was created by Article II of the Constitution, and relies on separation of powers principles that have structured our constitutional arrangement since the founding.

As a starting premise, petitioner contends that he occupies a unique office with powers and responsibilities so vast and important that the public interest demands that he devote his undivided time and attention to his public duties. He submits that—given the nature of the office—the doctrine of separation of powers places limits on the authority of the Federal Judiciary to interfere with the Executive Branch that would be transgressed by allowing this action to proceed.

We have no dispute with the initial premise of the argument . . . As Justice Jackson has pointed out, the Presidency concentrates executive authority "in a single head in whose choice the whole Nation has a part, making him the focus of public hopes and expectations. In drama, magnitude and finality his decisions so far overshadow any others that almost alone he fills the public eye and ear." *Youngstown Sheet & Tube Co. v. Sawyer, 343 U.S., at 653* (Jackson, J., concurring). We have, in short, long recognized the "unique position in the constitutional scheme" that this office occupies . . .

It does not follow, however, that separation of powers principles would be violated by allowing this action to proceed. The doctrine of separation of powers is concerned with the allocation of official power among the three co-equal branches of our Government. The Framers "built into the tripartite Federal Government . . . a self-executing safeguard against the encroachment or aggrandizement of one branch at the expense of the other." . . .

Of course the lines between the powers of the three branches are not always neatly defined. See *Mistretta v. United States, 488 U.S. 361, 380–381* (1989). But in this case there is no suggestion that the Federal Judiciary is being asked to perform any function that might in some way be described as "executive." Respondent is merely asking the courts to exercise their core Article III jurisdiction to decide cases and controversies. Whatever the outcome of this case, there is no possibility that the decision will curtail the scope of the official powers of the Executive Branch. The litigation of questions that relate entirely to the unofficial conduct of the individual who happens to be the President poses no perceptible risk of misallocation of either judicial power or executive power.

Rather than arguing that the decision of the case will produce either an aggrandizement of judicial power or a narrowing of executive power, petitioner contends that—as a by-product of an otherwise traditional exercise of judicial power—burdens will be placed on the President that will hamper the performance of his official duties. We have recognized that "[e]ven when a branch does not arrogate power to itself . . . the separation of powers doctrine requires that a branch not impair another in the performance of its constitutional duties." *Loving v. United States, 517 U.S. 748, 757* (1996) . . . As a factual matter, petitioner contends that this particular case—as well as the potential additional litigation that an affirmance of the Court of Appeals judgment might spawn—may impose an unacceptable burden on the President's time and energy, and

thereby impair the effective performance of his office.

Petitioner's predictive judgment finds little support in either history or the relatively narrow compass of the issues raised in this particular case. As we have already noted, in the more than 200 year history of the Republic, only three sitting Presidents have been subjected to suits for their private actions. If the past is any indicator, it seems unlikely that a deluge of such litigation will ever engulf the Presidency. As for the case at hand, if properly managed by the District Court, it appears to us highly unlikely to occupy any substantial amount of petitioner's time.

Of greater significance, petitioner errs by presuming that interactions between the Judicial Branch and the Executive, even quite burdensome interactions, necessarily rise to the level of constitutionally forbidden impairment of the Executive's ability to perform its constitutionally mandated functions. "[O]ur . . . system imposes upon the Branches a degree of overlapping responsibility, a duty of interdependence as well as independence the absence of which 'would preclude the establishment of a Nation capable of governing itself effectively.' " *Mistretta, 488 U.S., at 381* (quoting *Buckley, 424 U.S., at 121*). As Madison explained, separation of powers does not mean that the branches "ought to have no partial agency in, or no controul over the acts of each other." The fact that a federal court's exercise of its traditional Article III jurisdiction may significantly burden the time and attention of the Chief Executive is not sufficient to establish a violation of the Constitution. Two long settled propositions, first announced by Chief Justice Marshall, support that conclusion.

First, we have long held that when the President takes official action, the Court has the authority to determine whether he has acted within the law . . .

Second, it is also settled that the President is subject to judicial process in appropriate circumstances . . .

Sitting Presidents have responded to court orders to provide testimony and other information with sufficient frequency that such interactions between the Judicial and Executive Branches can scarcely be thought a novelty . . . Moreover, sitting Presidents have also voluntarily complied with judicial requests for testimony . . .

In sum, "[i]t is settled law that the separation of powers doctrine does not bar every exercise of jurisdiction over the President of the United States." *Fitzgerald, 457 U.S., at 753–754.* If the Judiciary may severely burden the Executive Branch by reviewing the legality of the President's official conduct, and if it may direct appropriate process to the President himself, it must follow that the federal courts have power to determine the legality of his unofficial conduct. The burden on the President's time and energy that is a mere by product of such review surely cannot be considered as onerous as the direct burden imposed by judicial review and the occasional invalidation of his official actions. We therefore hold that the doctrine of separation of powers does not require federal courts to stay all private actions against the President until he leaves office. . . .

We are persuaded that it was an abuse of discretion for the District Court to defer the trial until after the President leaves office. Such a lengthy and categorical stay takes no account whatever of the respondent's interest in bringing the case to trial. The complaint was filed within the statutory limitations period—albeit near the end of that period—and delaying trial would increase the danger of prejudice resulting from the loss of evidence, including the inability of witnesses to recall specific facts, or the possible death of a party.

The decision to postpone the trial was, furthermore, premature. The proponent of a stay bears the burden of establishing its need. In this case, at the stage at which the District Court made its ruling, there was no way to assess whether a stay of trial after the completion of discovery would be warranted. Other than the fact that a trial may consume some of the President's time and attention, there is nothing in the record to enable a judge to assess the potential harm that may ensue from scheduling the trial promptly after discovery is concluded.

We think the District Court may have given undue weight to the concern that a trial might generate unrelated civil actions that could conceivably hamper the President in conducting the duties of his office. If and when that should occur, the court's discretion would permit it to manage those actions in such fashion (including deferral of trial) that interference with the President's duties would not occur. But no such impingement upon the President's conduct of his office was shown here.

We add a final comment on two matters that are discussed at length in the briefs: the risk that our decision will generate a large volume of politically motivated harassing and frivolous litigation, and the danger that national security concerns might prevent the President from explaining a legitimate need for a continuance.

We are not persuaded that either of these risks is serious. Most frivolous and vexatious litigation is terminated at the pleading stage or on summary judgment, with little if any personal involvement by the defendant . . . History indicates that the likelihood that a significant number of such cases will be filed is remote. Although scheduling problems may arise, there is no reason to assume that the District Courts will be either unable to accommodate the President's needs or unfaithful to the tradition—especially in matters involving national security—of giving "the utmost deference to Presidential responsibilities." . . .

If Congress deems it appropriate to afford the President stronger protection, it may respond with appropriate legislation.

CHAPTER **6** | # Executive Privilege

The principle of executive privilege—the right of the president, and perhaps others in the executive branch, to withhold government documents and information from the Congress and the courts, and by extension the public—has been controversial since it was first claimed by President George Washington, who argued that some information could be withheld from the Congress if it was in the public interest to do so. (The Congress declined to argue the point.) Historians have argued that no such doctrine is allowable in a democratic society. Yet that opinion has been a minority view, and most have agreed that such a doctrine not only exists, but is important to the functioning of the presidency. Many executive privilege claims, however, have exceeded any reasonable definition of the power, including efforts to use the doctrine to avoid political embarrassment rather than to protect national security or other significant injury. In 1974, the doctrine received judicial legitimacy for the first time when the Supreme Court ruled in the landmark *United States v. Nixon* case that the doctrine did exist, even though the Court denied Nixon's attempt to apply it to documents from his administration. Although one may agree or disagree with the propriety or extent of this protection, there is no doubt that the presidency has firmly acquired and expanded the scope of this power over time. Bold assertion of privilege and challenge to that power provide clear evidence of the presidency's growing power, the role of the courts in defining and legitimizing that power, and how the courts also have underscored the distinction between domestic and foreign policy powers, noting the president's greater power in the latter area.

The special prosecutor appointed to investigate the Watergate scandal was denied access to tape recordings and other materials in the possession of the Nixon administration on the grounds of executive privilege. This right, asserted by many past presidents, says that the president may withhold documents or information from scrutiny by the other branches of the government in order to maintain proper confidentiality within the executive branch. Yet the doctrine of executive privilege had never been established by court ruling or law, and the basis for the special prosecutor's documents subpoena was his office's investigation into possible criminal wrongdoing by the president.

In its decision, the Supreme Court concluded that it had the right to judge the matter (that it was "justiciable"), that the special prosecutor's subpoena was legitimate, and that the Nixon administration had to turn over the requested materials. These materials confirmed that Nixon had been a party to illegal activities, and he resigned from office shortly after the Court handed down its decision.

Without question, this decision was a crushing blow to Nixon and his presidency. Yet it proved a stunning victory for the institution of the presidency, for four reasons. First, it established for the first time the legitimacy of the doctrine of executive privilege. Second, the opinion went out of its way to note that the Court's deference to executive privilege would be far greater if it involved a claim to protect information related to foreign policy—military, diplomatic, or national security matters—a concern referred to at least three times in the following decision. Thus the Court added to the long string of cases that accord the president greater prerogative in foreign affairs than in domestic matters—even though Nixon's lawyer made no argument for executive privilege based on foreign policy concerns.

Third, the Supreme Court also used the decision to stake out and solidify its own power claim, noting that it reserved to itself the power to define the parameters of the powers of another branch of government. And fourth, even though the court concluded that Nixon's claim to executive privilege was of lesser importance than the ongoing criminal investigation against him, it also noted that the president was entitled to more legal protection than an average citizen.

United States v. Nixon
418 U.S. 683 (1974)

Chief Justice Burger delivered the opinion of the Court.

. . . [W]e turn to the claim that the subpoena should be quashed because it demands "confidential conversations between a President and his close advisors that it would be inconsistent with the public interest to produce." The first contention is a broad claim that the separation of powers doctrine precludes judicial review of a President's claim of privilege. The second contention is that if he does not prevail on the claim of absolute privilege, the court should hold as a matter of constitutional law that the privilege prevails over the subpoena duces tecum [a subpoena requiring that the documents be produced—ed.].

In the performance of assigned constitutional duties each branch of the Government must initially interpret the Constitution, and the interpretation of its powers by any branch is due great respect from the others. The President's counsel, as we have noted, reads the Constitution as providing an absolute privilege of confidentiality for all Presidential communications. Many decisions of this Court, however,

have unequivocally reaffirmed the holding of *Marbury v. Madison, 1 Cranch 137* (1803), that "[i]t is emphatically the province and duty of the judicial department to say what the law is." *Id.*, at 177.

No holding of the Court has defined the scope of judicial power specifically relating to the enforcement of a subpoena for confidential Presidential communications for use in a criminal prosecution, but other exercises of power by the Executive Branch and the Legislative Branch have been found invalid as in conflict with the Constitution. . . . Since this Court has consistently exercised the power to construe and delineate claims arising under express powers, it must follow that the Court has authority to interpret claims with respect to powers alleged to derive from enumerated powers. . . .

Notwithstanding the deference each branch must accord the others, the "judicial Power of the United States" vested in the federal courts by Art. III, 1, of the Constitution can no more be shared with the Executive Branch than the Chief Executive, for example, can share with the Judiciary the veto power, or the Congress share with the Judiciary the power to override a Presidential veto. Any other conclusion would be contrary to the basic concept of separation of powers and the checks and balances that flow from the scheme of a tripartite government. . . . We therefore reaffirm that it is the province and duty of this Court "to say what the law is" with respect to the claim of privilege presented in this case. . . .

In support of his claim of absolute privilege, the President's counsel urges two grounds, one of which is common to all governments and one of which is peculiar to our system of separation of powers. The first ground is the valid need for protection of communications between high Government officials and those who advise and assist them in the performance of their manifold duties; the importance of this confidentiality is too plain to require further discussion. Human experience teaches that those who expect public dissemination of their remarks may well temper candor with a concern for appearances and for their own interests to the detriment of the decisionmaking process. Whatever the nature of the privilege of confidentiality of Presidential communications in the exercise of Art. II powers, the privilege can be said to derive from the supremacy of each branch within its own assigned area of constitutional duties. Certain powers and privileges flow from the nature of enumerated powers; the protection of the confidentiality of Presidential communications has similar constitutional underpinnings.

The second ground asserted by the President's counsel in support of the claim of absolute privilege rests on the doctrine of separation of powers. Here it is argued that the independence of the Executive Branch within its own sphere . . . insulates a President from a judicial subpoena in an ongoing criminal prosecution, and thereby protects confidential Presidential communications.

However, neither the doctrine of separation of powers, nor the need for confidentiality of high-level communications, without more, can sustain an absolute, unqualified Presidential privilege of immunity from judicial process under all circumstances. The President's need for complete candor and objectivity from advisers calls for great deference from the courts. However, when the privilege depends solely on the broad, undifferentiated claim of public interest in the confidentiality of such conversations, a confrontation with other values arises. Absent a claim of need to protect military, diplomatic, or sensitive national security secrets, we find it difficult to accept the argument that even the very important interest in confidentiality of Presidential communications is significantly diminished by production of such material for in camera inspection with all the protection that a district court will be obliged to provide.

The impediment that an absolute, unqualified privilege would place in the way of the primary constitutional duty of the Judicial Branch to do justice in criminal prosecutions would plainly conflict with the function of the courts under Art. III. In designing the structure of our Government and dividing and allocating the sovereign power among three co-equal branches, the Framers of the Constitution sought to provide a comprehensive system, but the separate powers were not intended to operate with absolute independence. . . .

To read the Art. II powers of the President as providing an absolute privilege as against a subpoena essential to enforcement of criminal statutes on no more than a generalized claim of the public interest in confidentiality of nonmilitary and nondiplomatic discussions would upset the constitutional balance of "a workable government" and gravely impair the role of the courts under Art. III.

Since we conclude that the legitimate needs of the judicial process may outweigh Presidential privilege, it is necessary to resolve those competing interests in a manner that preserves the essential functions of each branch. The right and indeed the duty to resolve that question does not free the Judiciary from according high respect to the representations made on behalf of the President. . . .

The expectation of a President to the confidentiality of his conversations and correspondence, like the claim of confidentiality of judicial deliberations, for example, has all the values to which we accord deference for the privacy of all citizens and, added to those values, is the necessity for protection of the public interest in candid, objective, and even blunt or harsh opinions in Presidential decision-making. A President and those who assist him must be free to explore alternatives in the process of shaping policies and making decisions and to do so in a way many would be unwilling to express except privately. These are the considerations justifying a presumptive privilege for Presidential communications. The privilege is fundamental to the operation of Government and inextricably rooted in the separation of powers under the Constitution. . . . But this presumptive privilege must be considered in light of our historic commitment to the rule of law. . . . We have elected to employ an adversary system of criminal justice in which the parties contest all issues before a court of law. The need to develop all relevant facts in the adversary system is both fundamental and comprehensive. The ends of criminal justice would be defeated if judgments were to be founded on a partial or speculative presentation of the facts. The very integrity of the judicial system and public confidence in the system depend on full disclosure of all the facts, within the framework of the rules of evidence. To ensure that justice is done, it is imperative to the function of courts that compulsory process be available for the production of evidence needed either by the prosecution or by the defense. . . .

In this case the President challenges a subpoena served on him as a third party requiring the production of materials for use in a criminal prosecution; he does so on the claim that he has a privilege against disclosure of confidential communications. He does not place his claim of privilege on the ground they are military or diplomatic secrets. As to these areas of Art. II duties the courts have traditionally shown the utmost deference to Presidential responsibilities. . . .

No case of the Court, however, has extended this high degree of deference to a President's generalized interest in confidentiality. Nowhere in the Constitution, as we have noted earlier, is there any explicit reference to a privilege of confidentiality, yet to the extent this interest relates to the effective discharge of a President's powers, it is constitutionally based.

The right to the production of all evidence at a criminal trial similarly has constitutional dimensions. The Sixth Amendment explicitly confers upon every defendant in a criminal trial the right "to be confronted with the witnesses against him" and "to have compulsory process for obtaining witnesses in his favor." Moreover, the Fifth Amendment also guarantees that no person shall be deprived of liberty without due process of law. It is the manifest duty of the courts to vindicate those guarantees, and to accomplish that it is essential that all relevant and admissible evidence be produced.

In this case we must weigh the importance of the general privilege of confidentiality of Presidential communications in performance of the President's responsibilities against the inroads of such a privilege on the fair administration of criminal justice. The interest in preserving confidentiality is weighty indeed and entitled to great respect. However, we

cannot conclude that advisers will be moved to temper the candor of their remarks by the infrequent occasions of disclosure because of the possibility that such conversations will be called for in the context of a criminal prosecution.

On the other hand, the allowance of the privilege to withhold evidence that is demonstrably relevant in a criminal trial would cut deeply into the guarantee of due process of law and gravely impair the basic function of the courts. A President's acknowledged need for confidentiality in the communications of his office is general in nature, whereas the constitutional need for production of relevant evidence in a criminal proceeding is specific and central to the fair adjudication of a particular criminal case in the administration of justice. Without access to specific facts a criminal prosecution may be totally frustrated. The President's broad interest in confidentiality of communications will not be vitiated by disclosure of a limited number of conversations preliminarily shown to have some bearing on the pending criminal cases.

We conclude that when the ground for asserting privilege as to subpoenaed materials sought for use in a criminal trial is based only on the generalized interest in confidentiality, it cannot prevail over the fundamental demands of due process of law in the fair administration of criminal justice. The generalized assertion of privilege must yield to the demonstrated, specific need for evidence in a pending criminal trial. . . .

Enforcement of the subpoena duces tecum was stayed pending this Court's resolution of the issues raised by the petitions for certiorari. Those issues now having been disposed of, the matter of implementation will rest with the District Court. . . . Statements that meet the test of admissibility and relevance must be isolated; all other material must be excised. At this stage the District Court is not limited to representations of the Special Prosecutor as to the evidence sought by the subpoena; the material will be available to the District Court. It is elementary that in camera inspection of evidence is always a procedure calling for scrupulous protection against any release or publication of material not found by the court, at that stage, probably admissible in evidence and relevant to the issues of the trial for which it is sought. That being true of an ordinary situation, it is obvious that the District Court has a very heavy responsibility to see to it that Presidential conversations, which are either not relevant or not admissible, are accorded that high degree of respect due the President of the United States. Mr. Chief Justice Marshall, sitting as a trial judge in the *Burr* case, *supra*, was extraordinarily careful to point out that

> "[i]n no case of this kind would a court be required to proceed against the president as against an ordinary individual." 25 F. Cas., at 192.

Marshall's statement cannot be read to mean in any sense that a President is above the law, but relates to the singularly unique role under Art. II of a President's communications and activities, related to the performance of duties under that Article. Moreover, a President's communications and activities encompass a vastly wider range of sensitive material than would be true of any "ordinary individual." It is therefore necessary in the public interest to afford Presidential confidentiality the greatest protection consistent with the fair administration of justice. The need for confidentiality even as to idle conversations with associates in which casual reference might be made concerning political leaders within the country or foreign statesmen is too obvious to call for further treatment. We have no doubt that the District Judge will at all times accord to Presidential records that high degree of deference suggested in *United States v. Burr, supra,* and will discharge his responsibility to see to it that until released to the Special Prosecutor no in camera material is revealed to anyone. This burden applies with even greater force to excised material; once the decision is made to excise, the material is restored to its privileged status and should be returned under seal to its lawful custodian.

Since this matter came before the Court during the pendency of a criminal prosecution, and on representations that time is of the essence, the mandate shall issue forthwith.

Affirmed.

During the investigation of the Clinton presidency that began with the Whitewater land deal and ended with the Monica Lewinsky sex scandal, independent counsel Kenneth Starr subpoenaed presidential aides Bruce Lindsey, Sidney Blumenthal, and a third, unnamed person to testify before a grand jury convened to examine possible criminal wrongdoing. Although the court noted that executive privilege includes the First Lady and others in the White House, even when the president is not directly involved, it concluded that neither that protection, which it considered "qualified" rather than "absolute" in the context of a criminal investigation, nor the attorney-client privilege outweighed the need to pursue the investigation. Judge Johnson ruled in favor of compelling the testimony of Lindsey and Blumenthal, but not that of the unnamed person. Note that bracketed insertions below—"REDACTED"—refer to sections of the decision not published for reasons of confidentiality.

In re Grand Jury Proceeding
5 F. Supp. 2d 21 (1998)
U.S. District Court for the District of Columbia

Judges: Norma Holloway Johnson, Chief Judge. Opinion by: Norma Holloway Johnson

. . . The Court does not have documents or tapes to review in camera [confidential review by the judge—ed.] that could establish whether the content of the subpoenaed communications relates only to private matters, nor does it know how Lindsey and Blumenthal might answer the grand jury's questions. The Court is aware of only the unanswered questions themselves. Furthermore. . . . the subpoenas here call for testimony, not documents that the Court could review in camera. The Court's ability to assess whether the subpoenaed materials relate to official decisions is thus greatly hindered. . . .

Although the Court must presume that presidential communications are privileged, the scope of the privilege is limited to "communications authored or solicited and received by those members of an immediate White House adviser's staff who have broad and significant responsibility for investigating and formulating the advice to be given to the President on the particular matter to which the communications relate." *In re Sealed Case*, 121 F.3d at 752. In other words, the President does not have to participate personally in the communication in order for it to be privileged.

Citing the presidential communications privilege, Lindsey refused to answer questions before the grand jury regarding a conversation he had with [REDACTED]. The White House did not mention [REDACTED] in its brief or at the hearings before this Court, much less argue that [REDACTED] is a presidential adviser. At any rate, the White House has not met its burden of showing that [REDACTED] communications with Lindsey "occurred in conjunction with the process of advising the President." *Id.* Accordingly, the Court finds that any conversations between Lindsey and [REDACTED] are not covered by the executive privilege.

Both Lindsey and Blumenthal refused to answer questions before the grand jury regarding conversations they had with the First Lady, citing executive privilege. [REDACTED] states: "The First Lady functions as a senior adviser to the President, and it was in that capacity that I had discussions with her about the Independent Counsel's investigation." [REDACTED] At the hearing on this matter, in response to a question from the Court, the attorney for the White House argued that First Ladies have traditionally held a position of senior adviser to the President and cited *Association of American Physicians & Surgeons, Inc. v. Clinton, 302 U.S. App. D.C. 208, 997* F.2d 898 (D.C. Cir. 1993). The OIC [Office of Independent Counsel] has not contested that Mrs. Clinton would be covered by the executive privilege. . . .

Mrs. Clinton is widely seen as an adviser to the President and "Congress itself has recognized that the President's spouse acts as the functional equivalent of an assistant to the President." *Id.* at 904 (citing 3 U.S.C. [*28] § 105(e)). The Court finds that conversations between the First Lady and Lindsey or Blumenthal fall under the executive privilege. . . .

The presumptive executive privilege is not absolute. Sirica, 487 F.2d at 716. The Court will not accept the President's "mere assertion of privilege as sufficient to overcome the need of the party subpoenaing the [testimony]." *Id.* at 713. The presumption of privilege may be rebutted by a sufficient showing of need by the Independent Counsel. . . .

The Court also finds that the OIC has met its burden of showing with specificity that the evidence is not available with due diligence elsewhere. See 121 F.3d at 754. The OIC seeks testimony regarding conversations that took place within the White House and the only sources of that testimony are those persons participating in the conversations. Further, the OIC presented the Court with detailed information about its unsuccessful efforts to obtain this evidence through other sources. The OIC has diligently pursued other alternatives where feasible.

In sum, the OIC has provided a substantial factual showing to demonstrate its "specific need" for the testimony. *Nixon, 418 U.S. at 713.* The Court finds that the evidence covered by the presumptive privilege remains necessary to the grand jury and cannot feasibly be obtained elsewhere. The Court will grant the OIC's motions to compel the testimony of Lindsey and Blumenthal insofar as they have asserted executive privilege. . . .

Although the Court finds that a governmental attorney-client privilege should apply in the federal grand jury context, the Court is not willing to recognize an absolute privilege. Even though this privilege is absolute in civil cases, such as FOIA [Freedom of Information Act] cases, this Court finds FOIA cases to be distinguishable from federal grand jury matters because the former involve civil litigation between the federal government and private parties seeking information from the government, whereas the latter involve criminal matters in which a government party seeks information from another government agency. . . . In the context of a federal grand jury investigation where one government agency needs information from another to determine if a crime has been committed, the Court finds that the governmental attorney-client privilege must be qualified in order to balance the needs of the criminal justice system against the government agency's need for confidential legal advice. . . .

The White House claims that candid legal advice will be chilled if the Court does not recognize an absolute governmental attorney-client privilege in the federal grand jury context. Similar arguments were rejected by the Supreme Court with respect to the assertions of executive privilege by President Nixon and with respect to a privilege asserted by state legislators comparable to that of members of Congress. Like the Supreme Court, this Court "cannot conclude that advisers will be moved to temper the candor of their remarks by the infrequent occasions of disclosure because of the possibility that such conversations will be called for in the context of a criminal prosecution." *Nixon, 418 U.S. at 712.* . . . Only a qualified governmental attorney-client privilege in the grand jury context can balance the President's need for frank legal advice against the grand jury's need for relevant evidence of criminal conduct.

Since the Nixon decision in 1974, the White House has operated effectively under a qualified executive privilege. The President continues to receive candid political advice from his top aides and the Court has no doubt that the President will continue to receive sound legal advice from White House attorneys under a qualified governmental attorney-client privilege. . . .

The Court's decision to make the attorney-client privilege qualified like the executive privilege not only respects the needs of the criminal justice system, but also saves courts from having to apply two different privilege standards to conversations commingling political and legal advice to the President. Many of the President's top advisers, such as Lindsey, provide both legal and political advice to the President and White House discussions often involve a mixture of the two. If no privilege applied to legal advice in the White House, as the OIC would have it, White House attorneys might be tempted to characterize their advice as political to acquire the qualified protection of the executive privilege. Similarly, if an absolute privilege applied to legal advice to the President while only a qualified executive privilege applied to political advice, the President and his staff might be tempted to characterize confidential political communications as legal in order to obtain greater protection. The Court finds that an absolute governmental attorney-client privilege would overly complicate communications to the President for both White House employees and the federal courts, that it would unduly frustrate the work of federal grand juries, and that it is not necessary to ensure candid legal advice to the President. . . .

For all of the reasons articulated above, the Court holds that although an absolute governmental attorney-client privilege applies to civil cases in which government attorneys represent government agencies or government employees, only a qualified governmental attorney-client privilege applies to a subpoena issued by a federal grand jury. The Court further holds that this privilege can be overcome if the subpoena proponent can show "first, that each discrete group of the subpoenaed materials [or testimony] likely contains important evidence; and second that this evidence is not available with due diligence elsewhere." 121 F.3d at 754. If the Court finds a sufficient showing of need, the Court shall order compliance with the subpoena subject to the relevancy standard established by *R. Enterprises, 498 U.S. at 300.* See *In re Sealed Case, 121 F.3d at 759.* . . .

The Court finds that the OIC's showing of need has overcome Lindsey's assertions of the governmental attorney-client privilege. Accordingly, the

Court orders Lindsey to comply with the subpoena by answering the questions posed to him by the OIC and the grand jurors. If Lindsey finds the questions do not meet the relevancy standard established by R. Enterprises, the Court will be available to make this determination. . . .

For the foregoing reasons, the Court will grant the motions of the Office of Independent Counsel to compel the testimony of Bruce Lindsey and Sidney Blumenthal and will deny as moot the motion to compel the testimony of [REDACTED]. An appropriate Order will issue on this date.

Investigations by independent counsel Kenneth Starr concerning the Whitewater land deal involving Bill Clinton before he became president eventually led a grand jury to subpoena White House lawyer Bruce Lindsey to testify about his knowledge of this and matters related to questions of perjury arising from the Monica Lewinsky investigation. (Lewinsky was a White House intern with whom Clinton had had an affair; Clinton denied the affair under oath, leading to a charge of perjury, which in turn was the basis of the unsuccessful effort to remove Clinton from office.) Lindsey refused to answer certain questions, claiming attorney-client privilege and executive privilege in regard to his conversations with Clinton. The Court of Appeals ruled against these protection claims in the face of a federal criminal investigation.

In Re: Bruce Lindsey
158 F.3d 1263 (1998)
United States Court of Appeals for the District of Columbia Circuit

Before: Randolph, Rogers, and Tatel, Circuit Judges (per curiam) . . . .

Recognizing that a government attorney-client privilege exists is one thing. Finding that the Office of the President is entitled to assert it here is quite another. . . .

We therefore turn to the question whether an attorney-client privilege permits a government lawyer to withhold from a grand jury information relating to the commission of possible crimes by government officials and others. Although the cases decided under FOIA [Freedom of Information Act] recognize a government attorney-client privilege that is rather absolute in civil litigation, those cases do not necessarily control the application of the privilege here. . . .although the traditional privilege between attorneys and clients shields private relationships from inquiry in either civil litigation or criminal prosecution, competing values arise when the Office of the President resists demands for information from a federal grand jury and the nation's chief law enforcement officer. . . .

When an executive branch attorney is called before a federal grand jury to give evidence about alleged crimes within the executive branch, reason and experience, duty, and tradition dictate that the attorney shall provide that evidence. With respect to investigations of federal criminal offenses, and especially offenses committed by those in government, government attorneys stand in a far different position from members of the private bar. Their duty is not to defend clients against criminal charges and it is not to protect wrongdoers from public exposure. The constitutional responsibility of the President, and all members of the Executive Branch, is to "take Care that the Laws be faithfully executed." U.S. Const. art. II, § 3. Investigation and prosecution of federal crimes is one of the most important and essential functions within that constitutional responsibility. Each of our Presidents has, in the words of the Constitution, sworn that he "will faithfully execute the Office of President of the United States, and will to the best of [his] Ability, preserve, protect and defend the Constitution of the United States." *Id.* art. II, § 1, cl. 8. And for more than two hundred years each officer of the Executive Branch has been bound by oath or affirmation to do the same. *See Id.* art. VI, cl. 3; *see also* 28 U.S.C. § 544 (1994). This is a solemn undertaking, a binding of the person to the cause of constitutional government, an expression of the individual's allegiance to the principles embodied in that document. Unlike a private practitioner, the loyalties of a government lawyer therefore cannot and must not lie solely with his or her client agency. . . .

This view of the proper allegiance of the government lawyer is complemented by the public's interest in uncovering illegality among its elected and appointed officials. While the President's constitutionally established role as superintendent of law enforcement provides one protection against wrongdoing by federal government officials, another protection of the public interest is through having transparent and accountable government. . . .

We may assume that if the government attorney-client privilege does not apply in certain contexts this may chill some communications between government officials and government lawyers. Even so, government officials will still enjoy the benefit of fully confidential communications with their attorneys unless the communications reveal information relating to possible criminal wrongdoing. And although the privacy of these communications may not be absolute before the grand jury, the Supreme Court has not been troubled by the potential chill on executive communications due to the qualified nature of executive privilege. . . .

Moreover, nothing prevents government officials who seek completely confidential communications with attorneys from consulting personal counsel. The President has retained several private lawyers, and he is entitled to engage in the completely confidential communications with those lawyers befitting an attorney and a client in a private relationship. . . .

The Supreme Court's recognition in *United States v. Nixon* of a qualified privilege for executive communications severely undercuts the argument of the Office of the President regarding the scope of the government attorney-client privilege. A President often has private conversations with his Vice President or his Cabinet Secretaries or other members of the Administration who are not lawyers or who are lawyers, but are not providing legal services. The advice these officials give the President is of vital importance to the security and prosperity of the nation, and to the President's discharge of his constitutional duties. Yet upon a proper showing, such conversations must be revealed in federal criminal proceedings. Only a certain conceit among those admitted to the bar could explain why legal advice should be on a higher plane than advice about policy, or politics, or why a President's conversation with the most junior lawyer in the White House Counsel's Office is deserving of more protection from disclosure in a grand jury investigation than a President's discussions with his Vice President or a Cabinet Secretary. In short, we do not believe that lawyers are more important to the operations of government than all other officials, or that the advice lawyers render is more crucial to the functioning of the Presidency than the advice coming from all other quarters. . . .

In sum, it would be contrary to tradition, common understanding, and our governmental system for the attorney-client privilege to attach to White House Counsel in the same manner as private counsel. When government attorneys learn, through communications with their clients, of information related to criminal misconduct, they may not rely on the government attorney-client privilege to shield such information from disclosure to a grand jury. . . .

As we have established, government officials have responsibilities not to withhold evidence relating to criminal offenses from the grand jury. The President cannot bring Lindsey within his personal attorney-client privilege as he could a private citizen, for Lindsey is in a fundamentally different position. Unlike in his role as an intermediary, Lindsey necessarily acts as a government attorney functioning in his official capacity as Deputy White House Counsel in those instances when the common interest doctrine might apply, just as in those instances when the government attorney-client privilege might apply. His obligation not to withhold relevant information acquired as a government attorney remains the same regardless of whether he acquired the information directly from the President or from the President's personal counsel. Thus, his status before the federal grand jury does not allow him to withhold evidence obtained in his official role under either the government attorney-client privilege or the President's personal attorney-client privilege applied through the common interest doctrine.

If the President wishes to discuss matters jointly between his private counsel and his official counsel, he must do so cognizant of the differing responsibilities of the two counsel and tailor his communications appropriately; undoubtedly, his counsel are alert to this need as well. Although his personal counsel remain fully protected by the absolute attorney-client privilege, a Deputy White House Counsel like Lindsey may not assert an absolute privilege in the face of a grand jury subpoena, but only the more limited protection of executive privilege. Consequently, although the President in his personal capacity has at least some areas of common interest with the Office of the Presidency, and although there may thus be reason for official and personal counsel to confer, the overarching duties of Lindsey in his role as a government attorney prevent him from withholding information about possible criminal misconduct from the grand jury. Accordingly, for the reasons stated in this opinion, we affirm in part and reverse in part. . . .

In 2001, President George W. Bush formed the National Energy Policy Development Group (NEPDC), headed by Vice President Dick Cheney, to advise him on energy policy. Environmental watchdog groups alleged that the group violated the Federal Advisory Committee Act (FACA), a federal law that imposes open meeting and disclosure requirements on any advisory board. Such advisory groups do not have to abide by the openness requirements, however, if all of the group members are federal employees. Although the Bush administration claimed that all members were government employees, two private groups brought suit to obtain information about the group's activities, arguing that nonfederal government employees and private energy industry lobbyists regularly attended meetings and participated in most important aspects of committee work, making them de facto *members of the group, and therefore meaning that the group's work fell under the openness requirements. A federal district court agreed to allow some "discovery" to reveal some*

information about the NEPDC's activities; on appeal, the Court of Appeals denied the administration's attempt to vacate the discovery order (through a writ of mandamus) and said that the administration must first assert executive privilege. In a 7 to 2 ruling, the court sent the case back to the district court, but told it that it must give greater weight to Cheney's arguments about separation of powers. Although this case did not end the matter, the decision emphasized the court's great deference to executive privilege (perhaps including the vice president, even though executive privilege does not extend to this office), and noted important differences between this case and U.S. v. Nixon, *where the president did have to turn over materials. On the other hand, the court did not agree with Cheney that the opposing groups had no right to make discovery claims, although the net effect of this decision will be to make such efforts at discovery more difficult. In May 2005 a federal appeals court ruled unanimously in favor of Cheney, saying that the administration was not obligated to disclose who attended the White House meetings.*

Cheney et al. *v. U.S. District Court* 159 L.Ed. 2d 459 (2004)

Justice Kennedy delivered the opinion of the Court. . . .

We now come to the central issue in the case—whether the Court of Appeals was correct to conclude it "ha[d] no authority to exercise the extraordinary remedy of mandamus [a petition to the court, usually granted only in drastic circumstances, asking it to set aside a discovery order to produce documents or other information—ed.]," 334 F. 3d, at 1105, on the ground that the Government could protect its rights by asserting executive privilege in the District Court. . . .

Were the Vice President not a party in the case, the argument that the Court of Appeals should have entertained an action in mandamus, notwithstanding the District Court's denial of the motion for certification, might present different considerations. Here, however, the Vice President and his comembers on the NEPDG are the subjects of the discovery orders. The mandamus petition alleges that the orders threaten "substantial intrusions on the process by which those in closest operational proximity to the President advise the President." App. 343. These facts and allegations remove this case from the category of ordinary discovery orders where interlocutory appellate review is unavailable, through mandamus or otherwise. It is well established that "a President's communications and activities encompass a vastly wider range of sensitive material than would be true of any 'ordinary individual.'" *United States v. Nixon, 418 U. S., at 715.* . . . As *United States v. Nixon* explained, these principles do not mean that the "President is above the law." *418 U. S., at 715.* Rather, they simply acknowledge that the public interest requires that a coequal branch of Government "afford Presidential confidentiality the greatest protection consistent with the fair administration of justice," *ibid.*, and give recognition to the paramount necessity of protecting the Executive Branch from vexatious litigation that might distract it from the energetic performance of its constitutional duties.

These separation-of-powers considerations should inform a court of appeals' evaluation of a mandamus petition involving the President or the Vice President. Accepted mandamus standards are broad enough to allow a court of appeals to prevent a lower court from interfering with a coequal branch's ability to discharge its constitutional responsibilities. . . .

The Court of Appeals dismissed these separation-of-powers concerns. Relying on *United States v. Nixon*, it held that even though respondents' discovery requests are overbroad and "go well beyond FACA's requirements," the Vice President and his former colleagues on the NEPDG "shall bear the burden" of invoking privilege with narrow specificity and objecting to the discovery requests with "detailed precision." *334 F. 3d, at 1105–1106.* In its view, this result was required by *Nixon's* rejection of an "absolute, unqualified Presidential privilege of immunity from judicial process under all circumstances." *418 U.S., at 706.* If *Nixon* refused to recognize broad claims of confidentiality where the President had asserted executive privilege, the majority reasoned, *Nixon* must have rejected, *a fortiori,*

petitioners' claim of discovery immunity where the privilege has not even been invoked. According to the majority, because the Executive Branch can invoke executive privilege to maintain the separation of powers, mandamus relief is premature.

This analysis, however, overlooks fundamental differences in the two cases. *Nixon* cannot bear the weight the Court of Appeals puts upon it. First, unlike this case, which concerns respondents' requests for information for use in a civil suit, *Nixon* involves the proper balance between the Executive's interest in the confidentiality of its communications and the "constitutional need for production of relevant evidence in a criminal proceeding." *Id.*, at 713. The Court's decision was explicit that it was "not . . . concerned with the balance between the President's generalized interest in confidentiality and the need for relevant evidence in civil litigation . . . . We address only the conflict between the President's assertion of a generalized privilege of confidentiality and the constitutional need for relevant evidence in criminal trials." *Id.*, at 712, n. 19.

The distinction *Nixon* drew between criminal and civil proceedings is not just a matter of formalism. As the Court explained, the need for information in the criminal context is much weightier because "our historic[al] commitment to the rule of law . . . is nowhere more profoundly manifest than in our view that 'the twofold aim [of criminal justice] is that guilt shall not escape or innocence suffer.'" *Id.*, at 708–709 (quoting *Berger v. United States, 295 U.S. 78, 88* (1935)). . . .

A party's need for information is only one facet of the problem. An important factor weighing in the opposite direction is the burden imposed by the discovery orders. This is not a routine discovery dispute. The discovery requests are directed to the Vice President and other senior Government officials who served on the NEPDG to give advice and makerecommendations to the President. The Executive Branch, at its highest level, is seeking the aid of the courts to protect its constitutional prerogatives. As we have already noted, special considerations control when the Executive Branch's interests in maintaining the autonomy of its office and safeguarding the confidentiality of its communications are implicated. . . .

Even when compared against *United States v. Nixon*'s criminal subpoenas, which did involve the President, the civil discovery here militates against respondents' position. The observation in *Nixon* that production of confidential information would not disrupt the functioning of the Executive Branch cannot be applied in a mechanistic fashion to civil litigation. In the criminal justice system, there are various constraints, albeit imperfect, to filter out insubstantial legal claims. The decision to prosecute a criminal case, for example, is made by a publicly accountable prosecutor subject to budgetary considerations and under an ethical obligation, not only to win and zealously to advocate for his client but also to serve the cause of justice. The rigors of the penal system are also mitigated by the responsible exercise of prosecutorial discretion. In contrast, there are no analogous checks in the civil discovery process here. Although under Federal Rule of Civil Procedure 11, sanctions are available, and private attorneys also owe an obligation of candor to the judicial tribunal, these safeguards have proved insufficient to discourage the filing of meritless claims against the Executive Branch. "In view of the visibility of" the Offices of the President and the Vice President and "the effect of their actions on countless people," they are "easily identifiable target[s] for suits for civil damages." *Nixon v. Fitzgerald, supra,* at 751. . . .

In contrast to *Nixon*'s subpoena orders that "precisely identified" and "specific[ally] . . . enumerated" the relevant materials, *id.*, at 688, and n. 5, the discovery requests here, as the panel majority acknowledged, ask for everything under the sky:

"1. All documents identifying or referring to any staff, personnel, contractors, consultants or employees of the Task Force.
"2. All documents establishing or referring to any Sub-Group.
"3. All documents identifying or referring to any staff, personnel, contractors, consultants or employees of any Sub-Group.

"4. All documents identifying or referring to any other persons participating in the preparation of the Report or in the activities of the Task Force or any Sub-Group.
"5. All documents concerning any communication relating to the activities of the Task Force, the activities of any Sub-Groups, or the preparation of the Report. . . .
"6. All documents concerning any communication relating to the activities of the Task Force, the activities of the Sub-Groups, or the preparation of the Report between any person . . . and [a list of agencies]." App. 220–221.

The preceding excerpt from respondents' "*First Request for Production of Documents,*" *id.*, at 215 (emphasis added), is only the beginning. Respondents' "First Set of Interrogatories" are similarly unbounded in scope. *Id.*, at 224. Given the breadth of the discovery requests in this case compared to the narrow subpoena orders in *United States v. Nixon*, our precedent provides no support for the proposition that the Executive Branch "shall bear the burden" of invoking executive privilege with sufficient specificity and of making particularized objections. *334 F. 3d, at 1105.* To be sure, *Nixon* held that the President cannot, through the assertion of a "broad [and] undifferentiated" need for confidentiality and the invocation of an "absolute, unqualified" executive privilege, withhold information in the face of subpoena orders. *418 U. S., at 706, 707.* It did so, however, only after the party requesting the information—the special prosecutor—had satisfied his burden of showing the propriety of the requests. Here, as the Court of Appeals acknowledged, the discovery requests are anything but appropriate. They provide respondents all the disclosure to which they would be entitled in the event they prevail on the merits, and much more besides. In these circumstances, *Nixon* does not require the Executive Branch to bear the onus of critiquing the unacceptable discovery requests line by line. Our precedents suggest just the opposite. . . .

Contrary to the District Court's and the Court of Appeals' conclusions, *Nixon* does not leave them the sole option of inviting the Executive Branch to invoke executive privilege while remaining otherwise powerless to modify a party's overly broad discovery requests. Executive privilege is an extraordinary assertion of power "not to be lightly invoked." *United States* v. *Reynolds, 345 U.S. 1, 7* (1953). Once executive privilege is asserted, coequal branches of the Government are set on a collision course. The Judiciary is forced into the difficult task of balancing the need for information in a judicial proceeding and the Executive's Article II prerogatives. This inquiry places courts in the awkward position of evaluating the Executive's claims of confidentiality and autonomy, and pushes to the fore difficult questions of separation of powers and checks and balances. These "occasion[s] for constitutional confrontation between the two branches" should be avoided whenever possible. *United States v. Nixon, supra*, at 692.

In recognition of these concerns, there is sound precedent in the District of Columbia itself for district courts to explore other avenues, short of forcing the Executive to invoke privilege, when they are asked to enforce against the Executive Branch unnecessarily broad subpoenas. . . .

In the absence of overriding concerns of the sort discussed in *Schlagenhauf, 379 U.S., at 111* (discussing, among other things, the need to avoid "piecemeal litigation" and to settle important issues of first impression in areas where this Court bears special responsibility), we decline petitioners' invitation to direct the Court of Appeals to issue the writ against the District Court. Moreover, this is not a case where, after having considered the issues, the Court of Appeals abused its discretion by failing to issue the writ. Instead, the Court of Appeals, relying on its mistaken reading of *United States v. Nixon*, prematurely terminated its inquiry after the Government refused to assert privilege and did so without even reaching the weighty separation-of-powers objections raised in the case, much less exercised its discretion to determine whether "the writ is appropriate under the circumstances." *Ante*, at 10. Because the issuance of the writ is a matter vested in the discretion of the court to which the petition is made, and because this Court is not presented with an original writ of mandamus, see, e.g., *Ex parte Peru, 318 U.S.,*

at 586, we leave to the Court of Appeals to address the parties' arguments with respect to the challenge to *AAPS* (Association of American Physicians and Surgeons) and the discovery orders. Other matters bearing on whether the writ of mandamus should issue should also be addressed, in the first instance, by the Court of Appeals after considering any additional briefs and arguments as it deems appropriate. We note only that all courts should be mindful of the burdens imposed on the Executive Branch in any future proceedings. Special considerations applicable to the President and the Vice President suggest that the courts should be sensitive to requests by the Government for interlocutory appeals to reexamine, for example, whether the statute embodies the *de facto* membership doctrine.

The judgment of the Court of Appeals for the District of Columbia is vacated, and the case is remanded for further proceedings consistent with this opinion.

It is so ordered.

Justice Ginsburg, with whom *Justice Souter* joins, dissenting.

The Government, in seeking a writ of mandamus from the Court of Appeals for the District of Columbia, and on brief to this Court, urged that this case should be resolved without *any* discovery. See App. 183–184, 339; Brief for Petitioners 45; Reply Brief 18. In vacating the judgment of the Court of Appeals, however, this Court remands for consideration whether mandamus is appropriate due to the *overbreadth* of the District Court's discovery orders. See *ante*, at 1, 16–20. But, as the Court of Appeals observed, it appeared that the Government "never asked the district court to *narrow* discovery." *In re Cheney*, 334 F. 3d 1096, 1106 (CADC 2003) (emphasis in original). Given the Government's decision to resist all discovery, mandamus relief based on the exorbitance of the discovery orders is at least "premature," *id.*, at 1104. I would therefore affirm the judgment of the Court of Appeals denying the writ, and allow the District Court, in the first instance, to pursue its expressed intention "tightly [to] rei[n] [in] discovery," *Judicial*

Watch, Inc. v. National Energy Policy Dev. Group, 219 F. Supp. 2d 20, 54 (DC 2002), should the Government so request. . . .

The discovery plan drawn by Judicial Watch and Sierra Club was indeed "unbounded in scope." *Ante*, at 17; accord 334 F. 3d, at 1106. Initial approval of that plan by the District Court, however, was not given in stunning disregard of separation-of-powers concerns. Cf. *ante*, at 16–20. In the order itself, the District Court invited "detailed and precise object[ions]" to any of the discovery requests, and instructed the Government to "identify and explain . . . invocations of privilege with particularity." App. to Pet. for Cert. 51a. To avoid duplication, the District Court provided that the Government could identify "documents or information [responsive to the discovery requests] that [it] ha[d] already released to [Judicial Watch or the Sierra Club] in different fora." *Ibid.* Anticipating further proceedings concerning discovery, the District Court suggested that the Government could "submit [any privileged documents] under seal for the court's consideration," or that "the court [could] appoint the equivalent of a Special Master, maybe a retired judge," to review allegedly privileged documents. App. 247.

The Government did not file specific objections; nor did it supply particulars to support assertions of privilege. Instead, the Government urged the District Court to rule that Judicial Watch and the Sierra Club could have no discovery at all. See *id.*, at 192 ("the governmen[t] position is that . . . no discovery is appropriate"); *id.*, at 205 (same); 334 F.3d, at 1106 ("As far as we can tell, petitioners never asked the district court to *narrow* discovery to those matters [respondents] need to support their allegation that FACA applies to the NEPDG." (Emphasis in original)). In the Government's view, "the resolution of the case ha[d] to flow from the administrative record" *sans* discovery. App. 192. Without taking up the District Court's suggestion of that court's readiness to rein in discovery, see 219 F. Supp. 2d, at 54, the Government, on behalf of the Vice President, moved, unsuccessfully, for a protective order and for certification of an interlocutory

appeal pursuant to 28 U.S.C. §1292(b). . . . At the District Court's hearing on the Government's motion for a stay pending interlocutory appeal, the Government argued that "the injury is submitting to discovery in the absence of a compelling showing of need by the [respondents]." App. 316; see 230 F. Supp. 2d 12 (DC 2002) (District Court order denying stay). . . .

Denied §1292(b) certification by the District Court, the Government sought a writ of mandamus from the Court of Appeals. See *Id.*, at 339–365. In its mandamus petition, the Government asked the appellate court to "vacate the discovery orders issued by the district court, direct the court to decide the case on the basis of the administrative record and such supplemental affidavits as it may require, and direct that the Vice President be dismissed as a defendant." *Id.*, at 364–365. In support of those requests, the Government again argued that the case should be adjudicated without discovery: "The Constitution and principles of comity preclude discovery of the President or Vice President, especially without a demonstration of compelling and focused countervailing interest." *Id.*, at 360.

The Court of Appeals acknowledged that the discovery plan presented by respondents and approved by the District Court "goes well beyond what [respondents] need." 334 F. 3d, at 1106. The appellate court nevertheless denied the mandamus petition, concluding that the Government's separation-of-powers concern "remain[ed] hypothetical." *Id.*, at 1105. Far from ordering immediate "disclosure of communications between senior executive branch officials and those with information relevant to advice that was being formulated for the President," the Court of Appeals observed, the District Court had directed the Government initially to produce only "non-privileged documents and a privilege log." *Id.*, at 1104 (citation and internal quotation marks omitted); see App. to Pet. for Cert. 47a.

The Court of Appeals stressed that the District Court could accommodate separation-of-powers concerns short of denying all discovery or compelling the invocation of executive privilege. See 334 F. 3d, at 1105–1106. Principally, the Court of Appeals stated, discovery could be narrowed, should the Government so move, to encompass only "whether non-federal officials participated [in NEPDG], and if so, to what extent." *Id.*, at 1106. The Government could identify relevant materials produced in other litigation, thus avoiding undue reproduction. *Id.*, at 1105; see App. to Pet. for Cert. 51a; *supra*, at 3. If, after appropriate narrowing, the discovery allowed still impels "the Vice President . . . to claim privilege," the District Court could "entertain [those] privilege claims" and "review allegedly privileged documents in camera." 334 F. 3d, at 1107. Mindful of "the judiciary's responsibility to police the separation of powers in litigation involving the executive," the Court of Appeals expressed confidence that the District Court would "respond to petitioners' concern and narrow discovery to ensure that [respondents]

obtain no more than they need to prove their case." *Id.*, at 1106. . . .

Review by mandamus at this stage of the proceedings would be at least comprehensible as a means to test the Government's position that *no* discovery is appropriate in this litigation. See Brief for Petitioners 45 ("[P]etitioners' separation-of-powers arguments are . . . in the nature of a claim of immunity from discovery."). But in remanding for consideration of discovery-tailoring measures, the Court apparently rejects that no-discovery position. Otherwise, a remand based on the overbreadth of the discovery requests would make no sense. Nothing in the record, however, intimates lower-court refusal to reduce discovery. Indeed, the appeals court has already suggested tailored discovery that would avoid "effectively prejudg[ing] the merits of respondents' claim," *ante*, at 2 (*Stevens, J.,* concurring). . . . I would therefore affirm the judgment of the Court of Appeals.

Congress

Major Pierre L'Enfant, principal designer of the nation's capital, had more than space in mind when he located the president and the Congress at opposite ends of the avenue. The Congress would be housed atop Jenkins Hill, giving it the high ground. The president would find his home about one mile away, at the end of a long street that would serve as a threadlike link connecting these two institutions. Not only did the Constitution separate the executive and legislative branches, but geography as well would keep these two branches apart.

But for the U.S. system to work, both branches must find ways to bridge the gap, to join what is separated. The founders saw the separation of powers not as a weakness (as some see it today) but as a source of strength, as a way to ensure deliberation and thoughtfulness, as a way to prevent tyranny. But how does a president adopt to the rythms of the branches to make the system of separate institutions sharing power work? How can a president couple what the founders decoupled?

Beyond question, the relationship between the president and the Congress is the most important one in the American system of government, and although the president spends a great deal of time and energy courting the media and appealing to the public, he does so in order to gain leverage with the Congress. For, in the long run, presidents must get the Congress to formally or tacitly accept their proposals, lest they run the risk of deadlock, delay, or failure. After all, only the Congress can allocate resources, and presidents who consistently attempt to go around the Congress cannot long succeed. Presidents may not like it, but they cannot live without the Congress.

Although there are a select few areas in which presidents may act semi-independently of the Congress, most presidential goals require a partnership with the Congress. This partnership is not easy to sustain.

In this sense, the Constitution sets up what constitutional scholar Edward S. Corwin refers to as an "invitation to struggle" over political control of the Constitution (power of the government).

Lest the system break down into hopeless gridlock, the president and the Congress must find ways to work together. The theory on which the U.S. government is based hinges on some cooperation between these two branches. As Justice Robert Jackson wrote in 1952, "While the Constitution diffuses power the better to secure liberty, it also contemplates that practice will integrate the dispersed powers into a workable government."

Must the president cite a law or specific constitutional authority in support of his actions for said actions to be deemed legitimate, or does the president possess broad executive or inherent powers on which to act? What, in short, are the scope and limits of executive power?

This case arose when David S. Terry threatened the life of Supreme Court Justice Stephen J. Field. The attorney general assigned David Neagle, a federal marshal, to protect Field. Terry approached Field in a threatening manner, and Neagle killed Terry.

Neagle was arrested and charged with murder. The federal government sought Neagle's release, arguing that Neagle had acted "in pursuance of a law of the United States." The only problem was that, in fact, Congress had passed no such law and had not authorized the president to post bodyguards to federal judges. The question then became: Does the president, acting on his own authority, have the power to act in the public interest as a function of his oath to "faithfully execute the law" absent congressional authority action?

In re Neagle
135 U.S. 1 (1890)

. . . Writing for the majority, Justice Miller . . .

It is urged . . . that there exists no statute authorizing any such protection as that which Neagle was instructed to give Judge Field in the present case, and, indeed, no protection whatever against a vindictive or malicious assault growing out of the faithful discharge of his official duties; and that the language of section 753 of the Revised Statutes, that the party seeking the benefit of the writ of habeas corpus must, in this connection, show that he is 'in custody for an act done or omitted in pursuance of a law of the United States,' makes it necessary that upon this occasion it should be shown that the act for which Neagle is imprisoned was done by virtue of an act of congress. It is not supposed that any special act of congress exists which authorizes the marshals or deputy-marshals of the United States, in express terms, to accompany the judges of the supreme court through their circuits, and act as a bodyguard to them, to defend them against malicious assaults against their persons. But we are of opinion that this view of the statute is an unwarranted restriction of the meaning of a law designed to extend in a liberal manner the benefit of the writ of habeas corpus to persons imprisoned for the performance of their duty; and we are satisfied that, if it was the duty of Neagle, under the circumstances,—a duty which could only arise under the laws of the United States,—to defend Mr. Justice Field from a murderous attack upon

him, he brings himself within the meaning of the section we have recited . . . In the view we take of the Constitution of the United States, any obligation fairly and properly inferable from that instrument, or any duty of the marshal to be derived from the general scope of his duties under the laws of the United States, is a 'law,' within the meaning of this phrase. It would be a great reproach to the system of government of the United States, declared to be within its sphere sovereign and supreme, if there is to be found within the domain of its powers no means of protecting the judges, in the conscientious and faithful discharge of their duties, from the malice and hatred of those upon whom their judgments may operate unfavorably . . .

. . . Where, then, are we to look for the protection which we have shown Judge Field was entitled to when engaged in the discharge of his official duties? Not to the courts of the United States, because, as has been more than once said in this court, in the division of the powers of government between the three great departments, executive, legislative, and judicial, the judicial is the weakest for the purposes of self-protection, and for the enforcement of the powers which it exercises. The ministerial officers through whom its commands must be executed are marshals of the United States, and belong emphatically to the executive department of the government. They are appointed by the president, with the advice and consent of the senate. They are removable from office at his pleasure . . . The legislative branch of the government can only protect the judicial officers by the enactment of laws for that purpose, and the argument we are now combating assumes that no such law has been passed by congress. If we turn to the executive department of the government, we find a very different condition of affairs. The constitution, 3, art. 2, declares that the president 'shall take care that the laws be faithfully executed'; and he is provided with the means of fulfilling this obligation by his authority to commission all the officers of the United States, and, by and with the advice and consent of the senate, to appoint the most important of them, and to fill vacancies. He is declared to be the commander in chief of the army and navy of the United States. The duties which are thus imposed upon him he is further enabled to perform by the recognition in the constitution, and the creation by acts of congress, of executive departments, which have varied in number from four or five to seven or eight, who are familiarly called 'cabinet ministers.' These aid him in the performance of the great duties of his office, and represent him in a thousand acts to which it can hardly be supposed his personal attention is called; and thus he is enabled to fulfill the duty of his great department, expressed in the phrase that 'he shall take care that the laws be faithfully executed.' Is this duty limited to the enforcement of acts of congress or of treaties of the United States according to their express terms; or does it include the rights, duties, and obligations growing out of the constitution itself, our international relations, and all the protection implied by the nature of the government under the constitution? . . .

We cannot doubt the power of the president to take measures for the protection of a judge of one of the courts of the United States who, while in the discharge of the duties of his office, is threatened with a personal attack which may probably result in his death; and we think it clear that where this protection is to be afforded through the civil power, the department of justice is the proper one to set in motion the necessary means of protection . . .

. . . To the objection, made in argument, that the prisoner is discharged by this writ from the power of the state court to try him for the whole offense, the reply is that if the prisoner is held in the state court to answer for an act which he was authorized to do by the law of the United States, which it was his duty to do as marshal of the United States, and if, in doing that act, he did no more than what was necessary and proper for him to do, he cannot be guilty of a crime under the law of the state of California. When these things are shown, it is established that he is innocent of any crime against the laws of the state, or of any other authority whatever. There is no occasion for any further trial in the state court, or in any court . . .

This case grew from the Pullman strike of 1894, when railroad workers refused to work on railroad cars until the Pullman Company agreed to arbitrate its dispute with labor organizations. Eugene Debs, the head of the workers' union, was enjoined from communications with rail workers and was arrested for conspiracy to obstruct the delivery of mail.

Interstate transportation of U.S. mail was interrupted, and the federal government intervened. Did the government have the authority to intervene and block a labor action to ensure interstate commerce and mail delivery? Can the government act absent an emergency? And what role should the president and the Congress play in these matters?

In re Debs
158 U.S. 564 (1895)

. . . Mr. Justice Brewer . . . delivered the opinion of the court.

The case presented by the bill is this: The United States, finding that the interstate transportation of persons and property, as well as the carriage of the mails, is forcibly obstructed, and that a combination and conspiracy exists to subject the control of such transportation to the will of the conspirators, applied to one of their courts, sitting as a court of equity, for an injunction to restrain such obstruction and prevent carrying into effect such conspiracy. Two questions of importance are presented: First. Are the relations of the general government to interstate commerce and the transportation of the mails such as authorized a direct interference to prevent a forcible obstruction thereof? Second. If authority exists, as authority in governmental affairs implies both power and duty, has a court of equity jurisdiction to issue an injunction in aid of the performance of such duty? What are the relations of the general government to interstate commerce and the transportation of the mails? They are those of direct supervision, control, and management. While, under the dual system which prevails with us, the powers of government are distributed between the state and the nation, and while the latter is properly styled a government of enumerated powers, yet within the limits of such enumeration it has all the attributes of sovereignty, and, in the exercise of those enumerated powers, acts directly upon the citizen, and not through the intermediate agency of the state . . .

As, under the constitution, power over interstate commerce and the transportation of the mails is vested in the national government, and congress, by virtue of such grant, has assumed actual and direct control, it follows that the national government may prevent any unlawful and forcible interference therewith. But how shall this be accomplished? Doubtless, it is within the competency of congress to prescribe by legislation that any interference's with these matters shall be offenses against the United States, and prosecuted and punished by indictment in the proper courts. But is that the only remedy? Have the vast interests of the nation in interstate commerce, and in the transportation of the mails, no other protection than lies in the possible punishment of those who interfere with it? To ask the question is to answer it . . . If . . . the national government had no other way to enforce the freedom of interstate commerce and the transportation of the mails than by prosecution and punishment for interference therewith, the whole interests of the nation in these respects would be at the absolute mercy of a portion of the inhabitants of that single state.

But there is no such impotency in the national government. The entire strength of the nation may be used to enforce in any part of the land the full and free exercise of all national powers and the security of all rights intrusted by the constitution to its care. The strong arm of the national government may be put forth to brush away all obstructions to the freedom of interstate commerce or the transportation of the mails. If the emergency arises, the army of the nation, and all its militia, are at the service of the nation, to compel obedience to its laws.

But, passing to the second question, is there no other alternative than the use of force on the part of the executive authorities whenever obstructions arise to the freedom of interstate commerce or the transportation of the mails? Is the army the only

instrument by which rights of the public can be enforced, and the peace of the nation preserved? Grant that any public nuisance may be forcibly abated, either at the instance of the authorities, or by any individual suffering private damage therefrom. The existence of this right of forcible abatement is not inconsistent with, nor does it destroy, the right of appeal, in an orderly way, to the courts for a judicial determination, and an exercise of their powers, by writ of injunction and otherwise, to accomplish the same result . . .

So, in the case before us, the right to use force does not exclude the right of appeal to the courts for a judicial determination, and for the exercise of all their powers of prevention. Indeed, it is more to the praise than to the blame of the government that, instead of determining for itself questions of right and wrong on the part of these petitioners and their associates, and enforcing that determination by the club of the policeman and the bayonet of the soldier, it submitted all those questions to the peaceful determination of judicial tribunals, and invoked their consideration and judgment as to the measure of its rights and powers, and the correlative obligations of those against whom it made complaint. And it is equally to the credit of the latter that the judgment of those tribunals was by the great body of them respected, and the troubles which threatened so much disaster terminated . . .

. . . Every government, intrusted by the very terms of its being with powers and duties to be exercised and discharged for the general welfare, has a right to apply to its own courts for any proper assistance in the exercise of the one and the discharge of the other, and it is no sufficient answer to its appeal to one of those courts that it has no pecuniary interest in the matter. The obligations which it is under to promote the interest of all and to prevent the wrongdoing of one, resulting in injury to the general welfare, is often of itself sufficient to give it a standing in court . . .

. . . While it is not the province of the government to interfere in any mere matter of private controversy between individuals, or to use its great powers to enforce the rights of one against another, yet, whenever the wrongs complained of are such as affect the public at large, and are in respect of matters which by the constitution are intrusted to the care of the nation, and concerning which the nation owes the duty to all the citizens of securing to them their common rights, then the mere fact that the government has no pecuniary interest in the controversy is not sufficient to exclude it from the courts, or prevent it from taking measures therein to fully discharge those constitutional duties.

The national government, given by the constitution power to regulate interstate commerce, has by express statute assumed jurisdiction over such commerce when carried upon railroads. It is charged, therefore, with the duty of keeping those highways of interstate commerce free from obstruction, for it has always been recognized as one of the powers and duties of a government to remove obstructions from the highways under its control . . .

. . . It is said by counsel in their brief:

'No case can be cited where such a bill in behalf of the sovereign has been entertained against riot and mob violence, though occurring on the highway. It is not such fitful and temporary obstruction that constitutes a nuisance. The strong hand of executive power is required to deal with such lawless demonstrations.

'The courts should stand aloof from them and not invade executive prerogative, nor, even at the behest or request of the executive, travel out of the beaten path of well-settled judicial authority. A mob cannot be suppressed by injunction; nor can its leaders be tried, convicted, and sentenced in equity.

'It is too great a strain upon the judicial branch of the government to impose this essentially executive and military power upon courts of chancery.'

We do not perceive that this argument questions the jurisdiction of the court, but only the expediency of the action of the government in applying for the process. It surely cannot be seriously contended that the court has jurisdiction to enjoin the obstruction of a highway by one person, but that its jurisdiction ceases when the obstruction is by a hundred persons . . . It is doubtless true that . . . in the throes of rebellion or revolution the processes of civil courts are of little avail, for the power of the courts rests on the general support of the people, and their recognition of the fact that peaceful remedies are the true resort for the correction of wrongs. But does not counsel's argument imply too much? Is it to be assumed that these defendants were conducting a rebellion or inaugurating a revolution, and that they and their associates were thus placing themselves beyond the reach of the civil process of the courts? We find in the opinion of the circuit court a quotation from the testimony given by one of the defendants before the United States strike commission, which is sufficient answer to this suggestion:

'As soon as the employees found that we were arrested, and taken from the scene of action, they became demoralized, and that ended the strike. It was not the soldiers that ended the strike. It was not the old brotherhoods that ended the strike. It was simply the United States courts that ended the strike. Our men were in a position that never would have been shaken, under any circumstances, if we had been permitted to remain upon the field, among them. Once we were taken from the scene of action, and restrained from sending telegrams or issuing orders or answering questions, then the minious of the corporations would be put to work . . . Our headquarters were temporarily demoralized and abandoned, and we could not answer any messages. The men went back to work, and the ranks were broken, and the strike was broken up, . . . not by the army, and not by any other power, but simply and solely by the action of the United States courts in restraining us from discharging our duties as officers and representatives of our employees.'

Whatever any single individual may have thought or planned, the great body of those who were engaged in these transactions contemplated neither rebellion nor revolution, and when in the due order of legal proceedings the question of right and wrong was submitted to the courts, and by them decided, they unhesitatingly yielded to their decisions. The outcome, by the very testimony of the defendants, attests the wisdom of the course pursued by the government, and that it was well not to oppose force simply by force, but to invoke the jurisdiction and judgment of those tribunals to whom by the constitution and in accordance with the settled conviction of all citizens is committed the determination of questions of right and wrong between individuals, masses, and states.

It must be borne in mind that this bill was not simply to enjoin a mob and mob violence. It was not a bill to command a keeping of the peace; much less was its purport to restrain the defendants from abandoning whatever employment they were engaged in. The right of any laborer, or any number of laborers, to quit work was not challenged. The scope and purpose of the bill was only to restrain forcible obstructions of the highways along which interstate commerce travels and the mails are carried. And the facts set forth at length are only those facts which tended to show that the defendants were engaged in such obstructions . . .

The petition for a writ of habeas corpus is denied.

In the late 1800s and early 1900s, the federal government's policy, via an 1897 act of the Congress, was to allow private interests to extract oil from public lands at virtually no cost. As the value of oil for both industry and the military became clearer, the government sought to put an end to this oil give-away program and reestablish control of public lands.

In 1909, President William H. Taft issued a proclamation restricting oil extraction from public lands. But in 1910, William T. Henshaw and others violated this proclamation. The government then sued the Midwest Oil Company seeking a recovery of land and oil.

The government claimed that the president, as commander in chief, had the authority to issue such an order for the protection of the nation and that the president, on his authority as chief executive, had the

constitutional power (Article 2, Section 1) with the tacit consent of the Congress, to withdraw public lands when deemed in the national interest. The Midwest Oil Company argued that the president had no right to suspend an act of Congress.

U.S. v. Midwest Oil Company
236 U.S. 459 (1915)

Mr. Justice Lamar delivered the opinion of the court . . .

. . . On the part of the government it is urged that the President, as Commander in Chief of the Army and Navy, had power to make the order for the purpose of retaining and preserving a source of supply of fuel for the Navy, instead of allowing the oil land to be taken up for a nominal sum, the government being then obliged to purchase at a great cost what it had previously owned. It is argued that the President, charged with the care of the public domain, could, by virtue of the executive power vested in him by the Constitution (art. 2, 1), and also in conformity with the tacit consent of Congress, withdraw, in the public interest, any public land from entry or location by private parties.

The appellees, on the other hand, insist that there is no dispensing power in the Executive, and that he could not suspend a statute or withdraw from entry or location any land which Congress had affirmatively declared should be free and open to acquisition by citizens of the United States. They further insist that the withdrawal order is absolutely void, since it appears on its face to be a mere attempt to suspend a statute—supposed to be unwise—in order to allow Congress to pass another more in accordance with what the Executive thought to be in the public interest.

We need not consider whether, as an original question, the President could have withdrawn from private acquisition what Congress had made free and open to occupation and purchase. The case can be determined on other grounds and in the light of the legal consequences flowing from a long-continued practice to make orders like the one here involved. For the President's proclamation of September 27, 1909, is by no means the first instance in which the Executive, by a special order, has withdrawn lands which Congress, by general statute, had thrown open to acquisition by citizens. And while it is not known when the first of these orders was made, it is certain that 'the practice dates from an early period in the history of the government.' *Grisar v. McDowell*, 6 Wall. 381 . . . Scores and hundreds of these orders have been made; and treating them as they must be . . . as the act of the President, an examination of official publications will show that . . . he has, during the past eighty years, without express statutory,—but under the claim of power so to do,—made a multitude of Executive orders which operated to withdraw public land that would otherwise have been open to private acquisition. They affected every kind of land—mineral and nonmineral. The size of the tracts varied from a few square rods to many square miles, and the amount withdrawn has aggregated millions of acres. The number of such instances cannot, of course, be accurately given, but the extent of the practice can best be appreciated by a consideration of what is believed to be a correct enumeration of such Executive orders mentioned in public documents.

They show that prior to the year 1910 there had been issued

99 Executive orders establishing or enlarging Indian reservations;

109 Executive orders establishing or enlarging military reservations and setting apart land for water, timber, fuel, hay, signal stations, target ranges, and rights of way for use in connection with military reservations;

44 Executive orders establishing bird reserves.

In the sense that these lands may have been intended for public use, they were reserved for a public purpose. But they were not reserved in pursuance of law, or by virtue of any general or special statutory authority. For it is to be specially noted that there was no act of Congress providing for bird reserves

or for these Indian reservations. There was no law for the establishment of these military reservations or defining their size or location. There was no statute empowering the President to withdraw any of these lands from settlement, or to reserve them for any of the purposes indicated.

But when it appeared that the public interest would be served by withdrawing or reserving parts of the public domain, nothing was more natural than to retain what the government already owned. And in making such orders, which were thus useful to the public, no private interest was injured. For, prior to the initiation of some right given by law, the citizen had no enforceable interest in the public statute, and no private right in land which was the property of the people. The President was in a position to know when the public interest required particular portions of the people's lands to be withdrawn from entry or location; his action inflicted no wrong upon any private citizen, and being subject to disaffirmance by Congress, could occasion no harm to the interest of the public at large. Congress did not repudiate the power claimed or the withdrawal orders made. On the contrary, it uniformly and repeatedly acquiesced in the practice, and, as shown by these records, there had been, prior to 1910, at least 252 Executive orders making reservations for useful, though nonstatutory, purposes.

This right of the President to make reservations— and thus withdraw land from private acquisition— was expressly recognized in *Grisar v. McDowell*, 6 Wall. 364 (9), 381, 18 L. ed. 863, 868, where (1867) it was said that 'from an early period in the history of the government it has been the practice of the President to order from time to time, as the exigencies of the public service required, parcels of land belonging to the United States, to be reserved from sale and set apart for public uses.'

But, notwithstanding this decision and the continuity of this practice, the absence of express statutory authority was the occasion of doubt being expressed as to the power of the President to make these orders. The matter was therefore several times referred to the law officers of the government for an opinion on the subject. One of them stated (1889) (19 Ops. Atty. Gen. 370) that the validity of such orders rested on 'a long-established and long-recognized power in the President to withhold from sale or settlement at discretion, portions of the public domain.' . . .

These decisions do not, of course, mean that private rights could be created by an officer withdrawing for a railroad more than had been authorized by Congress in the land grant act. *Southern P. R. Co. v. Bell*, 183 U.S. . . . *Brandon v. Ard, 211 U.S. 21* . . . Nor do these decisions mean that the Executive can, by his course of action, create a power. But they do clearly indicate that the long-continued practice, known to and acquiesced in by Congress, would raise a presumption that the withdrawals had been made in pursuance of its consent or of a recognized administrative power of the Executive in the management of the public lands. This is particularly true in view of the fact that the land is property of the United States, and that the land laws are not of a legislative character in the highest sense of the term (art. 4, 3), 'but savor somewhat of mere rules prescribed by an owner of property for its disposal.' *Butte City Water Co. v. Baker, 196 U.S. 126* . . .

For it must be borne in mind that Congress not only has a legislative power over the public domain, but it also exercises the powers of the proprietor therein. Congress 'may deal with such lands precisely as an ordinary individual may deal with farming property. It may sell or withhold them from sale.' *Camfield v. United States, 167 U.S. 524, 42* . . . *Light v. United States, 220 U.S. 536* . . . Like any other owner it may provide when, how, and to whom its land can be sold. It can permit it to be withdrawn from sale. Like any other owner, it can waive its strict rights, as it did when the valuable privilege of grazing cattle on this public land was held to be based upon an 'implied license growing out of the custom of nearly a hundred years.' *Buford v. Houtz, 133 U.S. 326* . . . So, too, in the early days, the 'government, by its silent acquiescence, assented to the general occupation of the public lands for mining.' *Atchison v. Peterson*, 20 Wall. 512, 22 . . . If private persons could acquire a privilege in public

land by virtue of an implied congressional consent, then, for a much stronger reason, an implied grant of power to preserve the public interest would arise out of like congressional acquiescence.

The Executive, as agent, was in charge of the public domain; by a multitude of orders extending over a long period of time, and affecting vast bodies of land, in many states and territories, he withdrew large areas in the public interest. These orders were known to Congress, as principal, and in not a single instance was the act of the agent disapproved. Its acquiescence all the more readily operated as an implied grant of power in view of the fact that its exercise was not only useful to the public, but did not interfere with any vested right of the citizen.

The appellees, however, argue that the practice thus approved related to reservations,—to cases where the land had been reserved for military or other special public purposes,—and they contend that even if the President could reserve land for a public purpose or naval uses, it does not follow that he can withdraw land in aid of legislation.

When analyzed, this proposition, in effect, seeks to make a distinction between a reservation and a withdrawal,—between a reservation for a purpose not provided for by existing legislation, and a withdrawal made in aid of future legislation. It would mean that a permanent reservation for a purpose designated by the President, but not provided for by a statute, would be valid, while a merely temporary withdrawal to enable Congress to legislate in the public interest would be invalid. It is only necessary to point out that, as the greater includes the less, the power to make permanent reservations includes power to make temporary withdrawals . . .

. . . That the existence of this power was recognized and its exercise by the Executive assented to by Congress is emphasized by the fact that the above-mentioned withdrawals were issued after the report which the Secretary of the Interior made in 1902, in response to a resolution of the Senate calling for information 'as to what, if any, of the public lands, have been withdrawn from disposition under the settlement or other laws by order the Commissioner of the General Land Office, and what, if any, authority of law exists for such order of withdrawal.' . . .

The answer to this specific inquiry was returned March 3, 1902 (Senate Doc. 232, 57th Cong. 1st Sess. vol. 17). On that date the Secretary transmitted to the Senate the elaborate and detailed report of the Commissioner of the Land Office . . . in response to the inquiry as to the authority by which withdrawals had been made . . .

This report refers to withdrawals, and not to reservations. It is most important in connection with the present inquiry as to whether Congress knew of the practice to make temporary withdrawals and knowingly assented thereto. It will be noted that the resolution called on the Department to state the extent of such withdrawals and the authority by which they were made. The officer of the Land Department, in his answer, shows that there have been a large number of withdrawals made for good, but for nonstatutory, reasons. He shows that these 92 orders had been made by virtue of a long-continued practice and under claim of a right to take such action in the public interest 'as exigencies might demand . . .' Congress, with notice of this practice and of this claim of authority, received the report. Neither at that session nor afterwards did it ever repudiate the action taken or the power claimed. Its silence was acquiescence. Its acquiescence was equivalent to consent to continue the practice until the power was revoked by some subsequent action by Congress.

. . . Nor is the position of the appellees strengthened by the act of June 25, 1910, (36 Stat. 847. . .), to authorize the President to make withdrawals of public lands, and requiring a list of the same to be filed with Congress . . .

The legislative history of the statute shows that there was no such intent and no purpose to make the act retroactive, or to disaffirm what the agent in charge had already done . . .

The case is therefore remanded to the District Court with directions that the decree dismissing the bill be reversed . . .

Mr. Justice McReynolds took no part in the decision of this case . . .

In an effort to reduce the budget deficit of the federal government, the Congress passed the Balanced Budget and Emergency Deficit Control Act of 1985, better known as the Gramm-Rudman-Hollings Act. This act set off automatic budget cuts if the budget deficit exceeded a preset amount.

Several members of the Congress, led by Mike Synar (D-Oklahoma), challenged the act on the grounds that the Congress had improperly delegated spending authority to the executive branch and violated the separation of powers, as the Congress had the authority to remove the officer, the comptroller general, charged with executing the cuts. On appeal, the Supreme Court took up the case, focusing only on the separation-of-powers question. This case is closely linked, and further clarifies, the Court's decisions in Humphrey's Executor *and* Myers.

Bowsher v. Synar
478 U.S. 714 (1986)

Chief Justice Burger delivered the opinion of the Court.

The question presented by these appeals is whether the assignment by Congress to the Comptroller General of the United States of certain functions under the Balanced Budget and Emergency Deficit Control Act of 1985 violates the doctrine of separation of powers . . .

A three-judge District Court, appointed pursuant to 2 U.S.C. 922(a)(5) (1982 ed., Supp. III), invalidated the reporting provisions. *Synar v. United States,* 626 F. Supp. 1374 (DC 1986) (Scalia, Johnson, and Gasch, JJ.) . . .

The District Court next rejected appellees' challenge that the Act violated the delegation doctrine. The court expressed no doubt that the Act delegated broad authority, but delegation of similarly broad authority has been upheld in past cases. The

District Court observed that in *Yakus v. United States, 321 U.S. 414, 420* (1944), this Court upheld a statute that delegated to an unelected "Price Administrator" the power "to promulgate regulations fixing prices of commodities." Moreover, in the District Court's view, the Act adequately confined the exercise of administrative discretion. The District Court concluded that "the totality of the Act's standards, definitions, context, and reference to past administrative practice provides an adequate 'intelligible principle' to guide and confine administrative decision making." 626 F. Supp., at 1389.

Although the District Court concluded that the Act survived a delegation doctrine challenge, it held that the role of the Comptroller General in the deficit reduction process violated the constitutionally imposed separation of powers. The court first explained that the Comptroller General exercises executive functions under the Act. However, the Comptroller General, while appointed by the President with the advice and consent of the Senate, is removable not by the President but only by a joint resolution of Congress or by impeachment. The District Court reasoned that this arrangement could not be sustained under this Court's decisions in *Myers v. United States, 272 U.S. 52* (1926), and *Humphrey's Executor v. United States, 295 U.S. 602* (1935). Under the separation of powers established by the Framers of the Constitution, the court concluded, Congress may not retain the power of removal over an officer performing executive functions. The congressional removal power created a "here-and-now subservience" of the Comptroller General to Congress. 626 F. Supp., at 1392. The District Court therefore held that

"since the powers conferred upon the Comptroller General as part of the automatic deficit reduction process are executive powers, which cannot constitutionally be exercised by an officer removable by Congress, those powers cannot be exercised and therefore the automatic deficit reduction process to which they are central cannot be implemented." . . .

Appeals were taken directly to this Court pursuant to 274(b) of the Act . . . We affirm . . .

. . . The declared purpose of separating and dividing the powers of government, of course, was to "diffus[e] power the better to secure liberty." *Youngstown Sheet & Tube Co. v. Sawyer, 343 U.S. 579, 635* (1952) (Jackson, J., concurring). Justice Jackson's words echo the famous warning of Montesquieu, quoted by James Madison in The Federalist No. 47, that " 'there can be no liberty where the legislative and executive powers are united in the same person, or body of magistrates' . . . ." . . .

The Constitution does not contemplate an active role for Congress in the supervision of officers charged with the execution of the laws it enacts. The President appoints "Officers of the United States" with the "Advice and Consent of the Senate . . . ." Once the appointment has been made and confirmed, however, the Constitution explicitly provides for removal of Officers of the United States by Congress only upon impeachment by the House of Representatives and conviction by the Senate. An impeachment by the House and trial by the Senate can rest only on "Treason, Bribery or other high Crimes and Misdemeanors." A direct congressional role in the removal of officers charged with the execution of the laws beyond this limited one is inconsistent with separation of powers . . .

This Court first directly addressed this issue in *Myers v. United States, 272 U.S. 52* . . . Chief Justice Taft, writing for the Court, declared the statute unconstitutional on the ground that for Congress to "draw to itself, or to either branch of it, the power to remove or the right to participate in the exercise of that power . . . would be . . . to infringe the constitutional principle of the separation of governmental powers." . . .

. . . A decade later, in *Humphrey's Executor v. United States, 295 U.S. 602* . . . a Federal Trade Commissioner who had been removed by the President sought back-pay. *Humphrey's Executor* involved an issue not presented either in the *Myers* case or in this case i.e., the power of Congress to limit the President's powers of removal of a Federal

Trade Commissioner . . . The Court distinguished *Myers*, reaffirming its holding that congressional participation in the removal of executive officers is unconstitutional . . .

In light of these precedents, we conclude that Congress cannot reserve for itself the power of removal of an officer charged with the execution of the laws except by impeachment. To permit the execution of the laws to be vested in an officer answerable only to Congress would, in practical terms, reserve in Congress control over the execution of the laws. As the District Court observed: "Once an officer is appointed, it is only the authority that can remove him, and not the authority that appointed him, that he must fear and, in the performance of his functions, obey." 626 . . . The structure of the Constitution does not permit Congress to execute the laws; it follows that Congress cannot grant to an officer under its control what it does not possess.

Our decision in *INS v. Chadha*, 462 U.S. 919 (1983), supports this conclusion. In *Chadha*, we struck down a one-House "legislative veto" provision by which each House of Congress retained the power to reverse a decision Congress had expressly authorized the Attorney General to make:

> "Disagreement with the Attorney General's decision on Chadha's deportation—that is, Congress' decision to deport Chadha—no less than Congress' original choice to delegate to the Attorney General the authority to make that decision, involves determinations of policy that Congress can implement in only one way; bicameral passage followed by presentment to the President. Congress must abide by its delegation of authority until that delegation is legislatively altered or revoked." . . .

To permit an officer controlled by Congress to execute the laws would be, in essence, to permit a congressional veto. Congress could simply remove, or threaten to remove, an officer for executing the laws in any fashion found to be unsatisfactory to Congress. This kind of congressional control over

the execution of the laws, *Chadha* makes clear, is constitutionally impermissible . . .

. . . Appellants urge that the Comptroller General performs his duties independently and is not subservient to Congress. We agree with the District Court that this contention does not bear close scrutiny.

The critical factor lies in the provisions of the statute defining the Comptroller General's office relating to removability. Although the Comptroller General is nominated by the President from a list of three individuals recommended by the Speaker of the House of Representatives and the President pro tempore of the Senate, see 31 U.S.C. 703 (a)(2), and confirmed by the Senate, he is removable only at the initiative of Congress. He may be removed not only by impeachment but also by joint resolution of Congress "at any time" resting on any one of the following bases:

> "(i) permanent disability;
> "(ii) inefficiency;
> "(iii) neglect of duty;
> "(iv) malfeasance; or
> "(v) a felony or conduct involving moral turpitude." 31 U.S.C. 703(e)(1)B.

This provision was included, as one Congressman explained in urging passage of the Act, because Congress "felt that [the Comptroller General] should be brought under the sole control of Congress, so that Congress at any moment when it found he was inefficient and was not carrying on the duties of his office as he should and as the Congress expected, could remove him without the long, tedious process of a trial by impeachment." 61 Cong. Rec. 1081 (1921) . . .

. . . The statute permits removal for "inefficiency," "neglect of duty," or "malfeasance." These terms are very broad and, as interpreted by Congress, could sustain removal of a Comptroller General for any number of actual or perceived transgressions of the legislative will. The Constitutional Convention chose to permit impeachment of executive officers only for "Treason, Bribery, or other high Crimes and Misdemeanors." It rejected language that would have permitted impeachment for "maladministration," with Madison arguing that "[s]o vague a term will be equivalent to a tenure during pleasure of the Senate." 2 M. Farrand . . . p. 550 . . .

Justice White, however, assures us that "[r]ealistic consideration" of the "practical result of the removal provision," . . . reveals that the Comptroller General is unlikely to be removed by Congress. The separated powers of our Government cannot be permitted to turn on judicial assessment of whether an officer exercising executive power is on good terms with Congress. The Framers recognized that, in the long term, structural protections against abuse of power were critical to preserving liberty. In constitutional terms, the removal powers over the Comptroller General's office dictate that he will be subservient to Congress.

This much said, we must also add that the dissent is simply in error to suggest that the political realities reveal that the Comptroller General is free from influence by Congress. The Comptroller General heads the General Accounting Office (GAO), "an instrumentality of the United States Government independent of the executive departments," 31 U.S.C. 702(a), which was created by Congress in 1921 as part of the Budget and Accounting Act of 1921, 42 Stat. 23. Congress created the office because it believed that it "needed an officer, responsible to it alone, to check upon the application of public funds in accordance with appropriations." H. Mansfield, The Comptroller General: A Study in the Law and Practice of Financial Administration 65 (1939).

It is clear that Congress has consistently viewed the Comptroller General as an officer of the Legislative Branch. The Reorganization Acts of 1945 and 1949, for example, both stated that the Comptroller General and the GAO are "a part of the legislative branch of the Government." 59 . . . Stat. 205. Similarly, in the Accounting and Auditing Act of 1950, Congress required the Comptroller General to conduct audits "as an agent of the Congress." . . .

Over the years, the Comptrollers General have also viewed themselves as part of the Legislative Branch . . .

. . . Against this background, we see no escape from the conclusion that, because Congress has retained removal authority over the Comptroller General, he may not be entrusted with executive powers. The remaining question is whether the Comptroller General has been assigned such powers in the Balanced Budget and Emergency Deficit Control Act of 1985.

. . . The primary responsibility of the Comptroller General under the instant Act is the preparation of a "report." This report must contain detailed estimates of projected federal revenues and expenditures. The report must also specify the reductions, if any, necessary to reduce the deficit to the target for the appropriate fiscal year. The reductions must be set forth on a program-by-program basis.

In preparing the report, the Comptroller General is to have "due regard" for the estimates and reductions set forth in a joint report submitted to him by the Director of CBO [Congressional Budget Office] and the Director of OMB [Office of Management and Budget], the President's fiscal and budgetary adviser. However, the Act plainly contemplates that the Comptroller General will exercise his independent judgment and evaluation with respect to those estimates. The Act also provides that the Comptroller General's report "shall explain fully any differences between the contents of such report and the report of the Directors." . . .

Appellants suggest that the duties assigned to the Comptroller General in the Act are essentially ministerial and mechanical so that their performance does not constitute "execution of the law" in a meaningful sense. On the contrary, we view these functions as plainly entailing execution of the law in constitutional terms. Interpreting a law enacted by Congress to implement the legislative mandate is the very essence of "execution" of the law. Under 251, the Comptroller General must exercise judgment concerning facts that affect the application of the Act. He must also interpret the provisions of the Act to determine precisely what budgetary calculations are required. Decisions of that kind are typically made by officers charged with executing a statute.

The executive nature of the Comptroller General's functions under the Act is revealed in 252(a)(3) which gives the Comptroller General the ultimate authority to determine the budget cuts to be made. Indeed, the Comptroller General commands the President himself to carry out, without the slightest variation (with exceptions not relevant to the constitutional issues presented), the directive of the Comptroller General as to the budget reductions:

> "The [Presidential] order *must provide* for reductions in the manner specified in section 251(a)(3), *must incorporate* the provisions of the [Comptroller General's] report submitted under section 251(b), and *must be consistent with such report in all respects.* The President *may not modify or recalculate any of the estimates, determinations, specifications, bases, amounts, or percentages* set forth in the report submitted under section 251(b) in determining the reductions to be specified in the order with respect to programs, projects, and activities, or with respect to budget activities, within an account . . . ." 252(a)(3) (emphasis added) . . .

. . . Congress of course initially determined the content of the Balanced Budget and Emergency Deficit Control Act; and undoubtedly the content of the Act determines the nature of the executive duty. However, as *Chadha* makes clear, once Congress makes its choice in enacting legislation, its participation ends. Congress can thereafter control the execution of its enactment only indirectly—by passing new legislation. *Chadha, 462 U.S., at 958.* By placing the responsibility for execution of the Balanced Budget and Emergency Deficit Control Act in the hands of an officer who is subject to removal only by itself, Congress in effect has retained control over the execution of the Act and has intruded into the executive function. The Constitution does not permit such intrusion . . .

. . . Justice Stevens, with whom Justice Marshall joins, concurring in the judgment.

. . . I disagree with the Court, however, on the reasons why the Constitution prohibits the Comptroller General from exercising the powers assigned to him by . . . the Act. It is not the dormant, carefully circumscribed congressional removal power that represents the primary constitutional evil. Nor do I agree with the conclusion of both the majority and the dissent that the analysis depends on a labeling of the functions assigned to the Comptroller General as "executive powers." . . . Rather, I am convinced that the Comptroller General must be characterized as an agent of Congress because of his long-standing statutory responsibilities; that the powers assigned to him under the Gramm-Rudman-Hollings Act require him to make policy that will bind the Nation; and that, when Congress, or a component or an agent of Congress, seeks to make policy that will bind the Nation, it must follow the procedures mandated by Article I of the Constitution—through passage by both Houses and presentment to the President . . .

The fact that Congress retained for itself the power to remove the Comptroller General is important evidence supporting the conclusion that he is a member of the Legislative Branch of the Government. Unlike the Court, however, I am not persuaded that the congressional removal power is either a necessary, or a sufficient, basis for concluding that his statutory assignment is invalid . . .

. . . The notion that the removal power at issue here automatically creates some kind of "here-and-now subservience" of the Comptroller General to Congress is belied by history. There is no evidence that Congress has ever removed, or threatened to remove, the Comptroller General for reasons of policy. Moreover, the President has long possessed a comparable power to remove members of the Federal Trade Commission, yet it is universally accepted that they are independent of, rather than subservient to, the President in performing their official duties . . .

The fact that Congress retained for itself the power to remove the Comptroller General thus is not necessarily an adequate reason for concluding that his role in the Gramm-Rudman-Hollings budget reduction process is unconstitutional. It is, however, a fact that lends support to my ultimate conclusion that, in exercising his functions under this Act, he serves as an agent of the Congress. . . .

The Court concludes that the Gramm-Rudman-Hollings Act impermissibly assigns the Comptroller General "executive powers." *Ante*, at 732. Justice White's dissent agrees that "the powers exercised by the Comptroller under the Act may be characterized as 'executive' in that they involve the interpretation and carrying out of the Act's mandate." This conclusion is not only far from obvious but also rests on the unstated and unsound premise that there is a definite line that distinguishes executive power from legislative power . . .

One reason that the exercise of legislative, executive, and judicial powers cannot be categorically distributed among three mutually exclusive branches of Government is that governmental power cannot always be readily characterized with only one of those three labels. On the contrary, as our cases demonstrate, a particular function, like a chameleon, will often take on the aspect of the office to which it is assigned . . .

The *Chadha* case itself illustrates this basic point. The governmental decision that was being made was whether a resident alien who had overstayed his student visa should be deported. From the point of view of the Administrative Law Judge who conducted a hearing on the issue—or as Justice Powell saw the issue in his concurrence—the decision took on a judicial coloring. From the point of view of the Attorney General of the United States to whom Congress had delegated the authority to suspend deportation of certain aliens, the decision appeared to have an executive character. But, as the Court held, when the House of Representatives finally decided that Chadha must be deported, its action "was essentially legislative in purpose and effect." . . .

The powers delegated to the Comptroller General by 251 of the Act before us today have a similar chameleon-like quality. The District Court

persuasively explained why they may be appropriately characterized as executive powers. But, when that delegation is held invalid, the "fallback provision" provides that the report that would otherwise be issued by the Comptroller General shall be issued by Congress itself . . . In the event that the resolution is enacted, the congressional report will have the same legal consequences as if it had been issued by the Comptroller General. In that event, moreover, surely no one would suggest that Congress had acted in any capacity other than "legislative." . . .

It is far from novel to acknowledge that independent agencies do indeed exercise legislative powers . . .

Thus, I do not agree that the Comptroller General's responsibilities under the Gramm-Rudman-Hollings Act must be termed "executive powers," or even that our inquiry is much advanced by using that term. For, whatever the label given the functions to be performed by the Comptroller General under 251—or by the Congress under 274—the District Court had no difficulty in concluding that Congress could delegate the performance of those functions to another branch of the Government. If the delegation to a stranger is permissible, why may not Congress delegate the same responsibilities to one of its own agents? That is the central question before us today . . .

The Gramm-Rudman-Hollings Act assigns to the Comptroller General the duty to make policy decisions that have the force of law. The Comptroller General's report is, in the current statute, the engine that gives life to the ambitious budget reduction process. It is the Comptroller General's report that "provide[s] for the determination of reductions" and that "contain[s] estimates, determinations, and specifications for all of the items contained in the report" submitted by the Office of Management and Budget and the Congressional Budget Office. 251(b). It is the Comptroller General's report that the President must follow and that will have conclusive effect. 252. It is, in short, the Comptroller General's report that will have a profound, dramatic, and immediate impact on the Government and on the Nation at large.

Article I of the Constitution specifies the procedures that Congress must follow when it makes policy that binds the Nation: its legislation must be approved by both of its Houses and presented to the President . . .

If Congress were free to delegate its policymaking authority to one of its components, or to one of its agents, it would be able to evade "the carefully crafted restraints spelled out in the Constitution." *Id.*, at 959. That danger—congressional action that evades constitutional restraints—is not present when Congress delegates lawmaking power to the executive or to an independent agency . . .

In my opinion, Congress itself could not exercise the Gramm-Rudman-Hollings functions through a concurrent resolution. The fact that the fallback provision in 274 requires a joint resolution rather than a concurrent resolution indicates that Congress endorsed this view. I think it equally clear that Congress may not simply delegate those functions to an agent such as the Congressional Budget Office. Since I am persuaded that the Comptroller General is also fairly deemed to be an agent of Congress, he too cannot exercise such functions . . .

In short, even though it is well settled that Congress may delegate legislative power to independent agencies or to the Executive, and thereby divest itself of a portion of its lawmaking power, when it elects to exercise such power itself, it may not authorize a lesser representative of the Legislative Branch to act on its behalf. It is for this reason that I believe 251(b) and 251(c)(2) of the Act are unconstitutional . . .

JUSTICE WHITE, dissenting . . .

Before examining the merits of the Court's argument, I wish to emphasize what it is that the Court quite pointedly and correctly does not hold: namely, that "executive" powers of the sort granted the Comptroller by the Act may only be exercised by officers removable at will by the President. The Court's apparent unwillingness to accept this argument, which has been tendered in this Court by the Solicitor General, is fully consistent with the Court's longstanding recognition that it is within the power of Congress under the "Necessary and Proper" Clause, Art. I, 8, to vest authority that falls within the Court's definition of executive power in officers who are not subject to removal at will by the President and are therefore not under the President's direct control. See, e.g., *Humphrey's Executor v. United States, 295 U.S. 602* (1935); *Wiener v. United States, 357 U.S. 349* (1958). In an earlier day, in which simpler notions of the role of government in society prevailed, it was perhaps plausible to insist that all "executive" officers be subject to an unqualified Presidential removal power, *see Myers v. United States 272 U.S. 52* (1926); but with the advent and triumph of the administrative state and the accompanying multiplication of the tasks undertaken by the Federal Government, the Court has been virtually compelled to recognize that Congress may reasonably deem it "necessary and proper" to vest some among the broad new array of governmental functions in officers who are free from the partisanship that may be expected of agents wholly dependent upon the President . . .

It is evident (and nothing in the Court's opinion is to the contrary) that the powers exercised by the Comptroller General under the Gramm-Rudman-Hollings Act are not such that vesting them in an officer not subject to removal at will by the President would in itself improperly interfere with Presidential powers. Determining the level of spending by the Federal Government is not by nature a function central either to the exercise of the President's enumerated powers or to his general duty to ensure execution of the laws; rather, appropriating funds is a peculiarly legislative function, and one expressly committed to Congress by Art. I, 9, which provides that "No Money shall be drawn from the Treasury, but in Consequence of Appropriations made by Law." In enacting Gramm-Rudman-Hollings, Congress has chosen to exercise this legislative power to establish the level of federal spending by providing a detailed set of criteria for reducing expenditures below the level of appropriations in the event that certain conditions are met. Delegating the execution of this legislation—that is, the power to apply the Act's criteria and make the required calculations—to an officer independent of the President's will does not deprive the President of any power that he would otherwise have or that is essential to the performance of the duties of his office. Rather, the result of such a delegation, from the standpoint of the President, is no different from the result of more traditional forms of appropriation: under either system, the level of funds available to the Executive Branch to carry out its duties is not within the President's discretionary control . . .

If, as the Court seems to agree, the assignment of "executive" powers under Gramm-Rudman-Hollings to an officer not removable at will by the President would not in itself represent a violation of the constitutional scheme of separated powers, the question remains whether, as the Court concludes, the fact that the officer to whom Congress has delegated the authority to implement the Act is removable by a joint resolution of Congress should require invalidation of the Act. The Court's decision, as I have stated above, is based on a syllogism: the Act vests the Comptroller with "executive power"; such power may not be exercised by Congress or its agents; the Comptroller is an agent of Congress because he is removable by Congress; therefore the Act is invalid. I have no quarrel with the proposition that the powers exercised by the Comptroller under the Act may be characterized as "executive" in that they involve the interpretation and carrying out of the Act's mandate. I can also accept the general proposition that although Congress has considerable authority in designating the officers who are to execute legislation, see *supra, at 760–764*, the constitutional scheme of separated powers does prevent Congress from reserving an executive role for itself or for its "agents." *Buckley v. Valeo, 424 U.S., at 120–141; id.,* at 267–282 (White, J., concurring in part and dissenting in part). I cannot accept, however, that the exercise of authority by an officer removable for cause by a joint resolution of Congress is analogous to the impermissible execution of the law by Congress itself, nor would I hold

that the congressional role in the removal process renders the Comptroller an "agent" of the Congress, incapable of receiving "executive" power . . .

That a joint resolution removing the Comptroller General would satisfy the requirements for legitimate legislative action laid down in Chadha does not fully answer the separation-of-powers argument, for it is apparent that even the results of the constitutional legislative process may be unconstitutional if those results are in fact destructive of the scheme of separation of powers . . . The question to be answered is whether the threat of removal of the Comptroller General for cause through joint resolution as authorized by the Budget and Accounting Act renders the Comptroller sufficiently subservient to Congress that investing him with "executive" power can be realistically equated with the unlawful retention of such power by Congress itself; more generally, the question is whether there is a genuine threat of "encroachment or aggrandizement of one branch at the expense of the other," *Buckley v. Valeo, 424 U.S., at 122*. Common sense indicates that the existence of the removal provision poses no such threat to the principle of separation of powers. . . .

More importantly, the substantial role played by the President in the process of removal through joint resolution reduces to utter insignificance the possibility that the threat of removal will induce subservience to the Congress. As I have pointed out above, a joint resolution must be presented to the President and is ineffective if it is vetoed by him, unless the veto is overridden by the constitutionally prescribed two-thirds majority of both Houses of Congress. The requirement of Presidential approval obviates the possibility that the Comptroller will perceive himself as so completely at the mercy of Congress that he will function as its tool. If the Comptroller's conduct in office is not so unsatisfactory to the President as to convince the latter that removal is required under the statutory standard, Congress will have no independent power to coerce the Comptroller unless it can muster a two-thirds majority in both Houses—a feat of bi-partisanship more difficult than that required to impeach and convict. The incremental in terrorem effect of the possibility of congressional removal in the face of a Presidential veto is therefore exceedingly unlikely to have any discernible impact on the extent of congressional influence over the Comptroller . . .

The practical result of the removal provision is not to render the Comptroller unduly dependent upon or subservient to Congress, but to render him one of the most independent officers in the entire federal establishment. Those who have studied the office agree that the procedural and substantive limits on the power of Congress and the President to remove the Comptroller make dislodging him against his will practically impossible. As one scholar put it nearly 50 years ago: "Under the statute the Comptroller General, once confirmed, is safe so long as he avoids a public exhibition of personal immorality, dishonesty, or failing mentality." H. Mansfield, The Comptroller General 75–76 (1939). The passage of time has done little to cast doubt on this view of the six Comptrollers who have served since 1921, none has been threatened with, much less subjected to, removal. Recent students of the office concur that "[b]arring resignation, death, physical or mental incapacity, or extremely bad behavior, the Comptroller General is assured his tenure if he wants it, and not a day more." F. Mosher, The GAO 242 (1979). The threat of "here-and-now subservience," *ante*, at 720, is obviously remote indeed . . .

Realistic consideration of the nature of the Comptroller General's relation to Congress thus reveals that the threat to separation of powers conjured up by the majority is wholly chimerical. The power over removal retained by the Congress is not a power that is exercised outside the legislative process as established by the Constitution, nor does it appear likely that it is a power that adds significantly to the influence Congress may exert over executive officers through other, undoubtedly constitutional exercises of legislative power and through the constitutionally guaranteed impeachment power . . .

The majority's contrary conclusion rests on the rigid dogma that, outside of the impeachment process, any "direct congressional role in the removal of officers charged with the execution of the laws . . . is inconsistent with separation of powers." *Ante*, at 723. Reliance on such an unyielding principle to strike down a statute posing no real danger of aggrandizement of congressional power is extremely misguided and insensitive to our constitutional role. The wisdom of vesting "executive" powers in an officer removable by joint resolution may indeed be debatable—as may be the wisdom of the entire scheme of permitting an unelected official to revise the budget enacted by Congress—but such matters are for the most part to be worked out between the Congress and the President through the legislative process, which affords each branch ample opportunity to defend its interests. The Act vesting budget-cutting authority in the Comptroller General represents Congress' judgment that the delegation of such authority to counteract ever-mounting deficits is "necessary and proper" to the exercise of the powers granted the Federal Government by the Constitution; and the President's approval of the statute signifies his unwillingness to reject the choice made by Congress . . . Under such circumstances, the role of this Court should be limited to determining whether the Act so alters the balance of authority among the branches of government as to pose a genuine threat to the basic division between the lawmaking power and the power to execute the law. Because I see no such threat, I cannot join the Court in striking down the Act . . .

JUSTICE BLACKMUN, dissenting . . .

. . . Appellees have not sought invalidation of the 1921 provision that authorizes Congress to remove the Comptroller General by joint resolution; indeed, it is far from clear they would have standing to request such a judgment. The only relief sought in this case is nullification of the automatic budget-reduction provisions of the Deficit Control Act, and that relief should not be awarded even if the Court is correct that those provisions are constitutionally incompatible with Congress' authority to remove the Comptroller General by joint resolution. Any incompatibility, I feel, should be cured by refusing to allow congressional removal—if it ever is attempted—and not by striking down the central provisions of the Deficit Control Act. However wise or foolish it may be, that statute unquestionably ranks among the most important federal enactments of the past several decades. I cannot see the sense of invalidating legislation of this magnitude in order to preserve a cumbersome, 65-year-old removal power that has never been exercised and appears to have been all but forgotten until this litigation . . . .

Domestic Policy

The five cases presented in this chapter deal with varying aspects of presidential power in the realm of domestic policy and rights, including cargo transport, free press, electronic surveillance, presidential documents, and the publishing rights of a former government employee. It is no coincidence that, in three of these cases, presidents lost in court. In the two instances where presidents prevailed, the key factor helping them involved national security or foreign policy: in *Chicago & Southern Airlines*, the court deferred to the president's commander-in-chief power; in the *Snepp* case, Frank Snepp was a former Central Intelligence Agency agent bound by a prior agreement, which he signed as part of his employment by the government, designed to avoid the release of information that might compromise national security. Although one often thinks of domestic and foreign policy as two different and separate policy realms, these cases show the extent to which foreign policy issues or concerns can affect domestic policy and therefore how the courts are liable to treat presidents attempting to legitimate their domestic actions by linking them to foreign policy or national security concerns.

When the Congress created the Civil Aeronautics Board (CAB), it gave the board special power to give American

companies permission to engage in international air transport. According to the law passed by the Congress, the CAB exercised this power differently for domestic than for foreign air transportation: In domestic travel, presidential review of CAB decisions was not required, but it was required in cases of international transport, as well as for foreign carriers that wished to fly into the United States. The CAB granted such a permission for international transport, called a "certificate of convenience and necessity," to Chicago & Southern Airlines but denied one to a business rival, the Waterman Steamship Corporation. This caused Waterman to sue in court. Chicago Airlines countered that, since the president had approved both decisions, the court had no right to review the decision. In this case, the Court sided with the CAB's and the President's decisions, in the process giving its approval to what it labeled an "unparalleled" administrative arrangement. The Court concluded, somewhat surprisingly, that it did not have the power to review the CAB's decisions pertaining to international flights, either before or after they were reviewed by the president, owing to the Court's view that the matter was political (and therefore outside of its jurisdiction), to the president's greater power in foreign policy matters arising from his powers as commander in chief and as "the Nation's organ in foreign affairs" (see the Curtiss-Wright *case), and to Congress's express power to regulate foreign commerce.*

Chicago & Southern Air Lines v. Waterman Steamship Corp.
333 U.S. 103 (1948)

Mr. Justice Jackson delivered the opinion of the Court. . . .

In the regulation of commercial aeronautics, the statute confers on the [Civil Aeronautics] Board many powers conventional in other carrier regulation under the Congressional commerce power. They are exercised through usual procedures and apply settled standards with only customary administrative finality. Congress evidently thought of the administrative function in terms used by this Court of another of its agencies in exercising interstate commerce power: 'Such a body cannot in any proper sense be characterized as an arm or an eye of the executive. Its duties are performed without executive leave and, in the contemplation of the statute, must be free from executive control.' . . . Those orders which do not require Presidential approval are subject to judicial review to assure application of the standards Congress has laid down.

But when a foreign carrier seeks to engage in public carriage over the territory or waters of this country, or any carrier seeks the sponsorship of this Government to engage in overseas or foreign air transportation, Congress has completely inverted the usual administrative process. Instead of acting independently of executive control, the agency is then subordinated to it. Instead of its order serving as a final disposition of the application, its force is exhausted when it serves as a recommendation to the President. Instead of being handed down to the parties as the conclusion of the administrative process, it must be submitted to the President, before publication even can take place. Nor is the President's control of the ultimate decision a mere right of veto. It is not alone issuance of such authorizations that are subject to his approval, but denial, transfer, amendment, cancellation or suspension, as well. And likewise subject to his approval are the terms, conditions and limitations of the order. . . . Thus, Presidential control is not limited to a negative but is a positive and detailed control over the Board's decisions, unparalleled in the history of American administrative bodies.

Congress may of course delegate very large grants of its power over foreign commerce to the President. . . . The President also possesses in his own right certain powers conferred by the Constitution on him as Commander-in-Chief and as the Nation's organ in foreign affairs. For present purposes, the order draws vitality from either or both sources. Legislative and Executive powers are pooled obviously to the end that commercial strategic and diplomatic interests of the country may be coordinated and advanced without collision or deadlock between agencies.

These considerations seem controlling on the question whether the Board's action on overseas and foreign air transportation applications by citizens are subject to revision or overthrow by the courts.

It may be conceded that a literal reading of 1006 subjects this order to re-examination by the courts. It also appears that the language was deliberately employed by Congress, although nothing indicates that Congress foresaw or intended the consequences ascribed to it by the decision of the Court below. The letter of the text might with equal consistency be construed to require any one of three things: first, judicial review of a decision by the President; second, judicial review of a Board order before it acquires finality through Presidential action, the court's decision on review being a binding limitation on the President's action; third, a judicial review before action by the President, the latter being at liberty wholly to disregard the court's judgment. We think none of these results is required by usual canons of construction.

In this case, submission of the Board's decision was made to the President, who disapproved certain portions of it and advised the Board of the changes which he required. The Board complied and submitted a revised order and opinion which the President approved. Only then were they made public, and that which was made public and which is before us is only the final order and opinion containing the President's amendments and bearing his approval. Only at that stage was review sought, and only then could it be pursued, for then only was the decision consummated, announced and available to the parties.

While the changes made at direction of the President may be identified, the reasons therefor are not disclosed beyond the statement that 'because of certain factors relating to our broad national welfare and other matters for which the Chief Executive has special responsibility, he has reached conclusions which require' changes in the Board's opinion.

The court below considered, and we think quite rightly, that it could not review such provisions of the order as resulted from Presidential direction. The President, both as Commander-in-Chief and as the Nation's organ for foreign affairs, has available intelligence services whose reports neither are nor ought to be published to the world. It would be intolerable that courts, without the relevant information, should review and perhaps nullify actions of the Executive taken on information properly held secret. Nor can courts sit in camera [confidential review by judge—ed.] in order to be taken into executive confidences. But even if courts could require full disclosure, the very nature of executive decisions as to foreign policy is political, not judicial. Such decisions are wholly confided by our Constitution to the political departments of the government, Executive and Legislative. They are delicate, complex, and involve large elements of prophecy. They are and should be undertaken only by those directly responsible to the people whose welfare they advance or imperil. They are decisions of a kind for which the Judiciary has neither aptitude, facilities nor responsibility and have long been held to belong in the domain of political power not subject to judicial intrusion or inquiry. . . . We therefore agree that whatever of this order emanates from the President is not susceptible of review by the Judicial Department. . . .

Until the decision of the Board has Presidential approval, it grants no privilege and denies no right. It can give nothing and can take nothing away from the applicant or a competitor. It may be a step, which if erroneous will mature into a prejudicial result, as an order fixing valuations in a rate proceeding may foreshow and compel a prejudicial rate order. But administrative orders are not reviewable unless and until they impose an obligation, deny a right or fix some legal relationship as a consummation of the administrative process. . . . The dilemma faced by those who demand judicial review of the Board's order is that, before Presidential approval, it is not a final determination even of the Board's ultimate action, and after Presidential approval, the whole order, both in what is approved without change, as well as in amendments which he directs, derives its vitality from the exercise of unreviewable Presidential discretion. . . .

To revise or review an administrative decision, which has only the force of a recommendation to the President, would be to render an advisory opinion in its most obnoxious form—advice that the President has not asked, tendered at the demand of a private litigant, on a subject concededly within the President's exclusive, ultimate control. This Court early and wisely determined that it would not give advisory opinions even when asked by the Chief Executive. It has also been the firm and unvarying practice of Constitutional Courts to render no judgments not binding and conclusive on the parties and none that are subject to later review or alteration by administrative action. . . .

We conclude that orders of the Board as to certificate for overseas or foreign air transportation are not mature and are therefore not susceptible to judicial review at anytime before they are finalized by Presidential approval. After such approval has been given, the final orders embody Presidential discretion as to political matters beyond the competence of the courts to adjudicate. This makes it unnecessary to examine the other questions raised. The petition of the Waterman Steamship Corp. should be dismissed.

Judgment reversed. . . .

In 1971, former Defense Department employee Daniel Ellsberg gave to several newspapers copies of a secret government report chronicling the long history of America's involvement in Vietnam. When the New York Times *began publication of report excerpts, the Nixon administration immediately obtained a restraining order to bar the* Times *and other newspapers from further publication. The imposition of this "prior restraint" by the federal government represented an unprecedented attempt by the president to bar further publication on the grounds that publication of the report would irreparably harm national security. Yet this injunction squarely collided with the First Amendment free press protection, considered a cornerstone of democracy. The case moved rapidly through the lower courts. In a 6 to 3 opinion, the majority rejected Nixon's effort to censor the press, saying that Nixon had failed to show that drastic and specific harm would ensue if the papers were published and noting also that the Congress had never given the president in law the power to stop publication during national emergencies. Note also that the Court showed little sympathy to arguments that the president could censor the press based on his constitutional powers in foreign policy. The three dissenters objected to the haste with which the case had been handled. This case, often referred to as The Pentagon Papers case, was a ringing affirmation of press freedom and a rejection of efforts by the president, and the government generally, to impose a "prior restraint."*

New York Times Co. v. United States
403 U.S. 713 (1971)

Mr. Justice Black, with whom
Mr. Justice Douglas joins, concurring.

. . . I believe that every moment's continuance of the injunctions against these newspapers amounts to a flagrant, indefensible, and continuing violation of the First Amendment. Furthermore, after oral argument, I agree completely that we must affirm the judgment of the Court of Appeals for the District of Columbia Circuit and reverse the judgment of the Court of Appeals for the Second Circuit for the reasons stated by my Brothers DOUGLAS and BRENNAN. In my view it is unfortunate that some of my Brethren are apparently willing to hold that the publication of news may sometimes be enjoined. Such a holding would make a shambles of the First Amendment.

. . . Now, for the first time in the 182 years since the founding of the Republic, the federal courts are asked to hold that the First Amendment does not mean what it says, but rather means that the Government can halt the publication of current news of vital importance to the people of this country.

In seeking injunctions against these newspapers and in its presentation to the Court, the Executive Branch seems to have forgotten the essential purpose and history of the First Amendment. When the Constitution was adopted, many people strongly opposed it because the document contained no Bill of Rights to safeguard certain basic freedoms. They especially feared that the new powers granted to a central government might be interpreted to permit the government to curtail freedom of religion, press, assembly, and speech. In response to an overwhelming public clamor, James Madison offered a series of amendments to satisfy citizens that these great liberties would remain safe and beyond the power of government to abridge. Madison proposed what later became the First Amendment in three parts, two of which are set out below, and one of which proclaimed: "The people shall not be deprived or abridged of their right to speak, to write, or to publish their sentiments; and the freedom of the press, as one of the great bulwarks of liberty, shall be inviolable." The amendments were offered to curtail and restrict the general powers granted to the Executive, Legislative, and Judicial Branches two years before in the original Constitution. The Bill of Rights changed the original Constitution into a new charter under which no branch of government could abridge the people's freedoms of press, speech, religion, and assembly. Yet the Solicitor General argues and some members of the Court appear to agree that the general powers of the Government adopted in the original Constitution should be interpreted to limit and restrict the specific and emphatic guarantees of the Bill of Rights adopted later. I can imagine no greater perversion of history. Madison and the other Framers of the First Amendment, able men that they were, wrote in language they earnestly believed could never be misunderstood: "Congress shall make no law . . . abridging the freedom . . . of the press . . . ." Both the history and language of the First Amendment support the view that the press must be left free to publish news, whatever the source, without censorship, injunctions, or prior restraints.

In the First Amendment the Founding Fathers gave the free press the protection it must have to fulfill its essential role in our democracy. The press was to serve the governed, not the governors. The Government's power to censor the press was abolished so that the press would remain forever free to censure the Government. The press was protected so that it could bare the secrets of government and inform the people. Only a free and unrestrained press can effectively expose deception in government. And paramount among the responsibilities of a free press is the duty to prevent any part of the government from deceiving the people and sending them off to distant lands to die of foreign fevers and foreign shot and shell. In my view, far from deserving condemnation for their courageous reporting, the New York Times, the Washington Post, and other newspapers should be commended for serving the purpose that the Founding Fathers saw so clearly. In revealing the workings of government that led to the Vietnam war, the newspapers nobly did precisely that which the Founders hoped and trusted they would do. . . .

[W]e are asked to hold that despite the First Amendment's emphatic command, the Executive Branch, the Congress, and the Judiciary can make laws enjoining [preventing] publication of current news and abridging freedom of the press in the name of "national security." The Government does not even attempt to rely on any act of Congress. Instead it makes the bold and dangerously far-reaching contention that the courts should take it upon themselves to "make" a law abridging freedom of the press in the name of equity, presidential power and national security, even when the representatives of the people in Congress have adhered to the command of the First Amendment and refused to make such a law. . . . To find that the President has "inherent power" to halt the publication of news by resort to the courts would wipe out the First Amendment and destroy the fundamental liberty and security of the very people the Government

hopes to make "secure." No one can read the history of the adoption of the First Amendment without being convinced beyond any doubt that it was injunctions like those sought here that Madison and his collaborators intended to outlaw in this Nation for all time. . . .

Mr. Justice Douglas, with whom
Mr. Justice Black joins, concurring.

. . . It should be noted at the outset that the First Amendment provides that "Congress shall make no law . . . abridging the freedom of speech, or of the press." That leaves, in my view, no room for governmental restraint on the press. There is, moreover, no statute barring the publication by the press of the material which the Times and the Post seek to use. . . . So any power that the Government possesses must come from its "inherent power."

The power to wage war is "the power to wage war successfully." But the war power stems from a declaration of war. The Constitution by Art. I, 8, gives Congress, not the President, power "[t]o declare War." Nowhere are presidential wars authorized. We need not decide therefore what leveling effect the war power of Congress might have.

These disclosures may have a serious impact. But that is no basis for sanctioning a previous restraint on the press. . . . The Government says that it has inherent powers to go into court and obtain an injunction to protect the national interest, which in this case is alleged to be national security. *Near v. Minnesota*, repudiated that expansive doctrine in no uncertain terms.

The dominant purpose of the First Amendment was to prohibit the widespread practice of governmental suppression of embarrassing information. It is common knowledge that the First Amendment was adopted against the widespread use of the common law of seditious libel to punish the dissemination of material that is embarrassing to the powers-that-be. . . .

Secrecy in government is fundamentally anti-democratic, perpetuating bureaucratic errors. Open debate and discussion of public issues are vital to our national health. On public questions there should be "uninhibited, robust, and wide-open" debate. *New York Times Co. v. Sullivan.* . . .

Mr. Justice Brennan, concurring.

. . . The error that has pervaded these cases from the outset was the granting of any injunctive relief whatsoever, interim or otherwise. The entire thrust of the Government's claim throughout these cases has been that publication of the material sought to be enjoined "could," or "might," or "may" prejudice the national interest in various ways. But the First Amendment tolerates absolutely no prior judicial restraints of the press predicated upon surmise or conjecture that untoward consequences may result. Our cases, it is true, have indicated that there is a single, extremely narrow class of cases in which the First Amendment's ban on prior judicial restraint may be overridden. Our cases have thus far indicated that such cases may arise only when the Nation "is at war," *Schenck v. United States* (1919), during which times "[n]o one would question but that a government might prevent actual obstruction to its recruiting service or the publication of the sailing dates of transports or the number and location of troops." *Near v. Minnesota* (1931). Even if the present world situation were assumed to be tantamount to a time of war, or if the power of presently available armaments would justify even in peacetime the suppression of information that would set in motion a nuclear holocaust, in neither of these actions has the Government presented or even alleged that publication of items from or based upon the material at issue would cause the happening of an event of that nature. . . .

Mr. Justice Stewart, with whom Mr. Justice White joins, concurring.

In the governmental structure created by our Constitution, the Executive is endowed with enormous power in the two related areas of national defense and international relations. This power, largely unchecked by the Legislative and Judicial branches, has been pressed to the very hilt since the advent of the nuclear missile age. For better or for worse, the simple fact is that a President of the United States possesses vastly greater constitutional independence in these two vital areas of power than does, say, a prime minister of a country with a parliamentary from of government.

In the absence of the governmental checks and balances present in other areas of our national life, the only effective restraint upon executive policy and power in the areas of national defense and international affairs may lie in an enlightened citizenry— in an informed and critical public opinion which alone can here protect the values of democratic government. For this reason, it is perhaps here that a press that is alert, aware, and free most vitally serves the basic purpose of the First Amendment. For without an informed and free press there cannot be an enlightened people.

Yet it is elementary that the successful conduct of international diplomacy and the maintenance of an effective national defense require both confidentiality and secrecy. Other nations can hardly deal with this Nation in an atmosphere of mutual trust unless they can be assured that their confidences will be kept. And within our own executive departments, the development of considered and intelligent international policies would be impossible if those charged with their formulation could not communicate with each other freely, frankly, and in confidence. In the area of basic national defense the frequent need for absolute secrecy is, of course, self-evident.

I think there can be but one answer to this dilemma, if dilemma it be. The responsibility must be where the power is. If the Constitution gives the Executive a large degree of unshared power in the conduct of foreign affairs and the maintenance of our national defense, then under the Constitution the Executive must have the largely unshared duty to determine and preserve the degree of internal security necessary to exercise that power successfully. It is an awesome responsibility, requiring judgment and wisdom of a high order. I should suppose that moral, political, and practical considerations would dictate that a very first principle of that wisdom would be an insistence upon avoiding secrecy for its own sake. For when everything is classified, then nothing is classified, and the system becomes one to be disregarded by the cynical or the careless, and to be manipulated by those intent on self-protection or self-promotion. I should suppose, in short, that the hallmark of a truly effective internal security system would be the maximum possible disclosure, recognizing that secrecy can best be preserved only when credibility is truly maintained. But be that as it may, it is clear to me that it is the constitutional duty of the Executive—as a matter of sovereign prerogative and not as a matter of law as the courts know law—through the promulgation and enforcement of executive regulations, to protect the confidentiality necessary to carry out its responsibilities in the fields of international relations and national defense.

This is not to say that Congress and the courts have no role to play. Undoubtedly Congress has the power to enact specific and appropriate criminal laws to protect government property and preserve government secrets. Congress has passed such laws, and several of them are of very colorable relevance to the apparent circumstances of these cases. And if a criminal prosecution is instituted, it will be the responsibility of the courts to decide the applicability of the criminal law under which the charge is brought. Moreover, if Congress should pass a specific law authorizing civil proceedings in this field, the courts would likewise have the duty to decide the constitutionality of such a law as well as its applicability to the facts proved.

But in the cases before us we are asked neither to construe specific regulations nor to apply specific laws. We are asked, instead, to perform a function that the Constitution gave to the Executive, not the Judiciary. We are asked, quite simply, to prevent the publication by two newspapers of material that the Executive Branch insists should not, in the national interest, be published. I am convinced that the Executive is correct with respect to some of the documents involved. But I cannot say that

disclosure of any of them will surely result in direct, immediate, and irreparable damage to our Nation or its people. That being so, there can under the First Amendment be but one judicial resolution of the issues before us. I join the judgments of the Court. . . .

Mr. Justice White, with whom Mr. Justice Stewart joins, concurring.

I concur in today's judgments, but only because of the concededly extraordinary protection against prior restraints enjoyed by the press under our constitutional system. I do not say that in no circumstances would the First Amendment permit an injunction against publishing information about government plans or operations. Nor, after examining the materials the Government characterizes as the most sensitive and destructive, can I deny that revelation of these documents will do substantial damage to public interests. Indeed, I am confident that their disclosure will have that result. But I nevertheless agree that the United States has not satisfied the very heavy burden that it must meet to warrant an injunction against publication in these cases, at least in the absence of express and appropriately limited congressional authorization for prior restraints in circumstances such as these.

The Government's position is simply stated: The responsibility of the Executive for the conduct of the foreign affairs and for the security of the Nation is so basic that the President is entitled to an injunction against publication of a newspaper story whenever he can convince a court that the information to be revealed threatens "grave and irreparable" injury to the public interest; and the injunction should issue whether or not the material to be published is classified, whether or not publication would be lawful under relevant criminal statutes enacted by Congress, and regardless of the circumstances by which the newspaper came into possession of the information.

At least in the absence of legislation by Congress, based on its own investigations and findings, I am quite unable to agree that the inherent powers of the Executive and the courts reach so far as to authorize remedies having such sweeping potential for inhibiting publications by the press. . . .

Mr. Justice Marshall, concurring.

. . .The Government argues that in addition to the inherent power of any government to protect itself, the President's power to conduct foreign affairs and his position as Commander in Chief give him authority to impose censorship on the press to protect his ability to deal effectively with foreign nations and to conduct the military affairs of the country. Of course, it is beyond cavil that the President has broad powers by virtue of his primary responsibility for the conduct of our foreign affairs and his position as Commander in Chief. . . . And in some situations it may be that under whatever inherent powers the Government may have, as well as the implicit authority derived from the President's mandate to conduct foreign affairs and to act as Commander in Chief, there is a basis for the invocation of the equity jurisdiction of this Court as an aid to prevent the publication of material damaging to "national security," however that term may be defined.

It would, however, be utterly inconsistent with the concept of separation of powers for this Court to use its power of contempt to prevent behavior that Congress has specifically declined to prohibit. There would be a similar damage to the basic concept of these co-equal branches of Government if when the Executive Branch has adequate authority granted by Congress to protect "national security" it can choose instead to invoke the contempt power of a court to enjoin the threatened conduct. The Constitution provides that Congress shall make laws, the President execute laws, and courts interpret laws. *Youngstown Sheet & Tube Co. v. Sawyer* (1952). It did not provide for government by injunction in which the courts and the Executive Branch can "make law" without regard to the action of Congress. It may be more convenient for the Executive Branch if it need only convince a judge to prohibit conduct rather than ask the Congress to pass a law, and it may be more convenient to

enforce a contempt order than to seek a criminal conviction in a jury trial. Moreover, it may be considered politically wise to get a court to share the responsibility for arresting those who the Executive Branch has probable cause to believe are violating the law. But convenience and political considerations of the moment do not justify a basic departure from the principles of our system of government.

In these cases we are not faced with a situation where Congress has failed to provide the Executive with broad power to protect the Nation from disclosure of damaging state secrets. Congress has on several occasions given extensive consideration to the problem of protecting the military and strategic secrets of the United States. This consideration has resulted in the enactment of statutes making it a crime to receive, disclose, communicate, withhold, and publish certain documents, photographs, instruments, appliances, and information. . . .

Either the Government has the power under statutory grant to use traditional criminal law to protect the country or, if there is no basis for arguing that Congress has made the activity a crime, it is plain that Congress has specifically refused to grant the authority the Government seeks from this Court. In either case this Court does not have authority to grant the requested relief. It is not for this Court to fling itself into every breach perceived by some Government official nor is it for this Court to take on itself the burden of enacting law, especially a law that Congress has refused to pass. . . .

MR. JUSTICE HARLAN, with whom THE CHIEF JUSTICE and MR. JUSTICE BLACKMUN join, dissenting.

. . . With all respect, I consider that the Court has been almost irresponsibly feverish in dealing with these cases.

Both the Court of Appeals for the Second Circuit and the Court of Appeals for the District of Columbia Circuit rendered judgment on June 23. The New York Times' petition for certiorari, its motion for accelerated consideration thereof, and its application for interim relief were filed in this

Court on June 24 at about 11 a.m. The application of the United States for interim relief in the Post case was also filed here on June 24 at about 7:15 p.m. This Court's order setting a hearing before us on June 26 at 11 a.m., a course which I joined only to avoid the possibility of even more peremptory action by the Court, was issued less than 24 hours before. The record in the [Washington] Post case was filed with the Clerk shortly before 1 p.m. on June 25; the record in the Times case did not arrive until 7 or 8 o'clock that same night. The briefs of the parties were received less than two hours before argument on June 26.

This frenzied train of events took place in the name of the presumption against prior restraints created by the First Amendment. Due regard for the extraordinarily important and difficult questions involved in these litigations should have led the Court to shun such a precipitate timetable. . . .

Forced as I am to reach the merits of these cases, I dissent from the opinion and judgments of the Court. Within the severe limitations imposed by the time constraints under which I have been required to operate, I can only state my reasons in telescoped form, even though in different circumstances I would have felt constrained to deal with the cases in the fuller sweep indicated above.

It is a sufficient basis for affirming the Court of Appeals for the Second Circuit in the Times litigation to observe that its order must rest on the conclusion that because of the time elements the Government had not been given an adequate opportunity to present its case to the District Court. At the least this conclusion was not an abuse of discretion. . . .

In a speech on the floor of the House of Representatives, Chief Justice John Marshall, then a member of that body, stated:

> "The President is the sole organ of the nation in its external relations, and its sole representative with foreign nations." 10 Annals of Cong. 613 (1800).

From that time, shortly after the founding of the Nation, to this, there has been no substantial challenge to this description of the scope of executive power. . . .

The power to evaluate the "pernicious influence" of premature disclosure is not, however, lodged in the Executive alone. I agree that, in performance of its duty to protect the values of the First Amendment against political pressures, the judiciary must review the initial Executive determination to the point of satisfying itself that the subject matter of the dispute does lie within the proper compass of the President's foreign relations power. Constitutional considerations forbid "a complete abandonment of judicial control." Moreover, the judiciary may properly insist that the determination that disclosure of the subject matter would irreparably impair the national security be made by the head of the Executive Department concerned— here the Secretary of State or the Secretary of Defense—after actual personal consideration by that officer. This safeguard is required in the analogous area of executive claims of privilege for secrets of state.

But in my judgment the judiciary may not properly go beyond these two inquiries and redetermine for itself the probable impact of disclosure on the national security. . . .

Even if there is some room for the judiciary to override the executive determination, it is plain that the scope of review must be exceedingly narrow. I can see no indication in the opinions of either the District Court or the Court of Appeals in the Post litigation that the conclusions of the Executive were given even the deference owing to an administrative agency, much less that owing to a co-equal branch of the Government operating within the field of its constitutional prerogative. . . .

Pending further hearings in each case conducted under the appropriate ground rules, I would continue the restraints on publication. I cannot believe that the doctrine prohibiting prior restraints reaches to the point of preventing courts from maintaining the status quo long enough to act responsibly in matters of such national importance as those involved here. . . .

Mr. JUSTICE BLACKMUN, dissenting.

I join Mr. Justice Harlan in his dissent. I also am in substantial accord with much that Mr. Justice White says, by way of admonition, in the latter part of his opinion.

. . . The New York Times clandestinely devoted a period of three months to examining the 47 volumes that came into its unauthorized possession. Once it had begun publication of material from those volumes, the New York case now before us emerged. It immediately assumed, and ever since has maintained, a frenetic pace and character. Seemingly, once publication started, the material could not be made public fast enough. Seemingly, from then on, every deferral or delay, by restraint or otherwise, was abhorrent and was to be deemed violative of the First Amendment and of the public's "right immediately to know." Yet that newspaper stood before us at oral argument and professed criticism of the Government for not lodging its protest earlier than by a Monday telegram following the initial Sunday publication. . . .

With such respect as may be due to the contrary view, this, in my opinion, is not the way to try a lawsuit of this magnitude and asserted importance. It is not the way for federal courts to adjudicate, and to be required to adjudicate, issues that allegedly concern the Nation's vital welfare. The country would be none the worse off were the cases tried quickly, to be sure, but in the customary and properly deliberative manner. The most recent of the material, it is said, dates no later than 1968, already about three years ago, and the Times itself took three months to formulate its plan of procedure and, thus, deprived its public for that period.

The First Amendment, after all, is only one part of an entire Constitution. Article II of the great document vests in the Executive Branch primary power over the conduct of foreign affairs and places in that branch the responsibility for the Nation's safety. Each provision of the Constitution is important, and I cannot subscribe to a doctrine of unlimited absolutism for the First Amendment at the cost of downgrading other provisions. First Amendment absolutism has never commanded a majority of this Court. See, for example, *Near v. Minnesota* (1931), and *Schenck v. United States* (1919). What is needed here is a weighing, upon properly developed standards, of the broad right of the press to print and of the very narrow right of the Government to prevent. Such standards are not yet developed. The parties here are in disagreement as to what those standards should be. But even the newspapers concede that there are situations where restraint is in order and is constitutional. Mr. Justice Holmes gave us a suggestion when he said in Schenck,

"It is a question of proximity and degree. When a nation is at war many things that might be said in time of peace are such a hindrance to its effort that their utterance will not be endured so long as men fight and that no Court could regard them as protected by any constitutional right."

I therefore would remand these cases to be developed expeditiously, of course, but on a schedule permitting the orderly presentation of evidence from both sides, with the use of discovery, if necessary, as authorized by the rules, and with the preparation of briefs, oral argument, and court opinions of a quality better than has been seen to this point. . . .

It may well be that if these cases were allowed to develop as they should be developed, and to be tried as lawyers should try them and as courts should hear them, free of pressure and panic and sensationalism, other light would be shed on the situation and contrary considerations, for me, might prevail. But that is not the present posture of the litigation. . . .

Three people were charged with conspiring to destroy government property in an action taken as a protest to the Vietnam War; one of the three was charged with dynamiting a Central Intelligence Agency office in Ann Arbor, Michigan. Key evidence implicating the three was obtained by the government through electronic surveillance conducted without a warrant. The defendants challenged the legality of the information obtained through the warrantless surveillance as a violation of their Fourth Amendment protection against warrantless searches and seizures, but the Nixon Justice Department argued that the surveillance was legal because the threat of domestic terrorism justified the government's actions under the president's power to protect national security and also under a 1968 law, the Omnibus Crime Control and Safe Streets Act. The Court rejected the government's arguments (and in doing so upheld lower court rulings), saying that, in the case of "domestic aspects of national security," warrantless information could not be used, although the Court was careful to separate this ruling from possible threats from abroad, where the president's power is considered greater.

United States v. United States District Court
407 U.S. 297 (1972)

Mr. Justice Powell delivered the opinion of the Court. . . .

Title III of the Omnibus Crime Control and Safe Streets Act, 18 U.S.C. 2510–2520, authorizes the use of electronic surveillance for classes of crimes carefully specified in 18 U.S.C. 2516. Such surveillance is subject to prior court order. Section 2518 sets forth the detailed and particularized application necessary to obtain such an order as well as carefully circumscribed conditions for its use. The Act represents a comprehensive attempt by Congress to promote more effective control of crime while protecting the privacy of individual thought and expression. . . .

The Government relies on 2511 (3). It argues that "in excepting national security surveillances from the Act's warrant requirement Congress recognized the President's authority to conduct such surveillances without prior judicial approval." Brief for United States 7, 28. The section thus is viewed as a recognition or affirmance of a constitutional authority in the President to conduct warrantless domestic security surveillance such as that involved in this case.

We think the language of 2511 (3), as well as the legislative history of the statute, refutes this interpretation. The relevant language is that:

> "Nothing contained in this chapter . . . shall limit the constitutional power of the President to take such measures as he deems necessary to protect . . ."

against the dangers specified. At most, this is an implicit recognition that the President does have certain powers in the specified areas. Few would doubt this, as the section refers—among other things—to protection "against actual or potential attack or other hostile acts of a foreign power." But so far as the use of the President's electronic surveillance power is concerned, the language is essentially neutral.

Section 2511 (3) certainly confers no power, as the language is wholly inappropriate for such a purpose. It merely provides that the Act shall not be interpreted to limit or disturb such power as the President may have under the Constitution. In short, Congress simply left presidential powers where it found them. . . .

In view of these and other interrelated provisions delineating permissible interceptions of particular criminal activity upon carefully specified conditions, it would have been incongruous for Congress to have legislated with respect to the important and complex area of national security in a single brief and nebulous paragraph. This would not comport with the sensitivity of the problem involved or with the extraordinary care Congress exercised in drafting other sections of the Act. We therefore think the conclusion inescapable that Congress only intended to make clear that the Act simply did not legislate with respect to national security surveillances. . . .

It is important at the outset to emphasize the limited nature of the question before the Court. This case raises no constitutional challenge to electronic surveillance as specifically authorized by Title III of the Omnibus Crime Control and Safe Streets Act of 1968. Nor is there any question or doubt as to the necessity of obtaining a warrant in the surveillance of crimes unrelated to the national security interest. Further, the instant case requires no judgment on the scope of the President's surveillance power with respect to the activities of foreign powers, within or without this country. The Attorney General's affidavit in this case states that the surveillances were "deemed necessary to protect the nation from attempts of domestic organizations to attack and subvert the existing structure of Government." There is no evidence of any involvement, directly or indirectly, of a foreign power. . . .

We begin the inquiry by noting that the President of the United States has the fundamental duty, under Art. II, 1, of the Constitution, to "preserve, protect and defend the Constitution of the United States." Implicit in that duty is the power to protect our Government against those who would subvert or overthrow it by unlawful means. In the discharge of this duty, the President—through the Attorney General—may find it necessary to employ electronic surveillance to obtain intelligence information on the plans of those who plot unlawful acts against the Government. The use of such surveillance in internal security cases has been sanctioned more or less continuously by various Presidents and Attorneys General since July 1946. Herbert Brownell, Attorney General under President Eisenhower, urged the use of electronic surveillance both in internal and international security matters on the grounds that those acting against the Government

> "turn to the telephone to carry on their intrigue. The success of their plans frequently rests upon piecing together shreds of information received from many sources and many nests. The participants in the conspiracy are often dispersed and stationed in various strategic positions in government and industry throughout the country."

Though the Government and respondents debate their seriousness and magnitude, threats and acts of sabotage against the Government exist in sufficient number to justify investigative powers with respect to them. The covertness and complexity of potential unlawful conduct against the Government and the necessary dependency of many conspirators

upon the telephone make electronic surveillance an effective investigatory instrument in certain circumstances. The marked acceleration in technological developments and sophistication in their use have resulted in new techniques for the planning, commission, and concealment of criminal activities. It would be contrary to the public interest for Government to deny to itself the prudent and lawful employment of those very techniques which are employed against the Government and its law-abiding citizens.

> It has been said that "[t]he most basic function of any government is to provide for the security of the individual and of his property." *Miranda v. Arizona, 384 U.S. 436, 539* (1966) (WHITE, J., dissenting). And unless Government safeguards its own capacity to function and to preserve the security of its people, society itself could become so disordered that all rights and liberties would be endangered. . . .

But a recognition of these elementary truths does not make the employment by Government of electronic surveillance a welcome development—even when employed with restraint and under judicial supervision. There is, understandably, a deep-seated uneasiness and apprehension that this capability will be used to intrude upon cherished privacy of law-abiding citizens. We look to the Bill of Rights to safeguard this privacy. Though physical entry of the home is the chief evil against which the wording of the Fourth Amendment is directed, its broader spirit now shields private speech from unreasonable surveillance. . . .

National security cases, moreover, often reflect a convergence of First and Fourth Amendment values not present in cases of "ordinary" crime. Though the investigative duty of the executive may be stronger in such cases, so also is there greater jeopardy to constitutionally protected speech . . . . History abundantly documents the tendency of Government—however benevolent and benign its motives—to view with suspicion those who most fervently dispute its policies. Fourth Amendment protections become the more necessary when the targets of official surveillance may be those suspected of unorthodoxy in their political beliefs. The danger to political dissent is acute where the Government attempts to act under so vague a concept as the power to protect "domestic security." Given the difficulty of defining the domestic security interest, the danger of abuse in acting to protect that interest becomes apparent. . . .

The price of lawful public dissent must not be a dread of subjection to an unchecked surveillance power. Nor must the fear of unauthorized official eavesdropping deter vigorous citizen dissent and discussion of Government action in private conversation. For private dissent, no less than open public discourse, is essential to our free society.

As the Fourth Amendment is not absolute in its terms, our task is to examine and balance the basic values at stake in this case: the duty of Government to protect the domestic security, and the potential danger posed by unreasonable surveillance to individual privacy and free expression. If the legitimate need of Government to safeguard domestic security requires the use of electronic surveillance, the question is whether the needs of citizens for privacy and free expression may not be better protected by requiring a warrant before such surveillance is undertaken. We must also ask whether a warrant requirement would unduly frustrate the efforts of Government to protect itself from acts of subversion and overthrow directed against it. . . .

These Fourth Amendment freedoms cannot properly be guaranteed if domestic security surveillances may be conducted solely within the discretion of the Executive Branch. The Fourth Amendment does not contemplate the executive officers of Government as neutral and disinterested magistrates. Their duty and responsibility are to enforce the laws, to investigate, and to prosecute. But those charged with this investigative and prosecutorial duty should not be the sole judges of when to utilize constitutionally sensitive means in pursuing their tasks. The historical judgment, which the Fourth Amendment accepts, is that unreviewed executive discretion may

yield too readily to pressures to obtain incriminating evidence and overlook potential invasions of privacy and protected speech.

It may well be that, in the instant case, the Government's surveillance of Plamondon's conversations was a reasonable one which readily would have gained prior judicial approval. But this Court "has never sustained a search upon the sole ground that officers reasonably expected to find evidence of a particular crime and voluntarily confined their activities to the least intrusive means consistent with that end." Katz, *supra*, at 356–357. The Fourth Amendment contemplates a prior judicial judgment, not the risk that executive discretion may be reasonably exercised. This judicial role accords with our basic constitutional doctrine that individual freedoms will best be preserved through a separation of powers and division of functions among the different branches and levels of Government. The independent check upon executive discretion is not satisfied, as the Government argues, by "extremely limited" post-surveillance judicial review. Indeed, post-surveillance review would never reach the surveillances which failed to result in prosecutions. Prior review by a neutral and detached magistrate is the time-tested means of effectuating Fourth Amendment rights.

It is true that there have been some exceptions to the warrant requirement. But those exceptions are few in number and carefully delineated; in general, they serve the legitimate needs of law enforcement officers to protect their own well-being and preserve evidence from destruction. Even while carving out those exceptions, the Court has reaffirmed the principle that the "police must, whenever practicable, obtain advance judicial approval of searches and seizures through the warrant procedure," *Terry v. Ohio, supra*, at 20; *Chimel v. California, supra*, at 762.

The Government argues that the special circumstances applicable to domestic security surveillances necessitate a further exception to the warrant requirement. It is urged that the requirement of prior judicial review would obstruct the President in the discharge of his constitutional duty to protect domestic security. We are told further that these surveillances are directed primarily to the collecting and maintaining of intelligence with respect to subversive forces, and are not an attempt to gather evidence for specific criminal prosecutions. It is said that this type of surveillance should not be subject to traditional warrant requirements which were established to govern investigation of criminal activity, not ongoing intelligence gathering.

The Government further insists that courts "as a practical matter would have neither the knowledge nor the techniques necessary to determine whether there was probable cause to believe that surveillance was necessary to protect national security." These security problems, the Government contends, involve "a large number of complex and subtle factors" beyond the competence of courts to evaluate.

As a final reason for exemption from a warrant requirement, the Government believes that disclosure to a magistrate of all or even a significant portion of the information involved in domestic security surveillances "would create serious potential dangers to the national security and to the lives of informants and agents. . . . Secrecy is the essential ingredient in intelligence gathering; requiring prior judicial authorization would create a greater 'danger of leaks . . . , because in addition to the judge, you have the clerk, the stenographer and some other officer like a law assistant or bailiff who may be apprised of the nature' of the surveillance."

These contentions in behalf of a complete exemption from the warrant requirement, when urged on behalf of the President and the national security in its domestic implications, merit the most careful consideration. We certainly do not reject them lightly, especially at a time of worldwide ferment and when civil disorders in this country are more prevalent than in the less turbulent periods of our history. There is, no doubt, pragmatic force to the Government's position.

But we do not think a case has been made for the requested departure from Fourth Amendment standards. The circumstances described do not justify complete exemption of domestic security surveillance from prior judicial scrutiny. Official surveillance, whether its purpose be criminal investigation or ongoing intelligence gathering, risks infringement of constitutionally protected privacy of speech. Security surveillances are especially sensitive because of the inherent vagueness of the domestic security concept, the necessarily broad and continuing nature of intelligence gathering, and the temptation to utilize such surveillances to oversee political dissent. We recognize, as we have before, the constitutional basis of the President's domestic security role, but we think it must be exercised in a manner compatible with the Fourth Amendment. In this case we hold that this requires an appropriate prior warrant procedure.

We cannot accept the Government's argument that internal security matters are too subtle and complex for judicial evaluation. Courts regularly deal with the most difficult issues of our society. There is no reason to believe that federal judges will be insensitive to or uncomprehending of the issues involved in domestic security cases. Certainly courts can recognize that domestic security surveillance involves different considerations from the surveillance of "ordinary crime." If the threat is too subtle or complex for our senior law enforcement officers to convey its significance to a court, one may question whether there is probable cause for surveillance.

Nor do we believe prior judicial approval will fracture the secrecy essential to official intelligence gathering. The investigation of criminal activity has long involved imparting sensitive information to judicial officers who have respected the confidentialities involved. Judges may be counted upon to be especially conscious of security requirements in national security cases. Title III of the Omnibus Crime Control and Safe Streets Act already has imposed this responsibility on the judiciary in connection with such crimes as espionage, sabotage, and treason, 2516(1)(a) and (c), each of which may involve domestic as well as foreign security threats. Moreover, a warrant application involves no public or adversary proceedings: it is an ex parte request [one that involves only the requestor and the judge—ed.] before a magistrate or judge.

Whatever security dangers clerical and secretarial personnel may pose can be minimized by proper administrative measures, possibly to the point of allowing the Government itself to provide the necessary clerical assistance.

Thus, we conclude that the Government's concerns do not justify departure in this case from the customary Fourth Amendment requirement of judicial approval prior to initiation of a search or surveillance. Although some added burden will be imposed upon the Attorney General, this inconvenience is justified in a free society to protect constitutional values. Nor do we think the Government's domestic surveillance powers will be impaired to any significant degree. A prior warrant establishes presumptive validity of the surveillance and will minimize the burden of justification in post-surveillance judicial review. By no means of least importance will be the reassurance of the public generally that indiscriminate wiretapping and bugging of law-abiding citizens cannot occur.

We emphasize, before concluding this opinion, the scope of our decision. As stated at the outset, this case involves only the domestic aspects of national security. We have not addressed, and express no opinion as to, the issues which may be involved with respect to activities of foreign powers or their agents. Nor does our decision rest on the language of 2511(3) or any other section of Title III of the Omnibus Crime Control and Safe Streets Act of 1968. That Act does not attempt to define or delineate the powers of the President to meet domestic threats to the national security.

Moreover, we do not hold that the same type of standards and procedures prescribed by Title III are necessarily applicable to this case. We recognize that domestic security surveillance may involve different policy and practical considerations from the surveillance of "ordinary crime." The gathering of security intelligence is often long range and involves the interrelation of various sources and types of information. The exact targets of such surveillance may be more difficult to identify than in surveillance operations against many types of crime specified in

Title III. Often, too, the emphasis of domestic intelligence gathering is on the prevention of unlawful activity or the enhancement of the Government's preparedness for some possible future crisis or emergency. Thus, the focus of domestic surveillance may be less precise than that directed against more conventional types of crime.

Given these potential distinctions between Title III criminal surveillances and those involving the domestic security, Congress may wish to consider protective standards for the latter which differ from those already prescribed for specified crimes in Title III. Different standards may be compatible with the Fourth Amendment if they are reasonable both in relation to the legitimate need of Government for intelligence information and the protected rights of our citizens. For the warrant application may vary according to the governmental interest to be enforced and the nature of citizen rights deserving protection. . . .

As the surveillance of Plamondon's conversations was unlawful, because conducted without prior judicial approval, the courts below correctly held that *Alderman v. United States*, 394 U.S. 165 (1969), is controlling and that it requires disclosure to the accused of his own impermissibly intercepted conversations. As stated in Alderman, "the trial court can and should, where appropriate, place a defendant and his counsel under enforceable orders against unwarranted disclosure of the materials which they may be entitled to inspect."

The judgment of the Court of Appeals is hereby Affirmed.

Shortly after President Richard Nixon resigned from the presidency in 1974 in the wake of the Watergate scandals, the public learned that Nixon had made an agreement with the General Services Administration (GSA) to take control of 42 million pages of documents and 880 tape recordings from his presidency, at least some of which he planned to destroy. The Congress responded by enacting the Presidential Recordings and Materials Preservation Act of 1974, which placed presidential papers under the control of the head of the GSA, who would oversee their screening by government archivists to separate purely personal papers, to be returned to the president, from those of historic importance, which would be preserved. Nixon challenged the law's constitutionality, arguing that it violated the separation of powers, executive privilege, his privacy rights, and his First Amendment rights, and that the law was an unconstitutional bill of attainder (a legislative enactment that imposes a punishment on a person without benefit of a judicial trial; bills of attainder are barred in Article I, section 9 of the Constitution). A seven-member majority of the Court upheld the law and rejected Nixon's arguments, although some expressed reservations about some of elements of the law. Most important, the 1974 law and this case firmly established the principle that most presidential records and documents accumulated during an administration belong to the public and are not the private property of a president.

Nixon v. Administrator of General Services
433 U.S. 425 (1977)

Mr. Justice Brennan delivered the opinion of the Court. . . .

We reject at the outset appellant's [Nixon's] argument that the Act's regulation of the disposition of Presidential materials within the Executive Branch constitutes . . . a violation of the principle of separation of powers. Neither President Ford nor President Carter supports this claim. The Executive Branch became a party to the Act's regulation when President Ford signed the Act into law, and the administration of President Carter, acting through the Solicitor General, vigorously supports affirmance of the District Court's judgment sustaining its constitutionality. Moreover, the control over the materials remains in the Executive Branch. The Administrator of General Services, who must promulgate and administer the regulations that are the keystone of the statutory scheme, is himself an official of the Executive Branch, appointed by the President. The career archivists appointed to do the initial screening for the purpose of selecting out and returning to appellant his private and personal papers similarly are Executive Branch employees.

Appellant's argument is in any event based on an interpretation of the separation-of-powers doctrine inconsistent with the origins of that doctrine, recent decisions of the Court, and the contemporary realities of our political system. True, it has been said that "each of the three general departments of government [must remain] entirely free from the control or coercive influence, direct or indirect, of either of the others . . . ," *Humphrey's Executor v. United States* (1935), and that "[t]he sound application of a principle that makes one master in his own house precludes him from imposing his control in the house of another who is master there." . . .

But the more pragmatic, flexible approach of Madison in the Federalist Papers and later of Mr. Justice Story was expressly affirmed by this Court only three years ago in United States v. Nixon. There the same broad argument concerning the separation of powers was made by appellant in the context of opposition to a subpoena duces tecum of the Watergate Special Prosecutor for certain Presidential tapes and documents of value to a pending criminal investigation. Although acknowledging that each branch of the Government has the duty initially to interpret the Constitution for itself, and that its interpretation of its powers is due great respect from the other branches, the Court squarely rejected the argument that the Constitution contemplates a complete division of authority between the three branches. Rather, the unanimous Court essentially embraced Mr. Justice Jackson's view, expressed in his concurrence in *Youngstown Sheet & Tube Co. v. Sawyer, 343 U.S. 579, 635 (1952).*

> "In designing the structure of our Government and dividing and allocating the sovereign power among three co-equal branches, the Framers of the Constitution sought to provide a comprehensive system, but the separate powers were not intended to operate with absolute independence." . . .

Like the District Court, we therefore find that appellant's argument rests upon an "archaic view of the separation of powers as requiring three airtight departments of government." Rather, in determining whether the Act disrupts the proper balance between the coordinate branches, the proper inquiry focuses on the extent to which it prevents the Executive Branch from accomplishing its constitutionally assigned functions. Only where the potential for disruption is present must we then determine whether that impact is justified by an overriding need to promote objectives within the constitutional authority of Congress.

It is therefore highly relevant that the Act provides for custody of the materials in officials of the Executive Branch and that employees of that branch have access to the materials only "for lawful Government use, subject to the [Administrator's] regulations." For it is clearly less intrusive to place custody and screening of the materials within the Executive Branch itself than to have Congress or some outside agency perform the screening function. While the materials may also be made available for use in judicial proceedings, this provision is expressly qualified by any rights, defense, or privileges that any person may invoke including, of course, a valid claim of executive privilege. Similarly, although some of the materials may eventually be made available for public access, the Act expressly recognizes the need both "to protect any party's opportunity to assert any legally or constitutionally based right or privilege," 104(a)(5), and to return purely private materials to appellant, 104(a)(7). These provisions plainly guard against disclosures barred by any defenses or privileges available to appellant or the Executive Branch. . . .

Thus, whatever are the future possibilities for constitutional conflict in the promulgation of regulations respecting public access to particular documents, nothing contained in the Act renders it unduly disruptive of the Executive Branch and, therefore, unconstitutional on its face. And, of course, there is abundant statutory precedent for the regulation and mandatory disclosure of documents in the possession of the Executive Branch. . . . Such regulation of material generated in the Executive Branch has never been considered invalid as an invasion of its autonomy. . . . Similar congressional power to regulate Executive Branch documents exists in this instance, a power that is augmented by the important interests that the Act seeks to attain. See *infra*, at 452–454.

. . . [W]e next consider appellant's more narrowly defined claim that the Presidential privilege shields these records from archival scrutiny. We start with what was established in *United States v. Nixon*— that the privilege is a qualified one. . . .

Unlike United States v. Nixon, in which appellant asserted a claim of absolute Presidential privilege against inquiry by the coordinate Judicial Branch, this case initially involves appellant's assertion of a privilege against the very Executive Branch in whose name the privilege is invoked. The nonfederal appellees rely on this apparent anomaly to contend that only an incumbent President can assert the privilege of the Presidency. Acceptance of that proposition would, of course, end this inquiry. The contention draws on *United States v. Reynolds, 345 U.S. 1, 7–8 (1953)*, where it was said that the privilege "belongs to the Government and must be asserted by it: it can neither be claimed nor waived by a private party." The District Court believed that this statement was strong support for the contention, but found resolution of the issue unnecessary. 408 F. Supp., at 343–345. It sufficed, said the District Court, that the privilege, if available to a former President, was at least one that "carries much less weight than a claim asserted by the incumbent himself." *Id.*, at 345.

It is true that only the incumbent is charged with performance of the executive duty under the Constitution. And an incumbent may be inhibited in disclosing confidences of a predecessor when he believes that the effect may be to discourage candid presentation of views by his contemporary advisers. Moreover, to the extent that the privilege serves as a shield for executive officials against burdensome requests for information which might interfere with the proper performance of their duties, . . . a former President is in less need of it than an incumbent. In addition, there are obvious political checks against an incumbent's abuse of the privilege. . . .

At the same time, however, the fact that neither President Ford nor President Carter supports appellant's claim detracts from the weight of his contention that the Act impermissibly intrudes into the executive function and the needs of the Executive Branch. This necessarily follows, for it must be presumed that the incumbent President is vitally concerned with and in the best position to assess the present and future needs of the Executive Branch, and to support invocation of the privilege accordingly.

The appellant may legitimately assert the Presidential privilege, of course, only as to those materials whose contents fall within the scope of the privilege recognized in *United States v. Nixon, supra.* In that case the Court held that the privilege is limited to communications "in performance of [a President's] responsibilities . . . of his office," *id.,* at 713, and made "in the process of shaping policies and making decisions," *id.,* at 708. Of the estimated 42 million pages of documents and 880 tape recordings whose custody is at stake, the District Court concluded that the appellant's claim of Presidential privilege could apply at most to the 200,000 items with which the appellant was personally familiar.

The appellant bases his claim of Presidential privilege in this case on the assertion that the potential disclosure of communications given to the appellant in confidence would adversely affect the ability of future Presidents to obtain the candid advice necessary for effective decisionmaking. We are called upon to adjudicate that claim, however, only with respect to the process by which the materials will be screened and catalogued by professional archivists. For any eventual public access will be governed by the guidelines of 104, which direct the Administrator to take into account "the need to protect any party's opportunity to assert any . . . constitutionally based right or privilege," 104(a)(5), and the need to return purely private materials to the appellant, 104(a)(7).

In view of these specific directions, there is no reason to believe that the restriction on public access ultimately established by regulation will not be adequate to preserve executive confidentiality. An absolute barrier to all outside disclosure is not practically or constitutionally necessary. As the careful research by the District Court clearly demonstrates, there has never been an expectation that the confidences of the Executive Office are absolute and unyielding. All former Presidents from President Hoover to President Johnson have deposited their papers in Presidential libraries (an example appellant has said he intended to follow) for governmental preservation and eventual disclosure. The screening processes for sorting materials for lodgment in these libraries also involved comprehensive review by archivists, often involving materials upon which access restrictions ultimately have been imposed. The expectation of the confidentiality of executive communications thus has always been limited and subject to erosion over time after an administration leaves office.

We are thus left with the bare claim that the mere screening of the materials by the archivists will impermissibly interfere with candid communication of views by Presidential advisers. We agree with the District Court that, thus framed, the question is readily resolved. The screening constitutes a very limited intrusion by personnel in the Executive Branch sensitive to executive concerns. These very personnel have performed the identical task in each of the Presidential libraries without any suggestion that such activity has in any way interfered with executive confidentiality. Indeed, in light of this consistent historical practice, past and present executive officials must be well aware of the possibility that, at some time in the future, their communications may be reviewed on a confidential basis by professional archivists. Appellant has suggested no reason why review under the instant Act, rather than the Presidential Libraries Act, is significantly more likely to impair confidentiality, nor has he called into question the District Court's finding that the archivists' "record for discretion in handling confidential material is unblemished." 408 F. Supp., at 347.

Moreover, adequate justifications are shown for this limited intrusion into executive confidentiality comparable to those held to justify the in camera inspection of the District Court sustained in *United States v. Nixon, supra.* Congress' purposes in enacting the Act are exhaustively treated in the opinion of the District Court. The legislative history of the Act clearly reveals that, among other purposes, Congress acted to establish regular procedures to deal with the perceived need to preserve the materials for legitimate historical and governmental purposes. An incumbent President should not be dependent on happenstance or the whim of a prior President when he seeks access to records of past decisions that define or channel current governmental obligations. Nor should the American people's ability to reconstruct and come to terms with their history be truncated by an analysis of Presidential privilege that focuses only on the needs of the present. Congress can legitimately act to rectify the hit-or-miss approach that has characterized past attempts to protect these substantial interests by entrusting the materials to expert handling by trusted and disinterested professionals.

Other substantial public interests that led Congress to seek to preserve appellant's materials were the desire to restore public confidence in our political processes by preserving the materials as a source for facilitating a full airing of the events leading to appellant's resignation, and Congress' need to understand how those political processes had in fact operated in order to gauge the necessity for remedial legislation. Thus by preserving these materials, the Act may be thought to aid the legislative process and thus to be within the scope of Congress' broad investigative power. And, of course, the Congress repeatedly referred to the importance of the materials to the Judiciary in the event that they shed light upon issues in civil or criminal litigation, a social interest that cannot be doubted.

In light of these objectives, the scheme adopted by Congress for preservation of the appellant's Presidential materials cannot be said to be overbroad. It is true that among the voluminous materials to be screened by archivists are some materials that bear no relationship to any of these objectives (and whose prompt return to appellant is therefore mandated by 104(a)(7)). But these materials are commingled with other materials whose preservation the Act requires, for the appellant, like his predecessors, made no systematic attempt to segregate official, personal, and private materials. Even individual documents and tapes often intermingle communications relating to governmental duties, and of great interest to historians or future policymakers, with private and confidential communications.

Thus, as in the Presidential libraries, the intermingled state of the materials requires the comprehensive review and classification contemplated by the Act if Congress' important objectives are to be furthered. In the course of that process, the archivists will be required to view the small fraction of the materials that implicate Presidential confidentiality, as well as personal and private materials to be returned to appellant. But given the safeguards built into the Act to prevent disclosure of such materials and the minimal nature of the intrusion into the confidentiality of the Presidency, we believe that the claims of Presidential privilege clearly must yield to the important congressional purposes of preserving the materials and maintaining access to them for lawful governmental and historical purposes.

In short, we conclude that the screening process contemplated by the Act will not constitute a more severe intrusion into Presidential confidentiality than the in camera inspection by the District Court approved in *United States v. Nixon.* We must, of course, presume that the Administrator and the career archivists concerned will carry out the duties assigned to them by the Act. Thus, there is no basis for appellant's claim that the Act "reverses" the presumption in favor of confidentiality of Presidential papers recognized in *United States v. Nixon.* Appellant's right to assert the privilege is specifically preserved by the Act. The guideline provisions on their face are as broad as the privilege itself. If the broadly written protections of the Act should nevertheless prove inadequate to safeguard appellant's rights or to prevent usurpation of executive powers, there will be time enough to consider that problem in a specific factual context. For the present, we hold, in agreement with the District Court, that the Act on its face does not violate the Presidential privilege. . . . The judgment of the District Court is

Affirmed. . . .

MR. CHIEF JUSTICE BURGER, dissenting.

In my view, the Court's holding is a grave repudiation of nearly 200 years of judicial precedent and historical practice. That repudiation arises out of an Act of Congress passed in the aftermath of a great national crisis which culminated in the resignation of a President. The Act (Title I of Pub. L. 93–526) violates firmly established constitutional principles in several respects.

I find it very disturbing that fundamental principles of constitutional law are subordinated to what seem the needs of a particular situation. That moments of great national distress give rise to passions reminds us why the three branches of Government were created as separate and coequal, each intended as a check, in turn, on possible excesses by one or both of the others. The Court, however, has now joined a Congress, in haste to "do something," and has invaded historic, fundamental principles of the separate powers of coequal branches of Government. To "punish" one person, Congress—and now the Court—tears into the fabric of our constitutional framework. . . .

The well-established principles of separation of powers, as developed in the decisions of this Court, are violated if Congress compels or coerces the President, in matters relating to the operation and conduct of his office. Next, the Act is an exercise of executive—not legislative—power by the Legislative Branch. Finally, Title I works a sweeping modification of the constitutional privilege and historical practice of confidentiality of every Chief Executive since 1789. . . .

The Presidency . . . stands on a very different footing [compared with cabinet departments]. Unlike the vast array of departments which the President oversees, the Presidency is in no sense a creature of the Legislature. The President's powers originate not from statute, but from the constitutional command to "take Care that the Laws be faithfully executed . . . ." These independent, constitutional origins of the Presidency have an important bearing on determining the appropriate extent of congressional power over the Chief Executive or his records and workpapers. For, although the branches of Government are obviously not divided into "watertight compartments," *Springer v. Philippine Islands* (1928) (Holmes, J., dissenting), the office of the Presidency, as a constitutional equal of Congress, must as a general proposition be free from Congress' coercive powers. This is not simply an abstract proposition of political philosophy; it is a fundamental prohibition plainly established by the decisions of this Court. . . .

Consistent with the principle of noncoercion, the unbroken practice since George Washington with respect to congressional demands for White House papers has been, in Mr. Chief Justice Taft's words, that "while either house [of Congress] may request information, it cannot compel it . . . ." W. Taft, The Presidency 110 (1916). President Washington established the tradition by declining to produce papers requested by the House of Representatives relating to matters of foreign policy. . . .

Part of our constitutional fabric, then, from the beginning has been the President's freedom from control or coercion by Congress, including attempts to procure documents that, though clearly pertaining to matters of important governmental interests, belong and pertain to the President. This freedom from Congress' coercive influence, in the words of *Humphrey's Executor*, "is implied in the very fact of the separation of the powers . . . ." *295 U.S., at 629–630.* Moreover, it is not constitutionally significant that Congress has not directed that the papers be turned over to it for examination or retention, rather than to GSA. Separation of powers is fully implicated simply by Congress' mandating what disposition is to be made of the papers of another branch. . . .

The statute, therefore, violates separation-of-powers principles because it exercises a coercive influence by another branch over the Presidency. The legislation is also invalid on another ground pertaining to separation of powers; it is an attempt by Congress to exercise powers vested exclusively in the President—the power to control files, records, and papers of the office, which are comparable to the internal workpapers of Members of the House and Senate. . . .

Finally, in my view, the Act violates principles of separation of powers by intruding into the confidentiality of Presidential communications protected by the constitutionally based doctrine of Presidential privilege. A unanimous Court in *United States v. Nixon* could not have been clearer in holding that the privilege guaranteeing confidentiality of such communications derives from the Constitution, subject to compelled disclosure only in narrowly limited circumstances. . . .

Frank Snepp, a former Central Intelligence Agency (CIA) agent, published a book in 1977 called Decent Interval, *which detailed his experiences as an agent during the Vietnam War. In doing so, Snepp violated an agreement he had signed when he joined the CIA in which he agreed not to publish anything related to his employment with the agency without first having the writing approved by the agency and not to disclose any classified information without CIA permission. The government prosecuted Snepp to require that all of his future writings be subject to prior government review and to confiscate all profits from the book. Even though the book did not contain any classified information, two lower courts ruled against Snepp, although he was not to be required to surrender his book profits. The Supreme Court sided with the government and against Snepp, but it also ruled that he forfeit his book royalties to the government (a "constructive trust"). Three dissenting justices argued that the penalty against Snepp was too drastic, noting that nothing he revealed was confidential, and so the actual harm caused was not sufficient to warrant the penalties imposed. (Note: "per curiam" means that the majority decision is a decision of the whole, not of a specific justice.)*

Snepp v. United States
444 U.S. 507 (1980)

PER CURIAM.

. . . Snepp's employment with the CIA involved an extremely high degree of trust. In the opening sentence of the agreement that he signed, Snepp explicitly recognized that he was entering a trust relationship. The trust agreement specifically imposed the obligation not to publish any information relating to the Agency without submitting the information for clearance. Snepp stipulated at trial that—after undertaking this obligation—he had been "assigned to various positions of trust" and that he had been granted "frequent access to classified information, including information regarding intelligence sources and methods." 456 F. Supp., at 178. Snepp published his book about CIA activities on the basis of this background and exposure. He deliberately and surreptitiously violated his obligation to submit all material for prepublication review. Thus, he exposed the classified information with which he had been entrusted to the risk of disclosure.

Whether Snepp violated his trust does not depend upon whether his book actually contained classified information. The Government does not deny—as a general principle—Snepp's right to publish unclassified information. Nor does it contend—at this stage of the litigation—that Snepp's book contains classified material. The Government simply claims that, in light of the special trust reposed in him and the agreement that he signed, Snepp should have given the CIA an opportunity to determine whether the material he proposed to publish would compromise classified information or sources. Neither of the Government's concessions undercuts its claim that Snepp's failure to submit to prepublication review was a breach of his trust.

Both the District Court and the Court of Appeals found that a former intelligence agent's publication of unreviewed material relating to intelligence activities can be detrimental to vital national interests even if the published information is unclassified. When a former agent relies on his own judgment about what information is detrimental, he may reveal information that the CIA—with its broader understanding of what may expose classified information and confidential sources—could have identified as harmful. In addition to receiving intelligence from domestically based or controlled sources, the CIA obtains information from the intelligence services of friendly nations and from agents operating in foreign countries. The continued availability of these foreign sources depends upon the CIA's ability to guarantee the security of information that might compromise them and even endanger the personal safety of foreign agents.

Undisputed evidence in this case shows that a CIA agent's violation of his obligation to submit writings about the Agency for prepublication review impairs the CIA's ability to perform its statutory duties. Admiral Turner, Director of the CIA, testified without contradiction that Snepp's book and others like it have seriously impaired the effectiveness of American intelligence operations. . . . Snepp's breach of his explicit obligation to submit his material—classified or not—for prepublication clearance has irreparably harmed the United States Government. . . .

A constructive trust . . . protects both the Government and the former agent from unwarranted risks. This remedy is the natural and customary consequence of a breach of trust. It deals fairly with both parties by conforming relief to the dimensions of the wrong. If the agent secures prepublication clearance, he can publish with no fear of liability. If the agent publishes unreviewed material in violation of his fiduciary and contractual obligation, the trust remedy simply requires him to disgorge the benefits of his faithlessness. Since the remedy is swift and sure, it is tailored to deter those who would place sensitive information at risk. And since the remedy reaches only funds attributable to the breach, it cannot saddle the former agent with exemplary damages out of all proportion to his gain. The decision of the Court of Appeals would deprive the Government of this equitable and effective means of protecting intelligence that may contribute to national security. We therefore reverse the judgment of the Court of Appeals insofar as it refused to impose a constructive trust on Snepp's

profits, and we remand the cases to the Court of Appeals for reinstatement of the full judgment of the District Court.

So ordered.

Mr. Justice Stevens, with whom Mr. Justice Brennan and Mr. Justice Marshall join, dissenting. . . .

The rule of law the Court announces today is not supported by statute, by the contract, or by the common law. Although Congress has enacted a number of criminal statutes punishing the unauthorized dissemination of certain types of classified information, it has not seen fit to authorize the constructive trust remedy the Court creates today. Nor does either of the contracts Snepp signed with the Agency provide for any such remedy in the event of a breach. The Court's per curiam opinion seems to suggest that its result is supported by a blend of the law of trusts and the law of contracts. But neither of these branches of the common law supports the imposition of a constructive trust under the circumstances of this case.

Plainly this is . . . an employment relationship in which the employee possesses fiduciary obligations arising out of his duty of loyalty to his employer. One of those obligations, long recognized by the common law even in the absence of a written employment agreement, is the duty to protect confidential or "classified" information. If Snepp had breached that obligation, the common law would support the implication of a constructive trust upon the benefits derived from his misuse of confidential information.

But Snepp did not breach his duty to protect confidential information. Rather, he breached a contractual duty, imposed in aid of the basic duty to maintain confidentiality, to obtain prepublication clearance. In order to justify the imposition of a constructive trust, the majority attempts to equate this contractual duty with Snepp's duty not to disclose, labeling them both as "fiduciary." I find nothing in the common law to support such an approach. . . .

But even assuming that Snepp's covenant to submit to prepublication review should be enforced, the constructive trust imposed by the Court is not an appropriate remedy. If an employee has used his employer's confidential information for his own personal profit, a constructive trust over those profits is obviously an appropriate remedy because the profits are the direct result of the breach. But Snepp admittedly did not use confidential information in his book; nor were the profits from his book in any sense a product of his failure to submit the book for prepublication review. For, even if Snepp had submitted the book to the Agency for prepublication review, the Government's censorship authority would surely have been limited to the excision of classified material. In this case, then, it would have been obliged to clear the book for publication in precisely the same form as it now stands. Thus, Snepp has not gained any profits as a result of his breach; the Government, rather than Snepp, will be unjustly enriched if he is required to disgorge profits attributable entirely to his own legitimate activity.

Despite the fact that Snepp has not caused the Government the type of harm that would ordinarily be remedied by the imposition of a constructive trust, the Court attempts to justify a constructive trust remedy on the ground that the Government has suffered some harm. The Court states that publication of "unreviewed material" by a former CIA agent "can be detrimental to vital national interests even if the published information is unclassified." *Ante*, at 511–512. It then seems to suggest that the injury in such cases stems from the Agency's inability to catch "harmful" but unclassified information before it is published. I do not believe, however, that the Agency has any authority to censor its employees' publication of unclassified information on the basis of its opinion that publication may be "detrimental to vital national interests" or otherwise "identified as harmful." *Ibid*. The CIA never attempted to assert such power over Snepp in either of the contracts he signed; rather, the Agency itself limited its censorship power to preventing the disclosure of "classified" information. Moreover, even if such a wide-ranging prior restraint would be good national security policy, I would have great difficulty reconciling it with the demands of the First Amendment.

The Court also relies to some extent on the Government's theory at trial that Snepp caused it harm by flouting his prepublication review obligation and thus making it appear that the CIA was powerless to prevent its agents from publishing any information they chose to publish, whether classified or not. The Government theorized that this appearance of weakness would discourage foreign governments from cooperating with the CIA because of a fear that their secrets might also be compromised. In support of its position that Snepp's book had in fact had such an impact, the Government introduced testimony by the Director of the CIA, Admiral Stansfield Turner, stating that Snepp's book and others like it had jeopardized the CIA's relationship with foreign intelligence services by making them unsure of the Agency's ability to maintain confidentiality. Admiral Turner's truncated testimony does not explain, however, whether these unidentified "other" books actually contained classified information. If so, it is difficult to believe that the publication of a book like Snepp's which does not reveal classified information, has significantly weakened the Agency's position. Nor does it explain whether the unidentified foreign agencies who have stopped cooperating with the CIA have done so because of a legitimate fear that secrets will be revealed or because they merely disagree with our Government's classification policies. . . .

[T]he Court seems unaware of the fact that its drastic new remedy has been fashioned to enforce a species of prior restraint on a citizen's right to criticize his government. Inherent in this prior restraint is the risk that the reviewing agency will misuse its authority to delay the publication of a critical work or to persuade an author to modify the contents of his work beyond the demands of secrecy. The character of the covenant as a prior restraint on free speech surely imposes an especially heavy burden on the censor to justify the remedy it seeks. It would take more than the Court has written to persuade me that that burden has been met.

I respectfully dissent.

Budgeting/Economy

Presidents are held responsible for the overall health of the U.S. economy. That presidents rarely have the constitutional authority or political power to exert control over the economy is a point often lost on voters. Especially since the New Deal, when the public demanded—and FDR provided— significantly increased federal involvement in economic management, presidents have been concerned with the overall health of the U.S. economy and with budgetary matters.

Understandably, presidents have sought to close the expectations/power gap in economic policy. Just as understandably, the Congress often pulls in the other direction. Thus, constitutional battles over the size of the federal budget, tax policy, economic stimulation programs, antipoverty legislation, the impoundment of funds, the defense budget, and a range of other issues become paramount.

The Constitution seems to give the Congress the upper hand in budget and economic policy making. But as is the case with so many policy areas, over time presidents have taken, the Congress has sometimes given, and the public has often demanded greater presidential involvement and control.

Budget allocations and economic policy remain key sources of reward and punishment for politicians. Thus the stakes are high and the potential rewards significant. That is why conflict is inevitable.

In the 1970s, busing to promote integration of racially segregated schools became a political hot potato.

Although the government sometimes ordered, as did the courts, school districts to desegregate, many were slow to do so. Thus, busing was a means to integrate schools.

Two students, Darryl and David Brown, along with sixteen others, challenged the constitutionality of this policy. What is the scope of federal power, and what limits can be placed on the government in pursuit of broad policy objectives?

Brown v. Califano
627 F.2d 1221 (D.C. Cir. 1980)

Bazelon, Senior Circuit Judge . . .

II. The Amendments and Effective Desegregation Enforcement

The amendments here at issue make no classification along impermissible lines, but that does not prevent an equal protection challenge. Interference with the remedies necessary to implement the promise of *Brown v. Board of Education, 347 U.S. 483* (1954), could well rise to the level of impermissible discriminatory effect and purpose. In essence, that is appellants' claim here. Appellants argue that, by restricting HEW's [The Department of Health, Education, and Welfare] ability to require busing remedies, the amendments demonstrate discriminatory intent to interfere with desegregation. Presumably, this claim attaches to HEW's statutory obligation under Title VI to achieve equality in federally-funded schools and to the Executive's duty to "take care that the Laws (are) faithfully executed.". . .

Thus, appellants assert that the amendments, by their plain terms, effect and purpose, violate the fifth amendment by eliminating "the single, proven, and most effective remedy for desegregating schools receiving federal aid." There are actually two prongs to this claim: the amendments will effectively inhibit desegregation and thereby dilute the guarantees of the fifth amendment; and the amendments reflect an impermissible legislative motivation to inhibit desegregation. Because the amendments on their face leave open many apparently effective avenues for desegregation, we are not persuaded by either argument . . .

A. Construing the Amendments

. . . The amendments can be interpreted here to advance a permissible purpose, with no general inhibition of desegregation . . . Although individual supporters broadly attacked busing as a desegregation remedy . . . we do not find these statements expressive of the entire legislature's intent. Were they representative, we would be confronted with grave constitutional difficulties. Instead, we recognize the primary focus of the congressional debates on the role of HEW as an enforcement agency. An explicit, major purpose of the amendments was to take "HEW out of the busing business." . . . In other words, Congress wanted to ensure that mandatory busing orders derive either from local school officials or federal courts . . .

Accordingly, the amendments only restrain HEW from using its fund-termination authority to induce school districts to require student transportation beyond schools closest to their homes. They do not in any way restrict HEW's authority to threaten or actually terminate funds with respect to any other desegregation remedy which would suffice. Thus, HEW can reject fund applications which fail to provide for magnet schools, faculty desegregation, school construction or school closings that enhance desegregation, or other nontransportation remedies it deems necessary for compliance with Title VI and the Constitution . . .

For those noncomplying school districts which HEW believes require transportation remedies, the amendments clearly eliminate use of the fund-termination option to induce busing. At the same time, nothing in their language or legislative history impairs two HEW activities in this context. First, the agency still may negotiate with the noncomplying district to encourage adoption of a voluntary transportation plan. . . . The second activity is obvious. As the district court concluded, nothing in the amendments precludes HEW from referring such cases to the Department of Justice, with recommendations for appropriate legal action . . .

Appellants contest the sufficiency of this referral option by claiming that time-consuming litigation will impermissibly forestall the requisite remedy . . . This is an issue which clearly requires concrete development, and is not susceptible to resolution in the abstract . . . Thus, as a facial challenge to the amendments, appellants' argument cannot succeed. Further, the Department of Justice is not limited to a litigative strategy; it may conduct negotiations and seek settlements, where appropriate . . .

B. Dilution of Equal Protection Guarantees

The amendments would be constitutionally flawed if they diluted rather than enforced equal protection guarantees . . . As construed, however, these amendments do not pose this problem. We concluded above that these amendments do not preclude the threat . . . The amendments also leave in place the enforcement options at the Department of Justice, we cannot find that on their face they "restrict, abrogate, or dilute" the guarantee of equal protection. Where a choice of alternative enforcement routes is available, and the one preferred is not demonstrably less effective, Congress has the power to exercise its preference . . .

C. Legislative Motivation

Absent discriminatory effect, judicial inquiry into legislative motivation is unnecessary, as well as undesirable . . . Obviously, the foreseeable effect of these amendments is increased litigation for court-ordered desegregation, and settlements supervised by HEW and the courts not unremedied segregation. Thus, statements by individual congressmen that reveal opposition to busing or to student assignment to achieve desegregation, do not by themselves establish constitutional flaws in the amendments . . .

III. Prohibition Against Government Support for Segregation

More problematic is appellants' charge that the amendments interfere with the government's obligation not to support segregated schools . . . Distinct from its duty to enforce the law, the Executive must not itself participate in unlawful discrimination. This prohibition is embodied in Title VI and in numerous subsequent statutory schemes . . . To avoid the cloud of constitutional doubt, we must assume that Congress did not intend the amendments to force federal financial support of illegal discrimination . . .

Thus, the amendments cannot be read to prevent HEW from fulfilling its obligation to assure no federal moneys support segregated schools. HEW has an obligation, as a government agency, not to participate in unlawful discrimination. In particular instances, HEW may be required to (1) refer a case to the Department of Justice for appropriate action; (2) terminate funds through HEW's administrative procedures; or (3) alert the President that a case may require Executive impoundment of funds. Appellants and other private individuals certainly are not barred from challenging HEW's failure to take any such steps . . .

. . . We agree, however, with the district court that the record does not establish sufficient factual evidence to permit a review of the amendments as applied. Therefore, we affirm the district court's judgment that the amendments survive facial challenge. We assume that the district court retained jurisdiction to entertain further motions challenging HEW's actions under the amendments and we affirm . . .

The impoundment (nonuse) of congressionally appropriated funds goes back nearly to the beginning of the

republic. During the Nixon presidency, this device was used not as a minor administrative tool, but as a way to pursue the president's policy goals when they conflicted with public law. In 1974, the Congress passed the Impoundment Control Act in an effort to limit the use of impoundment.

Could a president, as a function of his executive power, impound congressionally appropriated funds? In the 1974 law, the Congress spelled out the manner in which a president could impound funds, subject to a "legislative veto." Is this restriction constitutional?

City of New Haven v. U.S.
809 F.2d 900 (D.C. Cir. 1987)

Harry T. Edwards, Circuit Judge. . . .

I. Background

After thoroughly examining the statutory language, the legislative history and the historical political context surrounding passage of the Act, the District Court had little difficulty concluding that Congress would have preferred no statute at all to a statute that conferred unchecked deferral authority on the President . . . The court found that the *"raison d'etre"* of the entire legislative effort was to wrest *control* over the budgetary process from what Congress perceived as a usurping Executive:

> Control—how to regain and retain it—was studied and debated at length, on the floor and in committee, over a period of years by a Congress virtually united in its quest for a way to reassert its fiscal prerogative. A clearer case of congressional intent—obsession would be more accurate—is hard to imagine.

. . . This overwhelming evidence of congressional intent, the court concluded, conclusively demonstrated that Congress—had it known that it could not disapprove unwanted impoundments by means of a legislative veto—would never have enacted a statute that *conceded* impoundment authority to the

President. Indeed, it could be said with "conviction" that Congress

> would have preferred no statute to one without the one-House veto provision, for with no statute at all, the President would be remitted to such pre-ICA [Impoundment Control Act of 1974—ed.] authority as he might have had for particular deferrals which, in Congress' view (and that of most of the courts having passed upon it) was not much.

Having found that the legislative veto provision in section 1013 was inseverable from the remainder of the section, and that the President had therefore relied on an invalid statute in making the policy deferrals in question, the court imposed two remedies. First, it ordered the appellants to make the improperly deferred funds available for obligation. Second, it declared section 1013 void in its entirety. Subsequent to this decision, however, Congress duplicated the District Court's injunctive relief by enacting legislation (signed by the President) disapproving the deferrals and ordering that the funds be made available for obligation. It is in this posture that we review the appellants' appeal from the District Court's Memorandum and Order . . .

II. Analysis . . .

The appellants concede, as they must, that the legislative veto provision in section 1013 is unconstitutional under the Supreme Court's decision in *Immigration and Naturalization Service v. Chadha, 462 U.S. 919 (1983)*. The sole question for decision is whether that unconstitutional provision is severable from the remainder of section 1013, which ostensibly authorizes the President to defer congressional appropriations for a period not exceeding one fiscal year . . .

Before it was amended, the Anti-Deficiency Act authorized the President to "apportion[]" funds where justified by "other developments subsequent to the date on which such appropriation was made available." 31 U.S.C. § 665(c)(2) (1970). This open-ended language was amended to limit apportionments to three specified situations: "to provide for contingencies," "to achieve savings made possible by or through changes in requirements or greater efficiency of operations" or "as specifically provided by law." 31 U.S.C. § 1512(c)(1) (1982). The purpose of the amendment was to preclude the President from invoking the Act as authority for implementing "policy" impoundments, while preserving the President's authority to implement routine "programmatic" impoundments . . . President Nixon had attempted to use the Act as an instrument for shaping fiscal policy . . .

It is abundantly clear from both the statute and its legislative history that the overriding purpose of the deferral provision was to permit either House of Congress to veto any deferral proposed by the President—particularly policy deferrals. The title of the statute itself—"*Disapproval of proposed deferrals of budget authority*"—makes it plain that Congress was preoccupied with assuring for itself a ready means of disapproving proposed deferrals. The House Report accompanying H.R. 7130—from which the deferral provision was drawn—expressly states that the "basic purpose" of the bill was to provide each House an opportunity to veto an impoundment . . . The Conference Committee Report also emphasizes that the bill was designed to provide Congress with an effective system of impoundment control . . .

When the numerous statements of individual legislators urging the passage of legislation to control presidential impoundments are also considered, the evidence is incontrovertible that the "basic purpose" of section 1013 was to provide each House of Congress with a veto power over deferrals. Yet, the appellants would have us hold that Congress, had it foreseen *Chadha*, would nevertheless have gone ahead and enacted section 1013 *without* a legislative veto provision. As difficult (and precarious) as it may be at times to reconstruct what a particular Congress might have done had it been apprised of a particular set of facts, we refuse to entertain this remarkable proposition . . . It is simply untenable to suggest that a Congress precluded from achieving this goal would have turned around and ceded to the President the very power it was determined to curtail . . .

As noted earlier, the original bill passed by the House would have permitted both rescissions and deferrals to go into effect automatically, subject of course to a legislative veto . . . The House Report explained that the Committee favored a legislative veto mechanism because

> in the normal process of apportionment, the executive branch necessarily withholds funds on hundreds of occasions during the course of a fiscal year. If Congress adopts a procedure requiring it to approve every necessary impoundment, its legislative process would be disrupted by the flood of approvals that would be required for the normal and orderly operation of the government. The negative mechanism . . . will permit Congress to focus on critical and important matters, and save it from submersion in a sea of trivial ones.

. . . In the final analysis, however, the House approach prevailed only for deferrals for rescissions, Congress adopted the Senate approach, which required prior congressional approval before a rescission could go into effect. According to the appellants, this distinction is critical, for it demonstrates that Congress' intent in enacting section 1013 was to render deferrals "presumptively valid." . . . Because Congress did not want to trouble itself by approving deferrals in advance, they argue, Congress would have authorized the President to implement deferrals even had it known that it could not maintain oversight over those deferrals by means of a legislative veto.

This argument completely misreads the above-quoted passage and is completely at odds with Congress' expressed intention to *control* rather than *authorize* presidential deferrals. First, the quoted passage plainly speaks to "trivial," everyday *programmatic* deferrals. It is these "trivial" impoundments relating to the "normal and orderly operation of the government" that Congress expected to present

little controversy. Congress most certainly did not mean to suggest that impoundments designed to negate congressional budgetary *policies* would be "presumptively valid." It is precisely this sort of impoundment that Congress was determined to forestall.

Second, the quoted passage proves only that Congress preferred a system in which it need not enact legislation approving deferrals *because it could easily disapprove them* by the relatively simple expedient of the one-House veto. Nowhere in the legislative history is there the slightest suggestion that the President be given statutory authority to defer funds without the possible check of at least a one-House veto. Indeed, the House Report completely refutes the notion that Congress would have granted the President statutory authority to implement deferrals, thereby forcing itself to reenact an appropriations bill each time it disapproved of a deferral:

> [The one-House veto] is suggested on the ground that the impoundment situation established by the bill involves a presumption *against* the President's refusing to carry out the terms of an already considered and enacted statute. To make Congress go through a procedure involving agreement between the two Houses on an already settled matter would be to require both, in effect, to reconfirm what they have already decided.

. . . Yet, a finding of severability would create a presumption in favor of deferrals and require Congress to legislate a second time in order to effectuate its budgetary policies. We cannot conceive of a result more contrary to congressional intent.

The appellants further argue that Congress' more permissive treatment of deferrals suggests that the congressional furor over "impoundments" was principally a dissatisfaction with rescissions . . . Again, this contention has absolutely no basis in the legislative history. Although Congress certainly distinguished between rescissions and deferrals, it spoke in general terms of the need to control "impoundments," which it defined as "withholding or *delaying* the expenditure or obligation of budget authority . . . and the termination of authorized projects or activities for which appropriations have been made." . . . The appellants can point to nothing in the legislative history to suggest that members of Congress were disturbed with rescissions but tolerant of deferrals. Indeed, to the extent that Congress expressed any tolerance of deferrals at all, it was referring to routine programmatic deferrals, not policy deferrals . . . ("The Committee recognizes that a brief delay in expending or obligating funds may sometimes be legitimately necessary for purely administrative reasons.") . . .

We cannot emphasize enough in this context the critical distinction between programmatic and policy deferrals. As the appellants concede, *see* Brief of Defendants—Appellants at 33, our holding in this case will not impair the President's ability to implement routine programmatic deferrals. When Congress amended the Anti-Deficiency Act in the ICA, it did not disturb the President's authority to "impound" funds for purely administrative purposes. *See* note 18 *supra*. Thus, the President may still invoke the Anti-Deficiency Act as authority for implementing programmatic deferrals. By amending the Anti-Deficiency Act, however, Congress intended to foreclose the President from relying on that Act as separate statutory authority for *policy* deferrals. Congress intended to permit policy deferrals only under section 1013, and only if it could ensure itself a ready means of over-turning policy deferrals with which it disagreed. Had Congress known it could not employ such a mechanism, it most assuredly would not have nullified its own amendment to the Anti-Deficiency Act by creating new statutory authority for policy deferrals.

Finally, the appellants contend that if we invalidate section 1013 in its entirety, we must also strike down the ICA's other "deferral-related provision"— *i.e.*, Congress's amendment to the Anti-Deficiency Act . . . We find this argument to be wholly specious. As noted earlier, a court's duty in a severability case is to preserve as much of the statute as it can consistent with congressional intent . . . The amendment to the Anti-Deficiency Act, in contrast, is fully consistent with the expressed intent of Congress to control presidential impoundments. Thus, there is absolutely no basis for overturning Congress' amendment to the Anti-Deficiency Act . . .

Foreign Policy

It is widely understood that the president's power over foreign policy matters is greater than that over domestic policy, a relationship often referred to as the "two presidencies." The Congress and the courts historically have been much more willing to accede to presidential wishes and preferences in this realm, and presidents have been quick to exploit this greater deference. Constitutionally, foreign policy powers are divided between president and the Congress, but the Congress, and the country as a whole, often defer to the president's wishes because the office has come to represent the country as a whole when dealing with the rest of the world.

The preference for allowing the president to serve as the nation's single, unified voice in foreign affairs is clearly reflected in the court cases in this chapter. If the line of cases here shows anything, it is that the courts normally yield to presidential preferences in foreign policy, even though there is good reason to believe that the Constitution's founders, and the document itself, did not contemplate such a one-sided arrangement. Nevertheless, presidential dominance in foreign affairs has come to be accepted as the typical pattern. These cases show that the courts have played a major role in the evolution of presidency-centered foreign policy.

In 1934, the Congress passed a joint resolution giving President Franklin D. Roosevelt the power to halt arms shipments to two warring countries, Paraguay and Bolivia. Roosevelt used the power the day the law was passed, issuing a proclamation barring such sales. In 1936, the Curtiss-Wright Export Corporation was indicted for violating FDR's proclamation, but the corporation challenged the president's action, arguing that the Congress's delegation of power to the president was improper and excessive—in other words, that the Congress was improperly giving the president legislative power. The Court ruled that that Congress's actions were legal, as was the president's proclamation. But in a controversial move, Justice George Sutherland's decision went well beyond the particulars of the case to outline a sweeping and, many have argued, misguided view of executive power in foreign affairs. Not only did the decision note that presidential power was greater in foreign than in domestic affairs—an assertion often repeated in subsequent cases—but that the president was the "sole organ" of American foreign policy, Sutherland said, plucking this phrase from a speech given by then-Congressman (later Supreme Court Chief Justice) John Marshall. Critics noted that Marshall was simply talking about the president as sole communicator with other nations, not that the president somehow had sole right to make foreign policy. Nevertheless, this case, and the "sole organ" theory of presidential power in foreign affairs, often has been cited in law and politics to support a broad view of presidential foreign policy power.

United States v. Curtiss-Wright Export Corporation
299 U.S. 304 (1936)

Mr. Justice Sutherland delivered the opinion of the Court. . . .

First. It is contended that by the Joint Resolution the going into effect and continued operation of the resolution was conditioned (a) upon the President's judgment as to its beneficial effect upon the re-establishment of peace between the countries engaged in armed conflict in the Chaco; (b) upon the making of a proclamation, which was left to his unfettered discretion, thus constituting an attempted substitution of the President's will for that of Congress; (c) upon the making of a proclamation putting an end to the operation of the resolution, which again was left to the President's unfettered discretion; and (d) further, that the extent of its operation in particular cases was subject to limitation and exception by the President, controlled by no standard. In each of these particulars, appellees urge that Congress abdicated its essential functions and delegated them to the Executive.

Whether, if the Joint Resolution had related solely to internal affairs, it would be open to the challenge that it constituted an unlawful delegation of legislative power to the Executive, we find it unnecessary to determine. The whole aim of the resolution is to affect a situation entirely external to the United States, and falling within the category of foreign affairs. The determination which we are called to make, therefore, is whether the Joint Resolution, as applied to that situation, is vulnerable to attack under the rule that forbids a delegation of the lawmaking power. In other words, assuming (but not deciding) that the challenged delegation, if it were confined to internal affairs, would be invalid, may it nevertheless be sustained on the ground that its exclusive aim is to afford a remedy for a hurtful condition within foreign territory?

It will contribute to the elucidation of the question if we first consider the differences between the powers of the federal government in respect of foreign or external affairs and those in respect of domestic or internal affairs. That there are differences between them, and that these differences are fundamental, may not be doubted.

The two classes of powers are different, both in respect of their origin and their nature. The broad statement that the federal government can exercise no powers except those specifically enumerated in the Constitution, and such implied powers as are necessary and proper to carry into effect the enumerated powers, is categorically true only in respect of our internal affairs. In that field, the primary purpose of the Constitution was to carve from the general mass of legislative powers then possessed by the states such portions as it was thought desirable to vest in the federal government, leaving those not included in the enumeration still in the states. That this doctrine applies only to powers which the states had is self-evident. And since the states severally never possessed international powers, such powers could not have been carved from the mass of state powers but obviously were transmitted to the United States from some other source. During the Colonial period, those powers were possessed exclusively by and were entirely under the control of the Crown. By the Declaration of Independence, 'the Representatives of the United States of America' declared the United (not the several) Colonies to be free and independent states, and as such to have 'full Power to levy War, conclude Peace, contract Alliances, establish Commerce and to do all other Acts and Things which Independent States may of right do.'

As a result of the separation from Great Britain by the colonies, acting as a unit, the powers of external sovereignty passed from the Crown not to the colonies severally, but to the colonies in their collective and corporate capacity as the United States of America. Even before the Declaration, the colonies were a unit in foreign affairs, acting through a common agency—namely, the Continental Congress, composed of delegates from the thirteen colonies. That agency exercised the powers of war and peace, raised an army, created a navy, and finally adopted the Declaration of Independence. Rulers come and go; governments end and forms of government change; but sovereignty survives. A political society cannot endure without a supreme will somewhere. Sovereignty is never held in suspense. When, therefore, the external sovereignty of Great Britain in respect of the colonies ceased, it immediately passed to the Union. . . .

The Union existed before the Constitution, which was ordained and established among other things to form 'a more perfect Union.' Prior to that event, it is clear that the Union, declared by the Articles of Confederation to be 'perpetual,' was the sole possessor of external sovereignty, and in the Union it remained without change save in so far as the Constitution in express terms qualified its exercise. The Framers' Convention was called and exerted its powers upon the irrefutable postulate that though the states were several their people in respect of foreign affairs were one. . . .

It results that the investment of the federal government with the powers of external sovereignty did not depend upon the affirmative grants of the Constitution. The powers to declare and wage war, to conclude peace, to make treaties, to maintain diplomatic relations with other sovereignties, if they had never been mentioned in the Constitution, would have vested in the federal government as necessary concomitants of nationality. Neither the Constitution nor the laws passed in pursuance of it have any force in foreign territory unless in respect of our own citizens (see *American Banana Co. v. United Fruit Co., 213 U.S. 347, 356*, 29 S.Ct. 511, 16 Ann.Cas. 1047); and operations of the nation in such territory must be governed by treaties, international understandings and compacts, and the principles of international law. As a member of the family of nations, the right and power of the United States in that field are equal to the right and power of the other members of the international family. Otherwise, the United States is not completely

sovereign. The power to acquire territory by discovery and occupation (*Jones v. United States, 137 U.S. 202, 212*,11 S.Ct. 80), the power to expel undesirable aliens (*Fong Yue Ting v. United States, 149 U.S. 698*, 705 et seq., 13 S.Ct. 1016), the power to make such international agreements as do not constitute treaties in the constitutional sense (*Altman & Co. v. United States, 224 U.S. 583, 600*, 601 S., 32 S.Ct. 593; Crandall, Treaties, Their Making and Enforcement (2d Ed.) p. 102 and note 1), none of which is expressly affirmed by the Constitution, nevertheless exist as inherently inseparable from the conception of nationality. This the court recognized, and in each of the cases cited found the warrant for its conclusions not in the provisions of the Constitution, but in the law of nations. . . .

Not only, as we have shown, is the federal power over external affairs in origin and essential character different from that over internal affairs, but participation in the exercise of the power is significantly limited. In this vast external realm, with its important, complicated, delicate and manifold problems, the President alone has the power to speak or listen as a representative of the nation. He makes treaties with the advice and consent of the Senate; but he alone negotiates. Into the field of negotiation the Senate cannot intrude; and Congress itself is powerless to invade it. As Marshall said in his great argument of March 7, 1800, in the House of Representatives, 'The President is the sole organ of the nation in its external relations, and its sole representative with foreign nations.' Annals, 6th Cong., col. 613. The Senate Committee on Foreign Relations at a very early day in our history (February 15, 1816), reported to the Senate, among other things, as follows:

'The President is the constitutional representative of the United States with regard to foreign nations. He manages our concerns with foreign nations and must necessarily be most competent to determine when, how, and upon what subjects negotiation may be urged with the greatest prospect of success. For his conduct he is responsible to the Constitution. The committee considers this responsibility the surest pledge for the faithful discharge of his duty. They think the interference of the Senate in the direction of foreign negotiations calculated to diminish that responsibility and thereby to impair the best security for the national safety. The nature of transactions with foreign nations, moreover, requires caution and unity of design, and their success frequently depends on secrecy and dispatch.' 8 U.S. Sen. Reports Comm. on Foreign Relations, p. 24.

It is important to bear in mind that we are here dealing not alone with an authority vested in the President by an exertion of legislative power, but with such an authority plus the very delicate, plenary and exclusive power of the President as the sole organ of the federal government in the field of international relations—a power which does not require as a basis for its exercise an act of Congress, but which, of course, like every other governmental power, must be exercised in subordination to the applicable provisions of the Constitution. It is quite apparent that if, in the maintenance of our international relations, embarrassment—perhaps serious embarrassment—is to be avoided and success for our aims achieved, congressional legislation which is to be made effective through negotiation and inquiry within the international field must often accord to the President a degree of discretion and freedom from statutory restriction which would not be admissible were domestic affairs alone involved. Moreover, he, not Congress, has the better opportunity of knowing the conditions which prevail in foreign countries, and especially is this true in time of war. He has his confidential sources of information. He has his agents in the form of diplomatic, consular and other officials. Secrecy in respect of information gathered by them may be highly necessary, and the premature disclosure of it productive of harmful results. . . .

When the President is to be authorized by legislation to act in respect of a matter intended to affect a situation in foreign territory, the legislator properly bears in mind the important consideration that the form of the President's action—or, indeed, whether he shall act at all—may well depend, among other things, upon the nature of the confidential information which he has or may thereafter receive, or upon the effect which his action may have upon our foreign relations. This consideration, in connection with what we have already said on the subject discloses the unwisdom of requiring Congress in this field of governmental power to lay down narrowly definite standards by which the President is to be governed. . . .

In the light of the foregoing observations, it is evident that this court should not be in haste to apply a general rule which will have the effect of condemning legislation like that under review as constituting an unlawful delegation of legislative power. The principles which justify such legislation find overwhelming support in the unbroken legislative practice which has prevailed almost from the inception of the national government to the present day. . . .

Practically every volume of the United States Statutes contains one or more acts or joint resolutions of Congress authorizing action by the President in respect of subjects affecting foreign relations, which either leave the exercise of the power to his unrestricted judgment, or provide a standard far more general than that which has always been considered requisite with regard to domestic affairs. . . .

The result of holding that the joint resolution here under attack is void and unenforceable as constituting an unlawful delegation of legislative power would be to stamp this multitude of comparable acts and resolutions as likewise invalid. And while this court may not, and should not, hesitate to declare acts of Congress, however many times repeated, to be unconstitutional if beyond all rational doubt it finds them to be so, an impressive array of legislation such as we have just set forth, enacted by nearly every Congress from the beginning of our national existence to the present day, must be given unusual weight in the process of reaching a correct determination of the problem. A legislative practice such as we have here, evidenced not by only occasional instances, but marked by the movement of a steady stream for a century and a half of time, goes a long way in the direction of proving the presence of unassailable ground for the constitutionality of the practice, to be found in the origin and history of the power involved, or in its nature, or in both combined. . . .

The judgment of the court below must be reversed and the cause remanded for further proceedings in accordance with the foregoing opinion.

It is so ordered.

After years of hostility between the United States and the Soviet Union following the Bolshevik revolution of 1917, President Franklin D. Roosevelt established formal relations with the Soviet regime in 1933 through executive agreements—pacts made between the president and another nation that, unlike treaties, are not subject to Senate confirmation. (As early as 1912, the Supreme Court recognized the validity of executive agreements as international compacts in Altman & Co. v. US, *224 U.S. 583.) Included in this relationship was the settling of various claims between American and Soviet citizens, referred to as the Litvinov Assignment. One claimant, representing the estate of August Belmont, which had lost some holdings as a result of Roosevelt's agreement, challenged its legality, arguing that it was invalid because it was not approved by the Congress and that it could not supersede a state law that regulated funds in a New York bank. In its ruling, the Court upheld Roosevelt's actions and confirmed the legal validity of executive agreements. This ruling dramatically accelerated the use of executive agreements by presidents. In a subsequent case,* U.S. v. Pink *(315 U.S. 203; 1942) dealing with another financial dispute arising from the Litvinov Assignment, the Court reiterated the validity of executive agreements, noting that they possess a "similar dignity" as treaties and that they supersede state laws.*

United States v. Belmont
301 U.S. 324 (1937)

Mr. Justice Sutherland delivered the opinion of the Court. . . .

First. We do not pause to inquire whether in fact there was any policy of the state of New York to be infringed, since we are of opinion that no state policy can prevail against the international compact here involved.

This court has held, *Underhill v. Hernandez, 168 U.S. 250,* 18 S.Ct. 83, that every sovereign state must recognize the independence of every other sovereign state; and that the courts of one will not sit in judgment upon the acts of the government of another, done within its own territory. . . .

This court [has] held that the conduct of foreign relations was committed by the Constitution to the political departments of the government, and the propriety of what may be done in the exercise of this political power was not subject to judicial inquiry or decision; that who is the sovereign of a territory is not a judicial question, but one the determination of which by the political departments conclusively binds the courts; and that recognition by these departments is retroactive and validates all actions and conduct of the government so recognized from the commencement of its existence. 'The principle,' we said, *246 U.S. 297,* at page 303, 38 S.Ct. 309, 311, 'that the conduct of one independent government cannot be successfully questioned in the courts of another is as applicable to a case involving the title to property brought within the custody of a court, such as we have here, as it was held to be to the cases cited, in which claims for damages were based upon acts done in a foreign country, for it rests at last upon the highest considerations of international comity and expediency. To permit the validity of the acts of one sovereign state to be reexamined and perhaps condemned by the courts of another would very certainly 'imperil the amicable relations between governments and vex the peace of nations.' ' . . .

We take judicial notice of the fact that coincident with the assignment set forth in the complaint, the President recognized the Soviet government, and normal diplomatic relations were established between that government and the government of the United States, followed by an exchange of ambassadors. The effect of this was to validate, so far as this country is concerned, all acts of the Soviet government here involved from the commencement of its existence. The recognition, establishment of diplomatic relations, the assignment, and agreements with respect thereto, were all parts of one transaction, resulting in an international compact between the two governments. That the negotiations, acceptance of the assignment and agreements and understandings in respect thereof were within the competence of the President may not be doubted. Governmental power over internal affairs is distributed between the national government and the several states. Governmental power over external affairs is not distributed, but is vested exclusively in the national government. And in respect of what was done here, the Executive had authority to speak as the sole organ of that government. The assignment and the agreements in connection therewith did not, as in the case of treaties, as that term is used in the treaty making clause of the Constitution (article 2, 2), require the advice and consent of the Senate.

A treaty signifies 'a compact made between two or more independent nations, with a view to the public welfare.' *B. Altman & Co. v. United States, 224 U.S. 583, 600, 32 S.Ct. 593, 596.* But an international compact, as this was, is not always a treaty which requires the participation of the Senate. There are many such compacts, of which a protocol, a modus vivendi, a postal convention, and agreements like that now under consideration are illustrations. See 5 Moore, Int.Law Digest, 210–221. The distinction was pointed out by this court in the Altman Case, *supra*, which arose under section 3 of the Tariff Act of 1897 (30 Stat. 151, 203), authorizing the President to conclude commercial agreements with foreign countries in certain specified matters. We held that although

this might not be a treaty requiring ratification by the Senate, it was a compact negotiated and proclaimed under the authority of the President, and as such was a 'treaty' within the meaning of the Circuit Court of Appeals Act (26 Stat. 826), the construction of which might be reviewed upon direct appeal to this court.

Plainly, the external powers of the United States are to be exercised without regard to state laws or policies. The supremacy of a treaty in this respect has been recognized from the beginning. Mr. Madison, in the Virginia Convention, said that if a treaty does not supersede existing state laws, as far as they contravene its operation, the treaty would be ineffective. 'To counteract it by the supremacy of the state laws, would bring on the Union the just charge of national perfidy, and involve us in war.' 3 Elliot's Debates 515. And see *Ware v. Hylton*, 3 Dall. 199, 236, 237. And while this rule in respect of treaties is established by the express language of clause 2, article 6, of the Constitution, the same rule would result in the case of all international compacts and agreements from the very fact that complete power over international affairs is in the national government and is not and cannot be subject to any curtailment or interference on the part of the several states. Compare *United States v. Curtiss-Wright Export Corporation, 299 U.S. 304*, 316 et seq., 57 S.Ct. 216, 219. In respect of all international negotiations and compacts, and in respect of our foreign relations generally, state lines disappear. As to such purposes the state of New York does not exist. Within the field of its powers, what ever the United States rightfully undertakes, it necessarily has warrant to consummate. And when judicial authority is invoked in aid of such consummation, State Constitutions, state laws, and state policies are irrelevant to the inquiry and decision. It is inconceivable that any of them can be interposed as an obstacle to the effective operation of a federal constitutional power. Cf. *Missouri v. Holland, 252 U.S. 416*, 40 S. Ct. 382, 11 A.L.R. 984; *Asakura v. Seattle, 265 U.S. 332, 341*, 44 S.Ct. 515, 516.

Second. The public policy of the United States relied upon as a bar to the action is that declared by the Constitution, namely, that private property shall not be taken without just compensation. But the answer is that our Constitution, laws, and policies have no extraterritorial operation, unless in respect of our own citizens. *Compare United States v. Curtiss-Wright Export Corporation, supra, 299 U.S. 304,* at page 318, 57 S.Ct. 216, 220. What another country has done in the way of taking over property of its nationals, and especially of its corporations, is not a matter for judicial consideration here. Such nationals must look to their own government for any redress to which they may be entitled. So far as the record shows, only the rights of the Russian corporation have been affected by what has been done; and it will be time enough to consider the rights of our nationals when, if ever, by proper judicial proceeding, it shall be made to appear that they are so affected as to entitle them to judicial relief. The substantive right to the moneys, as now disclosed, became vested in the Soviet government as the successor to the corporation; and this right that government has passed to the United States. It does not appear that respondents have any interest in the matter beyond that of a custodian. Thus far no question under the Fifth Amendment is involved.

It results that the complaint states a cause of action and that the judgment of the court below to the contrary is erroneous. In so holding, we deal only with the case as now presented and with the parties now before us. We do not consider the status of adverse claims, if there be any, of others not parties to this action. And nothing we have said is to be construed as foreclosing the assertion of any such claim to the fund involved, by intervention or other appropriate proceeding. We decide only that the complaint alleges facts sufficient to constitute a cause of action against the respondents.

Judgment reversed. . . .

In 1948, American and Canadian officials entered into an agreement to protect American potato growers by barring the importation of potatoes, except for seed potatoes used for planting. Businessman Guy Capps imported and sold potatoes as "table stock" (for eating, not planting) in the United States, in contradiction to the executive agreement. He was prosecuted for violating the agreement, but challenged it by arguing that the executive agreement was contradicted, and therefore nullified, by a federal law, the Agricultural Act of 1948. The federal Court of Appeals agreed, ruling that the executive agreement was invalid because it conflicted with a prior law passed by the Congress; further, by the terms of the Constitution, the power to regulate foreign commerce rests squarely with the Congress. On appeal, the Supreme Court upheld the lower court ruling, but on different grounds (U.S. v. Capps, 348 U.S. 296, 1955).

U.S. v. Guy W. Capps, Inc.
U.S. Court of Appeals,
204 F.2d 655 (4th Cir. 1953)

Judges: Before Parker, Chief Judge, and Soper and Dobie, Circuit Judges.
Opinion by: Parker. . . .

On these facts we think that judgment was properly entered for the defendant, but for reasons other than those given by the District Court. We have little difficulty in seeing in the evidence breach of contract on the part of defendant and damage resulting to the United States from the breach. We think, however, that the executive agreement was void because it was not authorized by Congress and contravened provisions of a statute dealing with the very matter to which it related and that the contract relied on, which was based on the executive agreement, was unenforceable in the courts of the United States for like reason. We think, also, that no action can be maintained by the government to recover damages on account of what is essentially a breach of a trade regulation, in the absence of express authorization by Congress. The power to regulate foreign commerce is vested in Congress, not in the executive or the courts; and the executive may not exercise the power by entering into executive agreements and suing in the courts for damages resulting from breaches of contracts made on the basis of such agreements.

In the Agricultural Act of 1948, Congress had legislated specifically with respect to the limitations which might be imposed on imports if it was thought that they would render ineffective or materially interfere with any program or operation undertaken pursuant to that act. Section 3 of the act, which amended prior statutes, provided in the portion here pertinent, 62 Stat. 1248–1250, 7 U.S.C.A. § 624:

'(a) Whenever the President has reason to believe that any article or articles are being or are practically certain to be imported into the United States under such conditions and in such quantities as to render or tend to render ineffective, or materially interfere with, any program or operation undertaken under this title . . . he shall cause an immediate investigation to be made by the United States Tariff Commission, which shall give precedence to investigations under this section to determine such facts. Such investigation shall be made after due notice and opportunity for hearing to interested parties, and shall be conducted subject to such regulations as the President shall specify.

'(b) If, on the basis of such investigation and report to him of findings and recommendations made in connection therewith, the President finds the existence of such facts, he shall by proclamation impose such . . . quantitative limitations on any article or articles which may be entered . . . for consumption as he finds and declares shown by such investigation to be necessary in order that the entry of such article or articles will not render to tend to render ineffective, or materially interfere with, any program or operation referred to in subsection (a), of this section . . . *Provided*, That no proclamation under this section shall impose any limitation on the total quantity of any article or articles which may be entered . . . for consumption which reduces such permissible total quantity to proportionately less than 50 per centum of the total quantity of such article or articles which was entered . . . for consumption during a representative period as determined by the President: . . . .'

There was no pretense of complying with the requirements of this statute. The President did not cause an investigation to be made by the Tariff Commission, the Commission did not conduct an investigation or make findings or recommendations, and the President made no findings of fact and issued no proclamation imposing quantitative limitations and determined no representative period for the application of the 50 percent limitation contained in the proviso. All that occurred in the making of this executive agreement, the effect of which was to exclude entirely a food product of a foreign country from importation into the United States, was an exchange of correspondence between the Acting Secretary of State and the Canadian Ambassador. Since the purpose of the agreement as well as its effect was to bar imports which would interfere with the Agricultural Adjustment program, it was necessary that the provisions of this statute be complied with and an executive agreement excluding such imports which failed to comply with it was void. . . .

It is argued, however, that the validity of the executive agreement was not dependent upon the Act of Congress but was made pursuant to the inherent powers of the President under the Constitution. The answer is that while the President has certain inherent powers under the Constitution such as the power pertaining to his position as Commander in Chief of Army and Navy and the power necessary to see that the laws are faithfully executed, the power to regulate interstate and foreign commerce is not among the powers incident to the Presidential office, but is expressly vested by the Constitution in the Congress. It cannot be upheld as an exercise of the power to see that the laws are faithfully executed, for, as said by Mr. Justice Holmes in his dissenting opinion in *Myers v. United States*, 272 U.S. 52, 177, 47 S.Ct. 21, 85, 71 L.Ed. 160, 'The duty of the President to see that the laws be executed is a duty that does not go beyond the laws or require him to achieve more than Congress sees fit to leave within his power.' In the recent case of *Youngstown Sheet & Tube Co. v. Sawyer*, 343 U.S. 579, 72 S.Ct. 863, 867, 96 L.Ed. 1153, the

Supreme Court dealt with the question in the following pertinent language:

'Nor can the seizure order be sustained because of the several constitutional provisions that grant executive power to the President. In the framework of our Constitution, the President's power to see that the laws are faithfully executed refutes the idea that he is to be a lawmaker. The Constitution limits his functions in the lawmaking process to the recommending of laws he thinks wise and the vetoing of laws he thinks bad. And the Constitution is neither silent nor equivocal about who shall make laws which the President is to execute. The first section of the first article says that 'All legislative Powers herein granted shall be vested in a Congress of the United States . . . .' After granting many powers to the Congress, Article I goes on to provide that Congress may 'make all Laws which shall be necessary and proper for carrying into Execution the foregoing Powers and all other Powers vested by this Constitution in the Government of the United States, or in any Department or Officer thereof.'

The rule was well stated by Mr. Justice Jackson in his concurring opinion in the case last cited as follows:

'When the President takes measures incompatible with the expressed or implied will of Congress, his power is at its lowest ebb, for then he can rely only upon his own constitutional powers minus any constitutional powers of Congress over the matter. Courts can sustain exclusive Presidential control in such a case only by disabling the Congress from acting upon the subject. Presidential claim to a power at once so conclusive and preclusive must be scrutinized with caution, for what is at stake is the equilibrium established by our constitutional system.'

We think that whatever the power of the executive with respect to making executive trade agreements regulating foreign commerce in the absence of action by Congress, it is clear that the executive may not through entering into such an agreement avoid complying with a regulation prescribed by Congress.

Imports from a foreign country are foreign commerce subject to regulation, so far as this country is concerned, by Congress alone. The executive may not bypass congressional limitations regulating such commerce by entering into an agreement with the foreign country that the regulation be exercised by that country through its control over exports. Even though the regulation prescribed by the executive agreement be more desirable than that prescribed by Congressional action, it is the latter which must be accepted as the expression of national policy.

It is argued that irrespective of the validity of the executive agreement, the contract sued on was a valid contract between defendant and the Canadian exporter and that since the contract was made for the benefit of the United States, this country may maintain action upon it. The answer is that the contract was but the carrying out of the executive agreement entered into in contravention of the policy declared by Congress; and the courts of the United States will not lend their aid to enforcing it against the public policy of the country so declared. As stated, the regulation of imports from foreign countries is a matter for Congress and, when Congress has acted, the executive may not enforce different regulations by suing on contracts made with reference thereto. As said by the Supreme Court in *Oscanyan v. Arms. Co.*, 103 U.S. 261, 277, 26 L.Ed. 539, 'Contracts permissible by other countries are not enforceable in our courts, if they contravene our laws, our morality or our policy.'. . .

For the reasons stated, we do not think that the United States can maintain the action for damages. The judgment for defendant will accordingly be affirmed.

Affirmed.

An American citizen who wanted to travel to Cuba in 1962 was denied permission to do so by the State Department, as Cuba had been ruled off limits to Americans owing to hostility between the United States and the Cuban regime headed by Fidel Castro. The citizen sued, arguing that such travel was not barred by U.S. law, that the State Department's prohibition against traveling there was not valid, and that the ban violated his First Amendment rights. The Supreme Court disagreed, saying that the State Department's decision was authorized by past congressional enactments and by the absence of any effort by the Congress to block the ban, which amounted to an implicit statement of legislative intent supporting the executive branch's decision. Dissenters questioned whether the executive branch, in fact, possessed the power necessary to issue the no-travel ban.

Zemel v. Rusk
381 U.S. 1 (1965)

Mr. Chief Justice Warren delivered the opinion of the Court. . . .

We think that the Passport Act of 1926, 44 Stat. 887, 22 U.S.C. 211a (1958 ed.), embodies a grant of authority to the Executive to refuse to validate the passports of United States citizens for travel to Cuba. That Act provides, in pertinent part:

> "The Secretary of State may grant and issue passports . . . under such rules as the President shall [381 U.S. 1, 8] designate and prescribe for and on behalf of the United States. . . ."

This provision is derived from 23 of the Act of August 18, 1856, 11 Stat. 52, 60–61, which had, prior to 1926, been re-enacted several times without substantial change. The legislative history of the 1926 Act and its predecessors does not, it is true, affirmatively indicate an intention to authorize area restrictions. However, its language is surely broad enough to authorize area restrictions, and there is no legislative history indicating an intent to exclude such restrictions from the grant of authority; these factors take on added significance when viewed in light of the fact that during the decade preceding the passage of the Act, the Executive had imposed both peacetime and wartime area restrictions. . . .

On March 31, 1938, the President, purporting to act pursuant to the 1926 Act, specifically authorized the Secretary to impose area restrictions in the issuance of passports, Exec. Order No. 7856, 3 Fed. Reg. 681, 687:

> "The Secretary of State is authorized in his discretion to refuse to issue a passport to restrict a passport for use only in certain countries to restrict it against use in certain countries, to withdraw or cancel a passport already issued and to withdraw a passport for the purpose of restricting its validity or use in certain countries."

This Executive Order is still in force. 22 CFR 51.75. In September 1939, travel to Europe was prohibited except with a passport specially validated for such travel; passports were so validated only upon a showing of the "imperativeness" of the travel. Departmental Order No. 811, 4 Fed. Reg. 3892.

Area restrictions have also been imposed on numerous occasions since World War II. Travel to Yugoslavia was restricted in the late 1940s as a result of a series of incidents involving American citizens. Dept. State Press Conf., May 9, 1947. Travel to Hungary was restricted between December 1949 and May 1951, and after December 1951. In June 1951, the State Department began to stamp passports "not valid for travel in Czechoslovakia," and declared that all passports outstanding at that time were not valid for such travel. 24 Dept. State Bull. 932. In May 1952, the Department issued a general order that all new passports would be stamped not valid for travel to Albania, Bulgaria, Communist China, Czechoslovakia, Hungary, Poland, Rumania and the Soviet Union. 26 *id.*, at 736. In October 1955, the Secretary announced that passports would no longer require special validation for travel to Czechoslovakia, Hungary, Poland, Rumania, and the Soviet Union, but would be stamped invalid for travel "to the following areas under control of authorities with which the United States does not have diplomatic relations: Albania, Bulgaria, and those portions of China, Korea and Viet-Nam under communist control." 33 *id.*, at 777. In February 1956, the restriction on travel to Hungary was reimposed. 34 *id.*, at 246–248. And in late 1956, passports were for a brief period stamped invalid for travel to or in Egypt, Israel, Jordan, and Syria. 35 *id.*, at 756.

Even if there had been no passport legislation enacted since the 1926 Act, the post-1926 history of executive imposition of area restrictions, as well as the pre-1926 history, would be of relevance to our construction of the Act. The interpretation expressly placed on a statute by those charged with its administration must be given weight by courts faced with the task of construing the statute. Under some circumstances, Congress' failure to repeal or revise in the face of such administrative interpretation has been held to constitute persuasive evidence that that interpretation is the one intended by Congress. In this case, however, the inference is supported by more than mere congressional inaction. For in 1952 Congress, substantially re-enacting laws which had been passed during the First and Second World Wars, provided that after the issuance of a presidential proclamation of war or national emergency, it would be unlawful to leave or enter the United States without a valid passport. Section 215 of the Immigration and Nationality Act of 1952, 66 Stat. 190, 8 U.S.C. 1185 (1958 ed.). The Solicitor General urges that in view of the issuance in 1953 of a presidential proclamation of national emergency which is still outstanding, travel in violation of an area restriction imposed on an otherwise valid passport is unlawful under the 1952 Act. The correctness of this interpretation is a question we do not reach on this appeal, see infra, pp. 18–20. But whether or not the new legislation was intended to attach criminal penalties to the violation of area restrictions, it certainly was not meant to cut back upon the power to impose such restrictions, despite 26 years of executive interpretation of the 1926 Act as authorizing the imposition of area restrictions. Congress in 1952, though it once again enacted legislation relating to passports, left completely untouched the broad rule-making authority granted in the earlier Act. . . .

Having concluded that the Secretary of State's refusal to validate appellant's passport for travel to Cuba is supported by the authority granted by

Congress in the Passport Act of 1926, we must next consider whether that refusal abridges any constitutional right of appellant. Although we do not in this case reach the question of whether the 1952 Act should be read to attach criminal penalties to travel to an area for which one's passport is not validated, we must, if we are to approach the constitutional issues presented by this appeal candidly, proceed on the assumption that the Secretary's refusal to validate a passport for a given area acts as a deterrent to travel to that area. . . .

The requirements of due process are a function not only of the extent of the governmental restriction imposed, but also of the extent of the necessity for the restriction. Cuba is the only area in the Western Hemisphere controlled by a Communist government. It is, moreover, the judgment of the State Department that a major goal of the Castro regime is to export its Communist revolution to the rest of Latin America. The United States and other members of the Organization of American States have determined that travel between Cuba and the other countries of the Western Hemisphere is an important element in the spreading of subversion and many have therefore undertaken measures to discourage such travel. It also cannot be forgotten that in the early days of the Castro regime, United States citizens were arrested and imprisoned without charges. We think, particularly in view of the President's statutory obligation to "use such means, not amounting to acts of war, as he may think necessary and proper" to secure the release of an American citizen unjustly deprived of his liberty by a foreign government, that the Secretary has justifiably concluded that travel to Cuba by American citizens might involve the Nation in dangerous international incidents, and that the Constitution does not require him to validate passports for such travel.

The right to travel within the United States is of course also constitutionally protected, cf. *Edwards v. California, 314 U.S. 160.* But that freedom does not mean that areas ravaged by flood, fire or pestilence cannot be quarantined when it can be demonstrated that unlimited travel to the area would directly and materially interfere with the safety and welfare of the area or the Nation as a whole. So it is with international travel. That the restriction which is challenged in this case is supported by the weightiest considerations of national security is perhaps best pointed up by recalling that the Cuban missile crisis of October 1962 preceded the filing of appellant's complaint by less than two months.

Appellant also asserts that the Secretary's refusal to validate his passport for travel to Cuba denies him rights guaranteed by the First Amendment. . . . We must agree that the Secretary's refusal to validate passports for Cuba renders less than wholly free the flow of information concerning that country. While we further agree that this is a factor to be considered in determining whether appellant has been denied due process of law, we cannot accept the contention of appellant that it is a First Amendment right which is involved. For to the extent that the Secretary's refusal to validate passports for Cuba acts as an inhibition (and it would be unrealistic to assume that it does not), it is an inhibition of action. There are few restrictions on action which could not be clothed by ingenious argument in the garb of decreased data flow. For example, the prohibition of unauthorized entry into the White House diminishes the citizen's opportunities to gather information he might find relevant to his opinion of the way the country is being run, but that does not make entry into the White House a First Amendment right. The right to speak and publish does not carry with it the unrestrained right to gather information.

Finally, appellant challenges the 1926 Act on the ground that it does not contain sufficiently definite standards for the formulation of travel controls by the Executive. It is important to bear in mind, in appraising this argument, that because of the changeable and explosive nature of contemporary international relations, and the fact that the Executive is immediately privy to information which cannot be swiftly presented to, evaluated by, and acted upon by the legislature, Congress—in giving the Executive authority over matters of foreign affairs—must of necessity paint with a brush broader than that it customarily wields in domestic areas.

> "Practically every volume of the United States Statutes contains one or more acts or joint resolutions of Congress authorizing action by the President in respect of subjects affecting foreign relations, which either leave the exercise of the power to his unrestricted judgment, or provide a standard far more general than that which has always been considered requisite with regard to domestic affairs." *United States v. Curtiss-Wright Corp., 299 U.S. 304, 324.*

This does not mean that simply because a statute deals with foreign relations, it can grant the Executive totally unrestricted freedom of choice. However, the 1926 Act contains no such grant. We have held, *Kent v. Dulles, supra,* and reaffirm today, that the 1926 Act must take its content from history: it authorizes only those passport refusals and restrictions "which it could fairly be argued were adopted by Congress in light of prior administrative practice." *Kent v. Dulles, supra,* at 128. So limited, the Act does not constitute an invalid delegation. . . .

The District Court therefore correctly dismissed the complaint, and its judgment is

Affirmed. . . .

MR. JUSTICE BLACK, dissenting.

Article I of the Constitution provides that "All legislative Powers herein granted shall be vested in a Congress of the United States, which shall consist of a Senate and House of Representatives." I have no doubt that this provision grants Congress ample power to enact legislation regulating the issuance and use of passports for travel abroad, unless the particular legislation is forbidden by some specific constitutional prohibition such as, for example, the First Amendment. See *Aptheker v. Secretary of State, 378 U.S. 500, 517* (concurring opinion); cf. *Kent v. Dulles, 357 U.S. 116.* Since

Article I, however, vests "All legislative Powers" in the Congress, and no language in the Constitution purports to vest any such power in the President, it necessarily follows, if the Constitution is to control, that the President is completely devoid of power to make laws regulating passports or anything else. And he has no more power to make laws by labeling them regulations than to do so by calling them laws. Like my Brother Goldberg, I cannot accept the Government's argument that the President has "inherent" power to make regulations governing the issuance and use of passports. Post, pp. 28–30. We emphatically and I think properly rejected a similar argument advanced to support a seizure of the Nation's steel companies by the President. *Youngstown Sheet & Tube Co. v. Sawyer, 343 U.S. 579.* And regulation of passports, just like regulation of steel companies, is a law-making—not an executive, law-enforcing—function.

Nor can I accept the Government's contention that the passport regulations here involved are valid "because the Passport Act of 1926 in unequivocal words delegates to the President and Secretary a general discretionary power over passports. . . . " That Act does provide that "the Secretary of State may grant and issue passports, and cause passports to be granted, issued, and verified in foreign countries . . . under such rules as the President shall designate and prescribe. . . . " Quite obviously, the Government does not exaggerate in saying that this Act "does not provide any specific standards for the Secretary" and "delegates to the President and Secretary a general discretionary power over passports"—a power so broad, in fact, as to be marked by no bounds except an unlimited discretion. It is plain therefore that Congress has not itself passed a law regulating passports; it has merely referred the matter to the Secretary of State and the President in words that say in effect, "We delegate to you our constitutional power to make such laws regulating passports as you see fit." The Secretary of State has proceeded to exercise the power to make such laws regulating the issuance of passports by declaring that he will issue them for Cuba only to "persons whose travel may be regarded as being in the best interests of the United States," as he views those interests. For Congress to attempt to delegate such an undefined law-making power to the Secretary, the President, or both, makes applicable to this 1926 Act what Mr. Justice Cardozo said about the National Industrial Recovery Act: "This is delegation running riot. No such plenitude of power is susceptible of transfer." *A. L. A. Schechter Poultry Corp. v. United States, 295 U.S. 495, 553* (concurring opinion). See also *Panama Ref. Co. v. Ryan, 293 U.S. 388*; cf. *Kent v. Dulles, 357 U.S. 116, 129.*

Our Constitution has ordained that laws restricting the liberty of our people can be enacted by the Congress and by the Congress only. I do not think our Constitution intended that this vital legislative function could be farmed out in large blocks to any governmental official. Whoever he might be, or to any governmental department or bureau, whatever administrative expertise it might be thought to have. The Congress was created on the assumption that enactment of this free country's laws could be safely entrusted to the representatives of the people in Congress, and to no other official or government agency. The people who are called on to obey laws have a constitutional right to have them passed only in this constitutional way. This right becomes all the more essential when as here the person called on to obey may be punishable by five years' imprisonment and a $5,000 fine if he dares to travel without the consent of the Secretary or one of his subordinates. It is irksome enough for one who wishes to travel to be told by the Congress, the constitutional lawmaker with power to legislate in this field, that he cannot go where he wishes. It is bound to be far more irritating—and I do not think the authors of our Constitution, who gave "All" legislative power to Congress, intended—for a citizen of this country to be told that he cannot get a passport because Congress has given an unlimited discretion to an executive official (or viewed practically, to his subordinates) to decide when and where he may go. I repeat my belief that Congress has ample power to regulate foreign travel. And of course, the fact that there may be good and adequate reasons for

Congress to pass such a law is no argument whatever for holding valid a law written not by the Congress but by executive officials. See *Panama Ref. Co. v. Ryan, supra*, 293 U.S. at 420. I think the 1926 Act gives the lawmaking power of Congress to the Secretary and the President and that it therefore violates the constitutional command that "All" legislative power be vested in the Congress. I would therefore reverse the judgment.

In 1978, President Jimmy Carter announced the termination of the United States' Mutual Defense Treaty with Taiwan as a step toward formal recognition of the People's Republic of China. Several senators, including Barry Goldwater, argued that Carter needed a vote from the Senate to revoke the treaty. The Senate failed to act, provoking the lawsuit. Even though the Constitution requires Senate approval for treaty ratification, it is silent on treaty termination, and past history offered no clear guidance, as presidents sometimes had acted with Senate approval, sometimes with full congressional approval, and sometimes unilaterally. A splintered Supreme Court failed to address the matter fully: a majority decided that the case should not be decided on the merits (that is, whether Carter's action was legal), which had the effect of letting Carter's decision stand; three justices wanted to hear the case on the merits.

Goldwater v. Carter
444 U.S. 996 (1979)

Mr. Justice Powell, concurring.

Although I agree with the result reached by the Court, I would dismiss the complaint as not ripe for judicial review.

This Court has recognized that an issue should not be decided if it is not ripe for judicial review. *Buckley v. Valeo, 424 U.S. 1*, 113–114 (1976) (per curiam). Prudential considerations persuade me that a dispute between Congress and the President is not ready for judicial review unless and until each branch has taken action asserting its constitutional

authority. Differences between the President and the Congress are commonplace under our system. The differences should, and almost invariably do, turn on political rather than legal considerations. The Judicial Branch should not decide issues affecting the allocation of power between the President and Congress until the political branches reach a constitutional impasse. Otherwise, we would encourage small groups or even individual Members of Congress to seek judicial resolution of issues before the normal political process has the opportunity to resolve the conflict.

In this case, a few Members of Congress claim that the President's action in terminating the treaty with Taiwan has deprived them of their constitutional role with respect to a change in the supreme law of the land. Congress has taken no official action. In the present posture of this case, we do not know whether there ever will be an actual confrontation between the Legislative and Executive Branches. Although the Senate has considered a resolution declaring that Senate approval is necessary for the termination of any mutual defense treaty, see 125 Cong.Rec. S7015, S7038-S7039 (June 6, 1979), no final vote has been taken on the resolution. See *id.*, at S16683-S16692 (Nov. 15, 1979). Moreover, it is unclear whether the resolution would have retroactive effect. See *id.*, at S7054-S7064 (June 6, 1979); *id.*, at S7862 (June 18, 1979). It cannot be said that either the Senate or the House has rejected the President's claim. If the Congress chooses not to confront the President, it is not our task to do so. I therefore concur in the dismissal of this case.

Mr. Justice Rehnquist suggests, however, that the issue presented by this case is a nonjusticiable political question which can never be considered by this Court. I cannot agree. In my view, reliance upon the political-question doctrine is inconsistent with our precedents. As set forth in the seminal case of *Baker v. Carr, 369 U.S. 186, 217* (1962), the doctrine incorporates three inquiries: (i) Does the issue involve resolution of questions committed by the text of the Constitution to a coordinate branch of Government? (ii) Would resolution of the question demand that a court move beyond areas of judicial expertise? (iii) Do prudential considerations counsel against judicial intervention? In my opinion the answer to each of these inquiries would require us to decide this case if it were ready for review.

First, the existence of "a textually demonstrable constitutional commitment of the issue to a coordinate political department," *ibid.*, turns on an examination of the constitutional provisions governing the exercise of the power in question. *Powell v. McCormack, 395 U.S. 486, 519* (1969). No constitutional provision explicitly confers upon the President the power to terminate treaties. Further, Art. II, 2, of the Constitution authorizes the President to make treaties with the advice and consent of the Senate. Article VI provides that treaties shall be a part of the supreme law of the land. These provisions add support to the view that the text of the Constitution does not unquestionably commit the power to terminate treaties to the President alone. Cf. *Gilligan v. Morgan, 413 U.S. 1, 6* (1973); *Luther v. Borden, 7 How. 1, 42* (1849).

Second, there is no "lack of judicially discoverable and manageable standards for resolving" this case; nor is a decision impossible "without an initial policy determination of a kind clearly for nonjudicial discretion." *Baker v. Carr, supra, 369 U.S., at 217.* We are asked to decide whether the President may terminate a treaty under the Constitution without congressional approval. Resolution of the question may not be easy, but it only requires us to apply normal principles of interpretation to the constitutional provisions at issue. See *Powell v. McCormack, supra, 395 U.S., at 548–549.* The present case involves neither review of the President's activities as Commander in Chief nor impermissible interference in the field of foreign affairs. Such a case would arise if we were asked to decide, for example, whether a treaty required the President to order troops into a foreign country. But "it is error to suppose that every case or controversy which touches foreign relations lies beyond judicial cognizance." *Baker v. Carr, supra, 369 U.S., at 211.* This case "touches" foreign relations, but the question presented to us concerns only the constitutional division of power between Congress and the President.

A simple hypothetical demonstrates the confusion that I find inherent in Mr. Justice Rehnquist's opinion concurring in the judgment. Assume that the President signed a mutual defense treaty with a foreign country and announced that it would go into effect despite its rejection by the Senate. Under Mr. Justice Rehnquist's analysis that situation would present a political question even though Art. II, 2, clearly would resolve the dispute. Although the answer to the hypothetical case seems self-evident because it demands textual rather than interstitial analysis, the nature of the legal issue presented is no different from the issue presented in the case before us. In both cases, the Court would interpret the Constitution to decide whether congressional approval is necessary to give a Presidential decision on the validity of a treaty the force of law. Such an inquiry demands no special competence or information beyond the reach of the Judiciary. Cf. *Chicago & Southern Air Lines v. Waterman S.S. Corp., 333 U.S. 103, 111* (1948).

Finally, the political-question doctrine rests in part on prudential concerns calling for mutual respect among the three branches of Government. Thus, the Judicial Branch should avoid "the potentiality of embarrassment [that would result] from multifarious pronouncements by various departments on one question." Similarly, the doctrine restrains judicial action where there is an "unusual need for unquestioning adherence to a political decision already made." *Baker v. Carr, supra, 369 U.S., at 217.*

If this case were ripe for judicial review, see Part I *supra*, none of these prudential considerations would be present. Interpretation of the Constitution does not imply lack of respect for a coordinate branch. *Powell v. McCormack, supra, 395 U.S., at 548.* If the President and the Congress had reached irreconcilable positions, final disposition of the question presented by this case would eliminate, rather than create, multiple constitutional interpretations. The specter of the Federal Government brought to a halt because of the mutual intransigence of the President and the Congress would require this Court to provide a resolution pursuant to our duty " 'to say what the law is.' " *United States v. Nixon, 418 U.S. 683, 703* (1974), quoting *Marbury v. Madison, 1 Cranch 137, 177* (1803).

In my view, the suggestion that this case presents a political question is incompatible with this Court's willingness on previous occasions to decide whether one branch of our Government has impinged upon the power of another. See *Buckley v. Valeo, 424 U.S.,* at *138; United States v. Nixon, supra, 418 U.S.,* at *707; The Pocket Veto Case, 279 U.S. 655, 676–678* (1929); *Myers v. United States, 272 U.S. 52* (1926). Under the criteria enunciated in *Baker v. Carr,* we have the responsibility to decide whether both the Executive and Legislative Branches have constitutional roles to play in termination of a treaty. If the Congress, by appropriate formal action, had challenged the President's authority to terminate the treaty with Taiwan, the resulting uncertainty could have serious consequences for our country. In that situation, it would be the duty of this Court to resolve the issue.

Mr. Justice Rehnquist, with whom The Chief Justice, Mr. Justice Stewart, and Mr. Justice Stevens join, concurring in the judgment.

I am of the view that the basic question presented by the petitioners in this case is "political" and therefore nonjusticiable because it involves the authority of the President in the conduct of our country's foreign relations and the extent to which the Senate or the Congress is authorized to negate the action of the President. . . .

[T]he controversy in the instant case is a nonjusticiable political dispute that should be left for resolution by the Executive and Legislative Branches of the Government. Here, while the Constitution is express as to the manner in which the Senate shall participate in the ratification of a treaty, it is silent as to that body's participation in the abrogation of a treaty. . . .

In light of the absence of any constitutional provision governing the termination of a treaty, and the fact that different termination procedures may be appropriate for different treaties, the instant case in my view also "must surely be controlled by political standards."

I think that the justifications for concluding that the question here is political in nature are . . . compelling . . . because it involves foreign relations—specifically a treaty commitment to use military force in the defense of a foreign government if attacked. In *United States v. Curtiss-Wright Corp., 299 U.S. 304* (1936), this Court said:

"Whether, if the Joint Resolution had related solely to internal affairs it would be open to the challenge that it constituted an unlawful delegation of legislative power to the Executive, we find it unnecessary to determine. The whole aim of the resolution is to affect a situation entirely external to the United States, and falling within the category of foreign affairs. . . . " *Id.,* at 315.

The present case differs in several important respects from *Youngstown Sheet & Tube Co. v. Sawyer, 343 U.S. 579* (1952), cited by petitioners as authority both for reaching the merits of this dispute and for reversing the Court of Appeals. In *Youngstown,* private litigants brought a suit contesting the President's authority under his war powers to seize the Nation's steel industry, an action of profound and demonstrable domestic impact. Here, by contrast, we are asked to settle a dispute between coequal branches of our Government, each of which has resources available to protect and assert its interests, resources not available to private litigants outside the judicial forum. Moreover, as in *Curtiss-Wright,* the effect of this action, as far as we can tell, is "entirely external to the United States, and [falls] within the category of foreign affairs." Finally, as already noted, the situation presented here is closely akin to that presented in Coleman, where the Constitution spoke only to the procedure for ratification of an amendment, not to its rejection.

Having decided that the question presented in this action is nonjusticiable, I believe that the appropriate disposition is for this Court to vacate the decision of the Court of Appeals and remand with instructions for the District Court to dismiss the complaint. This procedure derives support from our practice in disposing of moot actions in federal courts. For more than 30 years, we have instructed lower courts to vacate any decision on the merits of an action that has become moot prior to a resolution of the case in this Court. *United States v. Munsingwear, Inc., 340 U.S. 36* (1950). The Court has required such decisions to be vacated in order to "prevent a judgment, unreviewable because of mootness, from spawning any legal consequences." *Id.*, at 41. It is even more imperative that this Court invoke this procedure to ensure that resolution of a "political question," which should not have been decided by a lower court, does not "spawn any legal consequences." An Art. III court's resolution of a question that is "political" in character can create far more disruption among the three coequal branches of Government than the resolution of a question presented in a moot controversy. Since the political nature of the questions presented should have precluded the lower courts from considering or deciding the merits of the controversy, the prior proceedings in the federal courts must be vacated, and the complaint dismissed. . . .

Mr. Justice BRENNAN, dissenting.

I respectfully dissent from the order directing the District Court to dismiss this case, and would affirm the judgment of the Court of Appeals insofar as it rests upon the President's well-established authority to recognize, and withdraw recognition from, foreign governments.

In stating that this case presents a nonjusticiable "political question," Mr. Justice Rehnquist, in my view, profoundly misapprehends the political-question principle as it applies to matters of foreign relations. Properly understood, the political-question doctrine restrains courts from reviewing an exercise of foreign policy judgment by the coordinate political branch to which authority to make that judgment has been "constitutional[ly] commit[ted]." *Baker v. Carr*, 369 U.S. 86, 211–213, 217 (1962). But the doctrine does not pertain when a court is faced with the antecedent question whether a particular branch has been constitutionally designated as the repository of political decisionmaking power. Cf. *Powell v. McCormack, 395 U.S. 486*, 519–521 (1969). The issue of decisionmaking authority must be resolved as a matter of constitutional law, not political discretion; accordingly, it falls within the competence of the courts.

The constitutional question raised here is prudently answered in narrow terms. Abrogation of the defense treaty with Taiwan was a necessary incident to Executive recognition of the Peking Government, because the defense treaty was predicated upon the now-abandoned view that the Taiwan Government was the only legitimate political authority in China. Our cases firmly establish that the Constitution commits to the President alone the power to recognize, and withdraw recognition from, foreign regimes. . . .

As part of the agreement between the United States and Iran to end the holding of American citizens in the Iranian hostage crisis, Presidents Jimmy Carter and Ronald Reagan issued several executive orders, pursuant to an executive agreement reached with Iran, to nullify liens on Iranian assets then held in the United States and to suspend American financial claims against Iran. Dames & Moore, an American company owed money by Iran, challenged the presidential actions in court, arguing that the actions exceeded constitutional authority and were not authorized by the Congress. The Supreme Court sided with the presidents, saying that Carter and Reagan's nullification of liens was justified by the International Emergency Economic Powers Act (IEEPA) and that the suspension of claims was justified because Congress's failure to act tacitly authorized the presidents' actions.

Dames & Moore v. Regan
453 U.S. 654 (1981)

Justice Rehnquist delivered the opinion of the Court. . . .

As we now turn to the factual and legal issues in this case, we freely confess that we are obviously deciding only one more episode in the never-ending tension between the President exercising the executive authority in a world that presents each day some new challenge with which he must deal and the Constitution under which we all live and which no one disputes embodies some sort of system of checks and balances. . . .

The parties and the lower courts, confronted with the instant questions, have all agreed that much relevant analysis is contained in *Youngstown Sheet & Tube Co. v. Sawyer, 343 U.S. 579* (1952). Justice Black's opinion for the Court in that case, involving the validity of President Truman's effort to seize the country's steel mills in the wake of a nationwide strike, recognized that "[t]he President's power, if any, to issue the order must stem either from an act of Congress or from the Constitution itself." *Id.*, at 585. Justice Jackson's concurring opinion elaborated in a general way the consequences of different types of interaction between the two democratic branches in assessing Presidential authority to act in any given case. When the President acts pursuant to an express or implied authorization from Congress, he exercises not only his powers but also those delegated by Congress. In such a case the executive action "would be supported by the strongest of presumptions and the widest latitude of judicial interpretation, and the burden of persuasion would rest heavily upon any who might attack it." *Id.*, at 637. When the President acts in the absence of congressional authorization he may enter "a zone of twilight in which he and Congress may have concurrent authority, or in which its distribution is uncertain." *Ibid.* In such a case the analysis becomes more complicated, and the validity of the President's action, at least so far as separation-of-powers principles are concerned, hinges on a consideration of all the circumstances which might shed light on the views of the Legislative Branch toward such action, including "congressional inertia, indifference or quiescence." *Ibid.* Finally, when the President acts in contravention of the will of Congress, "his power is at its lowest ebb," and the Court can sustain his actions "only by disabling the Congress from acting upon the subject." *Id.*, at 637–638.

Although we have in the past found and do today find Justice Jackson's classification of executive actions into three general categories analytically useful, we should be mindful of Justice Holmes' admonition, quoted by Justice Frankfurter in *Youngstown, supra*, at 597 (concurring opinion), that "[t]he great ordinances of the Constitution do not establish and divide fields of black and white." *Springer v. Philippine Islands, 277 U.S. 189, 209* (1928) (dissenting opinion). Justice Jackson himself recognized that his three categories represented "a somewhat over-simplified grouping," *343 U.S., 635*, and it is doubtless the case that executive action in any particular instance falls, not neatly in one of three pigeonholes, but rather at some point along a spectrum running from explicit congressional authorization to explicit congressional prohibition. This is particularly true as respects cases such as the one before us, involving responses to international crises the nature of which Congress can hardly have been expected to anticipate in any detail.

In nullifying post-November 14, 1979, attachments and directing those persons holding blocked Iranian funds and securities to transfer them to the Federal Reserve Bank of New York for ultimate transfer to Iran, President Carter cited five sources of express or inherent power. The Government, however, has principally relied on 203 of the IEEPA, 91 Stat. 1626, 50 U.S.C. 1702 (a) (1) (1976 ed., Supp. III), as authorization for these actions. Section 1702 (a) (1) provides in part:

"At the times and to the extent specified in section 1701 of this title, the President may, under such regulations as he may prescribe, by means of instructions, licenses, or otherwise—

"(A) investigate, regulate, or prohibit—

"(i) any transactions in foreign exchange,

"(ii) transfers of credit or payments between, by, through, or to any banking institution, to the extent that such transfers or payments involve any interest of any foreign country or a national thereof,

"(iii) the importing or exporting of currency or securities, and

"(B) investigate, regulate, direct and compel, nullify, void, prevent or prohibit, any acquisition, holding, withholding, use, transfer, withdrawal, transportation, importation or exportation of, or dealing in, or exercising any right, power, or privilege with respect to, or transactions involving, any property in which any foreign country or a national thereof has any interest;

"by any person, or with respect to any property, subject to the jurisdiction of the United States."

The Government contends that the acts of "nullifying" the attachments and ordering the "transfer" of the frozen assets are specifically authorized by the plain language of the above statute. The two Courts of Appeals that have considered the issue agreed with this contention. . . .

Petitioner contends that we should ignore the plain language of this statute because an examination of its legislative history as well as the history of 5 (b) of the Trading With the Enemy Act (hereinafter TWEA), 40 Stat. 411, as amended, 50 U.S.C. App. 5 (b) (1976 ed. and Supp. III), from which the pertinent language of 1702 is directly drawn, reveals that the statute was not intended to give the President such extensive power over the assets of a foreign state during times of national emergency. According to petitioner, once the President instituted the November 14, 1979, blocking order, 1702 authorized him "only to continue the freeze or to discontinue controls." Brief for Petitioner 32.

We do not agree and refuse to read out of 1702 all meaning to the words "transfer," "compel," or "nullify." Nothing in the legislative history of either 1702 or 5 (b) of the TWEA requires such a result. To the contrary, we think both the legislative history and cases interpreting the TWEA fully sustain the broad authority of the Executive when acting under this congressional grant of power. Although Congress intended to limit the President's emergency power in peacetime, we do not think the changes brought about by the enactment of the IEEPA in any way affected the authority of the President to take the specific actions taken here. We likewise note that by the time petitioner instituted

this action, the President had already entered the freeze order. Petitioner proceeded against the blocked assets only after the Treasury Department had issued revocable licenses authorizing such proceedings and attachments. . . .

This Court has previously recognized that the congressional purpose in authorizing blocking orders is "to put control of foreign assets in the hands of the President. . . . " *Propper v. Clark, 337 U.S. 472, 493* (1949). Such orders permit the President to maintain the foreign assets at his disposal for use in negotiating the resolution of a declared national emergency. The frozen assets serve as a "bargaining chip" to be used by the President when dealing with a hostile country. Accordingly, it is difficult to accept petitioner's argument because the practical effect of it is to allow individual claimants throughout the country to minimize or wholly eliminate this "bargaining chip" through attachments, garnishments, or similar encumbrances on property. Neither the purpose the statute was enacted to serve nor its plain language supports such a result.

Because the President's action in nullifying the attachments and ordering the transfer of the assets was taken pursuant to specific congressional authorization, it is "supported by the strongest of presumptions and the widest latitude of judicial interpretation, and the burden of persuasion would rest heavily upon any who might attack it." *Youngstown, 343 U.S., at 637* (Jackson, J., concurring). Under the circumstances of this case, we cannot say that petitioner has sustained that heavy burden. A contrary ruling would mean that the Federal Government as a whole lacked the power exercised by the President, see *id.*, at 636–637, and that we are not prepared to say.

Although we have concluded that the IEEPA constitutes specific congressional authorization to the President to nullify the attachments and order the transfer of Iranian assets, there remains the question of the President's authority to suspend claims pending in American courts. Such claims have, of course, an existence apart from the attachments which accompanied them. In terminating these claims through Executive Order No. 12294, the President purported to act under authority of both the IEEPA and 22 U.S.C. 1732, the so-called "Hostage Act." 46 Fed. Reg. 14111 (1981).

We conclude that although the IEEPA authorized the nullification of the attachments, it cannot be read to authorize the suspension of the claims. The claims of American citizens against Iran are not in themselves transactions involving Iranian property or efforts to exercise any rights with respect to such property. An in personam lawsuit [a suit against a person—ed.], although it might eventually be reduced to judgment and that judgment might be executed upon, is an effort to establish liability and fix damages and does not focus on any particular property within the jurisdiction. The terms of the IEEPA therefore do not authorize the President to suspend claims in American courts. This is the view of all the courts which have considered the question.

The Hostage Act, passed in 1868, provides:

> "Whenever it is made known to the President that any citizen of the United States has been unjustly deprived of his liberty by or under the authority of any foreign government, it shall be the duty of the President forthwith to demand of that government the reasons of such imprisonment; and if it appears to be wrongful and in violation of the rights of American citizenship, the President shall forthwith demand the release of such citizen, and if the release so demanded is unreasonably delayed or refused, the President shall use such means, not amounting to acts of war, as he may think necessary and proper to obtain or effectuate the release; and all the facts and proceedings relative thereto shall as soon as practicable be communicated by the President to Congress." Rev. Stat. 2001, 22 U.S.C. 1732.

We are reluctant to conclude that this provision constitutes specific authorization to the President to suspend claims in American courts. Although the broad language of the Hostage Act suggests it may cover this case, there are several difficulties with such a view. The legislative history indicates that the Act was passed in response to a situation unlike the recent Iranian crisis. Congress in 1868 was concerned with the activity of certain countries refusing to recognize the citizenship of naturalized Americans traveling abroad, and repatriating such citizens against their will. These countries were not interested in returning the citizens in exchange for any sort of ransom. This also explains the reference in the Act to imprisonment "in violation of the rights of American citizenship." Although the Iranian hostage-taking violated international law and common decency, the hostages were not seized out of any refusal to recognize their American citizenship—they were seized precisely because of their American citizenship. The legislative history is also somewhat ambiguous on the question whether Congress contemplated Presidential action such as that involved here or rather simply reprisals directed against the offending foreign country and its citizens.

Concluding that neither the IEEPA nor the Hostage Act constitutes specific authorization of the President's action suspending claims, however, is not to say that these statutory provisions are entirely irrelevant to the question of the validity of the President's action. We think both statutes highly relevant in the looser sense of indicating congressional acceptance of a broad scope for executive action in circumstances such as those presented in this case. . . .

Crucial to our decision today is the conclusion that Congress has implicitly approved the practice of claim settlement by executive agreement. This is best demonstrated by Congress' enactment of the International Claims Settlement Act of 1949, 64 Stat. 13, as amended, 22 U.S.C. 1621 et seq. (1976 ed. and Supp. IV). The Act had two purposes: (1) to allocate to United States nationals funds received in the course of an executive claims settlement with Yugoslavia, and (2) to provide a procedure whereby funds resulting from future settlements could be distributed. To achieve these ends Congress created the International Claims Commission, now the Foreign Claims Settlement Commission, and gave it jurisdiction to make final and binding decisions with respect to claims by United States nationals against settlement funds. 22 U.S.C. 1623 (a). By creating a procedure to implement future settlement agreements, Congress placed its stamp of approval on such agreements. Indeed, the legislative history of the Act observed that the United States was seeking settlements with countries other than Yugoslavia and that the bill contemplated settlements of a similar nature in the future. H. R. Rep. No. 770, 81st Cong., 1st Sess., 4, 8 (1949).

Over the years Congress has frequently amended the International Claims Settlement Act to provide for particular problems arising out of settlement agreements, thus demonstrating Congress' continuing acceptance of the President's claim settlement authority. . . .

In addition to congressional acquiescence in the President's power to settle claims, prior cases of this Court have also recognized that the President does have some measure of power to enter into executive agreements without obtaining the advice and consent of the Senate. In *United States v. Pink, 315 U.S. 203* (1942), for example, the Court upheld the validity of the Litvinov Assignment, which was part of an Executive Agreement whereby the Soviet Union assigned to the United States amounts owed to it by American nationals so that outstanding claims of other American nationals could be paid. . . .

Petitioner raises two arguments in opposition to the proposition that Congress has acquiesced in this longstanding practice of claims settlement by executive agreement. First, it suggests that all pre-1952 settlement claims, and corresponding court cases such as Pink, should be discounted because of the evolution of the doctrine of sovereign immunity. Petitioner observes that prior to 1952 the United States adhered to the doctrine of absolute sovereign immunity, so that absent action by the Executive there simply would be no remedy for a United States national against a foreign government. When the United States in 1952 adopted a more restrictive notion of sovereign immunity, by means of the so-called "Tate" letter, it is petitioner's view that United States nationals no longer needed executive aid to settle claims and that as a result, the President's authority to settle such claims in some sense "disappeared." Though petitioner's argument is not wholly without merit, it is refuted by the fact that since 1952 there have been at least 10 claims settlements by executive agreement. Thus, even if the pre-1952 cases should be disregarded, congressional acquiescence in settlement agreements since that time supports the President's power to act here.

Petitioner next asserts that Congress divested the President of the authority to settle claims when it enacted the Foreign Sovereign Immunities Act of 1976 (hereinafter FSIA). 28 U.S.C. 1330, 1602 et seq. The FSIA granted personal and subject-matter jurisdiction in the federal district courts over commercial suits brought by claimants against those foreign states which have waived immunity. 28 U.S.C. 1330. Prior to the enactment of the FSIA, a foreign government's immunity to suit was determined by the Executive Branch on a case-by-case basis. According to petitioner, the principal purpose of the FSIA was to depoliticize these commercial lawsuits by taking them out of the arena of foreign affairs—where the Executive Branch is subject to the pressures of foreign states seeking to avoid liability through a grant of immunity—and by placing them within the exclusive jurisdiction of the courts. Petitioner thus insists that the President, by suspending its claims, has circumscribed the jurisdiction of the United States courts in violation of Art. III of the Constitution.

We disagree. In the first place, we do not believe that the President has attempted to divest the federal courts of jurisdiction. Executive Order No. 12294 purports only to "suspend" the claims, not divest the federal court of "jurisdiction." As we read the Executive Order, those claims not within the jurisdiction of the Claims Tribunal will "revive" and become judicially enforceable in United States courts. This case, in short, illustrates the difference between modifying federal-court jurisdiction and directing the courts to apply a different rule of law.

The President has exercised the power, acquiesced in by Congress, to settle claims and, as such, has simply effected a change in the substantive law governing the lawsuit. . . .

In light of all of the foregoing—the inferences to be drawn from the character of the legislation Congress has enacted in the area, such as the IEEPA and the Hostage Act, and from the history of acquiescence in executive claims settlement—we conclude that the President was authorized to suspend pending claims pursuant to Executive Order No. 12294. As Justice Frankfurter pointed out in *Youngstown, 343 U.S., at 610–611,* "a systematic, unbroken, executive practice, long pursued to the knowledge of the Congress and never before questioned . . . may be treated as a gloss on 'Executive Power' vested in the President by 1 of Art. II." Past practice does not, by itself, create power, but "long-continued practice, known to and acquiesced in by Congress, would raise a presumption that the [action] had been [taken] in pursuance of its consent . . . ." *United States v. Midwest Oil Co., 236 U.S. 459, 474* (1915). Such practice is present here and such a presumption is also appropriate. In light of the fact that Congress may be considered to have consented to the President's action in suspending claims, we cannot say that action exceeded the President's powers. . . .

Just as importantly, Congress has not disapproved of the action taken here. Though Congress has held hearings on the Iranian Agreement itself, Congress has not enacted legislation, or even passed a resolution, indicating its displeasure with the Agreement. Quite the contrary, the relevant Senate Committee has stated that the establishment of the Tribunal is "of vital importance to the United States." S. Rep. No. 97–71, p. 5 (1981). We are thus clearly not confronted with a situation in which Congress has in some way resisted the exercise of Presidential authority.

Finally, we re-emphasize the narrowness of our decision. We do not decide that the President possesses plenary power to settle claims, even as against foreign governmental entities. As the Court of Appeals for the First Circuit stressed, "[t]he sheer magnitude of such a power, considered against the background of the diversity and complexity of modern international trade, cautions against any broader construction of authority than is necessary." *Chas. T. Main Int'l, Inc. v. Khuzestan Water & Power Authority,* 651 F.2d, at 814. But where, as here, the settlement of claims has been determined to be a necessary incident to the resolution of a major foreign policy dispute between our country and another, and where, as here, we can conclude that Congress acquiesced in the President's action, we are not prepared to say that the President lacks the power to settle such claims. . . .

The judgment of the District Court is accordingly affirmed, and the mandate shall issue forthwith.

It is so ordered. . . .

Philip Agee, former Central Intelligence Agency (CIA) officer turned author, began a campaign against his former employer to reveal the names of CIA agents in an effort to disrupt their activities and drive them from the countries where they were stationed. These activities prompted Secretary of State Alexander Haig to revoke Agee's passport. Agee sued, arguing that the secretary overstepped the authority granted by the Congress and violated his freedom to travel as well as his First Amendment rights to criticize the government and his Fifth Amendment due process rights. Two lower courts sided with Agee, but the Supreme Court overturned them, concluding that the government acted properly, in large measure because of Agee's perceived threat to national security.

Haig v. Agee
453 U.S. 280 (1981)

Chief Justice Burger delivered the opinion of the Court. . . .

[W]e begin with the language of the statute. The Passport Act of 1926 provides in pertinent part:

"The Secretary of State may grant and issue passports, and cause passports to be granted, issued, and verified in foreign countries by diplomatic representatives of the United States . . . under such rules as the President shall designated and prescribe for and on behalf of the United States, and no other person shall grant, issue, or verify such passports." 22 U.S.C. 211a (1976 ed., Supp. IV).

This language is unchanged since its original enactment in 1926.

The Passport Act does not in so many words confer upon the Secretary a power to revoke a passport. Nor, for that matter, does it expressly authorize denials of passport applications. Neither, however, does any statute expressly limit those powers. It is beyond dispute that the Secretary has the power to deny a passport for reasons not specified in the statutes. For example, in *Kent v. Dulles, 357 U.S. 116 (1958)*, the Court recognized congressional acquiescence in Executive policies of refusing passports to applicants "participating in illegal conduct, trying to escape the toils of the law, promoting passport frauds, or otherwise engaging in conduct which would violate the laws of the United States." *Id.,* at 127. In *Zemel,* the Court held that "the weightiest considerations of national security" authorized the Secretary to restrict travel to Cuba at the time of the Cuban missile crisis. *381 U.S., at 16.* Agee concedes that if the Secretary may deny a passport application for a certain reason, he may revoke a passport on the same ground.

Particularly in light of the "broad rule-making authority granted in the 1926 Act," *Zemel, 381 U.S., at 12*, a consistent administrative construction of that statute must be followed by the courts " 'unless there are compelling indications that it is wrong.' " This is especially so in the areas of foreign policy and national security, where congressional silence is not to be equated with congressional disapproval. In *United States v. Curtiss-Wright Export Corp., 299 U.S. 304 (1936)*, the volatile nature of problems confronting the Executive in foreign policy and national defense was underscored:

"In this vast external realm, with its important, complicated, delicate and manifold problems,

the President alone has the power to speak or listen as a representative of the nation. . . . As Marshall said in his great argument of March 7, 1800, in the House of Representatives, 'The President is the sole organ of the nation in its external relations, and its sole representative with foreign nations.' " *Id.,* at 319.

Applying these considerations to statutory construction, the Zemel Court observed:

"[B]ecause of the changeable and explosive nature of contemporary international relations, and the fact that the Executive is immediately privy to information which cannot be swiftly presented to, evaluated by, and acted upon by the legislature, Congress—in giving the Executive authority over matters of foreign affairs—must of necessity paint with a brush broader than that it customarily wields in domestic areas." *381 U.S., at 17.*

Matters intimately related to foreign policy and national security are rarely proper subjects for judicial intervention. In *Harisiades v. Shaughnessy, 342 U.S. 580 (1952)*, the Court observed that matters relating "to the conduct of foreign relations . . . are so exclusively entrusted to the political branches of government as to be largely immune from judicial inquiry or interference." *Id.,* at 589; accord, *Chicago & Southern Air Lines, Inc. v. Waterman S.S. Corp., 333 U.S. 103, 111 (1948)*. . . .

A passport is, in a sense, a letter of introduction in which the issuing sovereign vouches for the bearer and requests other sovereigns to aid the bearer. . . .

With the enactment of travel control legislation making a passport generally a requirement for travel abroad, a passport took on certain added characteristics. Most important for present purposes, the only means by which an American can lawfully leave the country or return to it—absent a Presidentially granted exception—is with a passport. See 8 U.S.C. 1185 (b) (1976 ed., Supp. IV). As a travel control document, a passport is both proof of identity and proof of allegiance to the

United States. Even under a travel control statute, however, a passport remains in a sense a document by which the Government vouches for the bearer and for his conduct.

The history of passport controls since the earliest days of the Republic shows congressional recognition of Executive authority to withhold passports on the basis of substantial reasons of national security and foreign policy. Prior to 1856, when there was no statute on the subject, the common perception was that the issuance of a passport was committed to the sole discretion of the Executive and that the Executive would exercise this power in the interests of the national security and foreign policy of the United States. This derived from the generally accepted view that foreign policy was the province and responsibility of the Executive. From the outset, Congress endorsed not only the underlying premise of Executive authority in the areas of foreign policy and national security, but also its specific application to the subject of passports. Early Congresses enacted statutes expressly recognizing the Executive authority with respect to passports. . . .

This history of administrative construction was repeatedly communicated to Congress, not only by routine promulgation of Executive Orders and regulations, but also by specific presentations, including 1957 and 1966 reports by the Department of State explaining the 1956 regulation and a 1960 Senate Staff Report which concluded that "the authority to issue or withhold passports has, by precedent and law, been vested in the Secretary of State as a part of his responsibility to protect American citizens traveling abroad, and what he considered to be the best interests of the Nation."

In 1966, the Secretary of State promulgated the regulations at issue in this case. 22 CFR 51.70 (b)(4), 51.71 (a) (1980). Closely paralleling the 1956 regulation, these provisions authorize revocation of a passport where "[t]he Secretary determines that the national's activities abroad are causing or are likely to cause serious damage to the national security or the foreign policy of the United States."

Zemel recognized that congressional acquiescence may sometimes be found from nothing more than silence in the face of an administrative policy. *381 U.S., at 11.* Here, however, the inference of congressional approval "is supported by more than mere congressional inaction." *Zemel, 381 U.S., at 11–12.* Twelve years after the promulgation of the regulations at issue and 22 years after promulgation of the similar 1956 regulation, Congress enacted the statute making it unlawful to travel abroad without a passport even in peacetime. 8 U.S.C. 1185 (b) (1976 ed., Supp. IV). Simultaneously, Congress amended the Passport Act of 1926 to provide that "[u]nless authorized by law," in the absence of war, armed hostilities, or imminent danger to travelers, a passport may not be geographically restricted. Title 8 U.S.C. 1185 (b) (1976 ed., Supp. IV) must be read in pari materia with [along with—ed.] the Passport Act.

The 1978 amendments are weighty evidence of congressional approval of the Secretary's interpretation, particularly that in the 1966 regulations. Despite the longstanding and officially promulgated view that the Executive had the power to withhold passports for reasons of national security and foreign policy, Congress in 1978, "though it once again enacted legislation relating to passports, left completely untouched the broad rulemaking authority granted in the earlier Act." *Zemel, supra,* at 12. . . .

The Secretary has construed and applied his regulations consistently, and it would be anomalous to fault the Government because there were so few occasions to exercise the announced policy and practice. Although a pattern of actual enforcement is one indicator of Executive policy, it suffices that the Executive has "openly asserted" the power at issue. *Zemel, 381 U.S., at 9*; see *id.,* at 10. . . .

Agee also contends that the statements of Executive policy are entitled to diminished weight because many of them concern the powers of the Executive in wartime. However, the statute provides no support for this argument. History eloquently attests that grave problems of national security and foreign policy are by no means limited to times of formally declared war. . . .

The protection accorded beliefs standing alone is very different from the protection accorded conduct. Thus, in *Aptheker v. Secretary of State, supra,* the Court held that a statute which, like the policy at issue in Kent, denied passports to Communists solely on the basis of political beliefs unconstitutionally "establishes an irrebuttable presumption that individuals who are members of the specified organizations will, if given passports, engage in activities inimical to the security of the United States." *378 U.S., at 511.* The Court recognized that the legitimacy of the objective of safeguarding our national security is "obvious and unarguable." . . .

Beliefs and speech are only part of Agee's "campaign to fight the United States CIA." In that sense, this case contrasts markedly with the facts in *Kent* and *Aptheker.* No presumptions, rebuttable or otherwise, are involved, for Agee's conduct in foreign countries presents a serious danger to American officials abroad and serious danger to the national security. . . .

Agee also attacks the Secretary's action on three constitutional grounds: first, that the revocation of his passport impermissibly burdens his freedom to travel; second, that the action was intended to penalize his exercise of free speech and deter his criticism of Government policies and practices; and third, that failure to accord him a prerevocation hearing violated his Fifth Amendment right to procedural due process.

In light of the express language of the passport regulations, which permits their application only in cases involving likelihood of "serious damage" to national security or foreign policy, these claims are without merit.

Revocation of a passport undeniably curtails travel, but the freedom to travel abroad with a "letter of introduction" in the form of a passport issued by the sovereign is subordinate to national security and foreign policy considerations; as such, it is subject to reasonable governmental regulation. The Court has made it plain that the freedom to travel outside the United States must be distinguished from the right to travel within the United States. . . .

Not only has Agee jeopardized the security of the United States, but he has also endangered the interests of countries other than the United States—thereby creating serious problems for American foreign relations and foreign policy. Restricting Agee's foreign travel, although perhaps not certain to prevent all of Agee's harmful activities, is the only avenue open to the Government to limit these activities.

Assuming, arguendo [in the course of an argument—ed.], that First Amendment protections reach beyond our national boundaries, Agee's First Amendment claim has no foundation. The revocation of Agee's passport rests in part on the content of his speech: specifically, his repeated disclosures of intelligence operations and names of intelligence personnel. Long ago, however, this Court recognized that "[n]o one would question but that a government might prevent actual obstruction to its recruiting service or the publication of the sailing dates of transports or the number and location of troops." *Near v. Minnesota* ex rel. Olson, *283 U.S. 697, 716* (1931), citing Z. Chafee, Freedom of Speech 10 (1920). Agee's disclosures, among other things, have the declared purpose of obstructing intelligence operations and the recruiting of intelligence personnel. They are clearly not protected by the Constitution. The mere fact that Agee is also engaged in criticism of the Government does not render his conduct beyond the reach of the law.

To the extent the revocation of his passport operates to inhibit Agee, "it is an inhibition of action," rather than of speech. *Zemel, 381 U.S., at 16–17.* Agee is as free to criticize the United States Government as he was when he held a passport—always subject, of course, to express limits on certain rights by virtue of his contract with the Government. See *Snepp v. United States, supra.*

On this record, the Government is not required to hold a prerevocation hearing. In *Cole v. Young, supra,* we held that federal employees who hold "sensitive" positions "where they could bring about any discernible adverse effects on the Nation's security" may be suspended without a presuspension hearing. *351 U.S., at 546–547.* For the same reasons, when there is a substantial likelihood of "serious damage" to national security or foreign policy as a result of a passport holder's activities in foreign countries, the Government may take action to ensure that the holder may not exploit the sponsorship of his travels by the United States. "[W]hile the Constitution protects against invasions of individual rights, it is not a suicide pact." *Kennedy v. Mendoza-Martinez, 372 U.S. 144,* 160 (1963). The Constitution's due process guarantees call for no more than what has been accorded here: a statement of reasons and an opportunity for a prompt postrevocation hearing.

We reverse the judgment of the Court of Appeals and remand for further proceedings consistent with this opinion.

Reversed and remanded. . . .

JUSTICE BRENNAN, with whom JUSTICE MARSHALL joins, dissenting. . . .

This is not a complicated case. The Court has twice articulated the proper mode of analysis for determining whether Congress has delegated to the Executive Branch the authority to deny a passport under the Passport Act of 1926. *Zemel v. Rusk, 381 U.S. 1* (1965); *Kent v. Dulles, 357 U.S. 116* (1958). The analysis is hardly confusing, and I expect that had the Court faithfully applied it, today's judgment would affirm the decision below.

In *Kent v. Dulles, supra,* the Court reviewed a challenge to a regulation of the Secretary denying passports to applicants because of their alleged Communist beliefs and associations and their refusals to file affidavits concerning present or past membership in the Communist Party. Observing that the right to travel into and out of this country is an important personal right included within the "liberty" guaranteed by the Fifth Amendment, *id.,* at 125–127, the Court stated that any infringement of that liberty can only "be pursuant to the law-making functions of the Congress," and that delegations to the Executive Branch that curtail that liberty must be construed narrowly, *id.,* at 129. Because the Passport Act of 1926—the same statute at issue here—did not expressly authorize the denial of passports to alleged Communists, the Court examined cases of actual passport refusals by the Secretary to determine whether "it could be fairly argued" that this category of passport refusals was "adopted by Congress in light of prior administrative practice." *Id.,* at 128. The Court was unable to find such prior administrative practice, and therefore held that the regulation was unauthorized. . . .

As in *Kent* and *Zemel,* there is no dispute here that the Passport Act of 1926 does not expressly authorize the Secretary to revoke Agee's passport. *Ante,* 290. Therefore, the sole remaining inquiry is whether there exists "with regard to the sort of passport [revocation] involved [here], an administrative practice sufficiently substantial and consistent to warrant the conclusion that Congress had implicitly approved it." *Zemel v. Rusk, supra,* at 12. The Court today, citing to this same page in Zemel, applies a test markedly different from that of Zemel and Kent and in fact expressly disavowed by the latter. The Court states: "We hold that the policy announced in the challenged regulations is 'sufficiently substantial and consistent' to compel the conclusion that Congress has approved it. See *Zemel, 381 U.S., at 12.*" *Ante,* at 306. The Court also observes that "a consistent administrative construction of [the Passport Act] must be followed by the courts ' "unless there are compelling indications that it is wrong." ' " *Ante,* at 291.

But clearly neither *Zemel* nor *Kent* holds that a longstanding Executive policy or construction is sufficient proof that Congress has implicitly authorized the Secretary's action. The cases hold that an administrative practice must be demonstrated; in fact *Kent* unequivocally states that mere construction by the Executive—no matter how longstanding and consistent—is not sufficient. . . . The Court's requirement in *Kent* of evidence of the Executive's exercise of discretion as opposed to its possession of discretion may best be understood as a preference for the strongest proof that Congress knew of and acquiesced in that authority. The presence of sensitive constitutional questions in the passport revocation context cautions against applying the normal rule that administrative constructions in cases of statutory construction are to be given great weight. Only when Congress had maintained its silence in the face of a consistent and substantial pattern of actual passport denials or revocations—where the parties will presumably object loudly, perhaps through legal action, to the Secretary's exercise of discretion—can this Court be sure that Congress is aware of the Secretary's actions and has implicitly approved that exercise of discretion. Moreover, broad statements by the Executive Branch relating to its discretion in the passport area lack the precision of definition that would follow from concrete applications of that discretion in specific cases. Although Congress might register general approval of the Executive's overall policy, it still might disapprove of the Executive's pattern of applying that broad rule in specific categories of cases. . . .

I suspect that this case is a prime example of the adage that "bad facts make bad law." Philip Agee is hardly a model representative of our Nation. And the Executive Branch has attempted to use one of the only means at its disposal, revocation of a passport, to stop respondent's damaging statements. But just as the Constitution protects both popular and unpopular speech, it likewise protects both popular and unpopular travelers. And it is important to remember that this decision applies not only to Philip Agee, whose activities could be perceived as harming the national security, but also to other citizens who may merely disagree with Government foreign policy and express their views.

The Constitution allocates the lawmaking function to Congress, and I fear that today's decision has handed over too much of that function to the Executive. In permitting the Secretary to stop this unpopular traveler and critic of the CIA, the Court professes to rely on, but in fact departs from, the two precedents in the passport regulation area, Zemel and Kent. Of course it is always easier to fit oneself within the safe haven of stare decisis [stick to precedent—ed.] than boldly to overrule precedents of several decades' standing. Because I find myself unable to reconcile those cases with the decision in this case, however, and because I disagree with the Court's sub silentio [unstated—ed.] overruling of those cases, I dissent.

The War Power and the Commander in Chief

No power of government is more momentous than that concerning war and peace. In the twentieth century, many presidents cited the commander-in-chief power as a basis for instituting military action, as if the power over military decisions rested with the president alone. Yet this is not what the Constitution says, nor was it the intention of the framers. As the wording of Article II of the Constitution says, "The President shall be Commander in Chief of the Army and Navy of the United States, and of the Militia of the several States, when called into the actual Service of the United States." The Congress does the calling.

In contrast with the British system, where the monarch possessed the powers over war, peace, and the military, America's framers vested final war-making and military authority in the Congress. Thus, the Congress could make war without the president, but the president could not make war without Congress. The framers would have met the idea of the president possessing sole and final power or war-related decisions with shock, if not outrage.

Yet it is equally true that, over time, presidents came to exercise more actual control over military decisions, owing in large measure to the Congress's willingness to acquiesce to the president's preferences.

The first cases in this chapter are often overlooked by those seeking the Supreme Court's view of the war and commander-in-chief powers. Yet they continue to stand as good law as they recognize the Congress's final power. The later cases pay greater deference to presidential preferences and initiative in military action. Even the most recent cases, from 2004, however, admonish the president's overly grandiose claims to sole power over war and the military.

The power of the Congress to declare war (what is also called a "perfect" or general war) is expressly stated in the Constitution. Yet the Congress also has the power to authorize limited military actions short of a full-blown declaration of war. Such limited, or "imperfect," conflicts often arise, including the so-called Quasi War with France from 1798 to 1800. In this case, a dispute arose concerning the fate of a ship and its cargo that had been seized by a French privateer, but later recaptured by America. In resolving the matter of what percentage of the recaptured ship's cargo should be returned to the owners, the Supreme Court addressed the broader question of the Congress's power over all forms of international conflict. Four justices wrote opinions, but they all agreed that the Congress had the right to authorize not only a general or declared war, but also a more limited conflict, as it may define in law.

Bas v. Tingy
4 Dall. 37 (1800)

The Judges delivered their opinions *seriatim* [one after the other—ed.] in the following manner. . . .

Washington, Justice. . . . The decision of this question must depend upon . . . whether, at the time of passing the act of congress of the 2d of March 1799, there subsisted a state of war between the two nations? It may, I believe, be safely laid down, that every contention by force between two nations, in external matters, under the authority of their respective governments, is not only war, but public war. If it be declared in form, it is called solemn, and is of the perfect kind; because one whole nation is at war with another whole nation; and all the members of the nation declaring war, are authorized to commit hostilities against all the members of the other, in every place, and under every circumstance. In such a war all the members act under a general authority, and all the rights and consequences of war attach to their condition.

But hostilities may subsist between two nations, more confined in its nature and extent; being limited as to places, persons, and things; and this is more properly termed imperfect war; because not solemn, and because those who are authorized to commit hostilities, act under special authority, and can go no farther than to the extent of their commission. Still, however, it is public war, because it is an external contention by force between some of the members of the two nations, authorized by the legitimate powers. It is a war between the two nations, though all the members are not authorized to commit hostilities such as in a solemn war, where the government restrain the general power. . . .

Chase, Justice. . . . Congress is empowered to declare a general war, or congress may wage a limited war; limited in place, in objects, and in time. If a general war is declared, its extent and operations are only restricted and regulated by the *jus belli* [the law of war—ed.], forming a part of the law of nations; but if a partial law is waged, its extent and operation depend on our municipal laws.

What then is the nature of the contest subsisting between America and France? In my judgment, it is a limited, partial, war. Congress has not declared war in general terms; but congress has authorized hostilities on the high seas by certain persons in certain cases. There is no authority given to commit hostilities on land; to capture unarmed French vessels, nor even to capture French armed vessels lying in a French port; and the authority is not given indiscriminately, to every citizen of America, against every citizen of France, but only to citizens appointed by commissions, or exposed to immediate outrage and violence. So far it is, unquestionably, a partial war; but, nevertheless, it is a public war, on account of the public authority from which it emanates. . . .

As there may be a public general war, and a public qualified war; so there may, upon correspondent principles, be a general enemy, and a partial enemy. The designation of "enemy" extends to a case of perfect war; but as a general designation, it surely includes the less, as well as the greater, species of warfare. If congress had chosen to declare a general war, France would have been a general enemy; having chosen to wage a partial war, France was, at the time of the capture, only a partial enemy; but still she was an enemy. . . .

Responding to specific instructions from President John Adams, American warships sought to seize any armed French shipping during America's Quasi War with France. In one case, an American ship seized an armed merchant ship flying under French colors that turned out to have been taken earlier by the French from another nation. This seizure set up a dispute over who had proper claim to the ship and its contents—the Americans or the original owners. Although the details of this dispute, covered at length in the Court's opinion, need not concern us, the guiding principle of the decision, written by Chief Justice John Marshall, does: Preeminent authority regarding war, whether full or limited, lies with Congress.

Talbot v. Seeman
5 U.S. (1 Cranch) 1 (1801)

Opinion by Marshall. . . .

The whole powers of war being, by the constitution of the United States, vested in congress, the acts of that body can alone be resorted to as our guides in this enquiry. It is not denied, nor in the course of the argument has it been denied, that congress may authorize general hostilities, in which case the general laws of war apply to our situation; or partial hostilities, in which case the laws of war, so far as they actually apply to our situation, must be noticed. . . .

Pursuant to a 1799 law passed by the Congress, the president was empowered to instruct American sea captains (by use of an executive order) to suspend trade between France and the United States during the Quasi War with France by stopping and impounding any American ships bound for France or other French ports. Yet the law said that only ships headed to French ports were to be stopped; those heading away from French ports were specifically excluded. In his executive order to American ship commanders, however, President John Adams said that "you are to be vigilant that vessels or cargoes really American . . . and bound to or from French ports, do not escape you." Ruling that law made by the Congress superseded Adams's executive order, the Court concluded that even though Captain Little was properly following the president's order, he was nonetheless "answerable in damages to the owner" for the improper seizure. Upholding a lower court ruling, the Court struck down Adams's executive order.

Little v. Barreme
6 U.S. 170 (Cranch) 1804

Chief Justice Marshall delivered the opinion of the court.

The Flying Fish, a Danish vessel, having on board Danish and neutral property, was captured on the 2d of December 1799, on a voyage from Jeremie to St. Thomas's, by the United States frigate Boston, commanded by Captain Little, and brought into the port of Boston, where she was libelled as an American vessel that had violated the non-intercourse law.

The judge before whom the cause was tried, directed a restoration of the vessel and cargo as neutral property, but refused to award damages for the capture and detention, because, in his opinion, there was probable cause to suspect the vessel to be American.

On an appeal to the circuit court this sentence was reversed, because the Flying Fish was on a voyage from, not to, a French port, and was therefore, had she even been an American vessel, not liable to capture on the high seas. During the hostilities between the United States and France, an act for the suspension of all intercourse between the two nations was annually passed. That under which the Flying Fish was condemned, declared every vessel, owned, hired or employed wholly or in part by an American, which should be employed in any traffic or commerce with or for any person resident within the jurisdiction or under the authority of the French Republic, to be forfeited together with her cargo; the one half to accrue to the United States, and the other to any person or persons, citizens of the United States, who will inform and prosecute for the same.

The fifth section of this act authorizes the president of the United States, to instruct the commanders of armed vessels, 'to stop and examine any ship or vessel of the United States on the high sea, which there may be reason to suspect to be engaged in any traffic or commerce contrary to the true tenor of the act, and if upon examination it should appear that such ship or vessel is bound or sailing to any or place within the territory of the French republic or her dependencies, it is rendered lawful to seize such vessel, and send her into the United States for adjudication.'

It is by no means clear that the president of the United States, whose high duty it is to 'take care that the laws be faithfully executed,' and who is commander in chief of the armies and navies of the United States, might not, without any special authority for that purpose, in the then existing state of things, have empowered the officers commanding the armed vessels of the United States, to seize and send into port for adjudication, American vessels which were forfeited by being engaged in this illicit commerce. But when it is observed that . . . the fifth section gives a special authority to seize on the high seas, and limits that authority to the seizure of vessels bound or sailing to a French port, the legislature seem to have prescribed that the manner in which this law shall be carried into execution, was to exclude a seizure of any vessel not bound to a French port. Of consequence, however strong the circumstances might be, which induced Captain Little to suspect the Flying Fish to be an American vessel, they could not excuse the detention of her, since he would not have been authorized to detain her had she been really American.

It was so obvious, that if only vessels sailing to a French port could be seized on the high seas, that the law would be very often evaded, that this act of congress appears to have received a different construction from the executive of the United States; a construction much better calculated to give it effect.

A copy of this act was transmitted by the secretary of the navy to the captains of the armed vessels, who were ordered to consider the fifth section as a part of their instructions. The same letter contained the following clause. 'A proper discharge of the important duties enjoined on you, arising out of this act, will require the exercise of a sound and an impartial judgment. You are not only to do all that in you lies, to prevent all intercourse, whether direct or circuitous, between the ports of the United States and those of France or her dependencies, where the vessels are apparently as well as really American, and protected by American papers only, but you are to be vigilant that vessels or cargoes really American, but covered by Danish or other foreign papers, and bound to or from French ports, do not escape you.'

These orders, given by the executive under the construction of the act of congress made by the department to which its execution was assigned, enjoin the seizure of American vessels sailing from a French port. Is the officer who obeys them liable for damages sustained by this misconstruction of the act, or will his orders excuse him? If his instructions afford him no protection, then the law must take its course, and he must pay such damages as are legally awarded against him. . . . [T]he instructions [sent from the president] cannot change the nature of the transaction, or legalize an act which without those instructions would have been a plain trespass.

It becomes therefore unnecessary to inquire whether the probable cause afforded by the conduct of the Flying Fish to suspect her of being an American, would excuse Captain Little from damages for having seized and sent her into port, since had she actually been an American, the seizure would have been unlawful.

Captain Little then must be answerable in damages to the owner of this neutral vessel, and as the account taken by order of the circuit court is not objectionable on its face, and has not been excepted to by counsel before the proper tribunal, this court can receive no objection to it.

There appears then to be no error in the judgment of the circuit court, and it must be affirmed with costs.

At the outset of the Civil War, newly elected president Abraham Lincoln ordered a blockade of southern ports in several proclamations issued in April 1861. As a result, a number of ships were seized by the Union Navy. The owners in turn sued for their return, based in part on the claim that the president had exceeded his authority. The Congress did not pass legislation to endorse Lincoln's actions until July—three months after the initial seizures. Although both the Supreme Court majority and minority here agreed that only the Congress can declare war, the majority upheld Lincoln's actions, arguing that he was obliged to confront the South's domestic insurrection and not wait for the Congress to convene and act. Note that the Congress never declared war against the South, because to do so would have recognized that the South was entitled to be considered a separate, sovereign nation; rather, the conflict was considered a domestic insurrection—yet one that the Court treats as the equivalent of war.

The Prize Cases
67 U.S. 635 (1863)

Mr. Justice Grier.

There are certain propositions of law which must necessarily affect the ultimate decision of these cases, and many others, which it will be proper to discuss and decide before we notice the special facts peculiar to each.

They are, 1st. Had the President a right to institute a blockade ofports in possession of persons in armed rebellion against the Government, on the principles of international law, as known and acknowledged among civilized States?

2d. Was the property of persons domiciled or residing within those States a proper subject of capture on the sea as 'enemies' property?'

I. Neutrals have a right to challenge the existence of a blockade *de facto* [in fact—ed.], and also the authority of the party exercising the right to institute it. They have a right to enter the ports of a friendly nation for the purposes of trade and commerce, but are bound to recognize the rights of a belligerent engaged in actual war, to use this mode of coercion, for the purpose of subduing the enemy.

That a blockade *de facto* actually existed, and was formally declared and notified by the President on the 27th and 30th of April, 1861, is an admitted fact in these cases.

That the President, as the Executive Chief of the Government and Commander-in-chief of the Army and Navy, was the proper person to make such notification, has not been, and cannot be disputed.

The right of prize and capture has its origin in the "jus belli," [the law of war—ed.] and is governed and adjudged under the law of nations. To legitimate the capture of a neutral vessel or property on the high seas, a war must exist *de facto*, and the neutral must have knowledge or notice of the intention of one of the parties belligerent to use this mode of coercion against a port, city, or territory, in possession of the other.

Let us enquire whether, at the time this blockade was instituted, a state of war existed which would justify a resort to these means of subduing the hostile force.

War has been well defined to be, 'That state in which a nation prosecutes its right by force.'

The parties belligerent in a public war are independent nations. But it is not necessary to constitute war, that both parties should be acknowledged as independent nations or sovereign States. A war may exist where one of the belligerents, claims sovereign rights as against the other.

Insurrection against a government may or may not culminate in an organized rebellion, but a civil war always begins by insurrection against the lawful authority of the Government. A civil war is never solemnly declared; it becomes such by its accidents— the number, power, and organization of the persons who originate and carry it on. When the party in rebellion occupy and hold in a hostile manner a certain portion of territory; have declared their independence; have cast off their allegiance; have organized armies; have commenced hostilities against their former sovereign, the world acknowledges them as belligerents, and the contest a war. They claim to be in arms to establish their liberty and independence, in order to become a sovereign State, while the sovereign party treats them as insurgents and rebels who owe allegiance, and who should be punished with death for their treason. . . .

As a civil war is never publicly proclaimed, eo nominee [by name—ed.], against insurgents, its actual existence is a fact in our domestic history which the Court is bound to notice and to know. . . .

By the Constitution, Congress alone has the power to declare a national or foreign war. It cannot declare war against a State, or any number of States, by virtue of any clause in the Constitution. The Constitution confers on the President the whole Executive power. He is bound to take care that the laws be faithfully executed. He is Commander-in-chief of the Army and Navy of the United States, and of the militia of the several States when called into the actual service of the United States. He has no power to initiate or declare a war either against a foreign nation or a domestic State. But by the Acts of Congress of February 28th, 1795, and 3d of March, 1807, he is authorized to called out the militia and use the military and naval forces of the United States in case of invasion by foreign nations, and to suppress insurrection against the government of a State or of the United States.

If a war be made by invasion of a foreign nation, the President is not only authorized but bound to resist force by force. He does not initiate the war, but is bound to accept the challenge without waiting for any special legislative authority. And whether the hostile party be a foreign invader, or States organized in rebellion, it is none the less a war, although the declaration of it be 'unilateral.' . . .

The battles of Palo Alto and Resaca de la Palma had been fought before the passage of the Act of Congress of May 13th, 1846, which recognized 'a state of war as existing by the act of the Republic of Mexico.' This act not only provided for the future prosecution of the war, but was itself a vindication and ratification of the Act of the President in accepting the challenge without a previous formal declaration of war by Congress.

This greatest of civil wars was not gradually developed by popular commotion, tumultuous assemblies, or local unorganized insurrections. However long may have been its previous conception, it nevertheless sprung forth suddenly from the parent brain, a Minerva in the full panoply of war. The President was bound to meet it in the shape it presented itself, without waiting for Congress to baptize it with a name; and no name given to it by him or them could change the fact. . . .

Whether the President in fulfilling his duties, as Commander-in-chief, in suppressing an insurrection, has met with such armed hostile resistance, and a civil war of such alarming proportions as will compel him to accord to them the character of belligerents, is a question to be decided by him, and this Court must be governed by the decisions and acts of the political department of the Government to which this power was entrusted. 'He must determine what degree of force the crisis demands.' The proclamation of blockade is itself official and conclusive evidence to the Court that a state of war existed which demanded and authorized a recourse to such a measure, under the circumstances peculiar to the case. . . .

If it were necessary to the technical existence of a war, that it should have a legislative sanction, we find it in almost every act passed at the extraordinary session of the Legislature [U.S. Congress—ed.] of 1861, which was wholly employed in enacting laws to enable the Government to prosecute the war with vigor and efficiency. And finally, in 1861, we find Congress 'ex majore cautela' [with the greatest care—ed.] and in anticipation of such astute objections, passing an act 'approving, legalizing, and making valid all the acts, proclamations, and orders of the President, &c., as if they had been issued and done under the previous express authority and direction of the Congress of the United States.'. . .

The objection made to this act of ratification, that it is ex post facto [after the fact—ed.], and therefore unconstitutional and void, might possibly have some weight on the trial of an indictment in a criminal Court. But precedents from that source cannot be received as authoritative in a tribunal administering public and international law.

On this first question therefore we are of the opinion that the President had a right, jure belli [by the law of war—ed.], to institute a blockade of ports in possession of the States in rebellion, which neutrals are bound to regard.

Mr. Justice NELSON, dissenting.

. . . We are of [the] opinion . . . that, according to the very terms of the proclamation, neutral ships wereentitled to a warning by one of the blockading squadron and could be lawfully seized only on the second attempt to enter or leave the port.

It is remarkable, also, that both the President and the Secretary, in referring to the blockade, treat the measure, not as a blockade under the law of nations, but as a restraint upon commerce at the interdicted portsunder the municipal laws of the Government. . . .

[T]he right of making war belongs exclusively to the supreme or sovereign power of the State.

This power in all civilized nations is regulated by the fundamental laws or municipal constitution of the country.

By our constitution this power is lodged in Congress. Congress shall have power 'to declare war, grant letters of marque and reprisal, and make rules concerning captures on land and water.'. . .

We have thus far been speaking of the war power under the Constitution of the United States, and as known and recognized by the law of nations. But we are asked, what would become of the peace and integrity of the Union in case of an insurrection at home or invasion from abroad if this power could not be exercised by the President in the recess of Congress, and until that body could be assembled?

The framers of the Constitution fully comprehended this question, and provided for the contingency. Indeed, it would have been surprising if they had not, as a rebellion had occurred in the State of Massachusetts while the Convention was in session, and which had become so general that it was quelled only by calling upon the military power of the State. The Constitution declares that Congress shall have power 'to provide for calling forth the militia to execute the laws of the Union, suppress insurrections, and repel invasions.' Another clause, 'that the President shall be Commander-in-chief of the Army and Navy of the United States, and of the militia of the several States when called into the actual service of United States;' and, again, 'He shall take care that the laws shall be faithfully executed.' Congress passed laws on this subject in 1792 and 1795. . . .

The law of war . . . is reserved to the legislative department by the express words of the Constitution. It cannot be delegated or surrendered to the Executive. Congress alone can determine whether war exists or should be declared; and until they have acted, no citizen of the State can be punished in his person or property, unless he has committed some offence against a law of Congress passed before the act was committed, which made it a crime, and defined the punishment. The penalty of confiscation for the acts of others with which he had no concern cannot lawfully be inflicted. . . .

Congress assembled on the call for an extra session the 4th of July, 1861, and among the first acts passed was one in which the President was authorized by proclamation to interdict all trade and intercourse between all the inhabitants of States in insurrection and the rest of the United States, subjecting vessel and cargo to capture and condemnation as prize, and also to direct the capture of any ship or vessel belonging in whole or in part to any inhabitant of a State whose inhabitants are declared by the proclamation to be in a state of insurrection, found at sea or in any part of the rest of the United States. Act of Congress of 13th of July, 1861, secs. 5, 6. The 4th section also authorized the President to close any port in a Collection District obstructed so that the revenue could not be collected, and provided for the capture and condemnation of any vessel attempting to enter.

The President's Proclamation was issued on the 16th of August following, and embraced Georgia, North and South Carolina, part of Virginia, Tennessee, Alabama, Louisiana, Texas, Arkansas, Mississippi and Florida.

This Act of Congress, we think, recognized a state of civil war between the Government and the Confederate States, and made it territorial. . . .

Upon the whole, after the most careful consideration of this case which the pressure of other duties has admitted, I am compelled to the conclusion that no civil war existed between this Government and the States in insurrection till recognized by the Act of Congress 13th of July, 1861; that the President does not possess the power under the Constitution to declare war or recognize its existence within the meaning of the law of nations, which carries with it belligerent rights, and thus change the country and all its citizens from a state of peace to a state of war; that this power belongs exclusively to the Congress of the United States, and, consequently, that the President had no power to set on foot a blockade under the law of nations, and that the capture of the vessel and cargo in this case, and in all cases before us in which the capture occurred before the 13th of July, 1861, for breach of blockade, or as enemies' property, are illegal and void, and that the decrees of condemnation should be reversed and the vessel and cargo restored.

Mr. Chief Justice Taney, Mr. Justice Catron and Mr. Justice Clifford, concurred in the dissenting opinion of Mr. Justice Nelson.

Lambdin Milligan was an Indiana citizen and Confederate sympathizer who was tried and convicted in a military court in 1864 of conspiring to release Confederate soldiers. He was convicted by a military tribunal, instead of in the regular criminal courts, and sentenced to death. Milligan appealed his conviction, arguing that the military tribunal had no jurisdiction over him, as he was a civilian, and that he was entitled to a jury trial. The Supreme Court sided with Milligan, but did so in a ruling handed down in 1866—after the Civil War had ended. Oddly, the Court did not know if Milligan was still alive when it handed down its decision (he was), but it assumed that he was, based on the case made for him by his lawyer. In its ringing majority decision, the Court rejected the idea that the government could try a northern citizen by military tribunal under martial law, in effect suspending the man's procedural rights, when the civil courts were available and functioning. "No graver question was ever considered by this court," the majority intoned. Supreme authority in the matter rested with the Congress; because it did not provide for such military tribunals, this executive action could not stand.

Ex Parte Milligan
71 U.S. 2 (1866)

Mr. Justice DAVIS delivered the opinion of the court.

On the 10th day of May, 1865, Lambdin P. Milligan presented a petition to the Circuit Court of the United States for the District of Indiana, to be discharged from an alleged unlawful imprisonment. The case made by the petition is this: Milligan is a citizen of the United States; has lived for twenty years in Indiana; and, at the time of the grievances complained of, was not, and never had been in the military or naval service of the United States. . . .

The importance of the main question presented by this record cannot be overstated; for it involves the very framework of the government and the fundamental principles of American liberty.

During the late wicked Rebellion, the temper of the times did not allow that calmness in deliberation and discussion so necessary to a correct conclusion of a purely judicial question. Then, considerations of safety were mingled with the exercise of power; and feelings and interests prevailed which are happily terminated. Now that the public safety is assured, this question, as well as all others, can be discussed and decided without passion or the admixture of any element not required to form a legal judgment. We approach the investigation of this case, fully sensible of the magnitude of the inquiry and the necessity of full and cautious deliberation. . . .

The controlling question in the case is this: Upon the facts stated in Milligan's petition, and the exhibits filed, had the military commission mentioned in it jurisdiction, legally, to try and sentence him? Milligan, not a resident of one of the rebellious states, or a prisoner of war, but a citizen of Indiana for twenty years past, and never in the military or naval service, is, while at his home, arrested by the military power of the United States, imprisoned, and, on certain criminal charges preferred against him, tried, convicted, and sentenced to be hanged by a military commission, organized under the direction of the military commander of the military district of Indiana. Had this tribunal the legal power and authority to try and punish this man?

No graver question was ever considered by this court, nor one which more nearly concerns the rights of the whole people; for it is the birthright of every American citizen when charged with crime, to be tried and punished according to law. . . .

The Constitution of the United States is a law for rulers and people, equally in war and in peace, and covers with the shield of its protection all classes of men, at all times, and under all circumstances. No doctrine, involving more pernicious consequences, was ever invented by the wit of man than that any of its provisions can be suspended during any of the great exigencies of government. Such a doctrine leads directly to anarchy or despotism, but the theory of necessity on which it is based is false; for the government, within the Constitution, has all the powers granted to it, which are necessary to preserve its existence; as has been happily proved by the result of the great effort to throw off its just authority. . . .

This nation, as experience has proved, cannot always remain at peace, and has no right to expect that it will always have wise and humane rulers, sincerely attached to the principles of the Constitution. Wicked men, ambitious of power, with hatred of liberty and contempt of law, may fill the place once occupied by Washington and Lincoln; and if this right is conceded, and the calamities of war again befall us, the dangers to human liberty are frightful to contemplate. If our fathers had failed to provide for just such a contingency, they would have been false to the trust reposed in them. They knew—the history of the world told them—the nation they were founding, be its existence short or long, would be involved in war; how often or how long continued, human foresight could not tell; and that unlimited power, wherever lodged at such a time, was especially hazardous to freemen. For this, and other equally weighty reasons, they secured the inheritance they had fought to maintain, by incorporating in a written constitution the safeguards which time had proved were essential to its preservation. Not one of these safeguards can the President, or Congress, or the Judiciary disturb, except the one concerning the writ of habeas corpus. . . .

Martial law cannot arise from a threatened invasion. The necessity must be actual and present; the invasion real, such as effectually closes the courts and deposes the civil administration.

It is difficult to see how the safety for the country required martial law in Indiana. If any of her citizens were plotting treason, the power of arrest could secure them, until the government was prepared for their trial, when the courts were open and ready to try them. It was as easy to protect witnesses before a civil as a military tribunal; and as there could be no wish to convict, except on sufficient legal evidence, surely an ordained and established court was better able to judge of this than a military tribunal composed of gentlemen not trained to the profession of the law.

. . . Martial rule can never exist where the courts are open, and in the proper and unobstructed exercise of their jurisdiction. It is also confined to the locality of actual war. Because, during the late Rebellion it could have been enforced in Virginia, where the national authority was overturned and the courts driven out, it does not follow that it should obtain in Indiana, where that authority was never disputed, and justice was always administered. . . .

But it is insisted that Milligan was a prisoner of war, and, therefore, excluded from the privileges of the statute. It is not easy to see how he can be treated as a prisoner of war, when he lived in Indiana for the past twenty years, was arrested there, and had not been, during the late troubles, a resident of any of the states in rebellion. If in Indiana he conspired with bad men to assist the enemy, he is punishable for it in the courts of Indiana; but, when tried for the offence, he cannot plead the rights of war; for he was not engaged in legal acts of hostility against the government, and only such persons, when captured, are prisoners of war. If he cannot enjoy the immunities attaching to the character of a prisoner of war, how can he be subject to their pains and penalties? . . .

The Chief Justice delivered the following opinion.

Four members of the court, concurring with their brethren in the order heretofore made in this cause, but unable to concur in some important particulars with the opinion which has just been read, think it their duty to make a separate statement of their views of the whole case.

... [T]he opinion which has just been read ... asserts not only that the military commission held in Indiana was not authorized by Congress, but that it was not in the power of Congress to authorize it; from which it may be thought to follow, that Congress has no power to indemnify the officers who composed the commission against liability in civil courts for acting as members of it.

We cannot agree to this.

We agree in the proposition that no department of the government of the United States—neither President, nor Congress, nor the Courts—possesses any power not given by the Constitution.

We assent, fully, to all that is said, in the opinion, of the inestimable value of the trial by jury, and of the other constitutional safeguards of civil liberty. And we concur, also, in what is said of the writ of habeas corpus [an order to bring the accused before a judge—ed.], and of its suspension, with two reservations: (1) That, in our judgment, when the writ is suspended, the Executive is authorized to arrest as well as to detain; and (2) that there are cases in which, the privilege of the writ being suspended, trial and punishment by military commission, in states where civil courts are open, may be authorized by Congress, as well as arrest and detention.

We think that Congress had power, though not exercised, to authorize the military commission which was held in Indiana. . . .

Congress has power to raise and support armies; to provide and maintain a navy; to make rules for the government and regulation of the land and naval forces; and to provide for governing such part of the militia as may be in the service of the United States.

It is not denied that the power to make rules for the government of the army and navy is a power to provide for trial and punishment by military courts without a jury. It has been so understood and exercised from the adoption of the Constitution to the present time. . . .

Congress has the power not only to raise and support and govern armies but to declare war. It has, therefore, the power to provide by law for carrying on war. This power necessarily extends to all legislation essential to the prosecution of war with vigor and success, except such as interferes with the command of the forces and the conduct of campaigns. That power and duty belong to the President as commander-in-chief. Both these powers are derived from the Constitution, but neither is defined by that instrument. Their extent must be determined by their nature, and by the principles of our institutions. . . .

We by no means assert that Congress can establish and apply the laws of war where no war has been declared or exists.

Where peace exists the laws of peace must prevail. What we do maintain is, that when the nation is involved in war, and some portions of the country are invaded, and all are exposed to invasion, it is within the power of Congress to determine in what states or district such great and imminent public danger exists as justifies the authorization of military tribunals for the trial of crimes and offences against the discipline or security of the army or against the public safety. . . .

Mr. Justice Wayne, Mr. Justice Swayne, and Mr. Justice Miller concur with me in these views.

During World War II, eight Germans (two of whom were naturalized American citizens) surreptitiously landed on American shores in 1942 to commit acts of sabotage, but all were promptly captured. A special, secret military commission convened by President Franklin D. Roosevelt tried them. All were found guilty; six were sentenced to death. They petitioned the Supreme Court, arguing that the president lacked authority to try them by military tribunal, deny them access to the civilian courts, and deprive them of procedural safeguards including trial by jury. A unanimous Court ruled that the military trial was justifiable under the president's commander-in-chief powers and congressional enactments. The decision later provoked much criticism by those who noted that it departed from the Milligan *decision, in that the civilian courts were functioning in America at the time, the United States was not an actual theater of war, and the decision placed much power in presidential hands.*

Ex Parte Quirin
317 U.S. 1 (1942)

PER CURIAM. . . .

Petitioners' main contention is that the President is without any statutory or constitutional authority to order the petitioners to be tried by military tribunal for offenses with which they are charged; that in consequence they are entitled to be tried in the civil courts with the safeguards, including trial by jury, which the Fifth and Sixth Amendments guarantee to all persons charged in such courts with criminal offenses. In any case it is urged that the President's Order, in prescribing the procedure of the [Military—ed.] Commission and the method for review of its findings and sentence, and the proceedings of the Commission under the Order, conflict with Articles of War adopted by Congress— particularly Articles 38, 43, 46, 50 1/2 and 70— and are illegal and void.

The Government challenges each of these propositions. But regardless of their merits, it also insists that petitioners must be denied access to the courts, both because they are enemy aliens or have entered our territory as enemy belligerents, and because the President's Proclamation undertakes in terms to deny such access to the class of persons defined by the Proclamation, which aptly describes the character and conduct of petitioners. It is urged that if they are enemy aliens or if the Proclamation has force no court may afford the petitioners a hearing. But there is certainly nothing in the Proclamation to preclude access to the courts for determining its applicability to the particular case. And neither the Proclamation nor the fact that they are enemy aliens forecloses consideration by the courts of petitioners' contentions that the Constitution and laws of the United States constitutionally enacted forbid their trial by military

commission. As announced in our per curiam opinion [decision of the whole—ed.] we have resolved those questions by our conclusion that the Commission has jurisdiction to try the charge preferred against petitioners. There is therefore no occasion to decide contentions of the parties unrelated to this issue. We pass at once to the consideration of the basis of the Commission's authority.

We are not here concerned with any question of the guilt or innocence of petitioners. Constitutional safeguards for the protection of all who are charged with offenses are not to be disregarded in order to inflict merited punishment on some who are guilty. But the detention and trial of petitioners—ordered by the President in the declared exercise of his powers as Commander in Chief of the Army in time of war and of grave public danger—are not to be set aside by the courts without the clear conviction that they are in conflict with the Constitution or laws of Congress constitutionally enacted. . . .

From the very beginning of its history this Court has recognized and applied the law of war as including that part of the law of nations which prescribes, for the conduct of war, the status, rights and duties of enemy nations as well as of enemy individuals. By the Articles of War, and especially Article 15, Congress has explicitly provided, so far as it may constitutionally do so, that military tribunals shall have jurisdiction to try offenders or offenses against the law of war in appropriate cases. Congress, in addition to making rules for the government of our Armed Forces, has thus exercised its authority to define and punish offenses against the law of nations by sanctioning, within constitutional limitations, the jurisdiction of military commissions to try persons for offenses which, according to the rules and precepts of the law of nations, and more particularly the law of war, are cognizable by such tribunals. And the President, as Commander in Chief, by his Proclamation in time of war his invoked that law. By his Order creating the present Commission he has undertaken to exercise the authority conferred upon him by Congress, and also such authority as the Constitution itself gives the Commander in Chief, to direct the performance of those functions which may constitutionally be performed by the military arm of the nation in time of war.

An important incident to the conduct of war is the adoption of measures by the military command not only to repel and defeat the enemy, but to seize and subject to disciplinary measures those enemies who in their attempt to thwart or impede our military effort have violated the law of war. It is unnecessary for present purposes to determine to what extent the President as Commander in Chief has constitutional power to create military commissions without the support of Congressional legislation. For here Congress has authorized trial of offenses against the law of war before such commissions. We are concerned only with the question whether it is within the constitutional power of the national government to place petitioners upon trial before a military commission for the offenses with which they are charged. We must therefore first inquire whether any of the acts charged is an offense against the law of war cognizable before a military tribunal, and if so whether the Constitution prohibits the trial. We may assume that there are acts regarded in other countries, or by some writers on international law, as offenses against the law of war which would not be triable by military tribunal here, either because they are not recognized by our courts as violations of the law of war or because they are of that class of offenses constitutionally triable only by a jury. It was upon such grounds that the Court denied the right to proceed by military tribunal in *Ex parte Milligan, supra.* But as we shall show, these petitioners were charged with an offense against the law of war which the Constitution does not require to be tried by jury.

It is no objection that Congress in providing for the trial of such offenses has not itself undertaken to codify that branch of international law or to mark its precise boundaries, or to enumerate or define by statute all the acts which that law condemns. An Act of Congress punishing 'the crime of piracy as defined by the law of nations' is an appropriate exercise of its constitutional authority, Art. I, 8, cl. 10, 'to define and punish' the offense since it has

adopted by reference the sufficiently precise definition of international law. . . .

By universal agreement and practice the law of war draws a distinction between the armed forces and the peaceful populations of belligerent nations and also between those who are lawful and unlawful combatants. Lawful combatants are subject to capture and detention as prisoners of war by opposing military forces. Unlawful combatants are likewise subject to capture and detention, but in addition they are subject to trial and punishment by military tribunals for acts which render their belligerency unlawful. The spy who secretly and without uniform passes the military lines of a belligerent in time of war, seeking to gather military information and communicate it to the enemy, or an enemy combatant who without uniform comes secretly through the lines for the purpose of waging war by destruction of life or property, are familiar examples of belligerents who are generally deemed not to be entitled to the status of prisoners of war, but to be offenders against the law of war subject to trial and punishment by military tribunals. . . .

Our Government, by thus defining lawful belligerents entitled to be treated as prisoners of war, has recognized that there is a class of unlawful belligerents not entitled to that privilege, including those who though combatants do not wear 'fixed and distinctive emblems'. And by Article 15 of the Articles of War Congress has made provision for their trial and punishment by military commission, according to 'the law of war'.

By a long course of practical administrative construction by its military authorities, our Government has likewise recognized that those who during time of war pass surreptitiously from enemy territory into our own, discarding their uniforms upon entry, for the commission of hostile acts involving destruction of life or property, have the status of unlawful combatants punishable as such by military commission. This precept of the law of war has been so recognized in practice both here and abroad, and has so generally been accepted as valid by authorities on international law that we think it must be regarded as a rule or principle of the law of war recognized by this Government. . . .

As we have seen, entry upon our territory in time of war by enemy belligerents, including those acting under the direction of the armed forces of the enemy, for the purpose of destroying property used or useful in prosecuting the war, is a hostile and war-like act. It subjects those who participate in it without uniform to the punishment prescribed by the law of war for unlawful belligerents. It is without significance that petitioners were not alleged to have borne conventional weapons or that their proposed hostile acts did not necessarily contemplate collision with the Armed Forces of the United States. Paragraphs 351 and 352 of the Rules of Land Warfare, already referred to, plainly contemplate that the hostile acts and purposes for which unlawful belligerents may be punished are not limited to assaults on the Armed Forces of the United States. Modern warfare is directed at the destruction of enemy war supplies and the implements of their production and transportation quite as much as at the armed forces. Every consideration which makes the unlawful belligerent punishable is equally applicable whether his objective is the one or the other. The law of war cannot rightly treat those agents of enemy armies who enter our territory, armed with explosives intended for the destruction of war industries and supplies, as any the less belligerent enemies than are agent similarly entering for the purpose of destroying fortified places or our Armed Forces. By passing our boundaries for such purposes without uniform or other emblem signifying their belligerent status, or by discarding that means of identification after entry, such enemies become unlawful belligerents subject to trial and punishment.

Citizenship in the United States of an enemy belligerent does not relieve him from the consequences of a belligerency which is unlawful because in violation of the law of war. Citizens who associate themselves with the military arm of the enemy government, and with its aid, guidance and direction enter this country bent on hostile acts are enemy belligerents within the meaning of the

Hague Convention and the law of war. Cf. *Gates v. Goodloe, 101 U.S. 612, 615*, 617 S., 618. It is as an enemy belligerent that petitioner Haupt is charged with entering the United States, and unlawful belligerency is the gravamen [the gist of a charge—ed.] of the offense of which he is accused. Nor are petitioners any the less belligerents if, as they argue, they have not actually committed or attempted to commit any act of depredation or entered the theatre or zone of active military operations. The argument leaves out of account the nature of the offense which the Government charges and which the Act of Congress, by incorporating the law of war, punishes. It is that each petitioner, in circumstances which gave him the status of an enemy belligerent, passed our military and naval lines and defenses or went behind those lines, in civilian dress and with hostile purpose. The offense was complete when with that purpose they entered—or, having so entered, they remained upon—our territory in time of war without uniform or other appropriate means of identification. For that reason, even when committed by a citizen, the offense is distinct from the crime of treason defined in Article III, 3 of the Constitution, since the absence of uniform essential to one is irrelevant to the other.

But petitioners insist that even if the offenses with which they are charged are offenses against the law of war, their trial is subject to the requirement of the Fifth Amendment that no person shall be held to answer for a capital or otherwise infamous crime unless on a presentment or indictment of a grand jury, and that such trials by Article III, 2, and the Sixth Amendment must be by jury in a civil court. Before the Amendments, 2 of Article III, the Judiciary Article, had provided: 'The Trial of all Crimes, except in Cases of Impeachment, shall be by Jury', and had directed that 'such Trial shall be held in the State where the said Crimes shall have been committed'. . . .

We cannot say that Congress in preparing the Fifth and Sixth Amendments intended to extend trial by jury to the cases of alien or citizen offenders against the law of war otherwise triable by military commission, while withholding it from members of our own armed forces charged with infractions of the Articles of War punishable by death. It is equally inadmissible to construe the Amendments—whose primary purpose was to continue unimpaired presentment by grand jury and trial by petit jury in all those cases in which they had been customary—as either abolishing all trials by military tribunals, save those of the personnel of our own armed forces, or what in effect comes to the same thing, as imposing on all such tribunals the necessity of proceeding against unlawful enemy belligerents only on presentment and trial by jury. We conclude that the Fifth and Sixth Amendments did not restrict whatever authority was conferred by the Constitution to try offenses against the law of war by military commission, and that petitioners, charged with such an offense not required to be tried by jury at common law, were lawfully placed on trial by the Commission without a jury.

Petitioners, and especially petitioner Haupt, stress the pronouncement of this Court in the *Milligan* case, 4 Wall. page 121, that the law of war 'can never be applied to citizens in states which have upheld the authority of the government, and where the courts are open and their process unobstructed'. Elsewhere in its opinion, 4 Wall. at pages 118, 121, 122, and 131, the Court was at pains to point out that Milligan, a citizen twenty years resident in Indiana, who had never been a resident of any of the states in rebellion, was not an enemy belligerent either entitled to the status of a prisoner of war or subject to the penalties imposed upon unlawful belligerents. We construe the Court's statement as to the inapplicability of the law of war to Milligan's case as having particular reference to the facts before it. From them the Court concluded that Milligan, not being a part of or associated with the armed forces of the enemy, was a non-belligerent, not subject to the law of war save as—in circumstances found not there to be present and not involved here—martial law might be constitutionally established.

The Court's opinion is inapplicable to the case presented by the present record. We have no occasion now to define with meticulous care the ultimate boundaries of the jurisdiction of military tribunals to try persons according to the law of war. It is enough that petitioners here, upon the conceded facts, were plainly within those boundaries, and were held in good faith for trial by military commission, charged with being enemies who, with the purpose of destroying war materials and utilities, entered or after entry remained in our territory without uniform—an offense against the law of war. We hold only that those particular acts constitute an offense against the law of war which the Constitution authorizes to be tried by military commission. . . .

There remains the contention that the President's Order of July 2, 1942, so far as it lays down the procedure to be followed on the trial before the Commission and on the review of its findings and sentence, and the procedure in fact followed by the Commission, are in conflict with Articles of War 38, 43, 46, 50 1/2 and 70. Petitioners argue that their trial by the Commission, for offenses against the law of war and the 81st and 82nd Articles of War, by a procedure which Congress has prohibited would invalidate any conviction which could be obtained against them and renders their detention for trial likewise unlawful; that the President's Order prescribes such an unlawful procedure; and that the secrecy surrounding the trial and all proceedings before the Commission, as well as any review of the decision, will preclude a later opportunity to test the lawfulness of the detention. . . .

We need not inquire whether Congress may restrict the power of the Commander in Chief to deal with enemy belligerents. For the Court is unanimous in its conclusion that the Articles in question could not at any stage of the proceedings afford any basis for issuing the writ. But a majority of the full Court are not agreed on the appropriate grounds for decision. Some members of the Court are of opinion that Congress did not intend the Articles of War to govern a Presidential military commission convened for the determination of questions relating to admitted enemy invaders and that the context of the Articles makes clear that they should not be construed to apply in that class of cases. Others are of the view that—even though this trial is subject to whatever provisions of the Articles of War Congress has in terms made applicable to 'commissions'—the particular Articles in question, rightly construed, do not foreclose the procedure prescribed by the President or that shown to have been employed by the Commission in a trial of offenses against the law of war and the 81st and 82nd Articles of War, by a military commission appointed by the President.

Accordingly, we conclude that Charge I, on which petitioners were detained for trial by the Military Commission, alleged an offense which the President is authorized to order tried by military commission; that his Order convening the Commission was a lawful order and that the Commission was lawfully constituted; that the petitioners were held in lawful custody and did not show cause for their discharge. It follows that the orders of the District Court should be affirmed, and that leave to file petitions for habeas corpus in this Court should be denied.

Mr. Justice Murphy took no part in the consideration or decision of these cases.

Orders of District Court affirmed and leave to file petitions for habeas corpus in the Supreme Court denied.

Fred Korematsu was an American citizen, by birth, of Japanese heritage. He was convicted of violating President Franklin Roosevelt's executive order, and a law passed by Congress, that ordered the exclusion of all Japanese Americans from areas of the West Coast placed under military jurisdiction and the forced placement of these persons in internment camps located farther inland. In upholding Korematsu's conviction (all agreed that he was otherwise a loyal and law-abiding citizen), the Court majority sustained the government's action as a regrettable but necessary exercise of the president's power as commander in chief during wartime and of the Congress's power. The decision relied on the Court's earlier ruling in the Hirabayashi *case, when it upheld a less drastic rule imposing a curfew on travel. It also accepted General J. L. DeWitt's assertion that these Japanese-descended people posed a general military*

threat justifying this extreme action in wartime. The three dissenters rejected what they considered to be weak and inadequate evidence from the government concerning the possible threat posed by Japanese Americans, considering it instead racism, and noting acidly that Americans of German and Italian extraction were subject to no similar mass evacuations or accusations. After the war, historians concluded that the government's dire predictions were indeed not supported by evidence.

Korematsu v. U.S.
323 U.S. 214 (1944)

Mr. Justice Black delivered the opinion of the Court. . . .

It should be noted, to begin with, that all legal restrictions which curtail the civil rights of a single racial group are immediately suspect. That is not to say that all such restrictions are unconstitutional. It is to say that courts must subject them to the most rigid scrutiny. Pressing public necessity may sometimes justify the existence of such restrictions; racial antagonism never can. . . .

Exclusion Order No. 34, which the petitioner knowingly and admittedly violated was one of a number of military orders and proclamations, all of which were substantially based upon Executive Order No. 9066, 7 Fed. Reg. 1407. That order, issued after we were at war with Japan, declared that 'the successful prosecution of the war requires every possible protection against espionage and against sabotage to national-defense material, national-defense premises, and national-defense utilities. . . .'

One of the series of orders and proclamations, a curfew order, which like the exclusion order here was promulgated pursuant to Executive Order 9066, subjected all persons of Japanese ancestry in prescribed West Coast military areas to remain in their residences from 8 p.m. to 6 a.m. As is the case with the exclusion order here, that prior curfew order was designed as a 'protection against espionage and against sabotage.' *In Kiyoshi Hirabayashi v.*

United States, we sustained a conviction obtained for violation of the curfew order. The Hirabayashi conviction and this one thus rest on the same 1942 Congressional Act and the same basic executive and military orders, all of which orders were aimed at the twin dangers of espionage and sabotage.

The 1942 Act was attacked in the *Hirabayashi* case as an unconstitutional delegation of power; it was contended that the curfew order and other orders on which it rested were beyond the war powers of the Congress, the military authorities and of the President, as Commander in Chief of the Army; and finally that to apply the curfew order against none but citizens of Japanese ancestry amounted to a constitutionally prohibited discrimination solely on account of race. To these questions, we gave the serious consideration which their importance justified. We upheld the curfew order as an exercise of the power of the government to take steps necessary to prevent espionage and sabotage in an area threatened by Japanese attack.

In the light of the principles we announced in the *Hirabayashi* case, we are unable to conclude that it was beyond the war power of Congress and the Executive to exclude those of Japanese ancestry from the West Coast war area at the time they did. True, exclusion from the area in which one's home is located is a far greater deprivation than constant confinement to the home from 8 p.m. to 6 a.m. Nothing short of apprehension by the proper military authorities of the gravest imminent danger to the public safety can constitutionally justify either. But exclusion from a threatened area, no less than curfew, has a definite and close relationship to the prevention of espionage and sabotage. The military authorities, charged with the primary responsibility of defending our shores, concluded that curfew provided inadequate protection and ordered exclusion. They did so, as pointed out in our *Hirabayashi* opinion, in accordance with Congressional authority to the military to say who should, and who should not, remain in the threatened areas.

In this case the petitioner challenges the assumptions upon which we rested our conclusions in the

Hirabayashi case. He also urges that by May 1942, when Order No. 34 was promulgated, all danger of Japanese invasion of the West Coast had disappeared. After careful consideration of these contentions we are compelled to reject them.

Here, as in the *Hirabayashi* case, '. . . we cannot reject as unfounded the judgment of the military authorities and of Congress that there were disloyal members of that population, whose number and strength could not be precisely and quickly ascertained. We cannot say that the war-making branches of the Government did not have ground for believing that in a critical hour such persons could not readily be isolated and separately dealt with, and constituted a menace to the national defense and safety, which demanded that prompt and adequate measures be taken to guard against it.'

Like curfew, exclusion of those of Japanese origin was deemed necessary because of the presence of an unascertained number of disloyal members of the group, most of whom we have no doubt were loyal to this country. It was because we could not reject the finding of the military authorities that it was impossible to bring about an immediate segregation of the disloyal from the loyal that we sustained the validity of the curfew order as applying to the whole group. In the instant case, temporary exclusion of the entire group was rested by the military on the same ground. The judgment that exclusion of the whole group was for the same reason a military imperative answers the contention that the exclusion was in the nature of group punishment based on antagonism to those of Japanese origin. That there were members of the group who retained loyalties to Japan has been confirmed by investigations made subsequent to the exclusion. Approximately five thousand American citizens of Japanese ancestry refused to swear unqualified allegiance to the United States and to renounce allegiance to the Japanese Emperor, and several thousand evacuees requested repatriation to Japan.

We uphold the exclusion order as of the time it was made and when the petitioner violated it. . . . In doing so, we are not unmindful of the hardships imposed by it upon a large group of American citizens. . . . But hardships are part of war, and war is an aggregation of hardships. All citizens alike, both in and out of uniform, feel the impact of war in greater or lesser measure. Citizenship has its responsibilities as well as its privileges, and in time of war the burden is always heavier. Compulsory exclusion of large groups of citizens from their homes, except under circumstances of direst emergency and peril, is inconsistent with our basic governmental institutions. But when under conditions of modern warfare our shores are threatened by hostile forces, the power to protect must be commensurate with the threatened danger.

It is said that we are dealing here with the case of imprisonment of a citizen in a concentration camp solely because of his ancestry, without evidence or inquiry concerning his loyalty and good disposition towards the United States. Our task would be simple, our duty clear, were this a case involving the imprisonment of a loyal citizen in a concentration camp because of racial prejudice. Regardless of the true nature of the assembly and relocation centers—and we deem it unjustifiable to call them concentration camps with all the ugly connotations that term implies—we are dealing specifically with nothing but an exclusion order. To cast this case into outlines of racial prejudice, without reference to the real military dangers which were presented, merely confuses the issue. Korematsu was not excluded from the Military Area because of hostility to him or his race. He was excluded because we are at war with the Japanese Empire, because the properly constituted military authorities feared an invasion of our West Coast and felt constrained to take proper security measures, because they decided that the military urgency of the situation demanded that all citizens of Japanese ancestry be segregated from the West Coast temporarily, and finally, because Congress, reposing its confidence in this time of war in our military leaders—as inevitably it must—determined that they should have the power to do just this. There was evidence of disloyalty on the part of some, the military authorities considered that the need for action was great, and time was short. We

cannot—by availing ourselves of the calm perspective of hindsight—now say that at that time these actions were unjustified.

AFFIRMED.

Mr. Justice Frankfurter, concurring. . . .

Mr. Justice Roberts.

I dissent, because I think the indisputable facts exhibit a clear violation of Constitutional rights.

This is not a case of keeping people off the streets at night as was Kiyoshi Hirabayashi v. United States, nor a case of temporary exclusion of a citizen from an area for his own safety or that of the community, nor a case of offering him an opportunity to go temporarily out of an area where his presence might cause danger to himself or to his fellows. On the contrary, it is the case of convicting a citizen as a punishment for not submitting to imprisonment in a concentration camp, based on his ancestry, and solely because of his ancestry, without evidence or inquiry concerning his loyalty and good disposition towards the United States. If this be a correct statement of the facts disclosed by this record, and facts of which we take judicial notice, I need hardly labor the conclusion that Constitutional rights have been violated. . . .

Mr. Justice MURPHY, dissenting.

This exclusion of 'all persons of Japanese ancestry, both alien and non-alien,' from the Pacific Coast area on a plea of military necessity in the absence of martial law ought not to be approved. Such exclusion goes over 'the very brink of constitutional power' and falls into the ugly abyss of racism. . . .

The judicial test of whether the Government, on a plea of military necessity, can validly deprive an individual of any of his constitutional rights is whether the deprivation is reasonably related to a public danger that is so 'immediate, imminent, and impending' as not to admit of delay and not to permit the intervention of ordinary constitutional processes to alleviate the danger. . . . Civilian Exclusion Order No. 34, banishing from a prescribed area of the Pacific Coast 'all persons of Japanese ancestry, both alien and non-alien,' clearly does not meet that test. Being an obvious racial discrimination, the order deprives all those within its scope of the equal protection of the laws as guaranteed by the Fifth Amendment. It further deprives these individuals of their constitutional rights to live and work where they will, to establish a home where they choose and to move about freely. In excommunicating them without benefit of hearings, this order also deprives them of all their constitutional rights to procedural due process. Yet no reasonable relation to an 'immediate, imminent, and impending' public danger is evident to support this racial restriction which is one of the most sweeping and complete deprivations of constitutional rights in the history of this nation in the absence of martial law. . . .

That this forced exclusion was the result in good measure of this erroneous assumption of racial guilt rather than bona fide military necessity is evidenced by the Commanding General's [J. L DeWitt—ed.] Final Report on the evacuation from the Pacific Coast area. In it he refers to all individuals of Japanese descent as 'subversive,' as belonging to 'an enemy race' whose 'racial strains are undiluted,' and as constituting 'over 112,000 potential enemies . . . at large today' along the Pacific Coast. In support of this blanket condemnation of all persons of Japanese descent, however, no reliable evidence is cited to show that such individuals were generally disloyal, or had generally so conducted themselves in this area as to constitute a special menace to defense installations or war industries, or had otherwise by their behavior furnished reasonable ground for their exclusion as a group.

Justification for the exclusion is sought, instead, mainly upon questionable racial and sociological grounds not ordinarily within the realm of expert military judgment, supplemented by certain semi-military conclusions drawn from an unwarranted use of circumstantial evidence. Individuals of Japanese ancestry are condemned because they are said to be 'a large, unassimilated, tightly knit racial group, bound to an enemy nation by strong ties of race, culture, custom and religion.' They are claimed to be given to 'emperor worshipping ceremonies' and to 'dual citizenship.' Japanese language schools and allegedly pro-Japanese organizations are cited as evidence of possible group disloyalty, together with facts as to certain persons being educated and residing at length in Japan. It is intimated that many of these individuals deliberately resided 'adjacent to strategic points,' thus enabling them 'to carry into execution a tremendous program of sabotage on a mass scale should any considerable number of them have been inclined to do so.' The need for protective custody is also asserted. The report refers without identity to 'numerous incidents of violence' as well as to other admittedly unverified or cumulative incidents. From this, plus certain other events not shown to have been connected with the Japanese Americans, it is concluded that the 'situation was fraught with danger to the Japanese population itself' and that the general public 'was ready to take matters into its own hands.' Finally, it is intimated, though not directly charged or proved, that persons of Japanese ancestry were responsible for three minor isolated shellings and bombings of the Pacific Coast area, as well as for unidentified radio transmissions and night signalling.

The main reasons relied upon by those responsible for the forced evacuation, therefore, do not prove a reasonable relation between the group characteristics of Japanese Americans and the dangers of invasion, sabotage and espionage. The reasons appear, instead, to be largely an accumulation of much of the misinformation, half-truths and insinuations that for years have been directed against Japanese Americans by people with racial and economic prejudices—the same people who have been among the foremost advocates of the evacuation. A military judgment based upon such racial and sociological considerations is not entitled to the great weight ordinarily given the judgments based upon strictly military considerations. Especially is this so when every charge relative to race, religion, culture, geographical location, and legal and economic status has been substantially discredited by independent studies made by experts in these matters.

The military necessity which is essential to the validity of the evacuation order thus resolves itself into a few intimations that certain individuals actively aided the enemy, from which it is inferred that the entire group of Japanese Americans could not be trusted to be or remain loyal to the United States. No one denies, of course, that there were some disloyal persons of Japanese descent on the Pacific Coast who did all in their power to aid their ancestral land. Similar disloyal activities have been engaged in by many persons of German, Italian and even more pioneer stock in our country. But to infer that examples of individual disloyalty prove group disloyalty and justify discriminatory action against the entire group is to deny that under our system of law individual guilt is the sole basis for deprivation of rights. Moreover, this inference, which is at the very heart of the evacuation orders, has been used in support of the abhorrent and despicable treatment of minority groups by the dictatorial tyrannies which this nation is now pledged to destroy. To give constitutional sanction to that inference in this case, however well-intentioned may have been the military command on the Pacific Coast, is to adopt one of the cruelest of the rationales used by our enemies to destroy the dignity of the individual and to encourage and open the door to discriminatory actions against other minority groups in the passions of tomorrow. No adequate reason is given for the failure to treat these Japanese Americans on an individual basis by holding investigations and hearings to separate the loyal from the disloyal, as was done in the case of persons of German and Italian ancestry. . . .

Moreover, there was no adequate proof that the Federal Bureau of Investigation and the military and naval intelligence services did not have the espionage and sabotage situation well in hand during this long period. Nor is there any denial of the fact that not one person of Japanese ancestry was accused or convicted of espionage or sabotage after Pearl Harbor while they were still free, a fact which is some evidence of the loyalty of the vast majority of these individuals and of the effectiveness of the established methods of combating these evils. It seems incredible that under these circumstances it would have been impossible to hold loyalty hearings for the mere 112,000 persons involved—or at least for the 70,000 American citizens—especially when a large part of this number represented children and elderly men and women. Any inconvenience that may have accompanied an attempt to conform to procedural due process cannot be said to justify violations of constitutional rights of individuals.

I dissent, therefore, from this legalization of racism. Racial discrimination in any form and in any degree has no justifiable part whatever in our democratic way of life. It is unattractive in any setting but it is utterly revolting among a free people who have embraced the principles set forth in the Constitution of the United States. All residents of this nation are kin in some way by blood or culture to a foreign land. Yet they are primarily and necessarily a part of the new and distinct civilization of the United States. They must accordingly be treated at all times as the heirs of the American experiment and as entitled to all the rights and freedoms guaranteed by the Constitution.

Mr. Justice JACKSON, dissenting.

Korematsu was born on our soil, of parents born in Japan. The Constitution makes him a citizen of the United States by nativity and a citizen of California by residence. No claim is made that he is not loyal to this country. There is no suggestion that apart from the matter involved here he is not law-abiding and well disposed. Korematsu, however, has been convicted of an act not commonly a crime. It consists merely of being present in the state whereof he is a citizen, near the place where he was born, and where all his life he has lived. . . .

A citizen's presence in the locality, however, was made a crime only if his parents were of Japanese birth. Had Korematsu been one of four—the others being, say, a German alien enemy, an Italian alien enemy, and a citizen of American-born ancestors, convicted of treason but out on parole—only Korematsu's presence would have violated the order. The difference between their innocence and his crime would result, not from anything he did, said, or thought, different than they, but only in that he was born of different racial stock.

Now, if any fundamental assumption underlies our system, it is that guilt is personal and not inheritable. Even if all of one's antecedents had been convicted of treason, the Constitution forbids its penalties to be visited upon him, for it provides that 'no Attainder of Treason shall work Corruption of Blood, or Forfeiture except during the Life of the Person attained.' Article 3, 3, cl. 2. But here is an attempt to make an otherwise innocent act a crime merely because this prisoner is the son of parents as to whom he had no choice, and belongs to a race from which there is no way to resign. If Congress in peace-time legislation should enact such a criminal law, I should suppose this Court would refuse to enforce it. . . .

America's longest and most controversial armed conflict was the Vietnam War—although Congress never officially declared war at all. Its most important action was to enact the Gulf of Tonkin Resolution in 1964, a measure that gave the president great discretion to prosecute the conflict as he thought best. Challenges to the constitutionality of this conflict were filed repeatedly, yet the courts mostly ducked the matter. In this case, the Supreme Court refused to hear a challenge from several men drafted into the military and slated to be sent to Vietnam who asked the Court to rule military activity in Vietnam illegal. Although the Court majority refused to hear the case (denying the petition for writ of certiorari), two justices wrote a dissent, arguing that the Court should hear the matter on its merits, citing numerous questions that go to the heart of the war power and the limits of court authority in war-related matters.

Mora v. McNamara
389 U.S. 934 (1967)

Mr. Justice STEWART, with whom Mr. Justice DOUGLAS joins, dissenting. . . .

There exist in this case questions of great magnitude. . . . : I. Is the present United States military activity in Vietnam a 'war' within the meaning of Article I, Section 8, Clause 11 of the Constitution? II. If so, may the Executive constitutionally order the petitioners to participate in that military activity, when no war has been declared by the Congress? III. Of what relevance to Question II are the present treaty obligations of the United States? IV. Of what relevance to Question II is the joint Congressional ('Tonkin Bay') Resolution of August 10, 1964?

(a) Do present United States military operations fall within the terms of the Joint Resolution?

(b) If the Joint Resolution purports to give the Chief Executive authority to commit United States forces to armed conflict limited in scope only by his own absolute discretion, is the Resolution a constitutionally impermissible delegation of all or part of Congress' power to declare war?

These are large and deeply troubling questions. Whether the Court would ultimately reach them depends, of course, upon the resolution of serious preliminary issues of justiciability. We cannot make these problems go away simply by refusing to hear the case of three obscure Army privates. I intimate not even tentative views upon any of these matters, but I think the Court should squarely face them by granting certiorari and setting this case for oral argument.

Mr. Justice DOUGLAS, with whom Mr. Justice STEWART concurs, dissenting.

Mr. Justice MARSHALL took no part in the consideration or decision of this petition.

The questions posed by Mr. Justice Stewart cover the wide range of problems which the Senate Committee on Foreign Relations recently explored, in connection with the SEATO [South East Asian Treaty Organization] Treaty of February 19, 1955, and the Tonkin Gulf Resolution.

Mr. Katzenbach, representing the Administration, testified that he did not regard the Tonkin Gulf Resolution to be 'a declaration of war' and that while the Resolution was not 'constitutionally necessary' it was 'politically, from an international viewpoint and from a domestic viewpoint, extremely important.' He added:

'The use of the phrase 'to declare war' as it was used in the Constitution of the United States had a particular meaning in terms of the events and the practices which existed at the time it was adopted. . . .

'[I]t was recognized by the Founding Fathers that the President might have to take emergency action to protect the security of the United States, but that if there was going to be another use of the armed forces of the United States, that was a decision which Congress should check the Executive on, which Congress should support. It was for that reason that the phrase was inserted in the Constitution.

'Now, over a long period of time, . . . there have been many uses of the military forces of the United States for a variety of purposes without a congressional declaration of war. But it would be fair to say that most of these were relatively minor uses of force. . . .

'A declaration of war would not, I think, correctly reflect the very limited objectives of the United States with respect to Vietnam. It would not correctly reflect our efforts there, what we are trying to do, the reasons why we are there, to use an outmoded phraseology, to declare war.'

The view that Congress was intended to play a more active role in the initiation and conduct of war than the above statements might suggest has been espoused by Senator Fulbright (Cong.Rec. Oct. 11, 1967, p. 14683–14690), quoting Thomas Jefferson who said: 'We have already given in example one effectual check to the Dog of war by transferring the power of letting him loose from the Executive to the Legislative body, from those who are to spend to those who are to pay.' These opposed views are reflected in the *Prize Cases*, 2 Black 635, a five-to-four decision rendered in 1863. Mr. Justice Grier, writing for the majority, emphasized the arguments for strong presidential powers. Justice Nelson, writing for the minority of four, read the Constitution more strictly, emphasizing that what is war in actuality may not constitute war in the constitutional sense. During all subsequent periods in our history—through the Spanish-American War, the Boxer Rebellion, two World Wars, Korea, and now Vietnam—the two points of view urged in the Prize Cases have continued to be voiced.

A host of problems is raised. Does the President's authority to repel invasions and quiet insurrections, his powers in foreign relations and his duty to execute faithfully the laws of the United States, including its treaties, justify what has been threatened of petitioners? What is the relevancy of the Gulf of Tonkin Resolution and the yearly appropriations in support of the Vietnam effort? . . .

There are other treaties or declarations that could be cited. Perhaps all of them are wide of the mark. There are sentences in our opinions which, detached from their context, indicate that what is happening is none of our business:

> 'Certainly it is not the function of the Judiciary to entertain private litigation—even by a citizen—which challenges the legality, the wisdom, or the propriety of the Commander-in-Chief in sending our armed forces abroad or to any particular region.' *Johnson v. Eisentrager, 339 U.S. 763, 789.*

We do not, of course, sit as a committee of oversight or supervision. What resolutions the President asks and what the Congress provides are not our concern. With respect to the Federal Government, we sit only to decide actual cases or controversies within judicial cognizance that arise as a result of what the Congress or the President or a judge does or attempts to do to a person or his property.

In *Ex parte Milligan*, 4 Wall. 2, the Court relieved a person of the death penalty imposed by a military tribunal, holding that only a civilian court had power to try him for the offense charged. Speaking of the purpose of the Founders in providing constitutional guarantees, the Court said:

> 'They knew . . . the nation they were founding, be its existence short or long, would be involved in war; how often or how long continued, human foresight could not tell; and that unlimited power, wherever lodged at such a time, was especially hazardous to freemen. For this, and other equally weighty reasons, they secured the inheritance they had fought to maintain, by incorporating in a written constitution the safeguards which time had proved were essential

to its preservation. Not one of these safeguards can the President, or Congress, or the Judiciary disturb, except the one concerning the writ of habeas corpus.' *Id.*, 125. . . .

These petitioners should be told whether their case is beyond judicial cognizance. If it is not, we should then reach the merits of their claims, on which I intimate no views whatsoever.

Shortly after Iraq invaded and occupied its neighbor Kuwait in August 1990, President George H. W. Bush ordered American troops to the Middle East to deter further Iraqi aggression. Bush continued the American military buildup in the region, stating that it was necessary to provide "an adequate offensive military option." But the Congress had not enacted a declaration of war. Fearing that the president would launch a war on his own, fifty three members of the House of Representatives and one U.S. Senator filed suit against the president, asking the court to issue an injunction to prevent the president from beginning a war without authorization from Congress. The Justice Department argued on behalf of the president that the lawsuit should be dismissed because it involved a political question (one to be resolved between the executive and legislative branches), that the fifty four members of the Congress had no grounds to sue, and that the matter was not ready for judicial action anyway, since the president had not taken any offensive military action. In this U.S. district court case, Judge Harold H. Green concluded that the members of the Congress were entitled, in principle, to appeal to the courts for relief and that the circumstances in the Middle East did represent a war situation where the Congress had the constitutional right to exercise authority. Nevertheless, the court concluded that, in this instance, the case was not yet "ripe," meaning that the plaintiffs in this case—the members of the Congress—had not yet been injured, so their case was, in effect, premature. Even so, the decision also rejected several Justice Department arguments about presidential power, including the assertion that the courts had no right to intervene.

Dellums v. Bush
752 F. Supp. 1141 (D.D.C. 1990)

Harold H. Greene, United States District Judge.

. . . In relation to the issues involved in this case the Department of Justice expands on its basic theme, contending that by their very nature the determination whether certain types of military actions require a declaration of war is not justiciable, but depends instead upon delicate judgment by the political branches. On that view, the question whether an offensive action taken by American armed forces constitutes an act of war (to be initiated by a declaration of war) or an "offensive military attack" (presumably undertaken by the President in his capacity as commander-in-chief) is not one of objective fact but involves an exercise of judgment based upon all the vagaries of foreign affairs and national security. Indeed, the Department contends that there are no judicially discoverable and manageable standards to apply, claiming that only the political branches are able to determine whether or not this country is at war. Such a determination, it is said, is based upon "a political judgment" about the significance of those facts. Under that rationale, a court cannot make an independent determination on this issue because it cannot take adequate account of these political considerations.

This claim on behalf of the Executive is far too sweeping to be accepted by the courts. If the Executive had the sole power to determine that any particular offensive military operation, no matter how vast, does not constitute war-making but only an offensive military attack, the congressional power to declare war will be at the mercy of a semantic decision by the Executive. Such an "interpretation" would evade the plain language of the Constitution, and it cannot stand. That is not to say that, assuming that the issue is factually close or ambiguous or fraught with intricate technical military and diplomatic baggage, the courts would not defer to the political branches to determine whether or not particular hostilities might qualify as a "war." However, here the forces involved are of such magnitude and significance as to present no serious claim that a war would not ensue if they became engaged in combat, and it is therefore clear that congressional approval is required if Congress desires to become involved. . . .

[T]he [Justice] Department goes on to suggest that the issue in this case is still political rather than legal, because in order to resolve the dispute the Court would have to inject itself into foreign affairs, a subject which the Constitution commits to the political branches. That argument, too, must fail. While the Constitution grants to the political branches, and in particular to the Executive, responsibility for conducting the nation's foreign affairs, it does not follow that the judicial power is excluded from the resolution of cases merely because they may touch upon such affairs. The court must instead look at "the particular question posed" in the case. In fact, courts are routinely deciding cases that touch upon or even have a substantial impact on foreign and defense policy.

The Department's argument also ignores the fact that courts have historically made determinations about whether this country was at war for many other purposes—the construction of treaties, statutes, and even insurance contracts. These judicial determinations of a *de facto* [in fact—ed.] state of war have occurred even in the absence of a congressional declaration.

Plaintiffs allege in their complaint that 230,000 American troops are currently deployed in Saudi Arabia and the Persian Gulf area, and that by the end of this month the number of American troops in the region will reach 380,000. They also allege, in light of the President's obtaining the support of the United Nations Security Council in a resolution allowing for the use of force against Iraq, that he is planning for an offensive military attack on Iraqi forces. Given these factual allegations and the legal principles outlined above, the Court has no hesitation in concluding that an offensive entry into Iraq by several hundred thousand United States servicemen under the conditions described above could be described as a "war" within the

meaning of Article I, Section 8, Clause 11, of the Constitution. To put it another way: the Court is not prepared to read out of the Constitution the clause granting to the Congress, and to it alone, the authority "to declare war." . . .

V. Ripeness

Although, as discussed above, the Court rejects several of defendant's objections to the maintenance of this lawsuit, and concludes that, in principle, an injunction may issue at the request of Members of Congress to prevent the conduct of a war which is about to be carried on without congressional authorization, it does not follow that these plaintiffs are entitled to relief at this juncture. For the plaintiffs are met with a significant obstacle to such relief: the doctrine of ripeness. It has long been held that, as a matter of the deference that is due to the other branches of government, the Judiciary will undertake to render decisions that compel action by the President or the Congress only if the dispute before the Court is truly ripe, in that all the factors necessary for a decision are present then and there. The need for ripeness as a prerequisite to judicial action has particular weight in a case such as this. The principle that the courts shall be prudent in the exercise of their authority is never more compelling than when they are called upon to adjudicate on such sensitive issues as those trenching upon military and foreign affairs. Judicial restraint must, of course, be even further enhanced when the issue is one—as here—on which the other two branches may be deeply divided. Hence the necessity for determining at the outset whether the controversy is truly "ripe" for decision or whether, on the other hand, the Judiciary should abstain from rendering a decision on ripeness grounds. In the context of this case, there are two aspects to ripeness, which the Court will now explore.

A. Actions By the Congress

No one knows the position of the Legislative Branch on the issue of war or peace with Iraq; certainly no one, including this Court, is able to ascertain the congressional position on that issue on the basis of this lawsuit brought by fifty-three members of the House of Representatives and one member of the U.S. Senate. It would be both premature and presumptuous for the Court to render a decision on the issue of whether a declaration of war is required at this time or in the near future when the Congress itself has provided no indication whether it deems such a declaration either necessary, on the one hand, or imprudent, on the other. . . .

The consequences of judicial action in the instant case with the facts in their present posture may be drastic, but unnecessarily so. What if the Court issued the injunction requested by the plaintiffs, but it subsequently turned out that a majority of the members of the Legislative Branch were of the view (a) that the President is free as a legal or constitutional matter to proceed with his plans toward Iraq without a congressional declaration of war, or (b) more broadly, that the majority of the members of this Branch, for whatever reason, are content to leave this diplomatically and politically delicate decision to the President?

It would hardly do to have the Court, in effect, force a choice upon the Congress by a blunt injunctive decision, called for by only about ten percent of its membership, to the effect that, unless the rest of the Congress votes in favor of a declaration of war, the President, and the several hundred thousand troops he has dispatched to the Saudi Arabian desert, must be immobilized. Similarly, the President is entitled to be protected from an injunctive order respecting a declaration of war when there is no evidence that this is what the Legislative Branch as such—as distinguished from a fraction thereof—regards as a necessary prerequisite to military moves in the Arabian desert.

All these difficulties are avoided by a requirement that the plaintiffs in an action of this kind be or represent a majority of the Members of the Congress: the majority of the body that under the Constitution is the only one competent to declare war, and therefore also the one with the ability to seek an order from the courts to prevent anyone

else, i.e., the Executive, from in effect declaring war. In short, unless the Congress as a whole, or by a majority, is heard from, the controversy here cannot be deemed ripe; it is only if the majority of the Congress seeks relief from an infringement on its constitutional war-declaration power that it may be entitled to receive it.

B. Actions Taken By the Executive

The second half of the ripeness issue involves the question whether the Executive Branch of government is so clearly committed to immediate military operations that may be equated with a "war" within the meaning of Article I, Section 8, Clause 11, of the Constitution that a judicial decision may properly be rendered regarding the application of that constitutional provision to the current situation.

Plaintiffs assert that the matter is currently ripe for judicial action because the President himself has stated that the present troop build-up is to provide an adequate offensive military option in the area. His successful effort to secure passage of United Nations Resolution 678, which authorizes the use of "all available means" to oust Iraqi forces remaining in Kuwait after January 15, 1991, is said to be an additional fact pointing toward the Executive's intention to initiate military hostilities against Iraq in the near future.

The Department of Justice, on the other hand, points to statements of the President that the troops already in Saudi Arabia are a peacekeeping force to prove that the President might not initiate more offensive military actions. In addition, and more realistically, it is possible that the meetings set for later this month and next between President Bush and the Foreign Minister of Iraq, Tariq Aziz, in Washington, and Secretary of State James Baker and Saddam Hussein in Baghdad, may result in a diplomatic solution to the present situation, and in any event under the U.N. Security Council resolution there will not be resort to force before January 15, 1991.

Given the facts currently available to this Court, it would seem that as of now the Executive Branch has not shown a commitment to a definitive course f action sufficient to support ripeness. In any vent, however, a final decision on that issue is not ecessary at this time.

hould the congressional ripeness issue discussed in 'art V-A above be resolved in favor of a finding of peness as a consequence of actions taken by the ˀongress as a whole, there will still be time enough ɔ determine whether, in view of the conditions as ˌey are found to exist at that time, the Executive is ɔ clearly committed to early military operations mounting to "war" in the constitutional sense that ˌe Court would be justified in concluding that the ːmainder of the test of ripeness has been met. And f course an injunction will be issued only if, on oth of the aspects of the doctrine discussed above, ˌe Court could find that the controversy is ripe for ˌdicial decision. That situation does not, or at least ot yet, prevail, and plaintiffs' request for a prelim-ˌary injunction will therefore not be granted.

or the reasons stated, it is this 13th day of ˈecember, 1990

ˈRDERED that plaintiffs' motion for preliminary ˌjunction be and it is hereby denied.

ˌaser Hamdi, an American citizen of Saudi Arabian *ˌescent, was captured in Afghanistan sometime after ˌeptember 11, 2001, and imprisoned indefinitely in ˌe United States in 2002 as an "enemy combatant" ˌr allegedly fighting with the Taliban. Aside from his ˌresence in Afghanistan, the government's only other ˌstification for detaining Hamdi was a nine-ˌaragraph statement from a military official saying ˌat Hamdi's detention was justified. Hamdi's father ˌaimed that his son was in Afghanistan to perform ˌlief work and argued in court that his son's contin-ˌed incarceration violated his habeas corpus rights ˌhe right to be brought before a magistrate and told ˌthe charges against him) and other basic civil liberties. ˌhe administration of George W. Bush argued that the ˌesident, as commander in chief, had full and sole ˌuthority to order the detention of citizens or nonciti-ˌns if they were deemed "enemy combatants" and that ˌeither Congress nor the courts had a right to intervene.*

In a landmark decision, the Supreme Court ruled 8 to 1 that Hamdi had been improperly detained (reversing a lower court ruling)—although the majority differed on particulars—and that he and other detainees had a right to be presented with charges and to an oppor-tunity to rebut the government's charges. While siding with Hamdi, the Court also agreed that the war on terrorism constituted a constitutional war and that the president's powers to conduct that war were great. Another case handed down the same day also involved an American citizen, José Padilla, who was arrested in Chicago for allegedly plotting to detonate a nuclear device. In Rumsfeld v. Padilla, *the Court declined to rule on the merits of the case, and sent it back to a lower court for rehearing. But the* Hamdi *ruling could only help Padilla, whose claims were similar to Hamdi's. A few months after the ruling, Hamdi was released by the government and allowed to return to Saudi Arabia.*

Hamdi et al. *v. Rumsfeld, Secretary of Defense* 159 L.Ed. 2d 578 (2004)

O'Connor, J., announced the judgment of the Court and delivered an opinion, in which *Rehnquist, C. J.*, and *Kennedy* and *Breyer, JJ.*, joined. *Souter, J.*, filed an opinion concurring in part, dissenting in part, and concurring in the judgment, in which *Ginsburg, J.*, joined. *Scalia, J.*, filed a dissenting opinion, in which *Stevens, J.*, joined. *Thomas, J.*, filed a dissenting opinion. . . .

At this difficult time in our Nation's history, we are called upon to consider the legality of the Government's detention of a United States citizen on United States soil as an "enemy combatant" and to address the process that is constitutionally owed to one who seeks to challenge his classification as such. The United States Court of Appeals for the Fourth Circuit held that petitioner's detention was legally authorized and that he was entitled to no fur-ther opportunity to challenge his enemy-combatant label. We now vacate and remand. We hold that although Congress authorized the detention of combatants in the narrow circumstances alleged here, due process demands that a citizen held in the United States as an enemy combatant be given a meaningful opportunity to contest the factual basis for that detention before a neutral decisionmaker. . . .

The threshold question before us is whether the Executive has the authority to detain citizens who qualify as "enemy combatants." There is some debate as to the proper scope of this term, and the Government has never provided any court with the full criteria that it uses in classifying individuals as such. It has made clear, however, that, for purposes of this case, the "enemy combatant" that it is seeking to detain is an individual who, it alleges, was " 'part of or supporting forces hostile to the United States or coalition partners' " in Afghanistan and who " 'engaged in an armed conflict against the United States' " there. Brief for Respondents 3. We therefore answer only the narrow question before us: whether the detention of citizens falling within that definition is authorized.

The Government maintains that no explicit congressional authorization is required, because the Executive possesses plenary authority to detain pursuant to Article II of the Constitution. We do not reach the question whether Article II provides such authority, however, because we agree with the Government's alternative position, that Congress has in fact authorized Hamdi's detention, through the AUMF [Authorization for Use of Military Force, passed in 2001—ed.] . . . .

The AUMF authorizes the President to use "all necessary and appropriate force" against "nations, organizations, or persons" associated with the September 11, 2001, terrorist attacks. 115 Stat. 224. There can be no doubt that individuals who fought against the United States in Afghanistan as part of the Taliban, an organization known to have supported the al Qaeda terrorist network responsible for those attacks, are individuals Congress sought to target in passing the AUMF. We conclude that detention of individuals falling into the limited category we are considering, for the duration of the particular conflict in which they were captured, i[s] so fundamental and accepted an incident to war a[s] to be an exercise of the "necessary and appropriat[e] force" Congress has authorized the President to use[.]

The capture and detention of lawful combatant[s] and the capture, detention, and trial of unlawfu[l] combatants, by "universal agreement and practice," are "important incident[s] of war." *Ex parte Quirin*, *317 U.S., at 28.* The purpose of detention is t[o] prevent captured individuals from returning to th[e] field of battle and taking up arms once again. . . .

There is no bar to this Nation's holding one of it[s] own citizens as an enemy combatant. . . . A citizen[,] no less than an alien, can be "part of or supportin[g] forces hostile to the United States or coalitio[n] partners" and "engaged in an armed conflict agains[t] the United States," Brief for Respondents 3; such [a] citizen, if released, would pose the same threat [of] returning to the front during the ongoing conflict[.]

In light of these principles, it is of no moment tha[t] the AUMF does not use specific language of deten[-] tion. Because detention to prevent a combatant['s] return to the battlefield is a fundamental inciden[t] of waging war, in permitting the use of "necessar[y] and appropriate force," Congress has clearly an[d] unmistakably authorized detention in the narro[w] circumstances considered here.

Hamdi objects, nevertheless, that Congress has n[ot] authorized the *indefinite* detention to which he [is] now subject. The Government responds that "th[e] detention of enemy combatants during World War I[I] was just as 'indefinite' while that war was bein[g] fought." *Id.,* at 16. We take Hamdi's objection t[o] be not to the lack of certainty regarding the date o[n] which the conflict will end, but to the substanti[al] prospect of perpetual detention. We recognize tha[t] the national security underpinnings of the "war o[n] terror," although crucially important, are broad an[d] malleable. As the Government concedes, "given i[ts] unconventional nature, the current conflict [is] unlikely to end with a formal cease-fire agreement[.]" *Ibid.* The prospect Hamdi raises is therefore not fa[r] fetched. If the Government does not consider th[is] unconventional war won for two generations, an[d] if it maintains during that time that Hamdi might, if released, rejoin forces fighting against the United States, then the position it has taken throughout the litigation of this case suggests that Hamdi's detention could last for the rest of his life. . . .

Hamdi contends that the AUMF does not authorize indefinite or perpetual detention. Certainly, we agree that indefinite detention for the purpose of interrogation is not authorized. Further, we understand Congress' grant of authority for the use of "necessary and appropriate force" to include the authority to detain for the duration of the relevant conflict, and our understanding is based on long-standing law-of-war principles. If the practical circumstances of a given conflict are entirely unlike those of the conflicts that informed the development of the law of war, that understanding may unravel. But that is not the situation we face as of this date. Active combat operations against Taliban fighters apparently are ongoing in Afghanistan. . . . The United States may detain, for the duration of these hostilities, individuals legitimately determined to be Taliban combatants who "engaged in an armed conflict against the United States." If the record establishes that United States troops are still involved in active combat in Afghanistan, those detentions are part of the exercise of "necessary and appropriate force," and therefore are authorized by the AUMF. . . .

[T]he "facts" . . . are insufficient to support Hamdi's detention. Under the definition of enemy combatant that we accept today as falling within the scope of Congress' authorization, Hamdi would need to be "part of or supporting forces hostile to the United States or coalition partners" and "engaged in an armed conflict against the United States" to justify his detention in the United States for the duration of the relevant conflict. Brief for Respondents 3. The habeas petition states only that "[w]hen seized by the United States Government, Mr. Hamdi resided in Afghanistan." App. 104. An assertion that one *resided* in a country in which combat operations are taking place is not a concession that one was "*captured*" in a zone of active combat operations in a foreign theater of war,"

316 F. 3d, at 459 (emphasis added), and certainly is not a concession that one was "part of or supporting forces hostile to the United States or coalition partners" and "engaged in an armed conflict against the United States." Accordingly, we reject any argument that Hamdi has made concessions that eliminate any right to further process. . . .

It is beyond question that substantial interests lie on both sides of the scale in this case. Hamdi's "private interest . . . affected by the official action," *ibid.*, is the most elemental of liberty interests—the interest in being free from physical detention by one's own government. . . .

Indeed, . . . the risk of erroneous deprivation of a citizen's liberty in the absence of sufficient process here is very real. . . . Moreover, as critical as the Government's interest may be in detaining those who actually pose an immediate threat to the national security of the United States during ongoing international conflict, history and common sense teach us that an unchecked system of detention carries the potential to become a means for oppression and abuse of others who do not present that sort of threat. . . . Because we live in a society in which "[m]ere public intolerance or animosity cannot constitutionally justify the deprivation of a person's physical liberty," *O'Connor v. Donaldson, 422 U.S. 563, 575* (1975), our starting point . . . is unaltered by the allegations surrounding the particular detainee or the organizations with which he is alleged to have associated. We reaffirm today the fundamental nature of a citizen's right to be free from involuntary confinement by his own government without due process of law, and we weigh the opposing governmental interests against the curtailment of liberty that such confinement entails. . . .

On the other side of the scale are the weighty and sensitive governmental interests in ensuring that those who have in fact fought with the enemy during a war do not return to battle against the United States. As discussed above, *supra*, at 10, the law of war and the realities of combat may render such detentions both necessary and appropriate, and our due process analysis need not blink at those realities.

Without doubt, our Constitution recognizes that core strategic matters of warmaking belong in the hands of those who are best positioned and most politically accountable for making them. . . .

Striking the proper constitutional balance here is of great importance to the Nation during this period of ongoing combat. But it is equally vital that our calculus not give short shrift to the values that this country holds dear or to the privilege that is American citizenship. It is during our most challenging and uncertain moments that our Nation's commitment to due process is most severely tested; and it is in those times that we must preserve our commitment at home to the principles for which we fight abroad. . . .

With due recognition of these competing concerns, we believe that neither the process proposed by the Government nor the process apparently envisioned by the District Court below strikes the proper constitutional balance when a United States citizen is detained in the United States as an enemy combatant. That is, "the risk of erroneous deprivation" of a detainee's liberty interest is unacceptably high under the Government's proposed rule, while some of the "additional or substitute procedural safeguards" suggested by the District Court are unwarranted in light of their limited "probable value" and the burdens they may impose on the military in such cases. . . .

We therefore hold that a citizen-detainee seeking to challenge his classification as an enemy combatant must receive notice of the factual basis for his classification, and a fair opportunity to rebut the Government's factual assertions before a neutral decisionmaker. . . .

We think it unlikely that this basic process will have the dire impact on the central functions of warmaking that the Government forecasts. The parties agree that initial captures on the battlefield need not receive the process we have discussed here; that process is due only when the determination is made to *continue* to hold those who have been seized. The Government has made clear in its briefing that documentation regarding battlefield detainees already

is kept in the ordinary course of military affairs. Brief for Respondents 3–4. Any factfinding imposition created by requiring a knowledgeable affiant to summarize these records to an independent tribunal is a minimal one. Likewise, arguments that military officers ought not have to wage war under the threat of litigation lose much of their steam when factual disputes at enemy-combatant hearings are limited to the alleged combatant's acts. This focus meddles little, if at all, in the strategy or conduct of war, inquiring only into the appropriateness of continuing to detain an individual claimed to have taken up arms against the United States. While we accord the greatest respect and consideration to the judgments of military authorities in matters relating to the actual prosecution of a war, and recognize that the scope of that discretion necessarily is wide, it does not infringe on the core role of the military for the courts to exercise their own time-honored and constitutionally mandated roles of reviewing and resolving claims like those presented here. . . .

In sum, while the full protections that accompany challenges to detentions in other settings may prove unworkable and inappropriate in the enemy-combatant setting, the threats to military operations posed by a basic system of independent review are not so weighty as to trump a citizen's core rights to challenge meaningfully the Government's case and to be heard by an impartial adjudicator. . . .

In so holding, we necessarily reject the Government's assertion that separation of powers principles mandate a heavily circumscribed role for the courts in such circumstances. Indeed, the position that the courts must forgo any examination of the individual case and focus exclusively on the legality of the broader detention scheme cannot be mandated by any reasonable view of separation of powers, as this approach serves only to *condense* power into a single branch of government. We have long since made clear that a state of war is not a blank check for the President when it comes to the rights of the Nation's citizens. *Youngstown Sheet & Tube, 343 U.S., at 587.* Whatever power the United States Constitution envisions for the Executive in its exchanges with other nations or with enemy organizations in times of conflict, it most assuredly envisions a role for all three branches when individual liberties are at stake. . . . Likewise, we have made clear that, unless Congress acts to suspend it, the Great Writ of habeas corpus allows the Judicial Branch to play a necessary role in maintaining this delicate balance of governance, serving as an important judicial check on the Executive's discretion in the realm of detentions. . . . Thus, while we do not question that our due process assessment must pay keen attention to the particular burdens faced by the Executive in the context of military action, it would turn our system of checks and balances on its head to suggest that a citizen could not make his way to court with a challenge to the factual basis for his detention by his government, simply because the Executive opposes making available such a challenge. Absent suspension of the writ by Congress, a citizen detained as an enemy combatant is entitled to this process. . . .

Hamdi asks us to hold that the Fourth Circuit also erred by denying him immediate access to counsel upon his detention and by disposing of the case without permitting him to meet with an attorney. Brief for Petitioners 19. Since our grant of certiorari in this case, Hamdi has been appointed counsel, with whom he has met for consultation purposes on several occasions, and with whom he is now being granted unmonitored meetings. He unquestionably has the right to access to counsel in connection with the proceedings on remand. No further consideration of this issue is necessary at this stage of the case.

The judgment of the United States Court of Appeals for the Fourth Circuit is vacated, and the case is remanded for further proceedings.

It is so ordered.

Justice Scalia, with whom *Justice Stevens* joins, dissenting. . . .

The very core of liberty secured by our Anglo-Saxon system of separated powers has been freedom from indefinite imprisonment at the will of the Executive. . . .

The gist of the Due Process Clause, as understood at the founding and since, was to force the Government to follow those common-law procedures traditionally deemed necessary before depriving a person of life, liberty, or property. When a citizen was deprived of liberty because of alleged criminal conduct, those procedures typically required committal by a magistrate followed by indictment and trial. . . .

It is unthinkable that the Executive could render otherwise criminal grounds for detention noncriminal merely by disclaiming an intent to prosecute, or by asserting that it was incapacitating dangerous offenders rather than punishing wrongdoing. Cf. *Kansas v. Hendricks, 521 U.S. 346, 358* (1997) ("A finding of dangerousness, standing alone, is ordinarily not a sufficient ground upon which to justify indefinite involuntary commitment"). . . .

The allegations here, of course, are no ordinary accusations of criminal activity. Yaser Esam Hamdi has been imprisoned because the Government believes he participated in the waging of war against the United States. The relevant question, then, is whether there is a different, special procedure for imprisonment of a citizen accused of wrongdoing *by aiding the enemy in wartime*. . . .

Justice O'Connor, writing for a plurality of this Court, asserts that captured enemy combatants (other than those suspected of war crimes) have traditionally been detained until the cessation of hostilities and then released. *Ante*, at 10–11. That is probably an accurate description of wartime practice with respect to enemy *aliens*. The tradition with respect to American citizens, however, has been quite different. Citizens aiding the enemy have been treated as traitors subject to the criminal process. . . .

The Founders inherited the understanding that a citizen's levying war against the Government was to be punished criminally. The Constitution provides: "Treason against the United States, shall consist only in levying War against them, or in adhering to their Enemies, giving them Aid and Comfort"; and establishes a heightened proof requirement (two witnesses) in order to "convic[t]" of that offense. Art. III, §3, cl. 1. . . .

Our Federal Constitution contains a provision explicitly permitting suspension [of habeas corpus], but limiting the situations in which it may be invoked: "The privilege of the Writ of Habeas Corpus shall not be suspended, unless when in Cases of Rebellion or Invasion the public Safety may require it." Art. I, §9, cl. 2. Although this provision does not state that suspension must be effected by, or authorized by, a legislative act, it has been so understood, consistent with English practice and the Clause's placement in Article I. . . .

The proposition that the Executive lacks indefinite wartime detention authority over citizens is consistent with the Founders' general mistrust of military power permanently at the Executive's disposal. In the Founders' view, the "blessings of liberty" were threatened by "those military establishments which must gradually poison its very fountain." The Federalist No. 45, p. 238 (J. Madison). No fewer than 10 issues of the Federalist were devoted in whole or part to allaying fears of oppression from the proposed Constitution's authorization of standing armies in peacetime. Many safeguards in the Constitution reflect these concerns. Congress's authority "[t]o raise and support Armies" was hedged with the proviso that "no Appropriation of Money to that Use shall be for a longer Term than two Years." U.S. Const., Art. 1, §8, cl. 12. Except for the actual command of military forces, all authorization for their maintenance and all explicit authorization for their use is placed in the control of Congress under Article I, rather than the President under Article II. As Hamilton explained, the President's military authority would be "much inferior" to that of the British King:

> "It would amount to nothing more than the supreme command and direction of the military and naval forces, as first general and admiral of the confederacy: while that of the British king extends to the *declaring* of war, and to the *raising* and *regulating* of fleets and armies; all which, by the constitution under consideration, would

appertain to the legislature." The Federalist No. 69, p. 357.

A view of the Constitution that gives the Executive authority to use military force rather than the force of law against citizens on American soil flies in the face of the mistrust that engendered these provisions. . . .

It follows from what I have said that Hamdi is entitled to a habeas decree requiring his release unless (1) criminal proceedings are promptly brought, or (2) Congress has suspended the writ of habeas corpus. A suspension of the writ could, of course, lay down conditions for continued detention, similar to those that today's opinion prescribes under the Due Process Clause. Cf. Act of Mar. 3, 1863, 12 Stat. 755. But there is a world of difference between the people's representatives' determining the need for that suspension (and prescribing the conditions for it), and this Court's doing so. . . .

If the situation demands it, the Executive can ask Congress to authorize suspension of the writ—which can be made subject to whatever conditions Congress deems appropriate, including even the procedural novelties invented by the plurality today. To be sure, suspension is limited by the Constitution to cases of rebellion or invasion. But whether the attacks of September 11, 2001, constitute an "invasion," and whether those attacks still justify suspension several years later, are questions for Congress rather than this Court. See 3 Story §1336, at 208–209.[6] If civil rights are to be curtailed during wartime, it must be done openly and democratically, as the Constitution requires, rather than by silent erosion through an opinion of this Court. . . .

Many think it not only inevitable but entirely proper that liberty give way to security in times of national crisis—that, at the extremes of military exigency, *inter arma silent leges* ["laws are silent amid arms—ed."]. Whatever the general merits of the view that war silences law or modulates its voice, that view has no place in the interpretation and application of a Constitution designed precisely to confront war and, in a manner that accords with democratic principles, to accommodate it

Because the Court has proceeded to meet the current emergency in a manner the Constitution does not envision, I respectfully dissent.

Justice Souter, with whom *Justice Ginsburg* joins, concurring in part, dissenting in part, and concurring in the judgment. . . .

The plurality rejects any such limit on the exercise of habeas jurisdiction and so far I agree with its opinion. The plurality does, however, accept the Government's position that if Hamdi's designation as an enemy combatant is correct, his detention (at least as to some period) is authorized by an Act of Congress as required by §4001(a), that is, by the Authorization for Use of Military Force, 115 Stat. 224 (hereinafter Force Resolution). *Ante*, at 9–14. Here, I disagree and respectfully dissent. The Government has failed to demonstrate that the Force Resolution authorizes the detention complained of here even on the facts the Government claims. If the Government raises nothing further than the record now shows, the Non-Detention Act entitles Hamdi to be released. . . .

The Government's first response to Hamdi's claim that holding him violates §4001(a), prohibiting detention of citizens "except pursuant to an Act of Congress," is that the statute does not even apply to military wartime detentions, being beyond the sphere of domestic criminal law. Next, the Government says that even if that statute does apply, two Acts of Congress provide the authority §4001(a) demands: a general authorization to the Department of Defense to pay for detaining "prisoners of war" and "similar" persons, 10 U.S.C. §956(5), and the Force Resolution, passed after the attacks of 2001. At the same time, the Government argues that in detaining Hamdi in the manner described, the President is in any event acting as Commander in Chief under Article II of the Constitution, which brings with it the right to invoke authority under the accepted customary rules for waging war. On the record in front of us, the Government has not made out a case on any theory. . . .

The threshold issue is how broadly or narrowly to read the Non-Detention Act, the tone of which is severe: "No citizen shall be imprisoned or otherwise detained by the United States except pursuant to an Act of Congress." Should the severity of the Act be relieved when the Government's stated factual justification for incommunicado detention is a war on terrorism, so that the Government may be said to act "pursuant" to congressional terms that fall short of explicit authority to imprison individuals? With one possible though important qualification, see *infra*, at 10–11, the answer has to be no. For a number of reasons, the prohibition within §4001(a) has to be read broadly to accord the statute a long reach and to impose a burden of justification on the Government. . . .

The defining character of American constitutional government is its constant tension between security and liberty, serving both by partial helpings of each. In a government of separated powers, deciding finally on what is a reasonable degree of guaranteed liberty whether in peace or war (or some condition in between) is not well entrusted to the Executive Branch of Government, whose particular responsibility is to maintain security. For reasons of inescapable human nature, the branch of the Government asked to counter a serious threat is not the branch on which to rest the Nation's entire reliance in striking the balance between the will to win and the cost in liberty on the way to victory; the responsibility for security will naturally amplify the claim that security legitimately raises. A reasonable balance is more likely to be reached on the judgment of a different branch, just as Madison said in remarking that "the constant aim is to divide and arrange the several offices in such a manner as that each may be a check on the other—that the private interest of every individual may be a sentinel over the public rights." The Federalist No. 51, p. 349 (J. Cooke ed. 1961). Hence the need for an assessment by Congress before citizens are subject to lockup, and likewise the need for a clearly expressed congressional resolution of the competing claims. . . .

[T]he Government has not made out its claim that in detaining Hamdi in the manner described, it is acting in accord with the laws of war authorized to be applied against citizens by the Force Resolution. I conclude accordingly that the Government has failed to support the position that the Force Resolution authorizes the described detention of Hamdi for purposes of §4001(a). . . .

[T]he weakness of the Government's mixed claim of inherent, extrastatutory authority under a combination of Article II of the Constitution and the usages of war. It is in fact in this connection that the Government developed its argument that the exercise of war powers justifies the detention, and what I have just said about its inadequacy applies here as well. Beyond that, it is instructive to recall Justice Jackson's observation that the President is not Commander in Chief of the country, only of the military. *Youngstown Sheet & Tube Co. v. Sawyer, 343 U.S. 579, 643–644 (1952)* (concurring opinion); see also *id.*, at 637–638 (Presidential authority is "at its lowest ebb" where the President acts contrary to congressional will).

There may be room for one qualification to Justice Jackson's statement, however: in a moment of genuine emergency, when the Government must act with no time for deliberation, the Executive may be able to detain a citizen if there is reason to fear he is an imminent threat to the safety of the Nation and its people (though I doubt there is any want of statutory authority, see *supra*, at 9–10). This case, however, does not present that question, because an emergency power of necessity must at least be limited by the emergency; Hamdi has been locked up for over two years. . . .

Subject to these qualifications, I join with the plurality in a judgment of the Court vacating the Fourth Circuit's judgment and remanding the case.

Justice Thomas, dissenting.

The Executive Branch, acting pursuant to the powers vested in the President by the Constitution and with explicit congressional approval, has determined that Yaser Hamdi is an enemy combatant and should be detained. This detention falls squarely within the Federal Government's war powers, and we lack the expertise and capacity to second-guess that decision. As such, petitioners' habeas challenge should fail, and there is no reason to remand the case. . . . Arguably, Congress could provide for additional procedural protections, but until it does, we have no right to insist upon them. But even if I were to agree with the general approach the plurality takes, I could not accept the particulars. The plurality utterly fails to account for the Government's compelling interests and for our own institutional inability to weigh competing concerns correctly. I respectfully dissent. . . .

The Founders intended that the President have primary responsibility—along with the necessary power—to protect the national security and to conduct the Nation's foreign relations. They did so principally because the structural advantages of a unitary Executive are essential in these domains. "Energy in the executive is a leading character in the definition of good government. It is essential to the protection of the community against foreign attacks." The Federalist No. 70, p. 471 (A. Hamilton). The principle "ingredien[t]" for "energy in the executive" is "unity." *Id.*, at 472. This is because "[d]ecision, activity, secrecy, and dispatch will generally characterise the proceedings of one man, in a much more eminent degree, than the proceedings of any greater number." *Ibid.*

These structural advantages are most important in the national-security and foreign-affairs contexts. "O[f] all the cares or concerns of government, the direction of war most peculiarly demands those qualities which distinguish the exercise of power by a single hand." The Federalist No. 74, p. 500 (A. Hamilton). Also for these reasons, John Marshall explained that "[t]he President is the sole organ of the nation in its external relations, and its sole representative with foreign nations." 10 Annals of Cong. 613 (1800); see *id.*, at 613–614. To this end, the Constitution vests in the President "[t]he executive Power," Art. II, §1, provides that he "shall be Commander in Chief of the" armed forces, §2, and places in him the power to recognize foreign governments, §3. . . .

Congress, to be sure, has a substantial and essential role in both foreign affairs and national security. But it is crucial to recognize that *judicial* interference in these domains destroys the purpose of vesting primary responsibility in a unitary Executive. . . .

I agree with the plurality that the Federal Government has power to detain those that the Executive Branch determines to be enemy combatants. See *ante*, at 10. But I do not think that the plurality has adequately explained the breadth of the President's authority to detain enemy combatants, an authority that includes making virtually conclusive factual findings. In my view, the structural considerations discussed above, as recognized in our precedent, demonstrate that we lack the capacity and responsibility to second-guess this determination. . . .

In this context, due process requires nothing more than a good-faith executive determination. To be clear: The Court has held that an executive, acting pursuant to statutory and constitutional authority may, consistent with the Due Process Clause, unilaterally decide to detain an individual if the executive deems this necessary for the public safety *even if he is mistaken.* . . .

The Government's asserted authority to detain an individual that the President has determined to be an enemy combatant, at least while hostilities continue, comports with the Due Process Clause. As these cases also show, the Executive's decision that a detention is necessary to protect the public need not and should not be subjected to judicial second-guessing. Indeed, at least in the context of enemy-combatant determinations, this would defeat the unity, secrecy, and dispatch that the Founders believed to be so important to the warmaking function. . . .

Accordingly, I conclude that the Government's detention of Hamdi as an enemy combatant does not violate the Constitution. By detaining Hamdi, the President, in the prosecution of a war authorized by Congress, has acted well within his authority. Hamdi thereby received all the process to which he was due under the circumstances. I therefore believe that this is no occasion to balance the competing interests, as the plurality unconvincingly attempts to do. . . .

Undeniably, Hamdi has been deprived of a serious interest, one actually protected by the Due Process Clause. Against this, however, is the Government's overriding interest in protecting the Nation. If a deprivation of liberty can be justified by the need to protect a town, the protection of the Nation, *a fortiori* [to believe strongly based on logic—ed.], justifies it.

For these reasons, I would affirm the judgment of the Court of Appeals.

Following the September 11, 2001, terrorist attacks, American troops invaded Afghanistan to dislodge and defeat al Qaeda and Taliban forces thought to have supported the attacks. Among hundreds captured and detained at the American naval base at Guantanamo Bay, Cuba, were two Australians and twelve Kuwaitis who filed suit in federal court to challenge the legality of their detention, saying that they had not been charged, were not terrorists, and wanted access to lawyers and access to American courts. The Bush administration claimed that the detainees had no right to court access, as they were non-U.S. citizens and that the Cuban base was outside of U.S. sovereign territory. In a 6 to 3 vote, the Court rejected administration arguments, citing past cases and a federal law to conclude that the Guantanamo Base with within federal court jurisdiction. The majority decision implied that access to American courts might also apply to detainees held elsewhere in the world. As with the Hamdi *case handed down on the same day, the Court rejected the Bush administration's assertion that it had no jurisdiction over such matters.*

Rasul et al. *v. Bush; al Odah v. U.S.* 159 L.Ed. 2d 548 (2004)

Justice Stevens delivered the opinion of the Court.

These two cases present the narrow but important question whether United States courts lack jurisdiction to consider challenges to the legality of the detention of foreign nationals captured abroad in connection with hostilities and incarcerated at the Guantanamo Bay Naval Base, Cuba. . . .

The question now before us is whether the habeas statute confers a right to judicial review of the legality of Executive detention of aliens in a territory over which the United States exercises plenary and exclusive jurisdiction, but not "ultimate sovereignty." . . .

Because [of] subsequent decisions of this Court . . . persons detained outside the territorial jurisdiction of any federal district court no longer need rely on the Constitution as the source of their right to federal habeas review. . . .

By the express terms of its agreements with Cuba, the United States exercises "complete jurisdiction and control" over the Guantanamo Bay Naval Base, and may continue to exercise such control permanently if it so chooses. 1903 Lease Agreement, Art. III; 1934 Treaty, Art. III. Respondents themselves concede that the habeas statute would create federal-court jurisdiction over the claims of an American citizen held at the base. Tr. of Oral Arg. 27. Considering that the statute draws no distinction between Americans and aliens held in federal custody, there is little reason to think that Congress intended the geographical coverage of the statute to vary depending on the detainee's citizenship. Aliens held at the base, no less than American citizens, are entitled to invoke the federal courts' authority under §2241 [a federal law authorizing federal courts to entertain habeas corpus applications, including aliens held in territories controlled by the United States—ed.].

Application of the habeas statute to persons detained at the base is consistent with the historical reach of the writ of habeas corpus. At common law, courts exercised habeas jurisdiction over the claims of aliens detained within sovereign territory of the realm, as well as the claims of persons detained in the so-called "exempt jurisdictions," where ordinary writs did not run, and all other dominions under the sovereign's control. . . .

In the end, the answer to the question presented is clear. Petitioners contend that they are being held

in federal custody in violation of the laws of the United States. No party questions the District Court's jurisdiction over petitioners' custodians. Section 2241, by its terms, requires nothing more. We therefore hold that §2241 confers on the District Court jurisdiction to hear petitioners' habeas corpus challenges to the legality of their detention at the Guantanamo Bay Naval Base. . . .

[N]othing in . . . any of our other cases categorically excludes aliens detained in military custody outside the United States from the " 'privilege of litigation' " in U. S. courts. 321 F. 3d, at 1139. The courts of the United States have traditionally been open to nonresident aliens. . . . And indeed, 28 U.S.C. §1350 explicitly confers the privilege of suing for an actionable "tort . . . committed in violation of the law of nations or a treaty of the United States" on aliens alone. The fact that petitioners in these cases are being held in military custody is immaterial to the question of the District Court's jurisdiction over their nonhabeas statutory claims. . . .

Whether and what further proceedings may become necessary after respondents make their response to the merits of petitioners' claims are matters that we need not address now. What is presently at stake is only whether the federal courts have jurisdiction to determine the legality of the Executive's potentially indefinite detention of individuals who claim to be wholly innocent of wrongdoing. Answering that question in the affirmative, we reverse the judgment of the Court of Appeals and remand for the District Court to consider in the first instance the merits of petitioners' claims.

It is so ordered. . . .

Justice Scalia, with whom *The Chief Justice* and *Justice Thomas* join, dissenting.

The Court today holds that the habeas statute, 28 U.S.C. §2241, extends to aliens detained by the United States military overseas, outside the sovereign borders of the United States and beyond the territorial jurisdictions of all its courts. This is not only a ovel holding; it contradicts a half-century-old recedent on which the military undoubtedly elied. . . . This is an irresponsible overturning of ettled law in a matter of extreme importance to ur forces currently in the field. I would leave it to Congress to change §2241, and dissent from the Court's unprecedented holding. . . .

No matter to whom the writ is directed, custodian r detainee, the statute could not be clearer that a ecessary requirement for issuing the writ is that me federal district court have territorial jurisdic- on over the detainee. Here, as the Court allows, ee *ante*, at 10, the Guantanamo Bay detainees are ot located within the territorial jurisdiction of any ederal district court. One would think that is the nd of this case.

he Court asserts, however, that the decisions f this Court have placed a gloss on the phrase within their respective jurisdictions" in §2241 which llows jurisdiction in this case. That is not so. . . .

oday, the Court springs a trap on the Executive, ubjecting Guantanamo Bay to the oversight of the ederal courts even though it has never before been nought to be within their jurisdiction—and thus naking it a foolish place to have housed alien artime detainees. . . .

n abandoning the venerable statutory line drawn 1 *Eisentrager*, the Court boldly extends the scope f the habeas statute to the four corners of the arth. . . .

he consequence of this holding, as applied aliens outside the country, is breathtaking. It ermits an alien captured in a foreign theater of ctive combat to bring a §2241 petition against the ecretary of Defense. Over the course of the last entury, the United States has held millions of alien risoners abroad. . . . A great many of these prison- rs would no doubt have complained about the ircumstances of their capture and the terms of neir confinement. The military is currently detain- ng over 600 prisoners at Guantanamo Bay alone; ach detainee undoubtedly has complaints—real or ontrived—about those terms and circumstances.

The Court's unheralded expansion of federal-court jurisdiction is not even mitigated by a comforting assurance that the legion of ensuing claims will be easily resolved on the merits. To the contrary, the Court says that the "[p]etitioners' allegations . . . unquestionably describe 'custody in violation of the Constitution or laws or treaties of the United States.' ". . . From this point forward, federal courts will entertain petitions from these prisoners, and others like them around the world, challenging actions and events far away, and forcing the courts to oversee one aspect of the Executive's conduct of a foreign war. . . .

Departure from our rule of *stare decisis* [stick to precedent—ed.] in statutory cases is always extraordi- nary; it ought to be unthinkable when the departure has a potentially harmful effect upon the Nation's conduct of a war. The Commander in Chief and his subordinates had every reason to expect that the internment of combatants at Guantanamo Bay would not have the consequence of bringing the cumbersome machinery of our domestic courts into military affairs. Congress is in session. If it wished to change federal judges' habeas jurisdiction from what this Court had previously held that to be, it could have done so. And it could have done so by intelligent revision of the statute, instead of by today's clumsy, countertextual reinterpretation that confers upon wartime prisoners greater habeas rights than domestic detainees. The latter must challenge their present physical confinement in the district of their confinement, see *Rumsfeld v. Padilla, ante*, whereas under today's strange holding Guantanamo Bay detainees can petition in any of the 94 federal judicial districts. The fact that extraterritorially located detainees lack the district of detention that the statute requires has been converted from a factor that precludes their ability to bring a petition at all into a factor that frees them to petition wherever they wish—and, as a result, to forum shop. For this Court to create such a mon- strous scheme in time of war, and in frustration of our military commanders' reliance upon clearly stated prior law, is judicial adventurism of the worst sort. I dissent.

Conclusion

"A republic, if you can keep it."

The quote introducing this chapter is from Benjamin Franklin, offered in response to a question from the crowd outside the Philadelphia Constitutional Convention in September of 1787 where the framers were about to unveil their handiwork: the newly minted Constitution of the United States of America. Convention delegate Franklin was asked, "What is it Mr. Franklin, a monarchy or a republic?" "A republic," Franklin replied, "if you can keep it."

The profound nature of Franklin's oft-quoted charge to future generations should not be lost on modern audiences. "If you can keep it"; if, indeed. It is up to our generation, and those to come, to study, know, and defend this Constitution, lest we run the danger of losing it.

Woodrow Wilson reminded us in 1885, long before he reached the presidency, that "[t]he Constitution in operation is manifestly a different thing from the Constitution of the books."[1] And nowhere is this more visible than in the area of presidential power. How did the presidency go from chief clerk to imperial potentate? How did this document, written in the eighteenth century for a newly formed, small, and relatively insignificant nation, come to guide a twenty-first-century global empire?

A reader of the Constitution's text in 1789 would find relatively few changes in the document as compared with the document's contemporary version. And the Constitution's text regarding presidential powers remains unchanged. Yet the actual powers of the President in 2005 are vastly expanded from the powers of the presidency in 1789. How we got from there to here is a long and complicated story, and not the central topic of this book.[2] But the fact that we have made this transition without altering the Constitution raises key questions regarding the role of law and constitutionalism in the development of the United States and of the presidency.

The cases chronicled in this book demonstrate that the Constitution is an elastic document—changing, evolving, even living and breathing. It is neither fixed nor static. As an organic document, it calls for our care and attention.

What lessons might we draw from the cases and controversies found in this work? Allow us to suggest just a few: First, basic constitutional relationships survive under the separation-of-powers system. Relationships between the president and the other branches of government shift according to historical era, the press of events, and the actions of particular presidents. The separation-of-powers system has never functioned as three coequal branches, like the three legs of an equilateral triangle. Instead, at various times, each branch has played a pivotal role in animating national policy, often marginalizing the role of one or both of the other branches. In the range of America's political development, the presidency has increasingly assumed this most central and pivotal role.

Second, the Constitution is not self-enforcing. Its health demands a vigilant, aware, and concerned citizenry, committed to the rule of law and to basic constitutional rights and liberties. Some of the key cases in this book involve moments where citizens with few resources and little hope were nevertheless able to obtain a hearing before the courts and win important victories under the constitutional system. If Lambdin Milligan (*Ex Parte Milligan*) from the Civil War era, or Daniel Ellsberg of *Pentagon Papers* case (*New York Times Co. v. United States*) fame, or accused enemy combatant Yaser Hamdi (*Hamdi et al. v. Rumsfeld*) from 2004 represent rarities in court annals, they nevertheless underscore the potential and actual role of a vigilant citizenry.

Third, the Constitution needs friends. Even in good times, the Constitution may come under siege, but in a crisis, whether war or other emergencies, it is especially in need of defenders. In the ongoing war against terrorism, the country has witnessed renewed debate over the proper balance between freedom and security, and the presidency sits at the very center of that debate.

Fourth, the presidency is—sometimes—a threat to the Constitution and the rule of law. Presidents attempt to draw power unto themselves. This should not surprise us, for it was exactly what James Madison warned us against in *Federalist No. 51*. And because presidents have such high demands and expectations placed on their shoulders, but lack the constitutional powers to meet these high expectations, it should not surprise us that often they attempt to cut constitutional corners and pull power into the presidential vortex. But this power is not theirs alone. It must, in our system, be shared with the Congress and at times, the courts. The separation of powers was designed to prevent one person from ruling. It is an unruly, cumbersome, slow, often frustrating system. The rule of law always is.

Fifth, one overwhelming trend regarding presidential power emerges from a surprising number of cases analyzed in this book. It is the extent to which the courts have paid special deference to presidential power in foreign affairs, especially in cases in the last hundred years. And court expressions of this deference have not been limited to cases involving foreign policy matters. Thus, even in cases purely domestic in nature, such as *United States v. Nixon*, the Supreme Court went out of its way to acknowledge what is, in its view, the greater deference

appropriate to presidential powers in foreign affairs, even though this case did not involve foreign policy concerns. This does not mean, however, that the Court always yields to the president in the foreign policy realm. In the recent *Hamdi* and *Rasul* cases, the Supreme Court rejected Bush administration power claims, noting in *Hamdi* that "a state of war is not a blank check for the president." True enough, but short of a blank check, presidential power in foreign affairs amounts to an awfully big check, and it is far bigger in the modern era than it was in the nineteenth century. And the magnitude of court deference to presidential foreign policy power has also had spillover effects for presidential power in domestic affairs. This finding is hardly a new one.

Writing in 1973, historian Arthur Schlesinger, Jr., popularized this very idea when he argued that "the imperial Presidency received its decisive impetus . . . from foreign policy."[3] The ongoing, post-9/11 war on terrorism brings this lesson to our attention in a most compelling way precisely because its formal declaration began with a terrorist strike against civilians within America's territory. Even during World War II, the largest war in world history, the continental United States never suffered a similarly devastating attack. Thus, the hunt for terrorists abroad combines and mixes with domestic security and liberty questions in a way that will further blur the traditional line between domestic and foreign policy. Under these circumstances, it is inevitable that presidents will want to use the deference presidents receive in foreign policy to enhance their powers at home.

A Typology of Presidency Cases

The cases offered in this book may be analyzed in terms of five possible types (see table 12.1), and we invite readers to consider the cases in light of this typology. Most of the time, as we have argued, the Supreme Court approves or *expands* presidential authority. It often also *legitimizes* presidential power. The Court also can *avoid* or duck the dispute with which it is presented, often on the

Table 12.1 Types of Court decisions regarding presidential power

Type of decision	Definition	Example
Expanding	Decision adding power to presidency	*U.S. v. Curtiss-Wright Export Corporation* (1936). Recognizes it is necessary for presidents to have more power in foreign than in domestic affairs.
Legitimizing	Decision giving Court approval for presidential activities that were questioned	*Korematsu v. U.S.* (1944). Approved FDR and executive powers to intern Japanese American citizens in World War II.
Avoiding	Decisions the Court decided "not to decide"; avoids getting involved	*Massachusetts v. Laird* (1970). Declined to hear a case that questioned the president's broad power in the Vietnam War, thus avoiding a decision on the war.
Two-sided	Decisions going against a president yet adding power to institution of the presidency	*United States v. Nixon* (1974). Nixon told to yield tapes, yet Court recognizes "executive privilege" as valid in serious national security situations.
Restricting	Decision curbing or even diminishing presidential power	*Youngstown Sheet & Tube Co. v. Sawyer* (1952). Truman and his secretary of commerce told they had exceeded their power in seizing the nation's steel mills to prevent a strike. Truman based his action on general powers of his office. Court held he could take no such action without express authorization from the Congress.

grounds that it is a political matter to be settled by the Congress and the president. This "political questions" doctrine means that the Court declines to rule based on the argument that the matter should be decided by the "political" branches—the Congress and the president. On rare occasions a *two-sided decision* is possible, when the Court may restrict an individual president but add to the power of the office. The Nixon tapes decision in 1974 is illustrative of a two-sided ruling. The Court ordered Nixon to yield his tapes; yet it also, and for the first time, recognized executive privilege as having constitutional standing. Sometimes, of course, in a clash of views the Supreme Court *restricts* or curbs a president and presidential powers.

Expanding and legitimizing decisions are common and are more likely than restricting decisions. Nearly every analyst of court–president relations emphasizes the Court's role in the expansion of presidential powers. Most of the time, the Supreme Court has supported the vigorous actions of our strong presidents. One scholar emphasizing this view in 1957 concluded that "in every major constitutional crisis between the executive and the judiciary, the president has emerged the victor." He also said the judiciary can neither force the president to do anything, "nor prevent him from doing anything he may decide to do."[4] Although this sweeping verdict arguably overstated the case, many students of presidential–judicial relations modify this judgment only slightly today, especially in the light of cases handed down since these words were written.[5]

Finally, we conclude with this observation: The Constitution is not enough. We acknowledge that not all issues, controversies, and concerns arise from, or can be answered by a court case or some line of text from the Constitution. Rights expressed as words on paper do not necessarily equal any guarantee of actual rights. The words must be brought to life by living, breathing beings. Judge Learned Hand reminded us of this in World War II:

I often wonder whether we do not rest our hope too much upon constitutions, upon laws, and upon courts. These are false hopes; believe me, these are false hopes. Liberty lies in the hearts of men and women; when it dies there, no constitution, no law, no court can save it. . . .[6]

Glossary of Legal Terms

a fortiori—to believe with strong reason that something must be true.

arguendo—in the course of an argument.

bill of attainder—A legislative enactment that imposes a punishment on a person without benefit of a judicial trial.

constructive trust—A trust in which the royalties go to the government.

de facto—In fact.

enjoin—to prevent something from occurring.

eo nominee—By name.

ex majore cautela—With the greatest care.

ex parte request—One that involves only the requestor and the judge.

ex post facto—After the fact.

gravamen—The gist or essence of a charge.

habeas corpus—A court order stipulated in the Constitution directing an official having a person in custody to produce the person in court and explain to the judge why he or she is being held.

impoundment—Nonuse.

in camera—Confidential review by the judge.

in pari materia—Along with.

in personam lawsuit—A lawsuit against a person.

in terrorem—A warning to terrify or deter others.

inter arma silent leges—Laws are silent amid arms.

jure belli—By the law of war.

jus belli—The law of war.

mandamus—A petition to the court, usually granted only in drastic circumstances, asking it to set aside a discovery order to produce documents or other information.

per curiam—The majority decision is a decision of the whole, not of a specific justice.

seriatim—one after the other.

stare decisis—stick to precedent.

sub silentio—allowing something to occur without question or objection.

subpoena duces tecum—A subpoena requiring that the documents be produced.

writ of certiorari—An appeal to the Supreme Court to hear a case.

Notes

Preface

1. The one exception is Peter M. Shane and Harold H. Bruff, *Separation of Powers Law* (Durham, NC: Carolina Academic Press, 1996). This 1,043-page law school casebook is an excellent resource, but its size and scope minimize its usefulness for average readers. One other good book, now out of print, presented some court cases and a variety of other materials related to the presidency: Christopher H. Pyle and Richard M. Pious, *The President, Congress, and the Constitution* (New York: Free Press, 1984).
2. See Louis Fisher, *Constitutional Dialogues: Interpretation as Political Process* (Princeton, NJ: Princeton University Press, 1988).

Chapter 1

1. Alexis de Tocqueville, *Democracy in America* (New York: New American Library, 1956), 73.
2. Edmund S. Morgan, *Inventing the People* (New York: Norton, 1988).
3. Bernard Bailyn, *The Ideological Origins of the American Revolution* (Cambridge, MA: Harvard University Press, 1967).
4. Charles C. Thach, *The Creation of the Presidency, 1775–1789: A Study in Constitutional History* (Baltimore, MD: Johns Hopkins University Press, 1922).
5. Thomas E. Cronin, ed. *Inventing the American Presidency* (Lawrence, KS: University Press of Kansas, 1989).
6. Harvey C. Mansfield, *Taming the Prince: The Ambivalence of Modern Executive Power* (New York: Free Press, 1989), 1.
7. Ralph Ketcham, *Presidents Above Party* (Chapel Hill: University of North Carolina Press, 1984), 9.
8. Alan Wolfe, "Presidential Power and the Crisis of Modernization," *Democracy* 1, no. 2 (1981): 21.
9. Charles Beard and Mary Beard, *The Rise of American Civilization* (New York: Macmillan, 1933), 317.
10. Robert J. Spitzer, *The Presidential Veto* (Albany, NY: SUNY Press, 1988).
11. James Madison, *The Writings of James Madison* ed. Gaillard Hunt, 9 vols. (New York: Putnam, 1900–1910), 6: 145.

12. David E. Haight and Larry D. Johnston, eds., *The President: Roles and Powers* (Chicago: Rand McNally & Company 1965), 1.
13. Louis Fisher, *Constitutional Dialogues* (Princeton, NJ: Princeton University Press, 1988).
14. Thomas E. Cronin and Michael A. Genovese, *The Paradox of the American Presidency* (New York: Oxford University Press, 1998), chapter 8.
15. Michael Kammen, *A Machine That Would Go of Itself* (NY: Random House, 1986).
16. See Aaron Wildavsky, "The Two Presidencies," *Transaction* (December 1966): 7–14.
17. Ibid.
18. Steven A. Shull, ed., *The Two Presidencies* (Chicago: Nelson-Hall, 1991).
19. Robert J. Spitzer, *President and Congress* (New York: McGraw-Hill, 1993), 142–46.
20. As Wolfram F. Hanrieder writes: "Separation not only sharpens a subsequent correlation of external and internal dimensions, but also acknowledges that both dimensions reach into significantly different analytical environments—namely, the external-international-operational and the internal-domestic-motivational." "Compatibility and Consensus: A Proposal for the Conceptual Linkage of External and Internal Dimensions of Foreign Policy," *American Political Science Review* 61, no. 4 (December 1967): 975.
21. A relationship of this sort was noted by Glendon Schubert when he wrote: "Emergency ordinances and those of extraterritorial effect are already almost beyond the pale of judicial review; but presidential action of domestic impact and not keyed to emergency powers—an area which is beginning to resemble, to borrow a mathematical concept, a disappearing function—may, under suitable conditions, be subjected to judicial review." *The Presidency in the Courts* (Minneapolis: University of Minnesota Press, 1957), 356.

Chapter 2

* Portions of this chapter are drawn from Thomas E. Cronin and Michael A. Genovese, *The Paradoxes of the American Presidency*, 2nd ed. (New York: Oxford University Press, 2004), 221–29.

1. *Ex-parte Merryman*, 17 Fed. Case No. 9487 (1861). See also on this clash David M. Silver, *Lincoln's Supreme Court* (Urbana: University of Illinois Press, 1957).
2. Clinton Rossiter, *The Supreme Court and the Commander-in-Chief* (Ithaca, NY: Cornell University Press, 1951), 25.
3. Richard N. Current, "The Lincoln Presidents," *Presidential Studies Quarterly* (Winter 1979): 32.
4. Robert H. Jackson, *The Struggle for Judicial Supremacy* (New York: Vintage, 1941).
5. Philip Abbott, *The Exemplary Presidency: Franklin D. Roosevelt and the American Political Tradition* (Amherst: University of Massachusetts Press, 1990), chapter 7.
6. William E. Leuchtenburg, "Court-Packing Plan," in Otis L. Graham and Meghan Robinson Wander, eds., *Franklin D. Roosevelt: His Life and Times* (Boston: G.K. Hall, 1985), 86.
7. David Gray Adler, "Court, Constitution, and Foreign Affairs," in Adler and Larry George, eds., *The Constitution and the Conduct of America Foreign Policy* (Lawrence: University Press of Kansas, 1996), 25.
8. David J. Danelski, "The Saboteurs' Case," *Journal of Supreme Court History* 1 (1996): 80. See also Louis Fisher, *Nazi Saboteurs on Trial* (Lawrence: University Press of Kansas, 2003).
9. *Korematsu v. United States*, 323 U.S. 214 (1944).
10. Richard M. Pious, "The Paradox of Clinton Winning and the Presidency Losing," *Political Science Quarterly* 114, no. 4 (1999–2000): 590.
11. David Gray Adler and Michael A. Genovese, eds., *The Presidency and the Law: The Clinton Legacy* (Lawrence: University Press of Kansas, 2002).

Chapter 4

1. James Ceaser and Andrew Busch, *The Perfect Tie* (Lanham, MD: Rowman & Littlefield, 2001), 171.

Chapter 12

1. Woodrow Wilson, *Congressional Government* (New Brunswick, NJ: Transaction, 2002), 9–10.
2. For chronicles of the rise and fall and rise of presidential power over time, see: Robert J. Spitzer, *President and Congress* (New York: McGraw-Hill, 1993), and Michael A. Genovese, *The Power of the American Presidency, 1789–2000* (New York: Oxford University Press, 2001).
3. Arthur Schlesinger, Jr., *The Imperial Presidency* (Boston: Houghton Mifflin, 1973), ix.
4. Glendon Schubert, *The Presidency in the Courts* (Minneapolis: University of Minnesota Press, 1957) 4, 354.
5. See, for example, David G. Adler, "Foreign Policy and the Separation of Powers under the Constitution: The Influence of the Judiciary," paper delivered at the 1987 Annual Meeting of the Western Political Science Association, Anaheim, California, March 26–28, 1987 and his more specialized book *The Constitution and the Termination of Treaties* (New York: Garland Publishing 1986). See also Francis D. Wormuth and Edwin B Firmage, *To Chain the Dog of War* (Dallas: Southern Methodist University Press, 1986). For a more modified verdict, see Louis Fisher, *The Politics of Shared Power,* 4th ed. (College Station, TX: Texas A&M University Press, 1998). For a much more modified view, see Robert Scigliano, "The Presidency and the Judiciary," in Michael Nelson, ed., *The Presidency and the Political System* (Washington, DC: Congressional Quarterly Press, 1984), 414. See also a helpful quantitative study by Craig R. Ducat and Robert L. Dudley, "Presidential Power in the Federal Courts during the Post War Era," paper delivered at the 1985 Annual Meeting of the American Political Science Association, New Orleans, August 1985.
6. Learned Hand, *The Spirit of Liberty* (New York: Knopf 1944), 190.

Index

Case and Statute Index